Real Exchange Rates, Devaluation, and Adjustment

Exchange Rate Policy in Developing Countries

Sebastian Edwards

The MIT Press
Cambridge, Massachusetts
London, England

This book was set in Palatino by Asco Trade Typesetting Ltd., Hong Kong, and printed and bound in the United States of America.

Library of Congress Cataloging-in-Publication Data

Edwards, Sebastian, 1953–
  Real exchange rates, devaluation, and adjustment: exchange rate policy in developing countries/by Sebastian Edwards.

        p.   cm.
  Bibliography: p.
  Includes index.
  ISBN 0-262-05039-0
  1. Foreign exchange administration—Developing countries. 2. Foreign exchange problem—Developing countries. 3. Devaluation of currency—Developing countries. 4. Developing countries—Economic policy. I. Title.
  HG3877.E383   1989
  332.4′56091724—dc19   88-39954
                                                               CIP

To my son Benjamin

Contents

Preface

For many years now the exchange rate has been at the center of policy discussions in the developing countries. Issues related to devaluations and their consequences have occupied the discourses of politicians and the writings of many political observers. Undoubtedly, devaluations constitute one of the most controversial policy measures in the poorer nations. Even under conditions of severe macroeconomic disequilibrium the authorities in these countries have many times resisted devaluing their currencies. Instead, they have tried to impose import tariffs, import licenses, and other forms of exchange, trade and capital controls in an effort to avoid the balance of payments deficits resulting from real exchange rate overvaluation and macroeconomic imbalances. How can we explain this historical regularity? Why do the authorities in these countries prefer to implement highly distorting controls instead of devaluing? What is, after all, the historical record of devaluations?

This book deals with the economics of devaluation and real exchange rates in the developing countries. It blends economic theory and empirical analysis in an effort to understand real exchange rate behavior and the circumstances surrounding devaluations in the developing nations. A central aim of the book is to evaluate the historical record of devaluations in the less developed countries (LDCs), trying to establish what had determined the "success" or "failure" of a devaluation package.

The book is divided into three parts. In part I (chapters 2 and 3) theoretical models of devaluation and real exchange rate behavior are developed, and the concept of real exchange rate misalignment is defined. The chapters in this part are based on modern economic theory and pay special attention to intertemporal channels in the transmission of disturbances. Part II (chapters 4 and 5) offers a detailed statistical analysis of real exchange rate behavior in a large number of LDCs. Finally, part III (chapters 6–8) analyze in detail 39 devaluation episodes, focusing on the evolution of a large number of variables, including trade controls, black markets, the current account, and income distribution. Chapter 9 contains the conclusions of the study. Although chapters 2 and 3 are somewhat technical, I have tried to make the rest of the book accessible to policy-makers, nontechnically oriented economists, and other social scientists interested in issues of stabilization and adjustment in the developing countries.

During the long gestation of this book I have incurred numerous intellectual debts. Fernando Ossa of the Catholic University of Chile first interested me in exchange rate issues more than 15 years ago. I was fortunate to be a student of Jacob Frenkel at the University of Chicago. My discussions with him have always been very fruitful. Throughout the years I have had the privilege of interacting with Al Harberger, first as his student, then as a coauthor, and more recently as a colleague. His insights have always proved to be extremely valuable. I have benefited from comments and suggestions by Mohsin Khan, Alejandra Cox-Edwards, Peter Montiel, Sweder van Wijnbergen, Carlos Massad, Saul Lizondo, Vittorio Corbo, Marcelo Selowsky, Edgardo Barandiarán, Guillermo Calvo, Deepak Lal, Brian Pinto, Armeane Choksi, Kathy Krumm, Demetris Papageorgiou, Ed Leamer, Max Corden, Angel Palerm, Arye Hillman, Mauricio González, Ken Froot, Raul Feliz, Inder Ruprah, Ignacio Trigueros, Miguel Kiguel, Roberto Villareal, Carlos Hurtado, Jesus Cervantes, Nora Lustig, Elías Mizralie, Klaus Schmidt-Hebbel, Bob Nobay, and Joshua Aizenman. I have also benefited from suggestions by participants at seminars and workshops at the University of Pennsylvania, Yale University, the University of California at San Diego, ILADES-Georgetown (Santiago, Chile), Konstanz University (Germany), the World Bank, the Research Department of the IMF, the National Bureau of Economic Research, ITAM (Mexico City), Banco de la Republica (Bogotá, Colombia), the American Economic Association Annual Meetings (New Orleans), Oklahoma State University, the University of North Carolina, Latin American Econometric Society Meetings (Córdoba, Argentina, and San José, Costa Rica), WIDER (Helsinki), CIDE (Mexico City), FEDESARROLLO (Bogotá, Colombia), the IMF Institute, UNAM (Mexico City) and the University of Chicago. I am also grateful to five anonymous reviewers for the MIT Press. Their perceptive comments were of great help in revising the manuscript. Finally, I want to express my gratitude to several generations of graduate students at UCLA on whom I first tried some of the material presented in this book.

Some of the empirical research for this book was started when I was visiting the Country Policy Department of the World Bank (1984–1985), and some of the chapters were written when I was visiting the Research

Department of the International Monetary Fund (summers of 1987 and 1988) and the Summer Institute of the National Bureau of Economic Research. I am grateful to these institutions for providing an ideal atmosphere for undertaking this kind of research.

A long and detailed empirical study such as this one requires efficient support by a large number of research assistants. I am grateful to Evan Tanner, Horng-Ji-Liu, Rogelio Arellano, Diane Cashman, David Gould, and Francis Ng for their assistance. I am particularly grateful to Miguel Savastano, who not only provided able research assistance but also read the complete manuscript, making important comments and suggestions.

I am grateful to UCLA's Academic Senate and to the National Science Foundation for providing financial support for this project. I thank Lorraine Grams from UCLA for her efficient typing of the many versions of this manuscript. I also wish to thank Terry Vaughn, the economics editor for MIT Press for his continuing interest in the project and for his support throughout its many stages.

As always, I have received great support from my family. My wife and children have had patience and understanding. Moreover, they usually managed not to tease me for my obsessions with devaluations and real exchange rates. I am grateful to all of them. It is, however, my son's turn to have a book dedicated to him.

Washington, DC
August 1988

1   Introduction

Exchange rate problems have become a dominant theme in policy discussions in the developing countries. Some analysts have argued that many of the economic misfortunes suffered by the LDCs during the 1980s—including the debt crisis (Cline, 1983), the disappointing outcome of the Southern Cone experiments with free market policies (Corbo et al., 1986), and the dismal performance of Africa's agricultural sector (World Bank, 1984)—have been the result, in one way or another, of inappropriate exchange rate policies. Two main issues regarding exchange rates have, in particular, attracted the attention of policymakers and academics. First, there has been increased interest in trying to understand real exchange rate fluctuations; and second, there has been mounting concern regarding the effectiveness of nominal devaluations as policy tools.[1]

In the last 15 years or so real exchange rates (RERs) have become increasingly volatile in the developed as well as in the developing countries. This has been true even for those developing countries that after the collapse of the Bretton Woods system maintained a fixed nominal exchange rate regime. In some countries the fluctuations in real exchange rates have been so pronounced that it is not at all surprising to find that the domestic real price of some tradable goods increases by two or three times in a matter of a few years. In fact, the Argentinian case of 1981, when a glass of Coca-Cola in the Buenos Aires Sheraton cost approximately U.S. $7, has become legendary.

Table 1.1 contains the ratio of highest to lowest real multilateral exchange rates in a group of LDCs for the periods 1965–1971 and 1972–1984. As can be seen in all but one of these countries this ratio was higher for the second period. The indexes in table 1.1 were constructed using official nominal exchange rates. If, however, data on parallel markets for foreign exchange are used, these ratios are even larger.[2]

Table 1.1
Ratio of highest to lowest real exchange rate (RER) in selected developing countries:
1965–1971 and 1972–1984

Country	1965–1971	1972–1984
Bolivia	1.3	2.6
Dominican Republic	1.1	2.9
El Salvador	1.2	2.5
Kenya	1.1	1.3
Korea	1.1	1.4
Paraguay	1.6	2.3
Sri Lanka	1.3	3.9
Yugoslavia	3.2	1.5
Zambia	1.3	2.7

Source: These ratios refer to multilateral RER indexes constructed using data on official nominal exchange rates. See chapter 4 for a detailed discussion on how they have been constructed.

It is now well accepted at the theoretical level that excess volatility in RERs, and in particular situations of real exchange rate misalignment, will be translated into important welfare costs. Maintaining the RER at the "wrong" level generates incorrect signals and greatly hurts the degree of competitiveness of the tradables sectors (Willet, 1986). Determining whether a country's RER is at a particular time out of line with its long-run equilibrium level is, both theoretically and practically, one of the most difficult challenges faced by macroeconomic analysts and policymakers under both predetermined and floating nominal exchange rates. The difficulties, however, do not end there. In a predetermined nominal exchange rates regime, once it is established that the RER is indeed misaligned, policy packages aimed at correcting this disequilibrium should be devised. Among the traditional policy measures to face exchange rate misalignment and external sector disequilibria, devaluation is one of the most important.

Historically, devaluations have generally been traumatic episodes in the developing countries. They have often been surrounded by political upheaval, and as a consequence of them finance ministers and even governments have many times fallen.[3] Even in the late 1980s, more than 15 years after the abandonment of the generalized fixed parities Bretton Woods system, devaluations continue to be a "touchy" subject in the developing nations. It is very common to find that even when facing major external disequilibria, these countries' authorities vehemently resist devaluing their currencies. Why have devaluations been so strongly opposed in so many countries, while at the same time they have been so single-mindedly pushed by the international multilateral institutions such as the World Bank and the International Monetary Fund? What is the historical record of devaluations in the developing nations? Why do they seem to work in some countries and not in others? What is, after all, the precise role of a devaluation from a theoretical perspective? These questions are of relevance not only to academics but also to policymakers. Obtaining answers to them will allow us to understand better one of the most controversial policy issues in the developing world.

The purpose of the present book is to tackle a number of policy questions related to equilibrium and disequilibrium real exchange rates, and to investigate empirically the extent to which devaluations have been successful (or unsuccessful) in the developing nations. The main hypotheses of this study can be summarized in a few lines: First, it is argued that contrary to some popular policy views not all observed movements in RERs—not even large movements—necessarily represent a disequilibrium situation.[4] The long-run equilibrium RER is a function of a number of *real* variables, and observed changes in RERs may well be an equilibrium phenomenon. Second, even though the equilibrium RER depends on real variables only, the actual RER responds to real and monetary variables. Unsustainable or inconsistent macroeconomic policies will, under most circumstances, generate large deviations between actual and equilibrium RERs, or real exchange rate misalignment. Determining whether observed RER measurements in a particular country and period of time are justified by structural changes or whether they primarily respond to macroeconomic instability is an empirical matter. Third, if the starting situation is one of disequilibrium, and if it is accompanied by appropriate macroeconomic policies, nominal devaluations can greatly help an economy to regain equilibrium in a rapid and efficient way. Whether a stepwise devaluation or a devaluation followed by a crawling peg is more effective will depend on a number of factors, including the country's ability to sustain fiscal discipline. The main theoretical underpinnings of these hypotheses are provided in chapters 2 and 3. Chapters 4–8 present an extensive cross-country empirical analysis that deals, among other things, with (a) real exchange rate measurement, (b) actual real exchange rate behavior, (c) real exchange rates and parallel (black) market premia, (d) measures of equilibrium RER movements, (e) consequences of RER volatility, (f) causes of devaluation crises, (g) exchange controls and balance of payments crises, (h) macroeconomic consistency and black markets for foreign exchange, (i) nominal and real devaluations, (j) devaluations and capital flight, (k) devaluations and real output, and (l) devaluations, real wages, and income distribution.

Although this book emphasizes exchange rate issues in the developing countries, many of the points made here are broader and apply as well to the industrialized nations. In particular, much of the theoretical discussion in chapters 2 and 3 is applicable to any *small* open economy. The empirical analysis, however, deals exclusively with developing nations, ranging from newly industrialized countries (NICs) to some of the poorest nations.

There are a number of reasons that justify separating developing from developed nations when analyzing exchange rate issues. First, after the collapse of the Bretton Woods system the vast majority of the developing countries maintained some type of predetermined (i.e., fixed or crawling peg) nominal exchange rate regime.[5] In that regard, most of the theoretical advances experienced by the economics of exchange rates during the 1970s and 1980—which have primarily dealt with an array of issues pertinent to freely fluctuating exchange rates—have had limited applicability for the developing countries. Second, most developing countries' currencies are nonconvertible; exchange controls are quite pervasive, greatly reducing the degree of capital mobility. Third, in only a handful of LDCs are there futures markets for foreign exchange, making exchange risk a major source of uncertainty for producers, exporters, and consumers. Fourth, multiple official exchange rates are also a common feature, imposing de facto taxes on a number of transactions. Fifth, in many countries parallel or black markets for foreign exchange are quite common, and at times even dominant. And sixth, in many of these countries, and in particular in Africa, domestic capital markets are highly repressed. This results in a reduced capacity for engaging in traditional monetary and fiscal policies. Although these institutional differences between the developed and developing nations are important, there are many other aspects common to both types of countries. In fact, as is argued in chapter 2, the more fundamental principles surrounding *long-run* equilibrium real exchange rates in the two groups can be analyzed using a very similar theoretical apparatus. Finally, it is important to notice that there are also differences across developing countries. Some of the NICs have institutions that are much more sophisticated than those in the poorer nations.

1.1 Preliminary Concepts

Alternative Definitions of Real Exchange Rates

Until now we have used the term real exchange rate in a rather vague way. This, in fact, reflects the state of affairs in the international economics literature, where a number of alternative definitions of real exchange rates are currently used. While this is not per se serious, it does generate some communication problems. Moreover, some economists from outside the field of international economics have objected altogether to the use of the concept of "real" exchange rates on the grounds that it involves a contradiction in terms. According to this view the (nominal) exchange rate is by definition a monetary variable; how, then, can we talk about a "real" exchange rate?[6] Although these professionals may have a (small) point, the term real exchange rate is too engrained in the modern literature on international and development economics to attempt here to rename it. What is very important, however, is to have a clear idea of what we exactly mean by "the" real exchange rate.

In most modern theoretical works "the" real exchange rate (e) is defined as the domestic relative price of tradable goods (P_T) to nontradable goods (P_N): $e = P_T/P_N$.[7] This definition summarizes incentives that guide resource allocation across the tradables and nontradables sectors; an increase in e will make the production of tradables relatively more profitable, inducing resources to move out of the nontradables sector and into the tradables sector. In addition, this definition of the real exchange rate provides a good index of the degree of international competitiveness of the country's tradables sector. Indeed, this relative price measures the cost of producing domestically the tradable goods. A decline in the RER, or a *real exchange rate appreciation*, reflects the fact that there has been an increase in the domestic cost of producing tradable goods. If there are no changes in relative prices in the rest of the world, this decline in RER represents a deterioration of the country's degree of international competitiveness— the country now produces tradable goods in a relatively (that is relative to the rest of the world) less efficient way than before. The interpretation of an increase in the relative price of tradables of RER, or *real depreciation*, is perfectly symmetrical, and represents an improvement in the degree of international competitiveness.[8] Although there are other indexes of a country's international degree of competitiveness, such as unit labor costs, these alternative indexes are usually unreliable in the case of the developing countries.[9]

A more traditional, but still popular, definition of the real exchange rate relies on the *purchasing power parity* (PPP) approach. According to the supporters of this view, the PPP real exchange rate (e_{PPP}) is equal to the nominal exchange rate (E) corrected (i.e., multiplied) by the ratio of "the" foreign price level (P^*) to "the" domestic price level: $e_{PPP} = EP^*/P$. Depending on whether P and P^* are consumer price indexes or producers price indexes, e_{PPP} will be the relative price of foreign to domestic consumption or production baskets. Although this definition of real exchange rates has not been popular in academic writing for quite sometime now, it is still widely used by policymakers and other practitioners. This is partially explained by the difficulties encountered in measuring the relative price of tradables to nontradables.

It is interesting to compare the tradables-nontradables relative price definition with the PPP definition of the real exchange rate. Assuming that P and P^* in the PPP definition are geometrically weighted averages of tradable and nontradable prices, with weights, α, $(1 - \alpha)$, β, and $(1 - \beta)$, it is possible to write $P = P_N^{\alpha} P_T^{1-\alpha}$ and $P^* = P_N^{*\beta} P_T^{*(1-\beta)}$. Further assuming that the country in question is small, that the law of one price holds for tradable goods (i.e., $P_T = P_T^* E$), that there are no taxes on trade, and that E is fixed and equal to 1, it is possible to find the relation between percentage changes in the real exchange rate (e) and in the PPP real exchange rate, where, as usual, the "hat" operator $(\hat{\ })$ represents percentage change: $\hat{e} = (1/\alpha)\hat{e}_{PPP} + (\beta/\alpha)(\hat{P}_T^* - \hat{P}_N^*)$. It may be seen, then, that in general changes in the two definitions of the real exchange rate will differ (i.e., $\hat{e} \neq \hat{e}_{PPP}$). Moreover, e and e_{PPP} can even move in opposite directions, depending on the behavior of foreign relative prices (P_T^*/P_N^*).

Although the PPP real exchange rate (e_{PPP}) is also an index of the degree of international competitiveness of the country in question, it fails to capture changes in the relative incentives guiding resource allocation across the tradables and nontradables sectors. Consequently, e_{PPP} does not provide precise information on how relative prices impinge on the evolution of the external sector and of the different accounts of the balance of payments. For this reason, in the theoretical chapters of this book the real exchange rate is defined as the relative price of tradables to nontradables. In chapter 4 we discuss some of the problems encountered in the attempt to measure this relative price, and propose some proxies for it.

The above discussion on the tradables to nontradables definition of the real exchange rate has ignored taxes on international trade. However, if there are these type of taxes, a decision should be made on whether to define a real exchange rate inclusive or exclusive of them. To the extent that we are interested in the allocation of resources between tradables and nontradables, the domestic relative price of tradables should be used. This is indeed the approach followed by most modern theoretical works. However, a limitation of this definition is that it (implicitly) assumes that all tradable goods are subject to the same tax. However, in a many-goods economy the different tradable goods are subject to taxes of different rates.

For example, most importables are subject to differentiated tariffs or import quotas, while some exportables are many times subject to taxes. Two basic ways have been devised for handling this problem. First, some authors have proposed to define sector-specific (or good-specific) indexes of the real exchange rate corrected by the effects of taxes (or subsidies).[10] For example, if sector j is subject to a tax of t_j, this index will be $e_{Tj} = EP_j^*(1 + t_j)/P_N$. A serious limitation of this approach is that it defeats the whole idea of having one comprehensive measure of competitiveness for the economy as a whole. The second way of handling the existence of differential trade taxes is by defining the economy-wide real exchange rate index exclusive of these taxes. In this case, then, $e = EP_T^*/P_N$. This approach has a number of advantages. First, this theoretical definition is quite close to available empirical measures; and second, once this index of the economy-wide RER is available, it is still possible to use information on the sectoral taxes on trade to compute more detailed relative price indexes.

Real Exchange Rate Measurement

When faced with the practical decision of constructing time series of real exchange rate indexes for the developing countries, analysts are confronted with significantly fewer options than those suggested by more theoretical discussions. In fact, the construction of actual indexes is surrounded by a number of problems, ranging from finding proxies for the analytical constructs to deciding which price indexes to use, and so on. Given the particularly severe data constraint encountered in the majority of the developing countries, measured RER indexes invariably take the following form:

$$\text{RER} = \frac{EP^*}{P},$$

where E is either the bilateral or the effective (i.e., multilateral) nominal exchange rate, P^* is some foreign price index, and P is a domestic price index. A problem with this measure refers to choosing price indexes—or components of price indexes—that are good proxies for the price of tradables and of nontradables. Some authors, for example, have suggested using the domestic consumer price index (CPI) as a proxy for nontradable prices, and a foreign wholesale (or producer) price index (WPI) as a proxy for the world price of tradables (Harberger, 1986). In a number of LDCs where there are multiple rates or generalized black markets, an additional problem involves choosing E. To the extent that the analyst requires periodicity and reliability, the choices of P^* and P are limited to CPIs and

WPIs (or its components). In chapter 4 we discuss a number of important issues of real exchange rate measurement and we analyze the behavior of different indexes of real exchange rates.

Real Exchange Rate Misalignment

Real exchange rate misalignment is a term commonly used in policy discussions, but seldom defined in a precise way. In this study real exchange rate misalignment is defined as *sustained deviations of the actual real exchange rate from its long-run equilibrium level*. If the actual real exchange rate is below the equilibrium RER value, we say that there is a real exchange rate *overvaluation*. If, on the other hand, the actual RER exceeds the equilibrium RER, we say that there is an *undervaluation*.

It follows immediately from this definition of misalignment that as a first step in understanding this phenomenon we need to have a theory on how the equilibrium real exchange rate behaves. Traditional policy analyses have tended to follow the purchasing power parity (PPP) doctrine of equilibrium real exchange rates. According to this theory the equilibrium real exchange rate is constant; its equilibrium level is found by looking at the value of the RER in some distant period that exhibited external equilibrium (see Dornbusch, 1982). The approach taken in this book differs significantly from the PPP view. The equilibrium real exchange rate (ERER) is defined as that relative price of tradables to nontradables that, for given sustainable (equilibrium) values of other relevant variables—such as taxes, international prices, and technology—results in the simultaneous attainment of *internal* and *external* equilibrium. *Internal equilibrium* means that the nontradable goods market clears in the current period, and is expected to be in equilibrium in future periods. In this definition of equilibrium RER it is implicit the idea that this equilibrium takes place with unemployment at the "natural" level. *External equilibrium*, on the other hand, is attained when the intertemporal budget constraint that states that the discounted sum of a country's current account has to be equal to zero is satisfied. In other words, external equilibrium means that the current account balances (current and future) are compatible with long-run sustainable capital flows.

From our definition of real exchange rate misalignment it also follows that in addition to understanding how equilibrium RERs behave, we need to have a theory on how the actual RER behaves, and on why the actual RER can indeed differ from its equilibrium value. This is done in chapter 3, where a monetary model of a small open economy with a parallel market for foreign exchange is developed.

1.2 Plan of the Book

The book is divided into three parts. Part I—chapters 2 and 3—deals with the theory of equilibrium and disequilibrium real exchange rates. Part II—chapters 4 and 5—presents the results from a large cross-country empirical analysis on real exchange rate behavior in developing countries. Part III—chapters 6–8—deals with devaluation and real exchange rate realignment.

The theoretical analysis is given mostly in chapters 2 and 3. In chapter 2 an intertemporal optimizing real model of a small open economy is developed to analyze the process of determination of equilibrium real exchange rates. The model considers the case of a two-period economy where three goods—exportables, importables, and nontradables—are consumed and produced. The equilibrium RER is defined as the relative price of nontradables compatible with the simultaneous attainment of external and internal equilibrium. Throughout the chapter we analyze in great detail how the equilibrium real exchange rate responds to a number of real disturbances, including terms of trade shocks, import tariff reforms, changes in government behavior, and technological progress.

The purpose of chapter 2 is to analyze the way in which the *equilibrium real* exchange rate responds to disturbances. Chapter 3, on the other hand, deals with *actual* real exchange rate behavior. In this chapter a monetary model of a small economy with a dual nominal exchange rate regime is developed. It is shown that unsustainable and inconsistent macroeconomic policies will generally lead to real exchange rate overvaluation, losses of international reserves, and balance of payments crises. The model is used to analyze the role of devaluations in the adjustment process, including issues related to exchange rate crises.

Chapters 4 and 5 present empirical cross-country evidence on real exchange rate behavior. In chapter 4 data for 33 countries are analyzed. The chapter starts by discussing problems related to RER measurement and comparing different RER indexes for the 33 countries in the sample. Then it deals with parallel market nominal rates and real exchange rates behavior. Finally, the time series properties of three alternative RER indexes for the 33 countries are analyzed. One of the main findings of the chapter is that there is massive evidence rejecting the PPP theory of real exchange rate behavior.

In chapter 5 we investigate empirically the roles played by nominal and real factors in real exchange rate movements for a group of 12 developing countries. For this purpose we derive a very general equation for RER dynamics that is able to capture the most important features of the theoretical constructs of chapters 2 and 3. The econometric results reported in this chapter support the hypothesis that real exchange rate movements respond, at least in the short run, to both monetary and real disturbances. These econometric estimates are then used to construct series on equilibrium real exchange rates for a number of countries. These estimated equilibrium RERs exhibit, for some of the countries, significant changes, as our model from chapter 2 suggested.

Chapters 6–8 deal with devaluation and real exchange rate realignment. In them 39 major devaluation episodes during 1960–1982 are analyzed in detail. Chapter 6 deals with the causes of devaluation in the light of the model developed in chapter 3. In particular, we inquire as to the extent to which devaluations have historically been the result of inconsistently expansive macroeconomic policies. In this empirical analysis we use a variety of statistical methods, both parametric and nonparametric. In addition to macroeconomic policies, we analyze the behavior of parallel markets for foreign exchange, as well as of exchange controls, trade impediments, and payments restrictions. To a large—even surprising—extent the results from this analysis support the implications of our model from chapter 3.

Chapter 7 deals with the effects of nominal devaluations, concentrating on whether they have been able to generate real exchange rate devaluations and, thus, help reestablish real exchange rate equilibrium. Here we make a clear distinction between stepwise devaluations and those devaluations followed by the adoption of a crawling peg. The analysis undertaken in this chapter closely follows the evolution of parallel market rates during the aftermath of the devaluation. Also, we look in detail at the interaction between devaluations and attempts to liberalize the external sector in these countries. In this chapter an effort is made to distinguish between successful and unsuccessful devaluations, and the causes behind the successes and failures are investigated.

The analysis in chapter 7 concentrates exclusively on the effects of devaluations on the external sector—the real exchange rate, the current account, capital movements, and the accumulation of foreign assets. In chapter 8 we move away from the external sector and inquire into the effects of devaluations on output, wages, and income distribution. The chapter makes a start on developing a model that captures the interactions between devaluations, employment, wages, and real economic activity. We then move to an empirical analysis focusing on two data sets: the 39 devaluation episodes of chapter 6 and 7 and the 12 countries of the regression analysis of chapter 5. This analysis looks into whether devaluations exhibit contractionary effects on output. The regression analysis also investigates the effects of external sector distortions on economic performance. The chapter finishes with an empirical analysis of the income distribution effects of devaluations. The book closes with chapter 9, where the main conclusions are presented.

Notes

1. The preoccupation with real exchange rate behavior has not been limited to the developing countries. Trying to explain real exchange rate movements in the industrialized world has indeed been a dominant subject in recent debates. See, for example, Williamson (1983b) and Marston (1988).

2. See chapter 4.

3. See Cooper (1971b). See also Denoon (1986).

4. These views have been based on the purchasing power parity (PPP) doctrine. See chapters 2 and 3.

5. In June 1988 the International Monetary Fund classified the developing nations' exchange regimes as follows: 88 had a pegged nominal exchange rate; 4 countries had "limited flexibility"; 4 adjusted their parity according to a set of indicators; 21 had a managed floating system; and only 10 had an independently floating system. (*International Financial Statistics*, July 1988).

6. Naturally these objections carry over to concepts such as the *real* quantity of money, which economists have used for many years.

7. See, for example, Dornbusch (1980), Frenkel and Mussa (1985), and the papers in Frenkel (1983).

8. See chapter 4. See also Edwards (1989e).

9. Recently, there has been some debate on whether the real exchange rate should be defined as P_T/P_N or as P_N/P_T. The International Monetary Fund has adopted the latter definition, while the tradition in the developing countries— and especially in Latin America—has been to use the former definition. Both approaches have pros and cons. The IMF definition is appealing because in that case a real appreciation is reflected by an increase in the RER index, while a decline represents a real depreciation. The P_T/P_N definition is particularly appealing because in this case both nominal and real depreciations (appreciations) will result in increases (decreases) of the respective indexes. In this book we shall follow the Latin American tradition by defining the real exchange rate as the relative price of tradable to nontradable goods.

10. See, for example, Krueger (1978). Sometimes this real exchange rate index that incorporates subsidies and taxes has been called the real effective exchange rate. This is another instance of confusing terminology, since other analysts—and most notably the International Monetary Fund—define real effective exchange rates as those real rates computed relative to a basket of currencies. In this study, and in order to avoid confusion, we call the basket rate the *real multilateral exchange rate*.

I

The Theory of Equilibrium and Disequilibrium Real Exchange Rates

2 The Determination of Equilibrium Real Exchange Rates

This chapter deals with the economics of equilibrium real exchange rates. It analyzes theoretically the way in which equilibrium real exchange rates react to a number of (real) disturbances, including terms of trade shocks, changes in the tax system, and technological progress. Since real exchange rate misalignment is defined as *sustained departures of the actual real exchange rate from its equilibrium value*, the understanding of the economics of equilibrium real exchange rates is a fundamental first step in any attempt to understand real exchange rate misalignment and overvaluation.

Simplified views based on the purchasing power parity (PPP) theory have suggested that the equilibrium RER is a constant that does not vary through time. Speaking rigorously, however, there is no reason why the value of the RER required to attain internal and external equilibrium should be a constant number; it would indeed be an extraordinary coincidence if it was. Changing world conditions, productivity improvements, adjustments to trade barriers, and changes in taxation, among many other factors, will affect the path of the RER compatible with the attainment of internal and external equilibrium. Only to the extent that we have a firm understanding of the way equilibrium RERs react to changes in their fundamental determinants can we meaningfully discuss issues related to sustained deviations of actual RERs from their equilibrium value, or RER misalignment.

In this chapter, a benchmark intertemporal general equilibrium model of a small open economy is developed to analyze how the equilibrium path of the real exchange rate responds to a series of disturbances. The benchmark model assumes that the economy is formed by optimizing consumers and producers, and by a government. It is also assumed that there is perfect foresight. The importation of commodities is subject to a tariff, while foreign borrowing is subject to a nonprohibitive tax. There is investment; however, it is assumed that the labor force does not grow. The model is set up using intertemporal duality theory, and emphasizes the intertemporal linkages between different shocks and relative prices. This model provides an abstract minimal real framework for analyzing the behavior of equilibrium RERs. Throughout most of the benchmark analysis it is assumed that prices are flexible, and that there is full employment and perfect competition. Later in the chapter some of these assumptions are relaxed and the way in which RERs react under alternative conditions—including rigid wages and unemployment—are discussed. The strategy followed in this chapter is to concentrate on essentials, eschewing unnecessary complications. For this reason the model is completely real; the role of monetary disturbances and their effect on actual RER behavior, misalignment, and overvaluation is relegated to chapter 3.

2.1 Equilibrium Real Exchange Rates

The equilibrium real exchange rate (ERER) is that relative price of tradables to nontradables that, for given sustainable (equilibrium) values of other relevant variables—such as taxes, international prices, and technology—results in the simultaneous attainment of *internal* and *external* equilibrium.[1] *Internal equilibrium* means that the nontradable goods market clears in the current period, and is expected to be in equilibrium in future periods. In this definition of equilibrium RER it is implicit the idea that this equilibrium takes place with unemployment at the "natural" level. *External equilibrium*, on the other hand, is attained when the intertemporal budget constraint that states that the discounted sum of a country's current account has to be equal to zero is satisfied. In other words, external equilibrium means that the current account balances (current and future) are compatible with long-run sustainable capital flows.[2]

A number of important implications follows from this definition of equilibrium real exchange rate. First, as noted above, the ERER is not an immutable number. When there are changes in any of the other variables that affect the country's internal and external equilibria, there will also be changes in the equilibrium real exchange rate. For example, the RER "required" to attain equilibrium will not be the same at a very low world price of the country's main export as it is at a very high price of that good. In a sense, then, the ERER is itself a function of a number of variables, including import tariffs, export taxes, real interest rates, and capital controls. These immediate determinants of the ERER are the *real exchange rate "fundamentals."* Second, the ERER will not only be affected by current "fundamentals" but also by the expected future evolution of these variables. To the extent that there are possibilities for intertemporal substitution of consumption via foreign borrowing and lending, and of intertemporal substitution in production via investment, expected future events—such as an expected future change in the international terms of trade—will have an effect on the current value of the ERER. In particular, the behavior of the equilibrium real exchange rate will depend on whether changes in fundamentals are perceived as being permanent or temporary. If there is perfect international borrowing, a temporary disturbance to, say, the terms of trade, will affect the complete future path of equilibrium RERs. However, if there is rationing in the international credit market, intertemporal substitution through consumption will be cut, and temporary disturbances will tend to affect the ERER in the short run only. In this case a distinction between short-run and long-run equilibrium real exchange rates becomes useful.

2.2 A Benchmark Model of Equilibrium Real Exchange Rates

In order to model the behavior of equilibrium real exchange rates formally, it is necessary to develop a complete intertemporal framework able to capture how both policy induced disturbances and exogenous shocks affect the path of equilibrium relative prices in the economy. In this chapter such a framework is developed, and the way in which equilibrium RERs react to a series of changes in "fundamentals" is analyzed. We start with the benchmark case, characterized by a highly stylized intertemporal model with full employment, no price rigidities and no international credit rationing. This allows us to understand the most fundamental aspects of the economics of equilibrium real exchange rates. We then relax some of these assumptions, and investigate the ways in which the results are altered.

Although the framework used in this chapter is general enough to accommodate many goods and factors, it is useful to think of this small economy as being comprised of a large number of profit maximizing firms that produce three goods—exportables (X), importables (M), and nontradables (N)—using constant returns to scale technology, under perfect competition. It is assumed that there are more factors than tradable goods, so that factor price equalization does not hold. One way to think about this is by assuming that each sector uses capital, labor, and natural resources.

There are two periods only—the present (period 1) and the future (period 2)—and there is perfect foresight. Residents of this small country can borrow or lend internationally. There are, however, taxes on foreign borrowing; the domestic (real) interest rate exceeds the world interest rate. The intertemporal constraint states that at the end of period 2 the country has paid its debts. The importation of M is subject to specific import tariffs both in periods 1 and 2. In this model the current account is equal to savings minus investment in each period. Consumers maximize intertemporal utility and consume all three goods.

There is a government that, in the general case, consumes both tradables and nontradables. Government expenditure is financed from four sources: nondistortionary taxes, proceeds from import tariffs, proceeds from the taxation of foreign borrowing by the private sector, and borrowing from abroad. As in the case of the private sector, the government is subject to an intertemporal constraint—the discounted value of government expenditure (including foreign debt service) has to equal the discounted value of income from taxation.

In addition to the private sector and government budget constraints, internal equilibrium requires that the nontradable market clears *in each period*. That is, the quantity supplied of nontradables has to equal the sum of the private and public sectors demands for these goods. The model is completely real; there is no money or other nominal assets.

Revenue and Expenditure Functions

A convenient and elegant way of setting up this intertemporal optimizing model is by using duality theory.[3] A tilde (˜) over a variable indicates that that is a period 2 variable (e.g., $\tilde{R}$ is the revenue function in period 2); subscripts refer to partial derivatives with respect to that variable (e.g., R_q is the partial derivative of R with respect to q; $\tilde{R}_{\tilde{q}\tilde{p}}$ is the second derivative of $\tilde{R}$ with respect to $\tilde{q}$ and $\tilde{p}$). Throughout the model we set the world price of exportables as the numeraire.

The production side of the model is characterized, in each period, by revenue functions—R and $\tilde{R}$ for periods 1 and 2—that give us the maximum revenue that optimizing firms obtain from producing X, M, and N, subject to prevailing domestic prices, available technology—summarized by the production possibilities function $F(\ )$—and available factors of production.[4] For period 1 the revenue function is given by

$$R = \max\{Q_X + pQ_M + qQ_N | F(Q, V) \leq 0\}, \tag{2.1}$$

where Q_X, Q_M, Q_N are quantities produced of exportables, importables, and nontradables in that period. Q is a vector that summarizes these quantities produced; V is a vector of factors of production; $F(\ )$ is the production function that summarizes existing technology; p is the domestic price of importables relative to exportables; and q is the price of nontradables relative to exportables in period 1. Equation (2.1) can then be rewritten in the following way:

$$R = R(p, q, V). \tag{2.2}$$

This is the maximized value of output in period 1 in terms of exportables. Naturally, the revenue function for period 2 can be written in a similar way.

Revenue functions have a number of convenient properties that make their use in formal modeling highly attractive. First, their derivatives with respect to prices yield the corresponding supply functions (Dixit and Norman, 1980, pp. 31–33). Thus, if we denote the partial derivatives with respect to a particular argument by a subindex, we have that

$$\frac{\partial R}{\partial p} = R_p = Q_M(p, \dots) \qquad \text{supply function of } M \text{ in period 1,}$$

$$\tag{2.3}$$

$$\frac{\partial \tilde{R}}{\partial \tilde{q}} = \tilde{R}_{\tilde{q}} = \tilde{Q}_N(\tilde{q}, \dots) \qquad \text{supply function of } N \text{ in period 2.}$$

Another convenient property of revenue functions is that they are convex, implying that $R_{pp} = \partial Q_M / \partial p \geq 0$ and that $R_{qq} = \partial Q_N / \partial q \geq 0$. That is, supply curves slope upward. We assume that the three goods compete for the given amount of resources, and that there are no intermediate inputs; thus, the cross-price derivatives of the revenue functions are negative.[5]

Consumers are assumed to maximize the present value of utility, subject to their intertemporal constraint. Assuming that the utility function is time separable, with each subutility function homothetic, the representative consumer problem can be stated as follows:

$$\max W\{U(C_N, C_M, C_X), \tilde{U}(\tilde{C}_N, \tilde{C}_M, \tilde{C}_X)\} \tag{2.4}$$

subject to

$$C_X + pC_M + qC_M + \delta(\tilde{C}_X + \tilde{p}\tilde{C}_M + \tilde{q}\tilde{C}_N) \leq \text{wealth,}$$

where W is the utility function; U and $\tilde{U}$ are periods 1 and 2 subutility functions; C_N, C_M, C_X ($\tilde{C}_N$, $\tilde{C}_M$, $\tilde{C}_X$) are consumption of N, M, and X in period 1 (2). As before, p and $\tilde{p}$ are the (domestic) price of importables relative to exportables in periods 1 and 2, and q and $\tilde{q}$ are the price of nontradables relative to exportables in periods 1 and 2. δ is the domestic discount factor, equal to $(1 + r)^{-1}$, and r is the domestic real interest rate in terms of the exportable good.

Wealth is the discounted sum of consumer's income in both periods. Income, in turn, is given in each period by three components: (1) income from labor services rendered to firms, (2) income from the renting of capital stock that consumers own to domestic firms, and (3) income obtained from government transfers. Given the nature of preferences, the consumer optimization problem can be thought of as taking place in two stages. First, the consumers decide how to allocate their wealth across periods. Second, they decide how to distribute each period (optimal) expenditure across the three goods.

The demand side of the model can be conveniently summarized by a twice-differentiable concave expenditure function that gives the minimum discounted value of expenditure required to attain a level of utility $\overline{W}$ for given domestic prices in periods 1 and 2:

$$E = \min\{C_X + pC_M + qC_N + \delta(\tilde{C}_X + \tilde{p}\tilde{C}_M + \tilde{q}\tilde{C}_X)\} \tag{2.5}$$

subject to $W(U, \tilde{U}) \geq \overline{W}$. Here C_X, C_M, C_N and $\tilde{C}_X$, $\tilde{C}_M$, $\tilde{C}_N$ refer to consumption of exportables, importables, and nontradables in periods 1 and 2. This expenditure function can be written as a function of prices and utility only (Dixit and Norman, 1980):

$$E = E\{p, q, \delta\tilde{p}, \delta\tilde{q}; W\}. \tag{2.6}$$

Furthermore, since we have assumed that the utility function is weakly separable with each period subutility homothetic, equation (2.6) can be written as

$$E = E\{\pi(p, q), \delta\tilde{\pi}(\tilde{p}, \tilde{q}); W\}, \tag{2.7}$$

where $\pi(\ )$ and $\tilde{\pi}(\ )$ are exact price indexes for periods 1 and 2, and are interpreted as unit expenditure functions (see Svensson and Razin, 1983). A convenient property of the expenditure function is that its partial derivatives with respect to prices are equal to the respective compensated (Hicksian) demand function. For example, the derivative of E with respect to p is equal to the compensated demand function for importables in period 1. In general, the following relations hold (where, as before, subindexes refer to partial derivatives with respect to that argument):

$$E_p = \frac{\partial E}{\partial \pi} \frac{\partial \pi}{\partial p} = E_\pi \pi_p = D_M(p, \ldots),$$

$$E_q = \frac{\partial E}{\partial \pi} \frac{\partial \pi}{\partial q} = E_\pi \pi_q = D_N(q, \ldots),$$

$$E_{\tilde{p}} = \frac{\partial E}{\partial \tilde{\pi}} \frac{\partial \tilde{\pi}}{\partial \tilde{p}} = E_{\tilde{\pi}} \tilde{\pi}_{\tilde{p}} = \tilde{D}_M(\tilde{p}, \ldots),$$

$$E_{\tilde{q}} = \frac{\partial E}{\partial \tilde{\pi}} \frac{\partial \tilde{\pi}}{\partial \tilde{q}} = E_{\tilde{\pi}} \tilde{\pi}_{\tilde{q}} = \tilde{D}_N(\tilde{q}, \ldots), \tag{2.8}$$

where D_M ($\tilde{D}_M$) and D_N ($\tilde{D}_N$) are the Hicksian demand functions for M and N in period 1 (2), and π_p and π_q are the derivatives of the exact price indexes with respect to the relative prices of importables and nontradables in period 1. Since the π's are unit expenditure functions, these derivatives can be interpreted as expenditure shares of M and N in period 1. By concacity of E it follows that the second derivatives are negative—E_{pp}, E_{qq}, $E_{\tilde{p}\tilde{p}}$, $E_{\tilde{q}\tilde{q}} < 0$—reflecting the fact that the demand curves slope downward. Given our assumption of a time separable utility function, expenditures in periods 1 and 2 are substitutes, implying that all intertemporal cross elasticities are positive. However, since in every period there are three goods, any two of them can be complements. It is possible, then, that in each period one of the *intra*temporal cross elasticities will be negative.

The Model

The general model is given by equations (2.9)–(2.17), where the (world) price of exportables has been taken as the numeraire:

$$R(1, p, q, V, K) + \delta \tilde{R}(1, \tilde{p}, \tilde{q}; \tilde{V}, K + I) - I(\delta) - T - \delta \tilde{T}$$

$$= E\{\pi(1, p, q), \delta \tilde{\pi}(1, \tilde{p}, \tilde{q}), W\}, \tag{2.9}$$

$$G_X + p^* G_M + q G_N + \delta^*(\tilde{G}_X + \tilde{p}^* \tilde{G}_M + \tilde{q} \tilde{G}_N)$$

$$= \tau(E_p - R_p) + \delta^* \tilde{\tau}(E_{\tilde{p}} - \tilde{R}_{\tilde{p}}) + b(NCA) + T + \delta^* \tilde{T}, \tag{2.10}$$

$$R_q = E_q + G_N, \tag{2.11}$$

$$\tilde{R}_{\tilde{q}} = E_{\tilde{q}} + \tilde{G}_N, \tag{2.12}$$

$$p = p^* + \tau, \tag{2.13}$$

$$\tilde{p} = \tilde{p}^* + \tilde{\tau}, \tag{2.14}$$

$$\delta \tilde{R}_K = 1, \tag{2.15}$$

$$P_T^* = \gamma P_M^* + (1 - \gamma) P_X^*, \quad \tilde{P}_T^* = \gamma \tilde{P}_M^* + (1 - \gamma) \tilde{P}_X^* \quad (P_X^* = \tilde{P}_X^* = 1), \tag{2.16}$$

$$RER = (P_T^*/P_N), \quad \widetilde{RER} = (\tilde{P}_T^*/\tilde{P}_N). \tag{2.17}$$

Table 2.1 gives the notation used.

Table 2.1
Notation used in model of equilibrium real exchange rates

$R(\ )$; $\tilde{R}(\ )$	Revenue functions in periods 1 and 2. Their partial derivatives with respect to each price are equal to the supply functions.
p; $\tilde{p}$	Domestic relative price of importables in periods 1 and 2.
q; $\tilde{q}$	Relative price of nontradables in periods 1 and 2.
V; $\tilde{V}$	Vector of factors of production, excluding capital.
K	Capital stock in period 1.
$I(\ )$	Investment in period 1.
δ^*	World discount factor, equal to $(1 + r^*)^{-1}$, where r^* is world real interest rate in terms of exportables.
δ	Domestic discount factor, equal to $(1 + r)^{-1}$. Since there is a tax on foreign borrowing, $\delta < \delta^*$
$b = (\delta^* - \delta)$	Discounted value of tax payments per unit borrowed from abroad.
p^*; $\tilde{p}^*$	World relative price of imports in periods 1 and 2.
τ; $\tilde{\tau}$	Import tariffs in periods 1 and 2.
T; $(\tilde{T})$	Lump sum tax in periods 1 and 2.
G_X, G_M, G_N; $\tilde{G}_X$, $\tilde{G}_M$, $\tilde{G}_N$	Quantities of goods X, M, and N consumed by the government in periods 1 and 2.
$E(\ )$	Intertemporal expenditure function.
$\pi(1, p, q)$; $\tilde{\pi}(\ )$	Exact price indexes for periods 1 and 2—which, under assumptions of homothecity and separability, corresponds to unit expenditure functions.
W	Total welfare.
NCA	Noninterest current account of the private sector in period 2.
P_M^*, P_X^*; $\tilde{P}_M^*$, $\tilde{P}_X^*$	Nominal world prices of M and X in periods 1 and 2. Notice that we assume that $P_X^* = \tilde{P}_X^* = 1$.
P_N; $\tilde{P}_N$	Nominal price of nontradables in periods 1 and 2.
P_T^*; $\tilde{P}_T^*$	World prices of tradables, computed as an index of the prices of X and M.
RER; $\widetilde{RER}$	Real exchange rates in periods 1 and 2.

Equation (2.9) is the intertemporal budget constraint for the private sector and states that the present value of income valued at domestic prices has to equal the present value of private expenditure. Given the assumption of a tax on foreign borrowing, the discount factor used in (2.9) is the domestic factor δ which is smaller than the world discount factor δ^*.

Equation (2.10) is the government intertemporal budget constraint. It states that the discounted value of government expenditure has to equal the present value of government income from taxation. Notice that since the government does not have to balance its budget period by period, equation (2.10) implicitly assumes that the government can borrow from abroad.[6] If period 1 income falls short of expenditure, the difference is made up with foreign loans. Since this is a two-period model, the amount of borrowing in period 1 is equal to the stock of public debt at the end of the period. Alternatively, one can assume that in period 1 the government "inherits" a certain stock of foreign debt (see Frenkel and Razin, 1987). There is, however, no domestic debt. NCA, which is equal to $(\tilde{R} - \tilde{\pi}E_{\tilde{\pi}})$ in (2.10), is the private sector current account surplus in period 2; $b(\mathrm{NCA})$ is the discounted value of taxes on foreign borrowing paid by the private sector. Notice that the use of the world discount factor δ^* in (2.10) reflects the assumption that in this model the government in not subject to the tax on foreign borrowing.

Equation (2.11) and (2.12) are the equilibrium conditions for the nontradables market in periods 1 and 2; in each of these periods the quantity supplied of N (R_q and $\tilde{R}_{\tilde{q}}$) has to equal the sum of the quantity demanded by the private sector (E_q and $E_{\tilde{q}}$) and by the government. Given the assumptions about preferences (separability and homotheticity) the demand for N by the private sector in period 1 can be written as

$$E_q = \pi_q E_{\pi},\tag{2.18}$$

where π_q is the share of nontradables in period 1's expenditure, and E_{π} is *real* consumption (on all goods) in period 1. A corresponding expression holds for period 2.

Equations (2.13) and (2.14) specify the relation between domestic prices of importables, world prices of imports, and tariffs. It is assumed that the initial level of the import tariffs is the one that the authorities deem compatible with, or conducive to, the desired long-run allocation of resources. In that sense, then, in this chapter we shall assume that tariffs are changed in order to generate a *new* desired allocation of resources, rather than to help establish balance of payments equilibrium. In chapter 3, however, we shall discuss the role of tariff hikes under conditions of balance of payments crises and real exchange rate overvaluation.

Equation (2.15) describes investment decisions, and states that profit maximizing firms will add to the capital stock until Tobin's "q" equals 1. This expression assumes that the stock of capital is made up of the numeraire good. This is only a simplifying assumption that helps clarify the exposition. Assuming that the capital is made up of other goods complicates the algebra without affecting in a significant way the results.

In this model we can distinguish between the "exportables real exchange rate" ($1/q$) and the "importables real exchange rate" (p/q). Since the relative price of X and M can change, we cannot really talk about a tradable goods composite. It is still possible, however, to *compute* how an index of tradables prices evolves through time. Equation (2.16) is the definition of the price index for tradables, where γ and $(1 - \gamma)$ are the weights of importables and exportables.[7] Equation (2.17) defines the real exchange rate index as the domestic relative price of tradables to nontradables. Equations (2.9)–(2.17) fully describe the inter and intratemporal (external and internal) equilibria in this economy.

Equilibrium Real Exchange Rates

In this model there is not *one* equilibrium value of the real exchange rate, but rather a vector of equilibrium relative prices and RERs. In fact, we can talk about the equilibrium path for the RER. Within this intertemporal framework the *equilibrium* RER in a particular period is defined as that relative price of tradables that, for given sustainable (equilibrium) values of other variables, such as world prices, technology and tariffs, equilibrates *simultaneously* the external and internal (i.e., nontradables) sectors. The vector of equilibrium RERs, **RER** = (RER, $\widetilde{\text{RER}}$), is composed of those RERs that satisfy equations (2.9)–(2.17) for given values of the other fundamental variables. Notice that since we have assumed no rigidities, externalities, or market failures, our equilibrium real exchange rates imply the existence of "full" employment (see, however, sections 2.3 and 2.6).

From the inspection of equations (2.9)–(2.17) it is apparent that exogenous shocks in, say, the international terms of trade will affect the vector of equilibrium relative prices and RERs through two interrelated channels. The first one is related to the *intratemporal* effects on resource allocation and consumption and production decisions. For example, as a result of a temporary worsening of the terms of trade, there will be a tendency to produce more and consume less of M in that period. This, plus the income effect resulting from the worsening of the terms of trade, will generate an incipient disequilibrium in the nontradables market that will have to be resolved by a change in relative prices and in the equilibrium RER. In fact, if we assume that there is an absence of foreign borrowing, these intratemporal effects will be the only relevant ones. However, with capital mobility and investment, as in the current model, there is an additional *inter*temporal channel through which changes in exogenous variables will affect the vector of equilibrium RERs. For example, in the case of a worsening of the terms of trade, the consumption discount factor $\tilde{\pi}\delta/\pi$ will be affected, altering the intertemporal allocation of consumption. Also, in that case the investment equilibrium condition (2.15) will be altered, affecting future output.

Naturally, without specifying the functional forms of the expenditure, revenue, and other functions in (2.9)–(2.17) it is not possible to write the vector of equilibrium relative prices of nontradables, or the equilibrium real exchange rates, in an explicit form. It is possible, however, to write them implicitly as functions of the sustainable levels of all exogenous variables (contemporaneous and anticipated) in the system:

$$\text{RER} = h(p^*, \tilde{p}^*, \tau, \tilde{\tau}, \delta, \delta^*, V, T, \tilde{T}, G_X, \tilde{G}_X, \dots), \tag{2.19}$$

$$\widetilde{\text{RER}} = \tilde{h}(p^*, \tilde{p}^*, \tau, \tilde{\tau}, \delta, \delta^*, \tilde{V}, T, \tilde{T}, G_X, \tilde{G}_X, \dots). \tag{2.20}$$

Since the equilibrium relative price of nontradables is directly related—through equation (2.17)—to the equilibrium RER index, once the equilibrium relative prices of nontradables have been found, it is straightforward to use equation (2.17) to compute the vector of equilibrium RERs (2.19) and (2.20).

A crucial question is related to the way in which the equilibrium vectors of relative prices and RERs will change in response to different types of disturbances. That is, we are interested in the (most plausible) signs of the partial derivatives of RER and $\widetilde{\text{RER}}$ with respect to their determinants. In the sections that follow the reactions of equilibrium RERs to exogenous changes in tariffs, terms of trade, exchange controls, government expenditure, and technology are analyzed in some detail. Since the model in (2.9)–(2.17) is fairly complicated, we have adopted a strategy where for each particular distortion we use a slightly simplified version of the general model that allows us to ignore aspects not essential to the question we are addressing.

2.3 Tariffs and Equilibrium Real Exchange Rates

In the economic development policy literature it has long been recognized that there is a relation between the sustainable (i.e., long-run) tariffs level and the equilibrium value of the real exchange rate. Much of this discussion has taken place within the context of trade liberalization reforms, and has dealt with the effect of (long-term) tariff reductions on the equilibrium real exchange rate. Most of the analyses, however, have been quite vague and have been carried out in a partial equilibrium context. The traditionally accepted view among policymakers has been that a reduction in tariffs in a small country will always "require" a real (equilibrium) depreciation to maintain external balance. The argument usually given is based on a partial equilibrium interpretation of the elasticities approach, and runs along the following lines: A lower tariff will reduce the domestic price of importables, and consequently increase the demand for imports. This, in turn, will generate an external imbalance (i.e., a trade account deficit), which, assuming that the Marshall-Lerner condition holds, will require a (real) devaluation to restore equilibrium. The view is clearly captured by the following quote from Balassa (1982, p. 16): "[E]liminating protective measures would necessitate a devaluation in order to offset the resulting deficit in the balance of payments."[8]

A common feature of most early models is that they were basically static, ignoring intertemporal effects. Also, these partial equilibrium models did not incorporate explicitly the role of nontradable goods.

In order to analyze formally the interaction between tariffs, terms of trade, and the RER, in this section we present a simplified version of the general model of equilibrium real exchange rates.[9] The main simplifications are that (1) we assume no government consumption, (2) we assume that there is no investment, and (3) we assume that there are no taxes on foreign borrowing. The domestic and foreign discount factors are thus equal, $\delta = \delta^*$. Later, however, we lift the noninvestment assumption. This simplified model is summarized in equations (2.21)–(2.25), where the same notation as in table 2.1 has been used:

$$R(1, p, q; V) + \delta^* \tilde{R}(1, \tilde{p}, \tilde{q}, \tilde{V}) + \tau(E_p - R_p) + \delta^* \tilde{\tau}(E_{\tilde{p}} - \tilde{R}_{\tilde{p}})$$

$$= E[\pi(1, p, q), \delta^* \tilde{\pi}(1, \tilde{p}, \tilde{q}), W], \tag{2.21}$$

$$R_q = E_q, \quad \tilde{R}_{\tilde{q}} = E_{\tilde{q}}, \tag{2.22}$$

$$p = p^* + \tau, \quad \tilde{p} = \tilde{p}^* + \tilde{\tau}, \tag{2.23}$$

$$CA = R(\ ) + \tau(E_p - R_p) - \pi E_\pi, \tag{2.24}$$

$$RER = (P_T^*/P_N), \quad \widetilde{RER} = (\tilde{P}_T^*/\tilde{P}_N). \tag{2.25}$$

Equations (2.21)–(2.25) can be manipulated to find out how the vector of equilibrium RERs and the current account respond to disturbances such as changes in tariffs, shocks to the international terms of trade, international transfers, and changes in world interest rates.

Equation (2.21) is the intertemporal budget constraint, and states that present value of income—generated through revenues from optimized production $R + \delta^*\tilde{R}$, plus tariffs collection—has to equal the present value of expenditure. Given the assumption of perfect access to the world capital market, the discount factor used in (2.21) is the world discount factor δ^*. Equations (2.22) are the equilibrium conditions for the nontradables market in periods 1 and 2. Equations (2.23) specify the relation between domestic prices of importables, world prices of imports, and tariffs. Equation (2.24) describes the current account in period 1 as the difference between income and total expenditure in that period. Finally, equation (2.25) is the definition of the real exchange rate for each period. Following the discussion above, the vector of equilibrium RERs is defined as the pair RER and $\widetilde{\text{RER}}$ for which equations (2.21)–(2.24) hold simultaneously. That is, it is the vector of real exchange rates for which external and internal equilibrium is jointly attained, for given values of other key variables, such as external terms of trade, tariffs, world interest rates, and tariffs. It is important to emphasize that in (2.21)–(2.25), as in the more general model, tariffs are used to alter long-run resource allocation, and not as a way to combat a balance of payments crisis. All exercises on tariff changes that follow should be viewed, then, as responding to efforts aimed at changing this long-run allocation of resources.

Figure 2.1 summarizes the initial equilibrium in the nontradables market

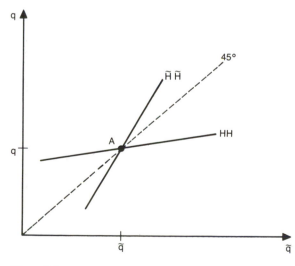

Figure 2.1

in periods 1 and 2. Schedule HH depicts the combination of q and $\tilde{q}$ consistent with equilibrium in the nontradable goods market in period 1. Its slope is equal to

$$\left.\frac{dq}{d\tilde{q}}\right|^{HH} = \frac{E_{q\tilde{q}}}{(R_{qq} - E_{qq})} > 0, \tag{2.26}$$

where $E_{q\tilde{q}}$ is an intertemporal cross-demand term that captures the reaction of the demand for N in period 1 (E_q) to an increase in nontradables prices in period 2. Since there are only two periods and the utility function is time separable, expenditure in periods 1 and 2 are substitutes, and thus this term is positive.[10] R_{qq} is the slope of the supply curve of N in period 1 and E_{qq} is the slope of the compensated demand curve. Thus, $(R_{qq} - E_{qq})$ is positive. The intuition behind the positive slope of HH is the following: An increase in the price of N in period 2 will make consumption in that period relatively more expensive. As a result there will be a substitution away from period 2 and towards period 1 expenditure. This will put pressure on the market for N in period 1, and an incipient excess demand for N in that period will develop. The reestablishment of nontradables equilibrium in period 1 will require an increase the relative price of N.

Schedule $\tilde{H}\tilde{H}$ depicts the locus of q and $\tilde{q}$ compatible with nontradable market equilibrium in period 2. Its slope is positive and equal to

$$\left.\frac{dq}{d\tilde{q}}\right|^{\tilde{H}\tilde{H}} = \frac{(\tilde{R}_{\tilde{q}\tilde{q}} - E_{\tilde{q}\tilde{q}})}{E_{q\tilde{q}}} > 0. \tag{2.27}$$

The intuition behind this positive slope is analogous to that of the HH schedule: An increase in q will make current consumption relatively more expensive, shifting expenditure into the future. As a result there will be a pressure on $\tilde{q}$, which will have to increase to reestablish equilibrium. Stability implies that the $\tilde{H}\tilde{H}$ schedule will be steeper than the HH curve (see the appendix).

The intersection of HH and $\tilde{H}\tilde{H}$ at A characterizes the (initial) relative prices of the nontradable goods market in periods 1 and 2 ($q, \tilde{q}$) compatible with the simultaneous attainment of intertemporal external equilibrium and internal equilibrium in both periods. In order to make the exposition clearer we have assumed that these equilibrium prices q and $\tilde{q}$ are equal; the 45° line passes through the initial equilibrium point A. Once the equilibrium values of q and $\tilde{q}$ are known, it is trivial to find RER and $\widetilde{\text{RER}}$. Notice that the existence of intertemporal substitution in consumption is what makes these schedules slope upward. If there were no intertemporal substitution, HH would be completely horizontal, while $\tilde{H}\tilde{H}$ would be vertical. Also, if this country had no access to borrowing in the international financial market, these schedules would be horizontal and vertical and there would be no intertemporal relation across nontradable markets.

Anticipated Future Import Tariffs and Equilibrium RERs

We now analyze how the anticipation of the future imposition of an import tariff will affect equilibrium RERs, and period 1's current account. In order to simplify the exposition we first assume that the initial condition is characterized by no import tariffs in either period ($\tau = \tilde{\tau} = 0$); this allows us to ignore first-order income effects. Later we discuss the more general case of positive initial tariffs.

Consider the case where, in period 1, economic agents (correctly) expect that the government will impose an import tariff $\tilde{\tau}$ in period 2. This will shift both the HH and $\tilde{H}\tilde{H}$ schedules, generating a new vector of equilibrium relative prices, and real exchange rates. Let us first consider the case of the HH schedule. An anticipated import tariff in 2 means that the expected price of imports in that period will increase, making future consumption relatively more expensive. Consequently, via the intertemporal substitution effect, consumers will substitute expenditure away from period 2 and into period 1. This will result in an increase in the demand for all goods in period 1, including nontradables, and in a higher q. Consequently the HH curve will shift upward. The magnitude of this vertical shift is equal to

$$dq|^{HH}_{d\tilde{q}=0} = \{E_{q\tilde{p}}/(R_{qq} - E_{qq})\}\, d\tilde{\tau}. \tag{2.28}$$

As this expression shows, the movement in the HH schedule is a reflection of the intertemporal degree of substitutability in consumption—it will be greater or smaller depending on whether $E_{q\tilde{p}}$ is large or small. In the extreme case of no intertemporal substitution ($E_{q\tilde{p}} = 0$), the HH schedule will be horizontal, and will *not* shift as a result of expected future tariffs.

The imposition of an (anticipated) import tariff in period 2 will also affect the $\tilde{H}\tilde{H}$ schedule. In this case, however, in addition to the intertemporal effect already discussed, there will also be an intratemporal effect related to the change in relative prices in period 2. Since the expected tariff will make future consumption more expensive, the *inter*temporal effect will generate forces toward a reduction in $\tilde{q}$, and a leftward movement of $\tilde{H}\tilde{H}$. The *intra*temporal effect, on the other hand, can either reinforce or tend to offset those forces. The higher domestic price of imports in period 2 will reduce the quantity demanded of M in that period. Depending on whether importables and nontradables are substitutes or complements in consumption, in

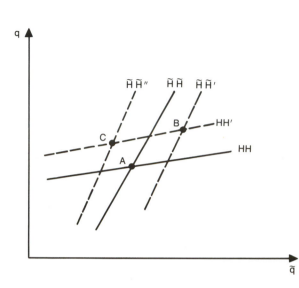

Figure 2.2

that period, the quantity demanded of N will increase or decline. If, as is the most plausible case at this level of aggregation, N and M are substitutes in consumption, the imposition of the period 2 tariff will increase the demand for N. In this case the $\tilde{H}\tilde{H}$ curve will shift to the right. Under the more implausible assumption of complementarity ($E_{\tilde{q}\tilde{p}} < 0$) it *may* shift to the left. Formally, the horizontal shift of $\tilde{H}\tilde{H}$ is equal to

$$d\tilde{q}|_{dq=0}^{\tilde{H}\tilde{H}} = \frac{(E_{\tilde{q}\tilde{p}} - R_{\tilde{p}\tilde{q}})}{(R_{\tilde{q}\tilde{q}} - E_{\tilde{q}\tilde{q}})} d\tilde{\tau}. \tag{2.29}$$

It is clear from (2.29) that a sufficient condition for $\tilde{H}\tilde{H}$ to shift to the right is that $E_{\tilde{p}\tilde{q}} > 0$. In fact, unless otherwise indicated, in the rest of this chapter we shall assume that M and N are substitutes in consumption, and that the intratemporal cross derivatives are positive.

Figure 2.2 illustrates the new equilibrium (point B) under our assumption that N and M are (net) substitutes: the new (after tariff anticipation) equilibrium schedules are HH' and $\tilde{H}\tilde{H}'$. In this case the anticipation of an import tariff results in a higher relative price of nontradables in periods 1 and 2. That is, the equilibrium RER appreciates in both periods, as a result of the expected tariff. Notice, however, that there is nothing in the model that tells us which of the two curves shifts by more [see below for the exact expression for $(dq/d\tilde{\tau})$ and $(d\tilde{q}/d\tilde{\tau})$]. This gives rise to the possibility of some interesting equilibrium paths for the RERs. For example, it is possible to observe an "equilibrium overshooting," where (relative to the nontariff case) q increases by more than $\tilde{q}$. This would be the case if the HH shifts to

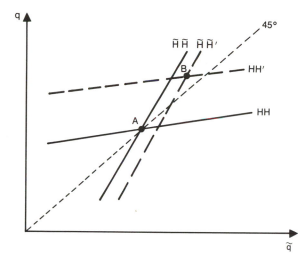

Figure 2.3

the left by more than what $\tilde{H}\tilde{H}$ shifts to the right. In this case the new equilibrium point is above the $45°$ line as illustrated in figure 2.3.[11]

Figure 2.4 shows four possible paths for the real exchange rate in periods 1 and 2 as a result of the anticipation of an import tariff. In these diagrams $\bar{q}$ is the equilibrium RER is both periods under the assumption of no tariffs, and is used as a benchmark for comparison. q and $\tilde{q}$ are the equilibrium relative prices in periods 1 and 2 in the anticipated tariff case. Panel (a) in figure 2.4 illustrates what we have called "equilibrium overshooting" of the relative price, where in the tariff case q and $\tilde{q}$ are higher than in the nontariff case, but the adjustment implies an equilibrium reduction of $\tilde{q}$ in period 2. By analogy, case (b) can be called "equilibrium undershooting." Here both q and $\tilde{q}$ are also higher than in the nontariff case. Now, however, the adjustment path requires an equilibrium increase of $\tilde{q}$ in period 2, over and above the higher q in period 1. Panel (c) is the most "traditional" case, where as a consequence of the anticipated tariff the RER appreciates by the same amount in both periods. Panel (d) depicts the case where the equilibrium RERs move in opposite directions in each period. In period 1 there is a real appreciation, relative to the nontariff case, while in period 2, the period when the tariff is actually imposed, there is a real depreciation.

From equations (2.21)–(2.25) it is possible to find formally the equilibrium changes in q and $\tilde{q}$ as a result of the anticipated import tariff:

$$\frac{dq}{d\tilde{\tau}} = -\left(\frac{1}{\Delta}\right)\{E_{q\tilde{p}}(\tilde{R}_{\tilde{q}\tilde{q}} - E_{\tilde{q}\tilde{q}}) + E_{q\tilde{q}}(E_{\tilde{q}\tilde{p}} - \tilde{R}_{\tilde{q}\tilde{p}})\}, \qquad (2.30)$$

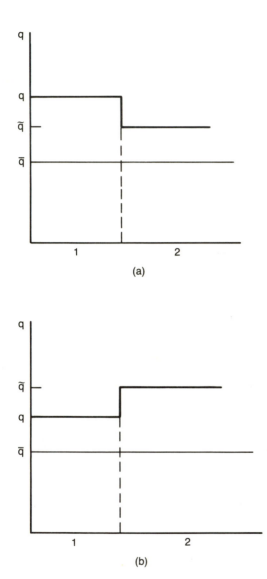

Figure 2.4

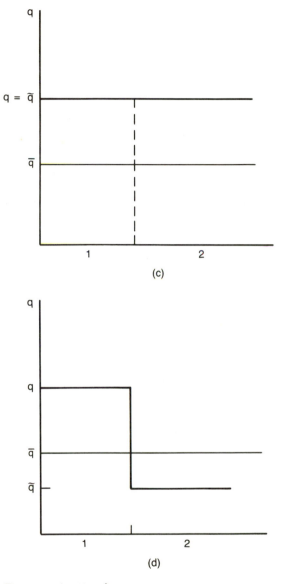

Figure 2.4 (continued)

$$\frac{d\tilde{q}}{d\tilde{\tau}} = -\left(\frac{1}{\Delta}\right)\{(R_{qq} - E_{qq})(E_{\tilde{q}\tilde{p}} - \tilde{R}_{\tilde{q}\tilde{p}}) + E_{q\tilde{p}}E_{\tilde{q}p}\}, \tag{2.31}$$

where (see the appendix)

$$\Delta = -[(R_{qq} - E_{qq})(\tilde{R}_{\tilde{q}\tilde{q}} - E_{\tilde{q}\tilde{q}}) - E_{\tilde{q}q}E_{q\tilde{q}}] < 0.$$

Equations (2.30) and (2.31) formally confirm the preceding diagrammatic analysis, showing that in this model of three goods and two periods, an anticipated import tariff can, in principle, generate interesting dynamic paths for the equilibrium real exchange rate under a pure real equilibrium analysis. They also show that substitutability everywhere in demand is a sufficient condition to guarantee that the exports real exchange rate will appreciate in both periods as a consequence of the anticipated tariff.

The discussion presented above has focused on the real exchange rate for exportables ($1/q$). The effects of the tariff on the domestic relative price of importables to nontradables can easily be found by analyzing the behavior of (p/q).

Although a tariff—and a terms of trade shock, for that matter—will alter the relative price of importables to exportables, it is still possible to analyze how the *index* of the equilibrium real exchange rate, or relative price of tradables to nontradables, will be affected by the tariff. In equation (2.25) we defined the real exchange rate as RER = (P_T^*/P_N), where P_T^* is the international price of tradables, defined as $P_T^* = \gamma P_M^* + (1 - \gamma)P_X^*$, where the γ's are weights. Since we have assumed that the world price of exports is the numeraire, we can rewrite the change in the equilibrium RER in period 1 as (there is a perfectly equivalent expression for period 2)

$$\frac{d(\text{RER})}{d\tilde{\tau}} = \frac{\gamma\, d(p^*/q)}{d\tilde{\tau}} + (1 - \gamma)\frac{d(1/q)}{d\tilde{\tau}}. \tag{2.32}$$

From our previous calculations of ($dq/d\tau$) we can easily compute the change in the index of equilibrium real exchange rates. It is straightforward to show that under substitutability everywhere the anticipated tariff will result in an *equilibrium real exchange* rate appreciation in the current period— as well as in the future—when the tariff is imposed.

The Current Account

From equation (2.24) it is possible to find out how the current account in period 1 will respond to the anticipated tariff:[12]

$$\frac{d\,CA}{d\tilde{\tau}} = -\delta^* \pi E_{\pi\tilde{\pi}} \tilde{\pi}_{\tilde{p}} - \pi E_{\pi\pi} \pi_q \left(\frac{dq}{d\tilde{\tau}}\right) - \delta^* \tilde{\pi}_{\tilde{q}} \pi E_{\pi\tilde{\pi}} \left(\frac{d\tilde{q}}{d\tilde{\tau}}\right). \tag{2.33}$$

The presence of an $E_{\pi\tilde{\pi}}$ or $E_{\pi\pi}$ term in every one of the terms on the right-hand side (RHS) of equation (2.33) clearly highlights the fact that the anticipated imposition of a future tariff will affect the current account via intertemporal channels. The first term in the RHS of equation (2.33) is negative and captures the direct effect of the anticipation of a tariff in period 2 on the current account in period 1. The intuition for this negative effect is straightforward. The anticipated higher period 2 tariff makes consumption in that period relatively more expensive, and as a result of this the public substitutes consumption away from period 2 into period 1, generating a worsening of the current account balance in period 1. The magnitude of this effect will depend both on the intertemporal substitution effect $E_{\pi\tilde{\pi}}$ and on the initial share of imports on period 2 expenditure $\tilde{\pi}_{\tilde{p}}$.

The second and third terms on the RHS of equation (2.33) are *indirect* effects that operate via changes in periods 1 and 2 equilibrium real exchange rates. The interpretation of these two indirect terms is quite straightforward within the intertemporal framework of the current model. If the anticipated tariff results in an equilibrium real appreciation in period 1, $(dq/d\tilde{\tau}) > 0$, there will be an offsetting force toward a current account improvement. The reasoning is simple. If the anticipated tariff results in a higher equilibrium price of nontradables in period 1 (i.e., in a real appreciation in 1), there will be substitution away from period 1 expenditure, generating an improvement in the current account in that period. The third term on the RHS relates the change in period 2's RER to period 1's current account. If as a consequence of the anticipated tariff $\tilde{q}$ increases [see equation (2.31) for the conditions under which this will take place], there will be a tendency to substitute expenditure away from period 2 into period 1, generating forces that will tend to worsen period 1's current account.

The total effect of the anticipation of an import tariff on period 1's current account will depend on the strength of the intertemporal price effects, on the initial expenditure on importables and nontradables, and on the effects of the tariff on the RER vector. This result contrasts with the traditional static view, where the conditions for tariffs improving the current account are related to imports and exports elasticities within each period. An important result of this analysis is that, under very plausible conditions, it is possible that the sole anticipation of the enactment of future protectionist policies will worsen today's current account. Moreover, it is possible to observe simultaneously a worsening of the current account and a real depreciation—a combination that would puzzle a number of observers, including the media.

Temporary and Permanent Tariffs

The model developed above can be easily used to analyze the effects of temporary and permanent tariffs on the path of equilibrium RERs and on the current account. In particular, the diagrammatic analysis can handle both of these cases. As is discussed in Edwards (1989c), in the case of temporary tariffs (i.e., a period 1 tariff only), it is easy to show that, once again, "equilibrium overshooting" can result where the initial equilibrium relative price of $N(q)$ increases—in relation to the nontariff benchmark case—by more than the equilibrium price of N in period 2.

It is interesting to compare the reaction of the RER in period 1 to the imposition of a temporary and a permanent tariff; we find unequivocally that a permanent tariff will appreciate the equilibrium real exchange rate in period 1 by more than a temporary tariff imposed in that period only (see Edwards, 1989c).

Positive Initial Tariffs

In the above discussion we have assumed that tariffs are initially equal to zero. This is a very convenient assumption since in this case there are no first-order income effects. In reality, however, things are different, since most countries have already (large) tariffs and other types of import restrictions in effect.

With positive initial tariffs further changes in protection will generate first-order income effects. Figuring out the nature, magnitude, and direction of these effects is not trivial. For example, if initially there are import tariffs in periods 1 and 2, a tariff liberalization in one of the periods only can have either a negative or a positive welfare effect, due to well known second-best reasons. Only in the rather extreme case where there is a *permanent* liberalization, with tariffs in both periods being reduced by the same amount $d\tau = d\bar{\tau}$, and where there are no other distortions, can we be sure that the tariff reduction will have a positive welfare effect.

Formal derivations for the case of positive tariffs can be found in Edwards (1986b). The resulting equations turn out to be quite cumbersome. However, these long equations tend to hide a somewhat straightforward intuition. If, for example, the hike in period 1's tariff reduces welfare via traditional efficiency costs, there will be a negative income effect in both periods. If nontradables are normal goods, there will be a decline in the demand for these goods and a tendency for their price to go down in each period. It is easy to establish that if all goods are substitutes in demand and the substitution effect dominates the income effect, a hike in period 1's tariffs will generate an *equilibrium real exchange rate appreciation in both periods.*[13] Notice that although this result is consistent with the traditional policy literature, we have reached it through a very different approach.

Investment

Up to now we have assumed that there is no investment. As a result, all of the intertemporal action has come from the demand side. If investment is incorporated, via equation (2.15), we shall also have intertemporal effects on the supply side. Once investment is added the capital stock in period 2 becomes an endogenous variable. More specifically, it is possible to relate additions to the capital stock (dK) to a permanent change in tariffs and to real exchange rate changes:

$$\left(\frac{dK}{d\tau}\right) = -\left(\frac{\tilde{R}_{K\tilde{p}}}{\tilde{R}_{KK}}\right) - \left(\frac{\tilde{R}_{K\tilde{q}}}{\tilde{R}_{KK}}\right)\left(\frac{d\tilde{q}}{d\tau}\right), \tag{2.34}$$

where $\tilde{R}_{KK} < 0$ is the slope of the marginal product of capital schedule; $\tilde{R}_{K\tilde{p}}$ and $\tilde{R}_{K\tilde{q}}$ are Rybczynski terms whose signs will depend on the relative ordering of factor intensities across sectors. Notice that the second term on the RHS includes ($d\tilde{q}/d\tau$), indicating that the permanent tariff will also affect investment via the *future* change in the equilibrium real exchange rate.

2.4 Terms of Trade and the Equilibrium Real Exchange Rate

In this section we investigate the way in which terms of trade changes affect the equilibrium path of real exchange rates. Since in section 2.3 we have already invested in understanding the way in which the model works, our discussion here will be rather brief.

The developing nations have traditionally been subject to important terms of trade shocks; many of the poorer countries, in fact, face highly volatile terms of trade. Naturally, these exogenous changes of the external terms of trade—or "world" relative price of exportables to importables— will affect the equilibrium path of real exchange rates. The traditional wisdom is that if the terms of trade deteriorate an equilibrium real depreciation will result. For example, Carlos Diaz-Alejandro (1982, p. 33) stated that "standard models ... predict that the following variables ... influence its real exchange rates...: an improvement [in terms of trade] will lead to appreciation."

Most traditional analyses of the effect of terms of trade changes on the equilibrium real exchange rate have emphasized almost exclusively the role of the *income effect* generated by the change in the external terms of trade. The argument usually goes the following way: A deterioration of the terms of trade reduces real income and results in a decline in the demand for nontradable goods. In order to restore equilibrium the relative price of nontradables has to decline (i.e., there has to be an equilibrium real depreciation). A problem with this view, however, is that the income effect is only part of the story—and under some circumstances, not even the most important one. In order to understand the way in which terms of trade shocks affect the equilibrium real exchange rate, both income and substitution effects, as well as intertemporal ramifications, should be analyzed.

In this section we briefly investigate how exogenous changes in international terms of trade (p^* and $\tilde{p}^*$) affect the equilibrium path of the real exchange rate, concentrating exclusively on a permanent terms of trade worsening (equiproportional increase in p^* and $\tilde{p}^*$).[14] Throughout the section we assume that initial tariffs are very low, so that we can evaluate our derivatives around $\tau = \tilde{\tau} \approx 0$. We maintain the assumptions of section 2.3—no government consumption, no investment, and no taxes on foreign borrowing—so that we still use the simplified model (2.21)–(2.25). Now, however, even if tariffs are zero, we cannot ignore the income effect associated with a change in the terms of trade.

Equations (2.35) and (2.36) capture the effect of a permanent terms of trade shock on the vector of equilibrium RERs:

$$\frac{dq}{dp^*} = \frac{dq}{d\tau} + \left(\frac{1}{\Delta}\right)\{E_{q\tilde{q}}\tilde{\pi}_{\tilde{q}}E_{\tilde{\pi}}E_{\tilde{\pi}W} + \pi_q E_{\pi W}(R_{\tilde{q}\tilde{q}} - E_{\tilde{q}\tilde{q}})\}$$

$$\cdot ((E_p - R_p) + \delta^*(E_{\tilde{p}} - \tilde{R}_{\tilde{p}})), \tag{2.35}$$

$$\frac{d\tilde{q}}{dp^*} = \frac{d\tilde{q}}{d\tau} + \left(\frac{1}{\Delta}\right)\{(R_{qq} - E_{qq})\tilde{\pi}_{\tilde{q}}E_{\tilde{\pi}W} + E_{\tilde{q}q}\pi_q E_{\pi W}\}$$

$$\cdot [(E_p - R_p) + \delta^*(E_{\tilde{p}} - \tilde{R}_{\tilde{p}})], \tag{2.36}$$

where $dq/d\tau$ and $d\tilde{q}/d\tau$ are the pure substitution effects. Under our assumption of (net) substitutability, these are positive. Notice that now the negative income effects are proportional to the *present value* of total imports. Again, as in the case of tariffs, it is not possible to know a priori which relative price of nontradables will be affected by more as a result of a permanent terms of trade shock.[15]

The analysis presented in this section is readily applicable to the "Dutch Disease" case, where there is a world price generated export boom in an enclave export sector (i.e., oil). The simplest way to address this case is by assuming that the country in question does not consume the booming commodity. In this way all intratemporal substitution effects on the consumption side are severed. Naturally, we would still have important intertemporal effects as well as substitution in supply.[16]

The cases of anticipated and temporary terms of trade shocks can be analyzed in the same way. As in the analysis just presented, the real exchange rate reaction to these disturbances will be the sum of a substitution effect and an income effect proportional to imports.

2.5 Exchange Controls, Capital Flows, and Equilibrium Real Exchange Rates

Most countries—developed or developing—have traditionally imposed several types of controls that result in some impediment to free borrowing and lending. In the general model of RER determination presented in section 2.2, these capital controls were modeled as a tax on foreign borrowing that resulted in a domestic interest rate that exceeds the world (real) rate of interest.[17] The extent of capital controls are many times altered by the economic authorities, generating adjustments of the amounts borrowed and lent, and in the equilibrium path of relative prices. For example, a liberalization of the capital account reduces the tax on foreign borrowing, bringing domestic interest rates more in line with world interest rates. Liberalization programs of this type have been implemented in the recent past by a number of developing countries. Perhaps the best known of these programs were pursued by the countries of the Southern Cone of Latin America in the late 1970s.[18] Changes in world interest rates will also have an important effect on decisions related to foreign borrowing, and on the equilibrium path of the real exchange rate. Also, from time to time, countries increase the extent of capital controls. Naturally, the analysis that follows will shed light on the reaction of the equilibrium RER in this case.

Some authors have investigated, at more or less informal levels, the relation between capital mobility and equilibrium real exchange rates. McKinnon (1976) provided an early analysis using a two-goods (tradables and nontradables) model with factor specificity, where he considers the effect of an *exogenous* capital inflow on the relative price of tradables to nontradables.

This inflow of capital allows expenditures to exceed income, generating an incipient excess demand for nontradables. To restore equilibrium, the relative price of nontradables has to rise—that is, a real appreciation has to take place.

The analysis of McKinnon (1976), as well as those by Corden (1981) and Harberger (1982, 1983) are carried out under the assumption that the change in the level of capital flows is largely exogenous. This, of course, need not be the case; in fact, in many cases capital movements tend to be endogenous, responding to a number of variables including interest rate differentials. In this section we use a simplified version of the general model in section 2.2 to investigate formally the way in which a change in the degree of capital account restrictions affect the path of equilibrium real exchange rates.[19] We also look at the effects of this deregulation policy on borrowing and lending decisions, analyzing whether one would observe comovements of equilibrium real exchange rates and capital flows. In order to make the exposition more clear we make some simplifying assumptions to the general model of section 2.2: (1) We first assume that there are no import tariffs (see below, however, for a discussion on what happens if $\tau \neq 0$). (2) We further assume that international prices of X and M do not change, so that these two goods can then be aggregated into a composite tradable good (T). We now denote the relative price of nontradables to tradables in periods 1 and 2 as f and $\tilde{f}$ (i.e., $f = P_N/P_T$). That is, $f, \tilde{f}$ are the inverses of each period's real exchange rate. Assuming, further, that there is no investment, and that the government hands back to the public the tax proceeds, the model in section 2.2 is now rewritten in the following way:

$$R(1, f; V) + \delta \bar{R}(1, \tilde{f}; \tilde{V}) + b(\text{NCA}) = E[\pi(1, f), \delta \tilde{\pi}(1, \tilde{f}), W], \tag{2.37}$$

$$b = (\delta^* - \delta) > 0, \tag{2.38}$$

$$R_f = E_f, \tag{2.39}$$

$$\tilde{R}_{\tilde{f}} = E_{\tilde{f}}, \tag{2.40}$$

$$\text{RER} = 1/f, \quad \widetilde{\text{RER}} = 1/\tilde{f}, \tag{2.41}$$

where a notation consistent with the preceding sections has been used. $R(\ )$ is a revenue function; $E(\ )$ is the intertemporal expenditure function; W is utility, $\pi(\ )$ an exact price index; R_f is supply of N in period 1; and E_f is demand of N in period 1. There are equivalent expressions for period 2 variables. Notice that contrary to the free capital mobility case, we have now used the domestic discount factor δ, instead of the world factor δ^*. The term $b(\text{NCA})$ is the discounted value of the proceeds from the taxation of foreign borrowing, where b is the tax.[20] Since we have assumed in this section that government consumption is zero, these tax proceeds are handed back to the public in a nondistortionary way.

Let us consider the case of a country with capital controls that decides to liberalize its capital account, reducing the extent to which foreign borrowing is taxed. Since $b = (\delta^* - \delta)$, a change in the tax on borrowing is equal to minus a change in the discount factor: $db = -d\delta$. The rest of the analysis will deal with changes in δ. Totally differentiating (2.39) and (2.40), we find out how the (inverse of the) equilibrium RER reacts to a liberalization of the capital account:

$$\frac{df}{d\delta} = - \left(\frac{E_W \pi}{\Delta''}\right)(\pi_f E_{\pi\tilde{\pi}}\tilde{R}_{\tilde{f}\tilde{f}} - \pi_f E_{\pi\tilde{\pi}}\tilde{\pi}_{\tilde{f}\tilde{f}})$$

$$- b\tilde{\pi}\left(\frac{\tilde{R}_{\tilde{f}\tilde{f}} - E_{\tilde{\pi}}\tilde{\pi}_{\tilde{f}\tilde{f}}}{\Delta''}\right)(E_{\tilde{\pi}W}\tilde{\pi}\pi_f E_{\pi\tilde{\pi}} - E_{\pi W}\tilde{\pi}\pi_f E_{\tilde{f}\tilde{f}}) > 0, \qquad (2.42)$$

where Δ'' is the determinant of the system and is negative (Edwards, 1989b).

The sign of the expression (2.42) is positive, indicating that a liberalization of the capital account (i.e., a reduction in the tax on foreign borrowing) will result in an increase in the relative price of nontradables, or in an *equilibrium real appreciation* in period 1. The intuition behind this real appreciation is simple. The adjustment takes place through two channels. The first, captured by the first term on the RHS of equation (2.42), is an intertemporal substitution effect, which operates via movements in the consumption rate of interest. The reduction of the tax on foreign borrowing (i.e., the increase in δ) makes future consumption relatively more expensive. As a result, people substitute intertemporally, consuming more of everything in period 1. This, of course, exercises pressure on the price of nontradables in period 1, generating an equilibrium real appreciation. Notice that if there is no intertemporal substitution (i.e., $E_{\pi\tilde{\pi}} = 0$), the first term on the RHS of (2.42) vanishes.

The second channel through which the liberalization of the capital account affects the real exchange rate is the income effect captured by the second term on the RHS of equation (2.42). An increase in δ toward its world level δ^* reduces the only distortion in this economy, generating a positive welfare effect. Consequently the public will increase consumption, exercising a positive pressure on f. The magnitude of this income effect basically depends on two factors: (1) the propensities to consume in periods 1 and 2, which are related to $E_{\pi W}$ and $E_{\tilde{\pi}W}$, and (2) the initial level of the distortion

b. If initially the tax is very low ($b \approx 0$), the second term on the RHS of (2.42) will tend to disappear.

Naturally, the relaxation of capital controls will affect the amount of foreign borrowing. In period 1 the amount of foreign borrowing by the nationals of this country will be given by the difference between expenditure and income in that period (this, of course, assumes nontradables equilibrium):

$$B = \pi E_\pi - R(\ ). \tag{2.43}$$

B can be either positive or negative, indicating a net borrower or net lender position in the first period. Notice that since in this real model there are no international reserves holdings, this expression for foreign borrowing in period 1 is the negative of the current account. It is easy to show from (2.43) that as a result of the relaxation of capital controls there will be an increase in B, reflecting an increase in net borrowing in period 1. This net capital inflow in period 1 is the result of the two effects—substitution and income—discussed above.

In sum, as a result of the reduction in tax on borrowing, in period 1 we shall simultaneously observe (1) an inflow of "capital," or higher net borrowing from abroad, (2) a real appreciation (i.e., a higher f), and (3) a worsening of the current account in that period.

The relaxation of barriers to foreign borrowing will affect period 2's real exchange rate via the same two channels. As is shown in Edwards (1989b), whether the equilibrium real exchange rate appreciates or depreciates in period 2 will depend on whether the intertemporal substitution or income effect dominates.

Transfers, Exogenous Capital Flows, and World Interest Rates

It is not unusual to find among the developing countries "exogenous" capital movements that do not necessarily have an origin on interest rate differentials. A common case is given by foreign aid, where the poorer country can increase expenditure above income due to a transfer made from abroad. Also, capital flight stemming from political uncertainty can, in principle, be modeled as a negative transfer. This type of "exogenous capital inflows" (or outflows) will usually have an effect on the equilibrium path of the RER.[21]

The model used in this section can be easily amended to handle this "transfer problem." Assuming that there is a transfer in period 1 only, and denoting the transfer from abroad by H, the intertemporal budget constraint has to be written as

$$R(1, f, V) + \delta \tilde{R}(1, \tilde{f}, \tilde{V}) + b(\text{NCA}) + H = E[\pi(1, f), \delta \tilde{\pi}(1, \tilde{f}), W]. \qquad (2.44)$$

It is easy to show now that as long as the propensities to consume non-tradables in periods 1 and 2 are different from zero, the transfers will result in equilibrium real appreciation in both periods:

$$\frac{df}{dH} > 0, \quad \frac{d\tilde{f}}{dH} > 0. \qquad (2.45)$$

Of course, if the income elasticities of demand for home goods are zero, (i.e., $\pi_f E_\pi = \tilde{\pi}_{\tilde{f}} E_{\tilde{\pi}} = 0$), the transfer will have *no effect on the equilibrium vector of RERs*. On the other hand, if for some reason, such as a prohibitive tax on foreign borrowing, there is no intertemporal substitution in consumption, the transfer will appreciate the real exchange rate in the first period only.[22]

Also, the model developed in this chapter can be easily used to analyze how exogenous changes in world interest rates—that is, changes in δ^*—will affect the path of equilibrium RERs. In the current two-period model changes in r^* will only create substitution effects. A higher r^* will make future consumption more expensive, generating the type of intertemporal substitution we discussed above.

2.6 The Composition of Government Expenditure, Fiscal Debt, and Equilibrium Real Exchange Rates

In this model the government faces an intertemporal budget constraint. In the long run (period 2) it pays all its debt. The sources of government revenue are limited to different forms of taxation and to foreign borrowing. Naturally, since this is a completely real model, the inflation tax is *not* an option faced by the government authorities. In that sense, then, although fiscal policy plays a real role, it does not operate through the traditional macroeconomic channels that are usually emphasized in policy discussions on the developing countries.

Government decisions regarding the allocation of expenditure across goods and the type of taxes used will, under certain cases, have effects on the equilibrium real exchange rate. It is in this sense that we can say that fiscal policy—or perhaps, more correctly, some real aspects of it—is a component of the fundamental determinants of the equilibrium real exchange rate. However, as discussed in detail in chapter 3, unsustainable fiscal expansions that are financed by the inflation tax will have no effect over the equilibrium real exchange rate; on the contrary, they will generate a divergence between the actual and equilibrium RER, or real exchange rate overvaluation. In this section we concentrate on how (real aspects of) fiscal policy will affect the behavior of equilibrium real exchange rates. We consider both changes in the composition of government expenditures as well as changes in the proportion of period 1 expenditures financed by issuing debt. The analysis of fiscal policies is particularly relevant for the case of the developing countries, where the government sector is usually prominent. Regarding taxation, we first assume that all taxes are of the nondistortionary type. We then briefly discuss two more realistic cases where distortionary taxes—consumption taxes and import tariffs—are used to raise revenue. Throughout the analysis government can borrow internationally but, as the private sector, it faces an intertemporal budget constraint.

A limitation of our two-period model is that, generally speaking, it is not possible to distinguish between fiscal borrowing and public debt. Period 1's fiscal borrowing becomes, after compounding it by the appropriate interest rate, the fiscal debt inherited in period 2. One possible way of introducing a distinction between borrowing and debt is by assuming that in period the government "inherits" some debt from previous periods (Frenkel and Razin, 1987).

In order to simplify the discussion and to concentrate fully on the relation between (real) fiscal policies and the equilibrium path of RERs, we develop a simplified version of the general model of section 2.2. It is first assumed that there are no import tariffs and that the terms of trade do not change. Consequently importables and exportables can again be aggregated into a single composite tradable good. Initially, it is assumed that the government raises revenue using non distortionary taxes T and $\tilde{T}$ in periods 1 and 2; the case of distortionary taxes is discussed later. As in section 2.5, f and $\tilde{f}$ are the relative prices of nontradables—or inverse of the RERs—in periods 1 and 2. As before, and to simplify the analysis, investment is ignored. Our simplified model is given by equations (2.46)–(2.50):

$$R(1, f, V) + \delta^* \tilde{R}(1, \tilde{f}, \tilde{V}) - T - \delta^* \tilde{T} = E(\pi(1, f), \delta^* \tilde{\pi}(1, \tilde{f}), W), \qquad (2.46)$$

$$G_T + f G_N + \delta^*(\tilde{G}_T + \tilde{f} \tilde{G}_N) = T + \delta^* \tilde{T}, \qquad (2.47)$$

$$R_f = E_f + G_N, \qquad (2.48)$$

$$\tilde{R}_{\tilde{f}} = E_{\tilde{f}} + \tilde{G}_N, \qquad (2.49)$$

$$\text{RER} = (1/f), \quad \widetilde{\text{RER}} = (1/\tilde{f}). \qquad (2.50)$$

Equation (2.46) is the budget constraint for the private sector. T and $\tilde{T}$ are (nondistortionary) taxes in each period. Equation (2.47) is the government's budget constraint. It has been assumed that the government consumes both tradables and nontradables, and that it can borrow from abroad at the same (exogenously given) interest rate as the private sector. This equation also establishes that the discounted value of the government's consumption has to be equal to the present value of taxes. If in period 1 there is an income shortcoming, it is financed by borrowing from abroad. In order to clarify the analysis it is possible to break down equation (2.47) into two equations:

$$(G_T + fG_N) - T = D, \tag{2.47'}$$

$$D + \delta^*(\tilde{G}_T + \tilde{f}\tilde{G}_N) = \delta^*\tilde{T}. \tag{2.47''}$$

Equation (2.47') is period 1's fiscal deficit, defined as the difference between real expenditure (in terms of tradables) and taxes. Equation (2.47'') says that the discounted value of period 2's revenue from taxes ($\delta^*\tilde{T}$) has to be enough to cover period 2's expenditure (in discounted value) *plus* period 1's deficit. It is clear from these two equations that in order to assure that the fiscal budget constraint will actually hold, either government expenditure or tax revenue in period 2 will now have to be endogenous. In this section we shall assume that period 2's tax revenue $\tilde{T}$ takes whatever value is required to assure government solvency.

Equations (2.48) and (2.49) are the equilibrium conditions for nontradables in each period. Notice that *total* demand for N by the private sector *plus* the government has to equal output of nontradables in each period.

Increase in Period 1 Borrowing Due to Tax Cut

Consider first the case where the government implements a tax cut in period 1 that results in an increase in its borrowing needs. Naturally, given the government budget constraint, this means that taxation in period 2 will have to go up in order for the intertemporal budget constraint to be satisfied. Given the perfect foresight assumptions of our model, households and firms will internalize this change in the timing of taxes and react accordingly. Taxation in period 2 will increase by $-(1/\delta^*)dT$, exactly the same amount by which household disposable income will go down. In this case we have perfect *Barro-Ricardo equivalence*, where the current tax cut has no effect on the equilibrium path of the real exchange rate:

$$\frac{df}{dT} = \frac{d\tilde{f}}{dT} = 0. \tag{2.51}$$

This result is by no means surprising. In fact, it has been built into the model through two key assumptions: (1) individuals and the government have the same rate of discount δ^* and (2) taxes are nondistortionary.

Changes in Government Consumption

Any change in the level of government consumption will have an impact on the equilibrium path of real exchange rates. The intuition behind this is very simple. Imagine, for example, an increase in the government's consumption of nontradables in period 1, which is financed by an increase in public debt. This will affect the path of equilibrium real exchange rates through two channels. First, the increased demand for N in 1 will tend to generate, on its own, a higher equilibrium relative price for those goods— or equilibrium real appreciation—in that period. Second, the higher level of government borrowing in period 1 will require a hike in taxes in period 2. This will reduce available income, tending to reduce the demand for N in periods 1 and 2. Whether as a result of the higher consumption of N by the government in period 1 there will or will not be an equilibrium real appreciation in that period will depend on the relative forces of the substitution and income effects. In the most plausible case, where the substitution effect dominates, there will be an equilibrium real appreciation in period 1.

An increase in the government's demand for tradables in period 1 financed by additional borrowing can be analyzed in a similar way; this time, however, there will be no direct pressure of the market for nontradables. Naturally, the indirect pressure via changes in the private sector disposable income will still be present. Formally, equation (2.52) gives us the effect of a temporary increase in the government's consumption of tradables in period 1 on the equilibrium of the (inverse of the) real exchange rate:

$$\frac{df}{dG_T} = -\frac{\delta^*}{\Delta''} \{E_{ff} E_{\tilde{\pi}} \tilde{\pi}_{\tilde{f}} \delta^* + (\tilde{R}_{\tilde{f}\tilde{f}} - E_{\tilde{f}\tilde{f}}) \tilde{\pi}_{\tilde{f}} E_{\pi W}\} < 0, \tag{2.52}$$

where Δ'' is the determinant from the system (2.46)–(2.49) and is positive. Equation (2.52) is negative, indicating that a temporary increase in the demand for tradables by the government will result in an equilibrium real depreciation in period 1. It is easy to show that a temporary increase in government consumption of tradables in period 1 only will also result in an equilibrium real depreciation in period 2.

Distortionary Taxes

A simplifying feature of our analysis in this section is that we have assumed that all of the government's revenue is obtained via nondistortionary taxes. A relaxation of this assumption will affect some of the results discussed above in several ways. In the general model of section 2.2 we discussed two possible ways of introducing distortionary taxes: import tariffs and taxes on foreign borrowing. By combining the positive tariffs analysis of section 2.3 with the discussion in this section, we can formally find out how changes in fiscal policy will affect the equilibrium paths of RERs. Frenkel and Razin (1987) discuss some of the ramifications of government deficits financed with distortionary taxes in open economies.

2.7 Technological Progress

David Ricardo (1821/1971) is considered to have been the first to postulate explicitly the existence of a negative relation between economic growth and the equilibrium relative price of tradables to nontradables. Later a number of authors, including Pigou (1922), pointed out within the context of the PPP debate that there is a tendency for the relative prices of tradables to nontradables to differ across countries; higher-income countries would tend to have a lower relative price between these two groups of goods. However, it was only in Balassa's (1964) reinterpretation of the PPP theory that the theoretical foundations of this proposition were clearly set forward. According to Balassa, the rate of productivity improvements is higher in countries with higher rates of growth than in countries with lower rates of growth. Moreover, the rate at which productivity improves is not uniform across sectors within each country; gains in productivity are larger in the tradable good sector than in the nontradable goods sector in all countries. This means that in each country the equilibrium relative price of tradables to nontradables will tend to decline through time. Since the prices of tradable goods will move together across countries, the differential in productivities improvements across countries and sectors will result in an appreciation of the PPP defined exchange rate. While sometimes this argument is presented in a dynamic form (i.e., growth of output rather than levels of income per capita), in Balassa's (1964) original article the analysis was presented from a static perspective.

The effects of productivity gains on the path of equilibrium real exchange rates can be analyzed formally using the model of section 2.2. Possibly the easiest way of incorporating technological progress is by adding a shift parameter ϕ in the revenue functions $R(\ )$ and $\tilde{R}(\ )$.[23] Depending on how the rate of technological progress affects the different sectors and the type of progress considered—product augmenting or factor augmenting—we shall have different effects on the equilibrium RERs. Any type of productivity shock will have a positive income effect, generating positive demand pressure on the nontradables market in both periods. As a result, there will be a tendency for the equilibrium price of N to go up in both periods.

Technological progress will also result in supply effects. If this progress is of the general factor augmenting variety, the results will be equivalent to those of an exogenously driven increase in factor availability and will be governed by the well known Rybczynski principle. Under some conditions it is possible that the supply effects of technological progress more than offset the demand effects, generating an equilibrium real depreciation. This would be the case, for example, of product augmenting technological improvement that increases the availability of N sufficiently to the point of generating an incipient excess supply, which will have to be resolved through an equilibrium real devaluation.

2.8 Credit Rationing, Price Rigidities, Unemployment, and Other Extensions

Intertemporal effects have played an important role in our discussion up to this point. We have shown that the effects of both anticipated and temporary disturbances are spread out throughout time via changes in the consumption rate of interest and in investment. Of course, this optimal intertemporal smoothing is possible due to our assumption that the nationals of this country can borrow internationally as much as they want at the exogenously given rate of interest, only subject to the constraint that the debt is paid.

The assumption of perfect access to foreign borrowing in some way reduces the need for making a distinction between short-term and long-term disturbances. With foreign borrowing and perfect foresight, agents react optimally and the resulting movements of equilibrium prices are "optimal." If, however, we assume that there is credit rationing, it will be important to make a distinction between *short-term* and *long-term* equilibrium RERs. For example, in the extreme case of *no* foreign borrowing, a temporary terms of trade shock will affect the equilibrium RER in period 1 only; in period 2, when the terms of trade return to their "long-run equilibrium," so will the RER. Moreover, if there are rigidities or transaction costs, it may not be completely desirable for a country to allow the actual real exchange rate to move toward its short-run equilibrium value for a very short period of time. This is because this move would then have to be reversed, generating additional potential costs (see Edwards, 1986b). Also, if we assume that there is uncertainty (i.e., we relax the perfect foreight assumption), observed price movements—that is, observed RER adjustments—will not be necessarily optimal.

Factor Price Rigidities

The exercises performed above have assumed that all prices, including those of factors, are fully flexible. Although this is a useful assumption for our benchmark analysis, it is not completely realistic for the case of the developing countries. Rigidities in some factor prices can be easily introduced into the analysis. Assume, for example, that the (real) wage rate (w) is fixed at a level $\bar{w} \geq R_L$, where R is the unconstrained revenue function and L is the labor force. In this case, then, we have to define a constrained revenue function for each period (RR) and ($\tilde{R}\tilde{R}$) (Neary, 1985):

$$RR(w, p, q, K) = \max_{Q,L} \{(Q^X + qQ^N + pQ^M) - \bar{w}L\}, \tag{2.53}$$

where Q^i, $i = X, M, N$, refers to output of exportables, importables, and nontradables. Also, the nontradable market equilibrium conditions are replaced by

$$RR_q = E_q, \qquad \tilde{R}\tilde{R}_{\tilde{q}} = E_{\tilde{q}}, \tag{2.54}$$

where RR_q is the partial derivative of the constrained revenue function (2.53) with respect to the price of nontradables in period 1 and $\tilde{R}\tilde{R}_{\tilde{q}}$ is the corresponding expression for period 2. Neary (1985) has shown that under fixed factor prices the following relation exists between restricted and unrestricted revenue functions:

$$RR = R[q, p, \hat{L}(\bar{w}, q, p, K)] - \bar{w}L(\bar{w}, q, p, K), \tag{2.55}$$

where $\hat{L}$ is the amount of labor employed in the constrained case. Once the revenue functions have been redefined in this way it is easy to find how the relative price of nontradables reacts to a tariff reduction in an economy with fixed real wages.

In this case (wage rigidity) there will not be full employment; some of the labor force is unemployed. For a number of years trade theorists have been preoccupied with the relation between tariffs and employment (Mundell, 1961; Eichengreen, 1981; Kimbrough, 1984; van Wijnbergen,

1987). In the model developed in this chapter, if wages are flexible, tariffs have no effects on aggregate employment. However, if there is real wage rigidity of the type described above, tariffs will indeed have an effect on the level of total employment in the economy. For example, equation (2.56) gives the response of labour employed in period 1 to a temporary tariff in that period:

$$\frac{d\hat{L}}{d\tau} = -(RR_{L_p}/RR_{L\hat{L}}) - (RR_{L_q}/RR_{L\hat{L}})\frac{dq}{d\tau}, \tag{2.56}$$

where the term $(dq/d\tau)$ captures the change in the relative price of N in period 1 to tariff increase. Both RR_{L_p} and RR_{L_q} are Rybczynski type terms whose signs will depend on factor intensities. Depending on the sign of $dq/d\tau$ and on factor intensities in the different sectors, $(d\hat{L}/d\tau)$ can be positive or negative.

Intermediate Inputs and Import Quotas

The intertemporal duality approach used here can be easily extended in order to incorporate import quotas and intermediate inputs. First, the case of import quotas can be analyzed in a quite straightforward fashion by defining "virtual prices" as in Neary and Roberts (1980). The use of virtual prices, of course, assumes that the quota is allocated competitively via an auction mechanism.

Intermediate goods can also be incorporated quite easily through the definition of net-outputs as in Dixit and Norman (1980). In this case an additional source of ambiguity with respect to the sign of $dq/d\tau$ emerges.

2.9 Summary

In this chapter an optimizing intertemporal real model of a small open economy has been developed to investigate how various exogenous changes in the real fundamental determinants of the equilibrium real exchange rate affect its path through time. This analysis is a fundamental step in any discussion dealing with issues related to real exchange rate misalignment. The model assumes that firms produce competitively three goods—exports, imports, and nontradables. Households maximize the present value of utility and consume all three goods. They have access to the international capital market, where they can borrow or lend at the given world interest rate. The only constraint they face is that the present value of the current account balances has to be zero. The model uses duality theory and exploits the properties of exact price indexes as developed by Svensson and Razin (1983).

The effects of changes in real exchange rate fundamentals, such as import tariffs and international terms of trade, were investigated, with emphasis placed on the distinction between temporary, permanent, and anticipated disturbances. In this setting a crucial channel through which exogenous shocks are transmitted is the consumption rate of interest (CRI). Changes in tariffs or in the international terms of trade will affect the CRI, intertemporal expenditure decisions, and consequently the equilibrium vector of RERs and the current account.

The formal analysis in this chapter showed that equilibrium real exchange rates can experience substantial, and some times even not easily predictable, changes as a result of disturbances to fundamentals. Given the very general nature of the model, in many cases it was not possible to establish unequivocally the direction in which the equilibrium real exchange rate will react. In most cases, however, it is possible to find definite signs under some plausible assumptions. The following is a very brief summary of our main results:

1. With low initial tariffs the imposition of important tariffs (either temporarily or permanently) will usually generate an *equilibrium real appreciation* in the current and future periods. A sufficient condition is that we have (net) substitutability in demand among all three goods X, M, and N. If initial tariffs are high, for this result to hold we need, in addition, that income effects do not dominate substitution effects. If, however, there is complementarity in consumption, it is possible that the imposition of import tariffs will generate a real equilibrium depreciation.

2. If the income effect associated with a terms of trade deterioration dominates the substitution effect, a worsening in the terms of trade will result in an *equilibrium real depreciation*.

3. Generally speaking, it is not possible to know how the effect of import tariffs and terms of trade shocks on the equilibrium real exchange rate will be distributed through time.

4. It is crucially important to distinguish between permanent and temporary shocks when analyzing the reaction of the equilibrium real exchange rate.

5. A relaxation of exchange controls will always result in an equilibrium real appreciation in period 1. Moreover, in that period we shall observe simultaneously a real appreciation and an increase in borrowing from abroad.

6. A transfer from the rest of the world—or an exogenously generated capital inflow for that matter—will always result in an equilibrium real appreciation.

7. The effect of an increase in government consumption on the equilibrium RERs will depend on the composition of this new consumption. If it falls fully on nontradables, there is a strong presumption that the RER will experience an equilibrium real appreciation. If it falls fully on tradables, there will be an equilibrium real depreciation.

The analysis in this chapter has ignored monetary considerations, focusing exclusively on movements in the equilibrium real exchange rates. In reality, of course, not all RER movements are equilibria ones. In chapter 3 we develop a model where macro disequilibria can indeed generate deviations between the actual and the equilibrium real exchange rates.

Appendix

A. Notation

$$E_{pp} = E_\pi \pi_{pp} + \pi_p E_{\pi\pi} \pi_{p'}$$

$$E_{pq} = E_\pi \pi_{pq} + \pi_p E_{\pi\pi} \pi_{q'}$$

$$E_{p\tilde{p}} = \pi_p E_{\pi\tilde{\pi}} \tilde{\pi}_{\tilde{p}} \delta^*,$$

$$E_{p\tilde{q}} = \delta^* \pi_p E_{\pi\tilde{\pi}} \tilde{\pi}_{\tilde{q}'}$$

$$E_{\tilde{p}\tilde{p}} = E_{\tilde{\pi}} \tilde{\pi}_{\tilde{p}\tilde{p}} + \tilde{\pi}_{\tilde{p}} E_{\tilde{\pi}\tilde{\pi}} \tilde{\pi}_{\tilde{p}'}$$

$$E_{qq} = E_\pi \pi_{qq} + \pi_q E_{\pi\pi} \pi_{q'}$$

$$E_{\tilde{q}\tilde{q}} = E_{\tilde{\pi}} \tilde{\pi}_{\tilde{q}\tilde{q}} + \tilde{\pi}_{\tilde{q}} E_{\tilde{\pi}\tilde{\pi}} \tilde{\pi}_{\tilde{q}'}$$

$$E_{q\tilde{q}} = \pi_q \delta^* E_{\pi\tilde{\pi}} \tilde{\pi}_{\tilde{q}'}$$

$$E_{q\tilde{p}} = \pi_q \delta^* E_{\pi\tilde{\pi}} \tilde{\pi}_{\tilde{p}'}$$

$$E_{\tilde{p}\tilde{q}} = E_{\tilde{\pi}} \tilde{\pi}_{\tilde{p}\tilde{q}} + \tilde{\pi}_{\tilde{p}} E_{\tilde{\pi}\tilde{\pi}} + \tilde{\pi}_{\tilde{p}} E_{\tilde{\pi}\tilde{\pi}} \tilde{\pi}_{\tilde{q}} \delta^*.$$

B. Stability

The dynamic behavior of nontradable prices are depicted by equations (2.B.1) and (2.B.2) where $\lambda_1, \lambda_2 > 0$:

$$\dot{q} = \lambda_1 [E_q - R_q], \tag{2.B.1}$$

$$\dot{\tilde{q}} = \lambda_2 [E_{\tilde{q}} - \tilde{R}_{\tilde{q}}]. \tag{2.B.2}$$

Using Taylor expansions of (2.B.1) and (2.B.2) around equilibrium prices, and dropping second- and higher-order terms, we obtain

$$\begin{pmatrix} \dot{q} \\ \dot{\tilde{q}} \end{pmatrix} = \begin{pmatrix} \lambda_1 (E_{qq} - R_{qq}) & \lambda_1 E_{q\tilde{q}} \\ \lambda_2 E_{\tilde{q}q} & \lambda_2 (E_{\tilde{q}\tilde{q}} - \tilde{R}_{\tilde{q}\tilde{q}}) \end{pmatrix} \begin{pmatrix} q - q^* \\ \tilde{q} - \tilde{q}^* \end{pmatrix}.$$

Denoting the RHS matrix as A, stability of the system requires

$\det A > 0,$

$\operatorname{tr} A < 0.$

This means that

$\{(E_{qq} - R_{qq})(E_{\tilde{q}\tilde{q}} - \tilde{R}_{\tilde{q}\tilde{q}}) - E_{\tilde{q}q} E_{q\tilde{q}}\} > 0,$

$\{(E_{qq} - R_{qq}) + (E_{\tilde{q}\tilde{q}} - \tilde{R}_{\tilde{q}\tilde{q}})\} < 0.$

These requirements can then be used to sign the determinant of the system of equations in the text. Also, it follows directly from these requirements that the $\tilde{H}\tilde{H}$ schedule is steeper than the HH schedule.

Notes

1. As pointed out in chapter 1, there is still disagreement among economists on how to define "the" real exchange rate. These discussions are mainly semantic and do not affect in any fundamental way the analytics. Once the behavior of the relative price of tradables—our definition of RER—is known, all that is required are algebraic manipulations to find how any other definition of "the" real exchange rate reacts to a particular shock.

2. This intertemporal budget constraint can be written in the following way— $\sum_i (1 + r)^{-i} C_{t+i} = 0$—and states that this country cannot be a net lender or net borrower forever. Eventually it has to pay its debts. See also the discussion in Williamson (1983b). Naturally here we are assuming that the initial stock of foreign debt is zero. If this is not the case, the intertemporal budget constraint will have to be rewritten.

3. Although the use of duality implies some setup costs, such as the mastering of new notation, its simplicity and elegance pay off, quite handsomely. Dixit and Norman (1980) use duality in static trade models. Svensson and Razin (1983), Edwards and van Wijnbergen (1986), and van Wijnbergen (1987) use duality theory to analyze intertemporal problems.

4. For further details on revenue and expenditure functions see Dixit and Norman (1980).

5. See however, chapter 8 for a model with imported intermediate inputs. If any of our goods is an input into another good, some of the cross-derivatives can be positive.

6. Notice that equations (2.9) and (2.10) imply that the government is not subject to import taxes.

7. The weights γ and $(1 - \gamma)$ can be related to the relative importance of imports and exports either in consumption *or* in production. In the former case they can be derived by using the properties of the exact price indexes.

8. The proposition that a reduction (or elimination) of tariffs will necessarily result in an equilibrium real depreciation has also been made in the developing countries shadow pricing literature. Some authors have proposed that the shadow exchange rate should be computed as the equilibrium real exchange rate under conditions of free trade (Bacha and Taylor, 1971). It has then been postulated that an elimination of existing trade impediments will result in a higher equilibrium real exchange rate (i.e., in a real depreciation). For example, for the case of a small country which faces initial trade equilibrium, Bacha and Taylor (1971, p. 216) proposed the following expression for the free trade real exchange rate: $e^F = e(1 + t)^\gamma$, where e^F is the free trade equilibrium (real) exchange rate, e is the (real) exchange rate prior to the elimination of tariffs, t is the level of the tariffs, and $\gamma = \eta_M/(\varepsilon_x + \eta_M)$, for η_M elasticity of demand for imports and ε_x elasticity of supply for exports.

9. The analysis of the effects of tariff changes on the equilibrium RER is highly relevant in the developing countries. Many LDCs have historically gone through major processes of trade liberalization and of trade restrictions. In the case of trade controls, there is a two-way relation that goes from tariff changes to the equilibrium RER and from the *actual* (as opposed to equilibrium) RER to changes in tariffs. In particular, if as a result of inconsistent macroeconomic policies the RER becomes overvalued, the authorities will usually hike tariffs. In the present chapter we shall only deal with the former effect: the implications of *exogenous* tariff changes on the equilibrium RER. In chapter 3 and in part III we discuss in detail the second aspect of this relation.

10. The exact expression for $E_{q\tilde{q}}$ is obtained after taking the derivative of $E_q = E_\pi \pi_q$.

11. Point C in figure 2.2 is the new equilibrium under the assumption that non-tradables and importables are complements in consumption in period 2, and that this effect dominates. In this case the $\tilde{H}\tilde{H}$ schedule has shifted to the left. A possible outcome is the one described in figure 2.2, where as a result of an anticipated tariff the *equilibrium* path of the real exchange rate will be characterized by wide swings—it will increase in period 1, and it will decline in period 2 below its initial (pretariff) level. Although this path is clearly characterized by equilibrium movements in each period, observers may think that the RER has moved in the "wrong direction" in period 1. Although this movement in the equilibrium RER in different directions is theoretically possible, it is not too likely in reality.

12. In Edwards (1989c) the effect of temporary import tariffs on the current account is analyzed in detail.

13. See Edwards (1986b) for a more detailed discussion.

14. See Edwards (1986b) for a detailed discussion on the effects of temporary shocks to the terms of trade on equilibrium real exchange rates and the current account.

15. It is also possible to analyze the effects of terms of trade disturbances on the current account. This, in fact, constitutes an extension of the analysis of Svensson and Razin (1983) to the case with nontradable goods. In the current setting, however, changes in equilibrium real exchange rates constitute an additional channel through which terms of trade disturbances get transmitted to the current account. For this, see Edwards (1989c).

16. On "Dutch Disease" see the volume edited by Neary and van Wijnbergen (1986).

17. There are, however, alternative ways of modeling capital controls. Edwards and van Wijnbergen (1986), for example, assume that there is a quantitative restriction that determines the maximum a country could borrow in any period of time. The domestic interest rate, then, adjusts to the level required to clear the market.

18. The caveats mentioned in the case of tariffs should be kept in mind when analyzing the role of capital controls as real exchange rate fundamentals. Only long-run changes in capital controls that respond to structural motives are relevant. The imposition of capital controls to avoid (or delay) a balance of payments crisis do not constitute a change in a "fundamental." On the Southern Cone liberalization attempts see Edwards and Cox-Edwards (1987), Corbo (1985), Corbo and de Melo (1985), and Calvo (1986).

19. Part of this section is based on Edwards (1989b).

20. Notice, however, that it is also possible that the capital account liberalization will result in massive capital outflows. See Edwards (1984). In this model the tax on borrowing is a policy variable. Alternatively one can assume, as in Edwards and van Wijnbergen (1986), that there is a quantitative limit to foreign borrowing. In that case δ becomes an endogenous variable.

21. This assumes that the transfer is made in the form of tradable goods. If actual capital is transferred, however, the results may be different.

22. The fact that transfers from abroad generate an equilibrium real appreciation has some important policy implications. In particular, it means that foreign aid will generally discourage tradable activities, including agriculture. Foreign aid, by increasing real income, will generate an "equilibrium overvaluation" that will squeeze profitability out of the exports and import competing sectors.

23. For a detailed analysis of technological progress using duality in a static general equilibrium model of trade see Dixit and Norman (1980, pp. 137–142).

3

Macroeconomic Policies, Real Exchange Rate Misalignment, and Devaluation

Even though long-run equilibrium real exchange rates are a function of real variables only, actual real exchange rates respond to both real and monetary variables. The existence of an equilibrium real exchange rate does not mean that the actual real rate has to be permanently equal to this equilibrium value. In fact, the actual RER will normally exhibit departures from its long-run equilibrium; short-run and even medium-run deviations of the actual from the equilibrium RER, which are typically not very large and stem from short-term frictions and adjustment costs, can be quite common. However, there are other types of deviations that can become persistent through time, generating major and sustained differentials between actual and equilibrium real exchange rates, or real exchange rate *misalignments*.

In the optimizing model of chapter 2 the RER was always in equilibrium. In this chapter, on the other hand, we deal with situations where the actual real exchange rate can become misaligned, exhibiting sustained departures from its long-run equilibrium value. In order to analyze these RER misalignments we develop a monetary model with a highly stylized real side. This, however, is not a serious limitation, since chapter 2 has provided an exhaustive analysis on equilibrium movements of real exchange rates.[1]

In this chapter the interaction between macroeconomic policies and the behavior of the actual real exchange rate is carried out for two different nominal exchange rate regimes: (1) fixed nominal exchange rates, and its variants including managed and crawling rates, and (2) nonunified exchange rate systems, including dual rates and the case where a significant parallel foreign exchange market coexists with the official market. The chapter also deals with the role of nominal devaluations in generating a real exchange rate *realignment* or return to long-run equilibrium. Here we emphasize the interaction between nominal devaluations and macroeconomic policies, and focus on both fixed and dual nominal rate regimes.

3.1 Macroeconomic Policies and Real Exchange Rate Misalignment in a Unified Fixed Nominal Exchange Rate Regime

A fundamental principle of open economy macroeconomics is that in order to have a sustainable macroeconomic equilibrium it is necessary that monetary and fiscal policies be *consistent* with the chosen nominal exchange rate regime. This means that the selection of an exchange rate system imposes certain limitations on the extent of macropolicies. If this consistency is violated, severe disequilibrium situations, which are usually reflected on real exchange rate misalignment, will take place.

Perhaps the case of a "high" fiscal deficit under fixed nominal exchange rates is the most clear example of macropolicies and exchange rate inconsistencies. In most developing countries fiscal imbalances are partially or wholly financed by money creation. The inflation required to finance a fiscal deficit equal to a fraction δ of GDP can be calculated as

$$\pi = \delta / \lambda, \tag{3.1}$$

where π is the rate of inflation required to finance the government deficit, and λ is the ratio of high-powered money to GDP. If the required rate of inflation is "too high," it will possibly result in the price of nontradables (P_N) growing faster than the international price of tradables (P_T^*) and in a real appreciation. This type of "inconsistent" fiscal policy will result in domestic credit creation above money demand growth. This, in turn, will be translated into an excess demand for tradable goods, nontradable goods, and financial assets. While the excess demand for tradables will be reflected in a higher trade deficit (or lower surplus), in a loss of international reserves, and in an increase in (net) foreign borrowing above its long-run sustainable level, the excess demand for nontradables will be translated into higher prices for those goods, and consequently into a real exchange rate appreciation. If there are no changes in the fundamental real determinants of the ERER, this real appreciation induced by the expansive domestic credit policy will represent a departure of the actual RER from its equilibrium value, or real exchange rate misalignment. Naturally, since this policy is unsustainable, something will have to give. Either the inconsistent macropolicies will have to be reverted, or at some time the central bank will "run out" of reserves and a balance of payments crisis will ensue.

The consistency between monetary and exchange rate policies is not only needed under fixed rates, but also under most types of predetermined and managed nominal exchange rates, such as an active crawling peg. Perhaps Argentina in the late 1970s is the most notorious recent case of an inconsistent fiscal and crawling nominal exchange rate policies. During that period the Argentinian government implemented the by-now famous pre-announced rate of devaluation or *"tablita"* as a means of reducing inflation. However, the preannounced rate of crawl was clearly inconsistent with the inflation tax required to finance the fiscal deficit (Calvo, 1986). This inconsistency not only generated a real appreciation but also a substantial speculative activity where the public basically bet on when the *"tablita"* would be abandoned.

A number of authors have analyzed the relation between macroeconomic policies, real exchange rates, and the external sector. Rodriguez (1978), for example, constructed a model of a small dependent economy with no capital mobility where inconsistent fiscal policies lead to real exchange rate overvaluation, losses in reserves, and eventually to a devaluation crisis. As long as the devaluation is not accompanied by a reversal of the unsustainable fiscal policies, all the nominal devaluation can accomplish is to generate a temporary improvement in the balance of payments. In the Rodriguez model, without fiscal restraint there will be recurrent balance of payments crises that will lead to a devaluation-inflation spiral. More recently, Khan and Lizondo (1987) have extended the Rodriguez model, allowing for a richer menu of policies. They also emphasize the relation between fiscal inconsistencies, real exchange rate overvaluation, and eventual balance of payments crises.

Neither of these papers incorporates the role of expectations of devaluation into the analysis. This, however, has been extensively done in the literature on speculative attacks and devaluations pioneered by Krugman (1979). A problem with most work along those lines, however, is that in these models, contrary to most historical episodes, the process leading to a devaluation crisis is not accompanied by a real exchange rate overvaluation. An exception to this is given by Calvo's (1987) optimizing model of a cash-in-advance economy where this real overvaluation does precede the devaluation crisis.[2] In section 3.3 we construct a model of a small economy that captures the most salient stylized facts of devaluation crises in the developing world.

3.2 Macroeconomic Policies and the Real Exchange Rates in the Presence of Parallel Nominal Exchange Rate Markets

Nonunified (or multiple) nominal exchange rates have traditionally had some appeal for the developing countries, and have recently become fairly common. Under this type of system different international transactions are subject to differential nominal exchange rates, giving rise to the possibility of having more than one real exchange rate.

Under nonunified exchange rates, the relation between macroeconomic policies and the rest of the economy will depend on the nature of the multiple rates system. If, for example, the multiple rates regime consists of two (or more) predetermined (i.e., fixed) nominal rates, the system will work almost in the same way as under unified predetermined nominal rates. This is because multiple fixed nominal exchange rates are perfectly equivalent to a unified rate system with taxes on certain external transactions. In this case, as with unified predetermined rates, inconsistent macroeconomic policies will result in loss of international reserves, a rate of domestic inflation that will exceed world inflation, and real exchange rate overvaluation. This situation, of course, will be unsustainable in the long run and the authorities will have to introduce corrective macropolicies.

A different kind of nonunified nominal exchange rates consists of a fixed official rate for current account transactions and an (official) freely fluctuating rate for capital account transactions. Although this type of arrangement has been more prevalent in the more advanced countries, in recent years a number of developing nations (e.g., Mexico, Venezuela) have experimented with it. The main purpose of this system is to delink the real side of the economy from the effects of supposedly highly unstable capital movements. In this dual exchange rate system, portfolio decisions are highly influenced by the differential between the free and fixed rates or exchange rate premium. The private sector decisions on what proportion of wealth to hold in the form of foreign currency denominated assets is directly influenced by the expected rate of devaluation of the free rate.

Under a dual exchange rate regime, even if no current account transactions slip into the free rate, changes in the fluctuating nominal rate will exercise an influence on the real exchange rate. Consider, for example, the case of an increase of domestic credit at a rate that exceeds the increase in the demand for domestic money. As before this will provoke an excess demand for goods and financial assets. As a result of this policy there will be a decline in the stock of international reserves, an increase in the price of nontradable goods, and consequently a real appreciation. In addition, there will be an increase in the demand for foreign assets, which will result in a nominal devaluation of the free rate, and in changes in the domestic interest rate. The devaluation of the free rate will, in turn, have secondary effects over the official *real* exchange rate via a wealth effect. The bottom line, however, is that in this case inconsistent macropolicies will eventually be also unsustainable, as international reserves are drained. By partially delinking the current from the capital account, all the dual rates system can hope to do is delay the eventual crisis.

3.3 A Dual Nominal Exchange Rate Model

In this section we construct a model to analyze the behavior of the key macroeconomic variables—including the real exchange rate—in a country with nonunified nominal exchange rates. This model provides a number of important insights regarding the relation between macroeconomic policies, real exchange rate misalignment, and devaluations. The model is an extension of the Calvo-Rodriguez (1977) model for the case where there are dual nominal rates and a government sector.[3] In this model the exportable and importable sectors are aggregated into a tradable sector.[4] It is assumed, consequently, that this small country produces and consumes two goods: tradables (T) and nontradables (N). Nationals of this country hold both domestic money (M) and foreign money (F). There is a government that consumes tradables and nontradables, and uses both nondistortionary taxes and domestic credit creation to finance its expenditures. Initially it is assumed that the government, as the private sector, cannot borrow from abroad. Later, however, we discuss several ways in which this assumption can be relaxed. Also, it is assumed that there is no domestic public debt. By assuming debt away we can ignore interest rates, greatly simplifying the exposition. Finally, it is assumed that there is a fixed nominal exchange rate for commercial transactions (E) and a freely floating nominal exchange rate (δ) for financial transactions. This latter rate takes whatever level is required to achieve asset market equilibrium. It is assumed that the price of tradables in terms of foreign currency is fixed and equal to 1 $(P_T^* = 1)$. Throughout the analysis it is also assumed that there is perfect foresight. The model is given by equations (3.2)–(3.16):

Portfolio Decisions

$$A = M + \delta F, \tag{3.2}$$

$$a = m + \rho F, \quad \text{where} \quad a = A/E, \quad m = M/E, \quad \rho = \delta/E, \tag{3.3}$$

$$m = \sigma(\dot{\delta}/\delta)\rho F, \quad \sigma' < 0, \tag{3.4}$$

$$\dot{F} = 0. \tag{3.5}$$

Demand Side

$$e = E/P_N, \tag{3.6}$$

$$C_T = C_T(e, a): \qquad \frac{\partial C_T}{\partial e} < 0, \quad \frac{\partial C_T}{\partial a} > 0, \qquad\qquad (3.7)$$

$$C_N = C_N(e, a): \qquad \frac{\partial C_N}{\partial e} > 0, \quad \frac{\partial C_N}{\partial a} > 0; \qquad\qquad (3.8)$$

Supply Side

$$Q_T = Q_T(e): \qquad \frac{\partial Q_T}{\partial e} > 0, \qquad\qquad (3.9)$$

$$Q_N = Q_N(e): \qquad \frac{\partial Q_N}{\partial e} < 0; \qquad\qquad (3.10)$$

Government Sector

$$G = P_N G_N + E G_T, \qquad\qquad (3.11)$$

$$\frac{E G_T}{G} = \lambda, \qquad\qquad (3.12)$$

$$G = t + \dot{D}; \qquad\qquad (3.13)$$

External Sector

$$CA = Q_T(e) - C_T(e, a) - G_T, \qquad\qquad (3.14)$$

$$\dot{R} = CA, \qquad\qquad (3.15)$$

$$\dot{M} = \dot{D} + E\dot{R}. \qquad\qquad (3.16)$$

Equation (3.2) defines total assets (A) in domestic currency as the sum of domestic money (M) plus foreign money (F) times the free market nominal exchange rate (δ). Equation (3.3) defines *real* assets in terms of tradable goods, where E is the (fixed) commercial rate and $\rho = \delta/E$ is the spread between the free and the commercial nominal exchange rates. Equation (3.4) is the portfolio composition equation and establishes that the desired ratio of real domestic money to real foreign money is a negative function of the expected rate of depreciation of the free rate δ. Since perfect foresight is assumed, in equation (3.4) expected depreciation has been replaced by actual depreciation $\dot{\delta}/\delta$. Equation (3.5) establishes that there is no capital mobility and that no commercial transactions are subject to the financial rate δ. It is assumed, however, that this economy has inherited a positive stock of foreign money, so that $F_0 \neq 0$.

Equations (3.6)–(3.10) summarize the demand and supply sides. Demands for nontradable and tradable goods depend on the real exchange rate and on the level of real assets; supply functions, on the other hand, depend on the real exchange rate only. Notice that a simplification is that taxes do not appear in the demand functions. Equations (3.11)–(3.13) summarize the government sector, where G_N and G_T are its consumption of N and T, respectively. It is convenient to express *real* government consumption in terms of tradables as

$$g = g_T + g_N, \tag{3.11'}$$

where $g = G/E$, $g_T = G_T$, and $g_N = P_N G_N/E = G_N/e$. Equation (3.12) defines the ratio of government consumption on tradable goods as λ. Notice that λ is also equal to (g_T/g). Equation (3.13) is the government budget constraint and says that government consumption has to be financed via nondistortionary taxes (t) and domestic credit creation ($\dot{D}$). However, under a fixed nominal exchange rate for commercial transactions a positive rate of growth of domestic credit ($\dot{D} > 0$) is not sustainable in the long run. Stationary equilibrium, then, is achieved when $G = t$ and $\dot{D} = 0$. If, however, a crawling peg is assumed for the commercial rate [i.e., $(\dot{E}/E) > 0)$], it is possible to have a positive $\dot{D}$ consistent with the rate of the crawl.

Equations (3.14), (3.15), and (3.16) summarize the external sector. Equation (3.14) defines the current account in foreign currency as the difference between output of tradables and total (private plus public sector) consumption of T. Equation (3.15) establishes that in this model, with no capital mobility and a freely determined financial exchange rate, the balance of payments ($\dot{R}$) is identical to the current account, where R is the stock of international reserves. It is also assumed that initially the central bank holds a positive stock of international reserves R_0.[5] Finally, the model is closed with equation (3.16), which provides the link between changes in international reserves, changes in domestic credit and changes in the domestic stock of money.

As in chapter 2, long-run sustainable equilibrium is attained when the nontradable goods market and the external sector (current account and balance of payments) are *simultaneously* in equilibrium. In this model this means that long-run sustainable equilibrium implies that the current account is in equilibrium in *every* period. In the short run and even the medium run, however, there can be departures from CA = 0. This, of course, will result in the accumulation or decumulation of international reserves. A steady state is attained when the following four conditions hold simultaneously: (1) the nontradables market clears, (2) the external sector is in equilibrium— $\dot{R} = 0 = \text{CA} = \dot{m}$; (3) fiscal policy is sustainable—$G = t$ and $\dot{D} = 0$, and (4) portfolio equilibrium holds. The real exchange rate prevailing under these steady state conditions is the *long-run equilibrium real exchange rate* ($\tilde{e}_{LR}$). This long-run equilibrium real exchange rate exchange rate is equivalent to **RER** in chapter 2.

The nontradables good market clears when

$$C_N(e, a) + eg_N = Q_N(e), \tag{3.17}$$

where g_N is *real* government consumption of N in terms of tradable goods. From (3.17) it is possible to find an *equilibrium* relation between e, a, and g_N.

$$e = v(a, g_N), \quad \text{where} \quad \frac{\partial v}{\partial a} < 0, \quad \frac{\partial v}{\partial g_N} < 0. \tag{3.18}$$

A higher value of real assets increases the demand for nontradables, requiring a higher P_N—or lower RER—to maintain equilibrium. The case of g_N is equivalent. Notice that equation (3.18) gives us the value of e that equilibrates the nontradable goods sector, without any reference to the external sector. In order to find the long-run equilibrium real exchange rate we have to look also at current account and balance of payments equilibrium.

Since the commercial rate is fixed, $(\dot{\delta}/\delta)$ in the money demand equation (3.4) can be substituted by the rate of change of the spread $(\dot{\rho}/\rho)$. Thus we can write $m/\rho F = \sigma(\dot{\rho}/\rho)$. Inverting this equation and solving for $\dot{\rho}$, we obtain

$$\dot{\rho} = \rho L\left(\frac{m}{\rho F}\right), \quad L'(\ ) < 0. \tag{3.19}$$

In steady state equilibrium $\dot{\rho} = 0$. In figure 3.1, the $\dot{\rho} = 0$ schedule has been drawn; it is positively sloped because in order for the public to hold larger amounts of m we need a higher ρ—the higher the spread, the lower the expectations of further increases of the free rate, and thus the higher the amount of (real) domestic money the public is willing to hold.

From equations (3.11), (3.14), (3.15), (3.16), the following expression for $\dot{m}$ can be derived:

$$\dot{m} = Q_T(e) - C_T(e, a) + \frac{G_N}{e} - \frac{t}{E}. \tag{3.20}$$

Equilibrium of the external sector requires that $\dot{m} = 0$. When government expenditures are fully financed with taxes, the $\dot{R} = 0$ schedule will coincide with the $\dot{m} = 0$ schedule. In figure 3.1, the $\dot{m} = 0$ schedule has been drawn. The intuition for its negative slope is related to the effects of wealth changes on the current account and on relative prices. An increase in m

results in higher real wealth (a) and in a current account deficit; in order to regain equilibrium real wealth (a) should go down via a decline in δ.

Long-run sustainable equilibrium is depicted in figure 3.1 by the intersection of the $\dot{p} = 0$ and the $\dot{m} = \dot{R} = 0$ schedules. S is the long-run equilibrium point with a steady state level of real balances m_0 and a steady state spread p_0. It is easy to show that this system is characterized by saddle path equilibrium. ss is the saddle path, and the arrows denote the dynamic forces at work in this system. Once the steady state values of p and m are determined, equation (3.18) can be used to find, for the corresponding value of g_N, the *long-run equilibrium real exchange rate*:

$$\tilde{e}_{LR} = v(m_0 + p_0 F_0, g_{N_0}). \tag{3.21}$$

Although the real side of this model is significantly simpler than the general equilibrium model of chapter 2, it is still the case that changes in the *real fundamental* determinants of the real exchange rate will affect the long-run sustainable equilibrium real exchange rate.[6] For example, a change in the composition of government consumption, or λ, will result in a change in e_{LR} If we assume that expenditure on tradables increases at the expense of government consumption of N—with total real government consumption constant—there will be an equilibrium real depreciation (increase in e).[7] In terms of the diagram this means that there will be a downward shift of $\dot{m} = 0$, with an unchanged $\dot{p} = 0$ schedule; the new steady state will be characterized by lower m and δ. From (3.21) we can then see that the new $\tilde{e}_{LR}$ will be higher.

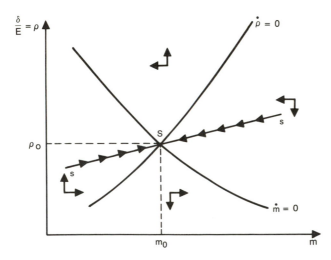

Figure 3.1

Macroeconomic Policies, Misalignment, and Dual Market Spread

Consider now how monetary disturbances will affect the real exchange rate and the external sector. In particular, we are interested in investigating how monetary disturbances will affect the evolution of the *actual* (as opposed to equilibrium) real exchange rate. This will allow us to discuss misalignment issues.

The simplest way to illustrate the working of the model is to consider a once-and-for-all *unanticipated* increase in the stock of domestic credit (D). On impact, this means that there will be a jump in the real stock of money, since $m = M/E = R + D/E$. This is illustrated in figure 3.2 by the new real stock of domestic money m_1. On impact the system moves from S to Q on the stationary saddle path, with a higher m_1 and spread ρ_1.[8] From equation (3.18) it is easy to see that at Q the *actual* real exchange rate has appreciated relative to its long-run equilibrium value:

$$de = \left(\frac{\partial v}{\partial a}\right) dm + \left(\frac{\partial v}{\partial a}\right) F_0 \, d\rho < 0. \tag{3.22}$$

The reason for this lower short-run real exchange rate e is that the demand for nontradables is a function of real assets and e. At Q, the higher m and the higher ρ imply a higher a ($= m + \rho F$) and, consequently, an incipient excess demand for N. This in turn requires a lower e to reestablish nontradable equilibrium. The higher δ, on the other hand, is required for the money market to be in equilibrium. In order to induce the public to

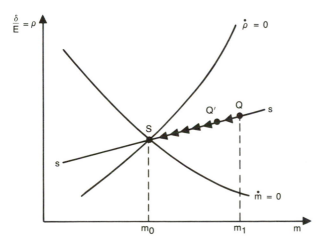

Figure 3.2

(temporarily) hold the higher m relative to F, it is required for them to expect an appreciation of δ [i.e., $(\dot{\delta}/\delta) < 0$]. This is exactly what will happen during the transition period.

The difference between the actual short-run real exchange rate e and its long-run equilibrium level is defined as real exchange rate overvaluation. In this case, however, the overvaluation will be short-lived, since there will be forces moving the system back toward equilibrium.[9]

Adjustment with Sufficient Reserves

After the initial once-and-for-all increase in D the economy will adjust along the saddle path ss moving from Q to S, with reductions of m and ρ. Throughout the transition two things will happen: (1) the stock of international reserves will decline as the public gets rid of the excess of domestic money, and (2) the real exchange rate will continuously depreciate—via reductions in P_N—moving back toward its long-run sustainable level. However, throughout the adjustment the actual real exchange rate will still be overvalued. (i.e., throughout the transition the actual e will be below $\tilde{e}_{LR}$). Only once the system gets back to S has the real exchange rate equilibrium been reestablished. In the final equilibrium m, ρ, and e are the same as before the domestic credit disturbance. However, now there is a new composition of domestic money with a higher level of D and a lower level of R. Figure 3.3 depicts the evolution of our key variables through time. At time t_0, D unexpectedly increases; the transition is assumed to be finished at time t_1. In panel (a) we depict the behavior of the real exchange rate, where as before $\tilde{e}_{LR}$ is the long-run sustainable level. Notice that since there are no changes in fundamentals, the equilibrium RER remains at its original level. The actual RER, however, moves down (i.e., appreciates) at time t_0, remaining below $\tilde{e}_{LR}$ throughout the transition. Finally, at time t_1 it gets back to its equilibrium value. Panel (b) depicts international reserves. Throughout the transition they decline, reaching at time t_1 their new long-run equilibrium level R_1. Finally, panel (c) depicts the evolution of the dual market spread.

The time taken to move back from Q to S in figure 3.2 will depend on a number of variables, including the magnitude of the original shock and the different elasticities involved. One possible way to accelerate the adjustment is by implementing an *unanticipated discrete nominal devaluation* of the commercial rate (E). From an economic perspective this once-and-for-all adjustment in E is the reverse of the increase in D. As a result of the higher E the real stock of money (M/E) will jump down. Notice, however, that an

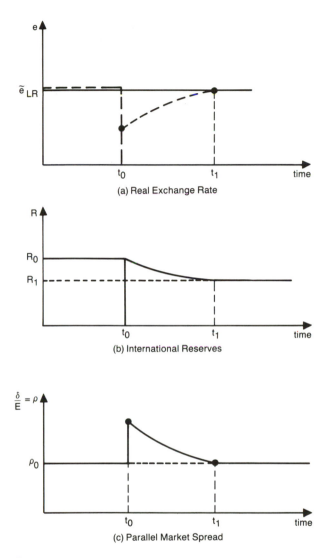

(a) Real Exchange Rate

(b) International Reserves

(c) Parallel Market Spread

Figure 3.3

important characteristic of discrete nominal devaluations is that if undertaken from the situation of equilibrium, they will only have short-run
effects on the real exchange rate. If, on the other hand, they are engineered
when the economy is out of equilibrium—such as in point Q' in figure
3.2—they can help speed up the adjustment process. For example, in our
case, an unanticipated nominal devaluation of the commercial rate of the
"right amount," implemented when the economy is at Q' in figure 3.2, will
result in a jump from Q' to S—the adjustment having been much faster
than if the system had been left to work its way back to S on its own.
Moreover, with the discrete devaluation the total loss of reserves would
have been reduced.

The Adjustment When International Reserves Are Insufficient

For the move from Q to S in figure 3.2 to be a feasible adjustment path we
have to assume that the initial stock of reserves (R_0) is sufficiently high to
cover the loss of reserves that takes place during the transition. If, however,
initial reserves are not high enough, the public will anticipate a balance of
payments crisis that will include a discrete devaluation of the commercial
rate. In this case the adjustment will be quite different from our previous
discussion—it is depicted in figure 3.4. Now, at the time of the actual
increase in D the public anticipates a future devaluation of E, and will want
to get out of domestic money. As a result there is a further jump in the free
rate δ, and thus in the spread ρ. On impact, then, the system moves to
point C in figure 3.4. As before, at this point the real exchange rate suffers

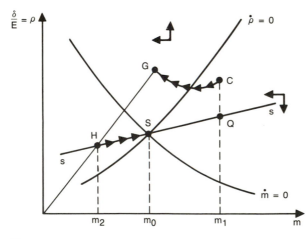

Figure 3.4

an appreciation relative to its long-run equilibrium level (i.e., it becomes overvalued). The system then moves along the divergent path CG. Throughout this path reserves are being lost, and the actual real exchange rate is still overvalued—that is, it is below its long-run sustainable level. The actual depreciation of the fixed rate E takes place when the central bank "runs out" of reserves—or more precisely when reserves reach a predetermined threshold. In figure 3.4 it is assumed that this happens when the system reaches point G. Exactly at this time E is devalued and the system jumps to point H; from there onward the adjustment continues on the saddle path ss. At the time of the devaluation the real stock of money is abruptly reduced, since $m = M/E$. The nominal free rate δ, however, does not jump.[10] The spread $\rho = \delta/E$, on the other hand, does jump down. In terms of the diagram the fact that δ does not jump when the anticipated devaluation of E actually takes place is captured by point H on the saddle path being along a ray from the origin that goes through G.

It is assumed that the magnitude of the devaluation is determined by the amount by which the central bank wants to replenish its international reserves. In figure 3.4 the magnitude of the devaluation of E is such that the new after-devaluation real stock of money m_2 is below the steady state level. This means that the final part of the adjustment will take place along the saddle path from H to S with some of the reserves previously lost being replenished. Notice that on H the real exchange rate has depreciated by more than what is required to achieve RER equilibrium. If the central bank wants to return to the initial stock of international reserves, the integral of $\dot{R}$ between points C and G has to be equal to (minus) the integral of $\dot{R}$ between H and S.

Figure 3.5 depicts, for the case of an unanticipated once-and-for-all domestic credit expansion with exchange rate crisis, the evolution through time of the real exchange rate, international reserves, the free market rate δ, and the spread. We now distinguish between three points in time: (1) The unanticipated increase in D takes place at time t_0. At this time the public also realizes that since reserves are low there will be a nominal devaluation of the official rate in the future. (2) At time t_1 the official devaluation actually takes place. (3) At time t_2 the adjustment has been completed. Notice that in panel (a) we have depicted two possible paths for the RER between periods t_0 and t_1. The reason is that, as can be seen in figure 3.4, during part of the transition m declines and ρ increases. Depending on which of these two forces dominates, e will go up or down [see equation (3.18)]. In panel (b) it has been assumed that the devaluation only partially replenishes the stock of international reserves. As discussed above this need not be the case.

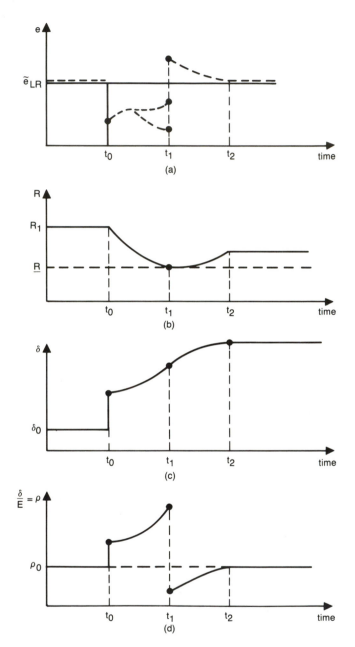

Figure 3.5

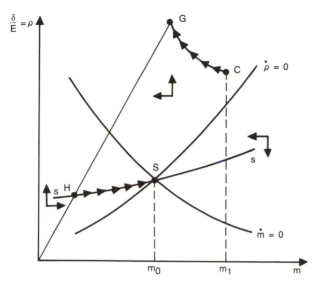

Figure 3.6

Figure 3.5 is highly revealing, since it provides a good depiction of the way the key variables behave during the period preceding a balance of payments crisis and devaluation. Basically our model predicts that before the devaluation we shall observe

a. real exchange rate overvaluation,

b. drainage of international reserves, and

c. increase in the dual market spread.

As mentioned, the initial level of international reserves plays an important role in determining the exact dynamic path followed by this economy. We know that throughout the transition from C to G reserves are being lost. Moreover, we know that the integral of reserves losses along the path from C to G has to be equal to the difference between initial reserves and the threshold level that triggers the devaluation. If the initial level of reserves is relatively large, we can have a relatively long transition. However, if initially reserves are very low, the transition period will be much shorter. In fact, in terms of figure 3.4, the initial level of reserves will determine the location of point C. If reserves are low, the crisis will take place soon after time t_0, and the initial jump in δ will be relatively large. The case of a shorter transition from the time of the domestic credit shock to the crisis is depicted in figure 3.6, where C is now above the $\dot{\rho} = 0$ schedule.

Changes in the Rate of Growth of Credit

Up to now we have considered once-and-for-all increases in domestic credit D. Let us now briefly analyze what happens when for a *limited* period of time $\dot{D}$ becomes positive. The easiest way to think about this is by considering an unanticipated *temporary* reduction in taxes t that results in a temporary positive $\dot{D}$. This exercise allows us to focus on the macro-economic aspects of the problem without getting sidetracked by real issues associated with *increases* in g.

It can be easily seen from equation (3.20) that the temporary reduction in taxes will result in a temporary shift of the $\dot{m} = 0$ schedule to the right. This is captured in figure 3.7, where $\dot{m}' = 0$ is the new schedule. Naturally, once the policy is reversed, the $\dot{m}' = 0$ schedule will shift back. On impact the spread will jump from S to B, below the "hypothetical" saddle path that goes through I. At this point, however, the dynamics are governed by the schedules $\dot{p} = 0$ and $\dot{m}' = 0$. Thus, the system will follow the divergent path BY, until the policy is reversed. Exactly at that time the system will reach point Y on the stationary saddle path ss, with the system now moving from Y to S. Throughout this process reserves are lost and there is a real exchange rate overvaluation. Notice that, as before, at any point during the second part of the adjustment a devaluation of E will help speed up the return to S, allowing the country to complete the adjustment with lower losses in international reserves.

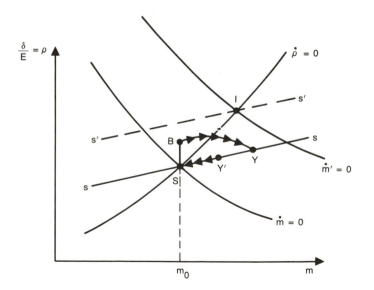

Figure 3.7

Again, in order for this adjustment path to be a feasible one, it is required that initial reserves R_0 exceed the losses that take place during the transition. If this is not the case, a balance of payments crisis and a devaluation of the commercial rate will take place. Figure 3.8 captures this case, where it has been assumed that the devaluation of E takes place exactly at the same time at which the temporary cut in taxes is reversed. At time t_0, when taxes are temporarily reduced, the public realizes that the stock of international reserves is insufficient and that there will be a devaluation of the commercial rate E. The public wants to reduce its holdings of domestic money; the free rate jumps by more than before, moving to B. From there on the system follows the divergent path BY. Throughout, international reserves are again being lost and the spread continues to go up. Moreover, the RER becomes overvalued, and during most of the path increasingly so. At time t_1, when the system is at Y, the lower bound of reserves is reached. At that time the official rate is devalued and taxes are hiked to their sustainable level. This latter measure means that the $\dot{m}' = 0$ schedule shifts back to $\dot{m} = 0$. Due to the nominal devaluation, on the other hand, the system jumps from Y to H, with *no* jump in the free market rate. At that point the system is back on the sustainable saddle path and moves from H to S with international reserves being (partially) replenished.

A simplifying assumption made in this model refers to the absence of capital flows. Perhaps the simplest way to incorporate capital movements

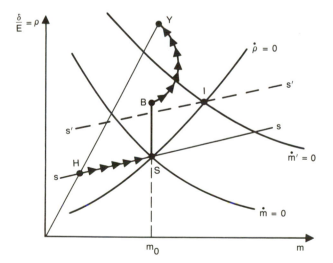

Figure 3.8

is to assume that these are restricted to the government and to model them as (autonomous) transfers. In that sense, foreign borrowing can be analyzed as a positive transfer today and a (larger) negative transfer in the future.[11] In this case it is easy to show that an (exogenous) increase in capital inflows into the country will result in an upward shift of $\dot{m} = 0$, generating an equilibrium real appreciation.[12]

Summary

Summarizing, the model developed here has illustrated some of the essential aspects of the functioning of an economy with dual exchange rates. It was shown that expansive macroeconomic policies will generally be associated with (1) losses of international reserves, (2) a current account deficit, (3) an increase in the spread between the free and the fixed nominal rates during the initial period, and (4) a real exchange rate overvaluation. The form in which the disequilibria is resolved will depend on the nature of the disturbances, the nominal exchange rate policy pursued, and the existing initial stock of international reserves. Although the assumption of perfect foresight has introduced some limitations into the analysis, the model is still able to capture some of the more important stylized facts related to expansionary macroeconomic policies in small open economies. In fact the empirical analysis of chapters 6 and 7 will be firmly based on this model.

3.4 Black Markets and Other Extensions

The analysis is somewhat more complex if some current account transactions are subject to the free nominal exchange rate. In this case we shall have an additional real exchange rate—defined as the price of tradables subject to the free nominal rate relative to nontradables, and macropolicies will affect both real exchange rates.[13] For example, an increase in domestic credit that exceeds the growth of domestic money demand will now result in lower reserves, higher prices on nontradables, a higher "free" market nominal exchange rate, and increased foreign indebtedness if there is capital mobility. The higher price of nontradables will generate a decline (i.e., appreciation) in the real exchange rate applicable to those goods subject to the official foreign exchange market. What will happen to the RER relevant to those goods subject to the free nominal rate? This will depend on whether as a result of the higher domestic credit the nominal exchange rate determined in the free market will increase by more or less than the price of nontradable goods. If the same type of behavior as under a freely floating rate is observed, we shall likely encounter exchange rate overshooting in this market, with the free nominal exchange rate increasing—at least on impact—by more than the price of domestic goods. The real exchange rate applicable to this type of good will, at least in the short run, depreciate. It is perfectly possible, then, that under this dual exchange rate system an expansionary monetary policy results in a real appreciation for a subset of goods—those subject to the official market—, and a real depreciation for a different subset of goods—those subject to the free nominal exchange rate.

Although as a first approximation we can think of a dual system of the type modeled in section 3.3 as equivalent to an economy with a black market for foreign exchange, this is not completely accurate. The case of a regime consisting of an official pegged (or predetermined) nominal exchange rate that coexists with an illegal black market for foreign exchange is rather complex. Although when there are exchange controls some kind of black market for foreign exchange always exist, there are times when this parallel market becomes very significant, and even dominant. Even though the combination of a fixed official rate with a black market works in a way similar to the dual rates regime, there are some important differences. First, to the extent that the black market is illegal, the expectations and costs of detection play an important role in determining the premium, or difference between the official and freely determined nominal exchange rates. Second, expectations regarding political events are fundamentally important, since they reflect possible future changes in the extent of exchange controls, and other important policies. Third, in this case exporters have to decide in each period what proportion of their foreign exchange earnings to surrender legally and what proportion to bring into the country via the parallel market. This decision, of course, will partially depend on the level of the premium itself.

An important question in the case of generalized black markets relates to determining what is the marginal exchange rate. Under these circumstances the black market rate will generally be the marginal rate for imports and import competing sectors. In the case of exports, the marginal rate will depend on the institutional arrangement and on whether exporters are required to surrender a certain proportion or a certain dollar amount of their export proceeds via the official market. If a certain proportion of these proceeds has to be surrendered, the marginal rate for exporters is a weighted average between the official and the black market rate. If, on the contrary, exporters have to surrender a given number of dollars, the black market rate is the marginal one.

In the case of a generalized illegal parallel market, an increase in domestic credit creation will result in higher domestic prices and in an increase in the black market premium. If the central bank has already lost all its international reserves, the increase in domestic credit will not be translated, as before, into losses of the official stock of foreign exchange. This expansive monetary policy will result in an appreciation of the official real exchange rate as well as in a decline of the relative price of exports surrendered via the official market relative to those that use the parallel market. As a result of this, a relatively smaller proportion of export proceeds will be surrendered at the official rate, making the crisis even worse. Eventually, the inconsistent macropolicies will become unsustainable, and corrective policies will have to be implemented. At this point, the issue of nominal exchange rate *unification* becomes important, since the authorities will usually try to devalue the nominal rate, and eliminate the (legal or de facto) multiple rates system.

Devaluations and Trade Impediments

In the model of the previous section there was no independent role for commercial policies. It is, however, quite straightforward to incorporate tariffs into the analysis. In that case it is necessary to distinguish between importables and exportables and specify, as in chapter 2, the relation between the domestic price of importables, the world price of importables, and tariffs. In this case the phase diagrams will still be the same, and, as long as tariffs do not change, our analysis from the previous section will still hold.

A model similar to that of section 3.3 can be derived for the case of three goods (Edwards, 1989d). That model can be summarized in a diagram identical to figure 3.1. In this case, however, changes in import tariffs will shift the $\dot{m} = 0$ schedule. Depending on the signs and magnitudes of the different cross-elasticities of demand, the $\dot{m} = 0$ schedule can go either up or down as a consequence of a tariff change. In the presence of import tariffs—and assuming that these do not change—devaluations will operate in exactly the same way as discussed above. They will help speed up the transition from a disequilibrium position to the long-run sustainable steady state equilibrium.

However, if, as in many developing countries, trade restrictions take the form of quotas rather than tariffs, devaluations will have some different effects. The main difference in the quota case is that a devaluation will not (necessarily) affect the domestic price of importable goods; instead, it will

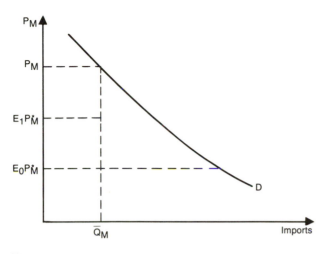

Figure 3.9

result in a reduction of the rents received by the holder of the quota. This means, then, that under quotas devaluations will reduce the domestic relative price of importables to exportables (Krueger, 1982; Bhagwati, 1978).

Although the model of the previous section cannot capture this aspect of devaluations under quotas, this can be easily illustrated by means of figure 3.9. Here D is the demand curve for a particular importable good, E_0 is the initial nominal exchange rate, and P_M^* is the (given) world price of the importable. $\bar{Q}_M$ is the amount of the quota. Consequently, the domestic price that clears the market is P_M higher than $E_0 P_M^*$. What the devaluation does is increase E_0 to E_1, reducing the rents, but not affecting the clearing price P_M.[14] In spite of this additional relative price effect, in an economy with quantitative restrictions, devaluations still play an important role in helping speed up the adjustment process. Again, however, if the sources of the initial disequilibrium condition—that is, the expansive macroeconomic policies—are not altered, the effects of the devaluation on the relative prices of nontradables will be short-lived.

3.5 Real Exchange Rate Misalignment, the Limits of Automatic Adjustment, and Nominal Devaluation

An important source of welfare and efficiency costs of real exchange rate misalignment, not captured by the stylized model of section 3.3, is related to the fact that RER overvaluation is usually accompanied by the imposition of a battery of exchange and trade controls aimed at slowing down the drainage of foreign exchange reserves that accompanies the process of RER overvaluation. These exchange and trade controls, on one hand, introduce major inefficiency costs and, on the other, encourage the creation of strong lobbies that compete for the rents generated by the protective measures (see Krueger, 1974). Also, a situation of exchange rate overvaluation greatly hurts exports and, if prolonged for a long period of time, it can generate irreversible costs by wiping out the agricultural infrastructure (see World Bank, 1984; Pfefferman, 1985). These types of costs can be significant if there are imperfections in local capital markets. Situations of RER misalignment are also conducive to speculation, and usually generate massive capital flights out of the country. Although these capital flights may be optimal from a purely private perspective, they can represent substantial social welfare costs (Cuddington, 1986).

Since RER misalignment generate major costs, how should policymakers deal with them? In the case of macroeconomic induced misalignment, a necessary step is to eliminate the source of the macroeconomic disequilibrium— i.e., the inconsistency between macroeconomic policies and the nominal exchange rate regime. The authorities can then supplement this policy with other measures or can simply wait for the economy to adjust on its own— that is, wait for the actual RER to converge on its own to the equilibrium RER.[15] However, this type of policy, based on *disinflation with automatic adjustment*, has a number of limitations that can be particularly severe under predetermined nominal exchange rates.

Once the inconsistent macroeconomic policies that generated the real exchange misalignment are controlled, the RER will still differ from the ERER. The question then is, How will the RER return to its equilibrium value? Consider the most common case, where the real exchange rate misalignment takes the form of real overvaluation and loss of competitiveness in the international market. In this case, and under fixed nominal rates for commercial transactions, a rapid return to real exchange rate equilibrium will require a *decline* in the nominal domestic price of nontradables. In terms of figure 3.2 this automatic adjustment corresponds to the move from Q to S on the saddle path. Naturally, if nominal prices of nontradables are fully flexible, as in our model of section 3.3, this adjustment will be attained at no cost. If, however, there are some rigidities or adjustment costs, a rapid reduction in this nominal price is, under most circumstances, quite unlikely. This implies that an automatic adjustment could take a substantial period of time, prolonging the situation of RER misalignment with all its related costs.

Under (nominal) domestic price and wage rate inflexibility the automatic adjustment approach can generate additional costs in the form of unemployment and reduced domestic output. The cut in aggregate expenditure resulting from the macrocorrective measures will generate an excess supply (or smaller excess demand) for all types of goods and assets. At the tradables goods level this will be reflected in a smaller trade deficit and, with capital mobility, in a reduction in (net) foreign indebtedness. In the nontradables market, if nominal prices are rigid, the required relative price realignment will not take place, and unemployment will result.

The restoration of real exchange rate equilibrium can be greatly aided by policies, such as nominal devaluations, that help the domestic price of tradables to adjust. In terms of the real exchange rate definition, (RER $=$ P_T/P_N), these policies are aimed at generating a higher RER via an increase in P_T ($= EP_T^*$). This contrasts with the automatic adjustment approach, whose aim is to generate the complete return of the RER to equilibrium via its effect on P_N. Once again, in terms of figure 3.2, a nominal devaluation taken at point Q' will allow the system to jump to S, rather than continue to move along the saddle path.

In theory, and under the most common conditions, nominal devaluations will affect an economy via three main channels. First, a devaluation will have an *expenditure reducing* effect. To the extent that as a result of the devaluation the domestic price level goes up, there will a negative wealth effect that will reduce the real value of domestic currency denominated nominal assets, including domestic money. In terms of our model this expenditure reduction effect of a devaluation is manifested via the reduction in real domestic money m and real assets a. A lower value of real assets (a) will reduce expenditure on all goods. Second, a nominal devaluation will tend to have an *expenditure switching* effect. If the nominal devaluation succeeds in altering the real exchange rate, there will be a substitution in expenditure away from tradables, and a substitution in production towards tradables. In the model of section 3.3 it is clear that a higher e will result in a higher Q_T and a lower C_T. The opposite will happen to nontradable goods. The combination of the expenditure reducing and expenditure switching effects will, of course, result in an improved external situation for the country. While the expenditure switching effect results in an increased demand for nontradables, the expenditure reducing effect generates a decline in demand for those goods. Depending on which of these effects dominate, there will be an increase or a decline in the demand for nontradable goods. Third, a devaluation will result in an increase in the domestic currency price of imported intermediate inputs. This will result in an upward shift of the supply schedules for the final goods, including nontradables.[16]

An important characteristic of nominal devaluation is that, under unified nominal exchange rates and with no quantitative restrictions, it is not discriminatory, and increases the domestic price of *all* tradable goods, services, and assets. This, however, will not be the case if there is a parallel (or dual) market, with some commercial transactions subject to the free rate, and the devaluation is restricted to the official rate only. In this case, only those transactions affected by the official rate will be directly affected by the devaluation. Of course, since the parallel (or free) market will be affected by the devaluation, transactions conducted in that market will be subject to an indirect effect. Notice, however, that in general it is not possible to know a priori whether a devaluation of the official rate will increase or reduce the parallel market premium. Naturally, with parallel markets there will be additional relative price changes, with the price of transactions subject to the official rate changing relative to those subject to the parallel rate.

Whether a nominal devaluation will be successful in accomplishing these objectives will depend on (a) accompanying policies implemented alongside the devaluation and (b) the initial conditions prevailing prior to the devaluation. If the country implements a devaluation at a time when the real exchange rate is greatly misaligned (i.e., overvalued), the nominal devaluation will generally be helpful in restoring equilibrium in the external sector. Under these starting conditions a nominal devaluation, if accompanied by the appropriate macropolicies, will generally have a medium-to-long-run positive effect on the real exchange rate. In practice, what the nominal devaluation will do is help the country follow a smoother transition path toward reestablishing equilibrium in the external sector. If the initial condition of real exchange rate misalignment has been generated by unsustainable macroeconomic policies, a discrete once-and-for-all devaluation will only have a lasting effect on the real exchange rate if at the same time as the devaluation the unsustainable policies are corrected. If, however, the initial condition is one of equilibrium—that is, the actual real exchange rate does not diverge from its long-run equilibrium level—a nominal devaluation will have *no* medium- or long-run effect. Very quickly after the nominal devaluation has been implemented, the price of nontradables will increase and the real exchange rate will not be affected. It should be noticed, however, that devaluations—and in particular those devaluations that succeed in generating a RER change—can have severe fiscal effects by hiking the domestic currency costs of servicing the foreign debt.

This was, in fact, an important source of fiscal pressures in Latin America during the 1980s (Edwards, 1989f).

Import Tariffs and Export Subsidies as Alternatives to Devaluations

Many times policymakers are confronted with the question of whether the simultaneous imposition of import tariffs and export subsidies (of the same rate) will replicate the effects of a devaluation. The answer is that the tariffs *cum* subsidies policy will only replicate some of the effects of a devaluation. Import tariffs will result in an increase in the domestic price of the importable goods; export subsidies will likewise result in an increase in the domestic price of the exportable goods. As long as both the tariffs and the subsidies are of the same rate, the relative price between importables and exportables (the tradables) will not be affected, but their relative price with respect to nontradables will increase. In this way, the domestic relative price of tradables as a group will increase, which is indeed what will happen in the case of a successful devaluation. In that respect, then, both policies are equivalent.

There are, however, a number of other important respects in which these two policies differ quite sharply. First, while a devaluation affects both visible and invisible trade, (i.e., trade on goods and services), the tariff *cum* subsidies policy affects only visible trade. Consequently the relative price between goods and international traded services is altered in the case of the tariffs *cum* subsidies policy, but not in the case of a devaluation. Second, a devaluation affects the domestic currency price of both tradable goods and tradable assets. A tariff *cum* subsidies policy, on the other hand, affects only the domestic price of tradable goods and services. Third, under some circumstances devaluations may affect the level of the domestic interest rate. This will happen as long as a devaluation generates expectations of further devaluations. In this case, as pointed out in Edwards (1985b), some fraction of the expected devaluation will be passed on to the domestic interest rate, even if the capital account of the economy in question is partially closed. On the other hand, the tariffs *cum* subsidies policy will not have this type of effect on the domestic interest rate. Fourth, devaluations and tariffs *cum* subsidies policies will usually have different fiscal effects. While, in general, devaluations will not have first-order direct effects on the fiscal budget, the tariffs *cum* subsidies policy will generally result in fiscal imbalances. Finally (fifth), perhaps the most important difference between the devaluation and tariff *cum* subsidies policies are related to the political economy of these two strategies. Generally, the imposition of tariffs and export subsidies will generate important reactions from the affected interest groups, which will seek an exemption to the application of this measure to their particular industries. As the history of many cases has shown, more often than not these interest groups partially succeed in getting exemptions applied to their products. The argument used by the interest groups lobbyists are well known—the good in question is a necessity, or vital to the geopolitical survival of the country.

3.6 Summary

In this chapter we have discussed the relation between macroeconomic policies, real exchange rates, the external sector, and devaluation. Once monetary and fiscal sectors are introduced into the analysis, it is possible to start talking about *real exchange rate misalignment*, or departures of the actual real rate from its long-run equilibrium value. The discussion presented in this chapter has emphasized the causality that goes from inconsistent macro—fiscal and monetary—policies to real exchange rate misalignment and eventual balance of payments crises.

A perfect foresight model of an economy with a dual exchange rates regime was constructed to analyze formally the behavior of some key variables in the process leading to a balance of payments crisis. The model assumes that a fixed nominal rate is applied to commercial transactions while a fully fluctuating rate applies to the financial sector. It was shown that even temporary inconsistent macropolicies may lead to a balance of payments crisis and devaluation of the rate for commercial transactions. The process leading to a devaluation is characterized by

a. real exchange rate overvaluation,

b. loss of international reserves, and current account deficits, and

c. increasing spread between the commercial and free rates.

It was shown that nominal devaluations are only effective if accompanied by a reversal of the inconsistent macropolicies. It also was shown that even if there is not a crisis (in the sense of a *required* abandonment of the peg), a nominal devaluation, if supplemented by the appropriate macropolicies, can greatly help the country regain equilibrium.

Although this model is highly stylized, it captures very neatly some of the more salient aspects of exchange rate and macroeconomic disequilibrium. This model, and its complementary model developed in chapter 2, will provide the general analytical framework used in much of the empirical analysis in part III of this book.

Notes

1. Although the model developed here complements that of chapter 2, its purpose is to focus on aspects of the problem ignored in that chapter. For that reason, in this chapter the real side has been simplified significantly.

2. See also Connolly and Taylor (1984). On speculative attacks see the work by Obstfeld (1986) and Flood and Garber (1984).

3. Lizondo (1987a,b), Dornbusch (1986a,b), Kiguel and Lizondo (1987), and Edwards (1989d) have developed similar models based on Calvo and Rodriguez (1977).

4. Since this chapter does not consider disturbances to the relative price of exportables to importables, it is highly convenient to aggregate these goods into tradables. See Edwards (1989d) for a version of the model with X, M, and N.

5. If we assume that the central bank has a well defined and stable demand for international reserves, R_0 can be considered as the desired long-run level of official reserves. On the demand for reserves by the developing nations see Edwards (1983b). For a model somewhat similar to the one in this chapter that incorporates an explicit demand for reserves see Edwards and Montiel (1989).

6. In Edwards (1989d) the implications of different real disturbances, including tariffs and terms of trade changes, are analyzed in detail.

7. This assumes that the direct effect of the change dominates indirect effects.

8. Instead of assuming an unanticipated increase in D, we can think of a fully expected increase in D. In this case ρ will jump when the public anticipates the future increase of D. Then the system will move toward the northwest on a divergent path; the spread will continue to increase, and reserves will begin to go down even before the shock. At the time when D actually goes up, we shall observe the jump in m. The free rate δ, and the spread, however, will not jump at that time. The system will then move to the saddle path, and the more conventional adjustment will take place.

9. This assumes that the central bank holds a sufficiently large stock of international reserves. If it does not, a devaluation will have to take place. See below.

10. The reason for this is that even without capital mobility, a fully anticipated jump in δ will result in infinite capital gains. On this see Krugman (1979), Obstfeld (1984), and Connolly and Taylor (1984).

11. There are some difficulties associated with the incorporation of interest rates and endogenous capital movements. Under most cases in this setting, an expansive domestic credit policy will not result in a real exchange rate overvaluation. See, however, Calvo (1987).

12. The effect of capital inflows on the real exchange rate has played a central role in recent interpretations of the experience of the Southern Cone countries with liberalization and stabilization during the late 1970s and early 1980s. See Edwards and Cox-Edwards (1987) and Corbo and de Melo (1987).

13. See Lizondo (1987a,b) for such an analysis.

14. Notice, however, that with imperfect competition or externalities the results may differ. See Bhagwati (1978) for a thorough discussion of devaluations in the presence of QRs (quantitative restrictions).

15. Recall the discussion in section 3.3.

16. The simple model of section 3.3 does not have intermediate inputs. See, however, the model in chapter 8.

II

**Real Exchange Rates in
Developing Countries:
The Empirical Evidence**

4

Real Exchange Rate Behavior in Developing Countries: The Cross-Country Evidence

In spite of the prominent role that real exchange rates have attained in recent economic debates in developing countries, relatively few empirical studies have dealt in any systematic way with the subject. In this and the following chapters the findings from a detailed investigation on real exchange rate behavior in a large number of LDCs is reported. This empirical analysis is based on the theoretical models of chapters 2 and 3. The present chapter provides a broad preliminary look at real exchange rate behavior in 33 countries between 1965 and 1985. The chapter deals with (1) alternative measures of RERs, (2) trends and variability in real exchange rates, (3) black markets for foreign exchange and RERs behavior, and (4) time series properties of the alternative RER indexes.

In the theoretical chapters of this book the real exchange rate was defined as the relative price of tradables to nontradables: $RER = EP_T^*/P_N$. Unfortunately, it is not possible to find an exact empirical counterpart to this analytical construct.[1] For this reason, proxies for the world price of tradables (P_T^*) and the domestic price of nontradables have to be chosen. In the empirical chapters of this book P_T^* has been proxied by the wholesale price indexes (WPIs) of the country's trade partners. Since WPIs contain mainly tradable goods, they do provide a reasonable proxy for P_T^* (Harberger, 1986). With respect to the domestic price of nontradables, we have proxied it by the country's consumer price index (CPI). Obviously, since the CPI contains some tradables, it is not the ideal measure of P_N. Still, however, the fact that consumer price indexes are heavily influenced by nontradable goods and nontradable activities, such as retail, makes them a reasonable proxy for P_N. An additional advantage of using the CPI is that it is readily and periodically available for most countries. Thus, it is possible to make cross-country comparisons.

Another important measurement problem is related to which nominal exchange rate is the most appropriate when calculating $RER = EP_T^*/P_N$.

Should a bilateral rate with respect to the U.S. dollar be used? Or should a multilateral rate that considers the variability of exchange rates of a larger number of partners be used? What to do when there are multiple official nominal exchange rates? What about black or parallel markets? Given the difficulties in computing "an" index for the RER, five different indexes were constructed and their statistical properties were compared. These indexes include two bilateral RER indexes with respect to the United States dollar constructed using official nominal exchange rates, two multilateral indexes also constructed with official rates, and a bilateral RER index constructed using data on the nominal exchange rate in the parallel market.

4.1 Official Nominal Exchange Rates and RER Behavior in 33 Developing Countries

Multilateral Real Exchange Rates and Bilateral Exchange Rates

Multilateral real exchange rates provide a measure of the degree of competitiveness of a country relative to a group of its trade partners. It should be noted that in a world where the principal currencies are floating, multilateral real exchange rates can exhibit significant departures from bilateral real exchange rates.[2]

In the construction of the multilateral indexes of real effective exchange rate the following equation was used:

$$\text{MRER}_{jt} = \frac{\sum_{i=1}^{k} \alpha_i E_{it} P_{it}^*}{P_{jt}}, \tag{4.1}$$

where MRER_{jt} is the index of the multilateral real rate in period t for country j; E_{it} is an *index* of the nominal rate between country i and country j in period t; $i = 1, \ldots, k$ refers to the k partner countries used in the construction of the MRER index; α_i is the weight corresponding to partner i in the computation of MRER_{jt}; P_{it}^* is the price *index* of partner i in period t; and P_{jt} is the price index of the home country in period t. An increase in the value of this index of MRER reflects real depreciation, whereas a decline implies a real appreciation of the domestic currency.

Two indexes of multilateral real exchange rates were constructed and their behavior compared. The first index—which corresponds to our proxy for the relative price of tradables to nontradables—used the partner countries' WPIs as the P_{it}^* values and the home country's CPI as P_{jt}. For notation purposes this index was called MRER1. The second index—which is related to the more traditional PPP measure of the real exchange rate—used consumer price indexes for both partner countries and the home country. This index was called MRER2.

In the construction of both indexes the following procedure was followed: (1) The weights (α's) were trade weights constructed using data from the International Monetary Fund *Directions of Trade*. The actual values of these weights can be found in the appendix to this chapter. (2) For each country the 10 largest trade partners in 1975 were used for the construction of the real exchange rate indexes. (3) In all cases the nominal exchange rate indexes (E_{ij}) were constructed from data on official nominal exchange rates obtained from *International Financial Statistics (IFS)*. In those cases where there were multiple official exchange rates, the "most common" rate, as listed by the *IFS*, was used. This means that these indexes are capturing some of the distortions introduced by the existence of multiple rates. What they do not capture, however, is the role of nonofficial black or parallel markets for foreign exchange. For this reason in the next section we report results obtained when RER indexes using parallel market data are used. The actual need to construct these indexes resides in the fact that there are no long-run series on multilateral real exchange rates readily available from any of the multilateral agencies. Although both the IMF and the World Bank have constructed these types of indicators, they are not currently available to the public. Morgan Guarantee publishes a multilateral real exchange rates index for a number of developing nations. Those series, however, only cover the most recent period.

Two indexes of bilateral real exchange rates with respect to the United States were also constructed using data on official nominal rates. These indexes were defined as

$$BRER1 = \frac{E\,WPI^{US}}{CPI} \tag{4.2}$$

and

$$BRER2 = \frac{E\,CPI^{US}}{CPI}, \tag{4.3}$$

where E is the bilateral (official) nominal exchange rate with respect to the U.S. dollar; WPI^{US} and CPI^{US} are the wholesale and consumer price indexes; and CPI is, as before, the domestic country's consumer price index. BRER1, then, is the bilateral counterpart of MRER1. On the other hand, BRER2 uses both the domestic country and the U.S. CPIs and has historically been the most popular RER index in policy analyses.

Figures 4.1–4.8 show the evolution of two real exchange rate indexes, the multilateral MRER1 index and the bilateral BRER1 index, for 33 developing countries.[3] As may be seen, in most cases both indexes tended to move roughly in the same direction throughout most of the period, and in particular between 1960 and 1971. After the collapse of the Bretton Woods system, in many of the countries depicted in these diagrams the multilateral and bilateral indexes started to exhibit some difference in behavior. This is especially the case during the 1980s, where often the bilateral and multilateral real exchange rate indexes even moved in opposite directions. This reflects the fact that in most of these countries nominal exchange rate policies have traditionally been pursued using the U.S. dollar as the reference currency; between 1980 and 1985, however, as the U.S. dollar appreciated steeply against the other major currencies, so did the currencies of many of these developing countries. As a result, for this period the index of the real multilateral rate is below the index of the bilateral rate in most countries.[4]

In order to compare formally the behavior of the four alternative indexes of the real exchange rate constructed using official data, coefficients of correlations between the multilateral and the bilateral real exchange rate indexes were computed using quarterly data for the period that goes from the first quarter of 1965 up to the second quarter of 1985. The following regularities emerged from this analysis. First, in most countries the two alternative definitions of the bilateral real exchange rate index moved closely together during this period. In 27 out of the 33 countries considered the coefficient of correlation between log(BRER1) and log(BRER2) was above 0.9, and in all cases it exceeded 0.8. Second, the two indexes of trade weighted multilateral RER also moved closely together. In 30 out of the 33 countries the coefficient of correlation between the logs of MRER1 and MRER2 exceeded 0.9. And third, the behavior of the bilateral and multilateral RER indexes has been quite different in many of these countries. In 16 cases the coefficient of correlation between log(MRER) and log(BRER) was below 0.5, and in 2 countries it was even negative.

These findings indicate that for most countries, and within a particular type of index—bilateral or multilateral—the selection of the price indexes used in the construction of the RER measure is not a major practical problem. The results also show that the bilateral and multilateral real exchange rate indexes move in different, and even opposite, directions. This means that when evaluating policy related situations it is necessary to use or construct a broad multilateral index of real exchange rate. A failure to do

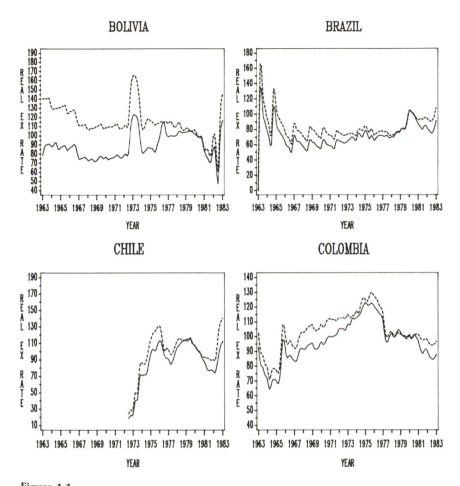

Figure 4.1
Multilateral (———) and bilateral (---) real exchange rates. Source: constructed from raw
data obtained from the *IFS*.

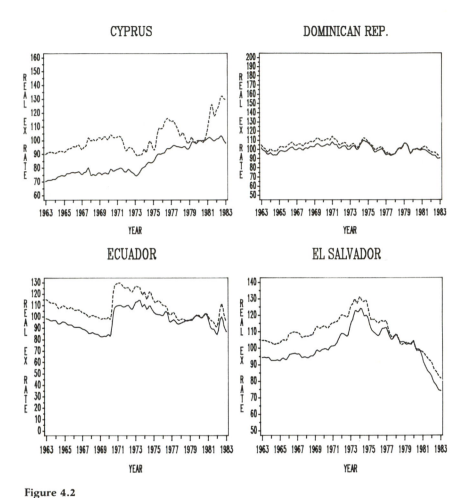

Figure 4.2
Multilateral (———) and bilateral (---) real exchange rates. Source: constructed from raw data obtained from the *IFS*.

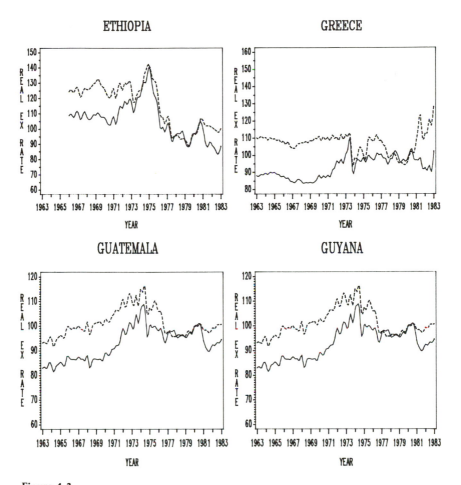

Figure 4.3
Multilateral (————) and bilateral (---) real exchange rates. Source: constructed from raw data obtained from the *IFS*.

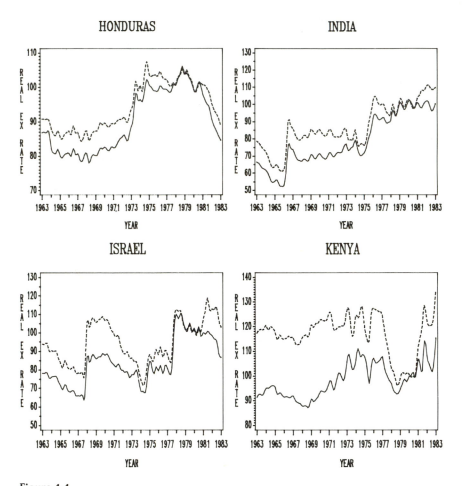

Figure 4.4
Multilateral (———) and bilateral (---) real exchange rates. Source: constructed from raw data obtained from the *IFS*.

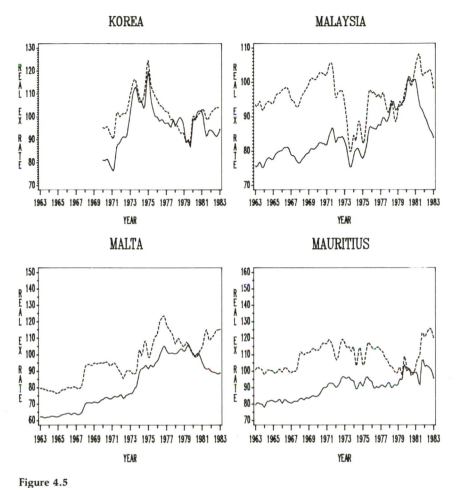

Figure 4.5
Multilateral (———) and bilateral (---) real exchange rates. Source: constructed from raw
data obtained from the *IFS*.

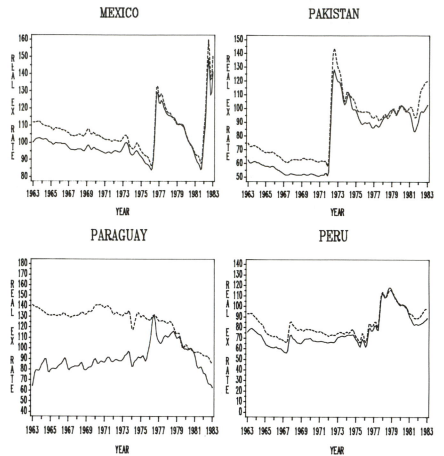

Figure 4.6
Multilateral (———) and bilateral (---) real exchange rates. Source: constructed from raw data obtained from the *IFS*.

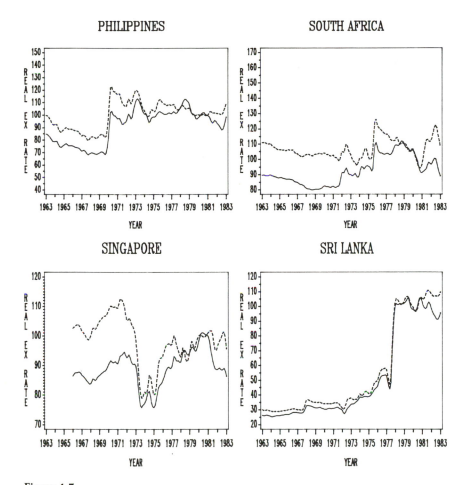

Figure 4.7
Multilateral (———) and bilateral (---) real exchange rates. Source: constructed from raw
data obtained from the *IFS*.

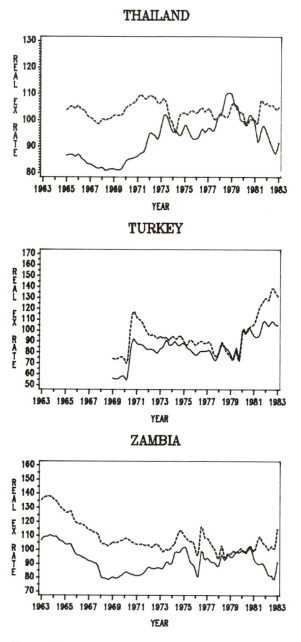

Figure 4.8

Multilateral (————) and bilateral (---) real exchange rates. Source: constructed from raw data obtained from the *IFS*.

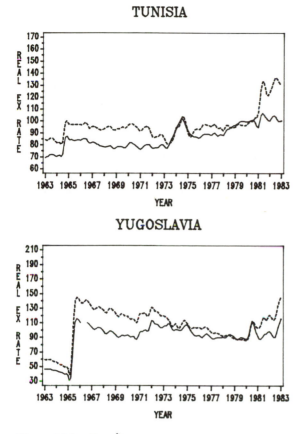

Figure 4.8 (continued)

this can result in misleading and incorrect inferences regarding the evolution of a country's degree of competitiveness.[5]

Some authors—and in particular the IMF—have recommended using wages at home and abroad to construct indexes of real exchange rates or competitiveness. In order to compare these wage based real exchange rate indexes to the more traditional ones, data on manufacturing wages for 13 out of the 33 countries were collected and bilateral (with respect to the U.S. dollar) real exchange rate indexes based on the wage rate were constructed.[6] Coefficients of correlation were then computed between this bilateral rate and some of the more traditional indexes of bilateral real exchange rates. The results showed that there has been a wide divergence between these indexes. For example, in 10 of 13 cases the correlation coefficient between BRER2 and the wage based real exchange rate index was below 0.7, and in 6 of the cases it was lower than 0.5. In a way this result is not too surprising, since it is well known that wage rate figures are not very reliable for these small countries; also the indexes used were actual wages, not corrected by productivity changes (see *IFS*, April 1984, p. 63).

Trends and Variability

The real exchange rate indexes depicted in figures 4.1−4.8 have two important characteristics. First, they show that in most countries the real exchange rate has been fairly variable. Second, in spite of the observed variability, in several of these countries it appears that these indexes have not had significant long-term trends during the whole period under consideration. For the shorter, more recent, periods, however, negative trends can be detected in a number of cases.

Tables 4.1−4.3 contain data on the main statistical properties of the multilateral real exchange rate index MRER1 for the 33 countries considered in this chapter. These indicators have been calculated for three alternative periods of time: 1965−1985, 1965−1971, and 1972−1985. The years 1965−1971 correspond to the last years of the Bretton Woods period, where a majority of countries were pegged to the U.S. dollar. The last period, 1972−1985, corresponds to the post−Bretton Woods era, a period during which most advanced countries have followed a dirty (or managed) floating nominal exchange rates system and most of the developing nations have maintained some kind of peg. The more important findings that emerge from these tables can be summarized as follows: First, as the diagrams suggested, real exchange rates have been quite volatile in many of these countries, with the extent of this variability being quite different

Table 4.1
Basic statistical properties of multilateral real exchange rate index MRER1
(quarterly data 1965−1985)

	Mean	Standard deviation	Coefficient of variation	Maximum	Minimum
Bolivia	86.78	15.93	18.35	122.92	47.17
Brazil	75.83	17.02	22.44	115.23	50.02
Chile	93.47	26.44	28.29	147.66	18.67
Colombia	99.08	11.76	11.87	124.12	68.26
Cyprus	88.04	10.61	12.05	103.40	74.33
Dominican Republic	101.17	14.46	14.29	175.51	59.95
Ecuador	96.63	8.96	9.27	114.38	79.60
El Salvador	96.24	17.42	18.10	123.94	51.07
Ethiopia	102.51	15.22	14.84	140.18	64.27
Greece	94.45	6.45	6.96	112.29	83.65
Guatemala	92.22	7.38	8.00	108.46	67.93
Guyana	82.03	14.17	17.27	105.08	62.40
Honduras	89.00	9.58	10.76	106.10	74.58
India	82.92	15.00	18.09	105.30	52.45
Israel	85.64	11.91	13.90	110.68	65.72
Kenya	100.31	7.89	7.86	118.96	87.60
Korea	96.75	8.51	8.80	119.72	77.12
Malaysia	84.68	6.43	7.59	101.72	75.49
Malta	85.02	13.65	16.05	106.03	62.31
Mauritius	93.02	8.10	8.00	—	—
Mexico	103.42	13.66	13.21	148.95	85.06
Pakistan	82.83	22.80	27.53	125.48	51.09
Paraguay	88.72	14.64	16.50	131.60	56.82
Peru	79.69	17.14	21.51	117.96	56.39
Philippines	94.00	13.74	14.62	123.87	68.40
Singapore	88.56	5.60	6.32	100.99	75.84
South Africa	93.60	10.10	10.79	116.21	80.08
Sri Lanka	58.36	30.62	52.46	105.63	26.22
Thailand	92.43	7.52	8.14	110.21	80.99
Tunisia	90.46	10.11	11.18	107.50	76.41
Turkey	89.03	15.88	17.83	123.08	55.68
Yugoslavia	100.42	15.77	15.70	133.93	35.65
Zambia	92.86	15.31	16.48	213.73	78.96

Source: See text.

Table 4.2
Basic statistical properties of multilateral real exchange rate index MRER1
(quarterly data 1965–1971)

	Mean	Standard deviation	Coefficient of variation	Maximum	Minimum
Bolivia	78.95	5.79	7.33	90.62	72.05
Brazil	62.73	9.05	14.43	92.37	50.02
Colombia	90.93	8.39	9.23	101.59	68.26
Cyprus	76.98	1.58	2.05	80.26	74.34
Dominican Republic	102.35	2.82	2.75	108.43	97.67
Ecuador	92.17	7.36	10.15	110.19	82.69
El Salvador	97.31	3.37	3.46	106.49	92.30
Ethiopia	108.06	2.82	2.60	115.09	102.51
Greece	86.66	2.34	2.70	92.53	83.65
Guatemala	87.48	2.63	3.00	94.02	83.13
Guyana	68.64	4.32	6.30	75.59	62.46
Honduras	81.11	1.61	1.98	85.14	78.03
India	66.90	6.77	10.12	76.53	52.45
Israel	78.10	9.12	11.68	88.88	65.72
Kenya	91.94	2.85	3.10	97.83	87.60
Korea	81.57	3.98	4.87	88.29	77.12
Malaysia	80.43	2.43	3.02	86.18	76.48
Malta	68.81	4.49	6.53	74.88	62.31
Mauritius	84.61	3.79	4.48	92.65	80.91
Mexico	96.82	2.00	2.06	100.04	51.09
Pakistan	53.31	2.32	4.35	58.12	—
Paraguay	84.53	3.63	4.29	91.40	56.82
Peru	64.95	4.20	6.47	72.29	56.39
Philippines	78.78	11.65	14.79	102.45	68.40
Singapore	88.28	3.04	3.45	94.47	83.89
South Africa	83.37	2.65	3.18	88.03	80.08
Sri Lanka	29.82	2.11	7.10	32.91	26.22
Thailand	84.45	2.67	3.16	91.09	80.99
Tunisia	80.74	2.68	3.32	85.23	76.41
Turkey	71.88	15.78	21.95	92.35	55.68
Yugoslavia	94.77	17.87	18.85	115.91	35.65
Zambia	87.72	8.25	9.41	104.05	78.96

Source: See text.

Table 4.3
Basic statistical properties of multilateral real exchange rate index MRER1
(quarterly data 1972–1985)

	Mean	Standard deviation	Coefficient of variation	Maximum	Minimum
Bolivia	91.00	17.99	19.76	122.92	47.17
Brazil	82.38	16.30	19.79	115.23	61.85
Chile	93.47	26.44	28.29	147.66	18.67
Colombia	103.15	11.12	10.78	124.12	84.71
Cyprus	93.57	8.68	9.27	103.40	74.73
Dominican Republic	100.57	17.68	17.58	175.51	59.95
Ecuador	98.86	7.93	8.03	114.38	79.60
El Salvador	95.71	21.25	22.20	123.94	51.07
Ethiopia	100.09	17.65	17.63	140.18	64.27
Greece	98.35	4.03	4.10	112.29	90.38
Guatemala	94.60	7.85	8.30	108.46	67.93
Guyana	89.38	12.15	13.59	105.08	63.03
Honduras	92.94	9.47	10.79	106.10	74.58
India	90.93	11.01	12.10	105.30	70.44
Israel	89.42	11.39	12.74	110.68	67.91
Kenya	104.49	6.04	5.78	118.96	92.83
Korea	98.92	6.54	6.61	119.72	87.02
Malaysia	86.80	6.76	7.79	101.72	75.49
Malta	93.12	8.40	9.02	106.02	73.43
Mauritius	97.23	6.17	6.34	111.62	89.15
Mexico	106.72	15.70	14.72	148.95	85.06
Pakistan	97.59	10.81	11.07	125.48	54.81
Paraguay	90.81	17.43	19.19	131.60	56.82
Peru	87.07	16.40	18.83	117.96	61.64
Philippines	101.61	6.43	6.33	123.87	87.99
Singapore	88.68	6.41	7.23	100.99	75.84
South Africa	98.91	8.26	8.35	116.21	84.50
Sri Lanka	72.64	28.11	38.70	105.63	27.41
Thailand	96.42	5.77	5.98	110.21	84.85
Tunisia	95.32	8.87	9.30	107.50	77.51
Turkey	92.70	13.39	14.45	123.08	73.11
Yugoslavia	103.25	13.94	13.50	133.93	87.76
Zambia	95.43	17.32	18.15	213.73	79.12

Source: See text.

across countries. For example, while in Zambia the difference between the maximum and minimum values of the index for the complete 1965–1985 period surpasses 130 points, it was only 25 points in Singapore. The differential in real exchange rate variability across countries can be better illustrated by looking at the ratio of the highest to the lowest coefficients of variation. For the complete period under consideration (1965–1985) this ratio is above 8! A second fact that emerges from tables 4.1, 4.2, and 4.3 refers to the increased real exchange rate variability through time. A comparison of the coefficients of variation for 1965–1971 and 1972–1985 (tables 4.2 and 4.3) reveals that in all but 4 countries (Ecuador, the Philippines, Turkey, and Yugoslavia), the multilateral real exchange rate has been significantly more volatile during the post–Bretton Woods era. This reflects, among other things, the fact that during the post-1972 period exchange rates across industrial countries have experienced significant increases in variability, affecting the stability of real exchange rates in those smaller countries that either peg to one of the large industrial countries or use one of the major currencies as a point of reference when conducting (nominal) exchange rate policy (see Edwards, 1988b).

From a preliminary analysis of the RER diagrams, it is possible to classify these countries into four broad groups. The rules for classifying them are only approximate and take into account the behavior of the real effective exchange rate throughout the period. A first group can be labeled "two-regime countries" and includes Sri Lanka, Pakistan, Chile, the Philippines, Yugoslavia, and Peru. In these countries two distinct periods—each relatively stable—can be distinguished. The two periods are separated either by an abrupt real depreciation or an abrupt real appreciation. A second group of countries has been grouped under the label of "inverted-U countries" and includes Colombia, the Dominican Republic, El Salvador, Guatemala, Guyana, and Honduras. In all of these countries a steady real multilateral depreciation was observed until a certain date—usually the late 1970s—and a fairly steep real appreciation has been detected since. Not surprisingly, a number of these countries have pegged or managed their currency against the U.S. dollar; as the U.S. dollar appreciated in the first part of the 1980s, so did these countries' real exchange rates. A third group is comprised of those countries whose RERs have exhibited clear long-term trends: Cyprus, India, Malta, Mauritius, Tunisia, and Turkey have a definitively strong positive trend (i.e., the RER has depreciated through time), while Bolivia, Ecuador, Ethiopia, Paraguay, and Zambia have exhibited a negative (real appreciation) long-run trend. The final group includes all other countries, whose RERs do not show a strong long-term trend. However, in spite of the absence of a long-term trend, in some of these cases, as in Kenya and Mexico, there have been some fairly abrupt jumps in RERs, usually as a result of major nominal devaluations. The degree of RER instability across these countries has also been fairly different, with Kenya, for example, being quite stable, while Mexico has exhibited a fair amount of instability.

Table 4.4 contains estimates of the trend coefficients for the multilateral real exchange rate index MRER1. Linear trends regressions were estimated for four time periods: 1965–1985, 1965–1971, 1972–1985, and the more recent period 1978–1985. For most countries the absolute value of the estimated coefficients for the whole period are small, although in most cases they are significant. A comparison of the number of negative signs of the trend coefficients in the earlier Bretton Woods era and the more recent period shows that during 1965–1971 in only 8 out of the 33 countries the trend coefficient was small but negative, indicating a weak tendency toward appreciation. However, during 1978–1985 in 23 out of the 33 countries the trend coefficient was negative, and in some cases, such as El Salvador, Paraguay, and Bolivia, fairly large. Undoubtedly, this tendency toward real appreciation in a larger number of countries has been primarily determined by the behavior of the U.S. dollar in the first half of the 1980s. Since most of these countries used the U.S. dollar as the reference currency when formulating their nominal exchange rate policies, the real appreciation of the dollar with respect to other major industrial currencies necessarily resulted in a real appreciation of these small countries' currencies. This effect is clearer when the small country has a fixed nominal rate with respect to the U.S. dollar—as is the case of most of the "inverted-U countries" in our sample—Guatemala, Honduras, and the Dominican Republic, for example. It should be emphasized, however, that without looking at other variables it is not possible to infer from the trend regressions whether these countries' currencies were at any particular time misaligned.

4.2 Parallel Markets and RER Behavior: The Cross-Country Evidence

The RER indexes used in the analysis of section 4.1 were constructed using data on official nominal exchange rates.[7] However, as pointed out in chapters 1 and 3, in many developing countries at different times there have been quite significant parallel (or black) markets for foreign exchange. The coverage and importance of these parallel market vary from country to country and period to period. In some cases they are quite thin, and are

Table 4.4
Estimated trend coefficients for multilateral real exchange rate indexes (MRER1)[a]

	1965–1985	1965–1971	1972–1985	1978–1985
Bolivia	0.001	−0.006	−0.005	−0.021
	(1.112)	(−4.656)	(−2.797)	(−4.373)
Brazil	0.006	−0.008	0.009	0.011
	(9.454)	(−2.702)	(10.216)	(3.758)
Chile	0.017	0.009	0.017	−0.005
	(4.639)	(6.521)	(4.639)	(−1.297)
Colombia	0.001	0.003	−0.006	−0.007
	(1.797)	(7.491)	(−8.998)	(−6.253)
Cyprus	0.005	0.001	0.006	0.003
	(23.766)	(3.001)	(16.164)	(6.092)
Dominican Republic	−0.002	0.004	−0.005	−0.013
	(−5.678)	(2.085)	(−6.242)	(−6.382)
Ecuador	0.001	0.004	−0.004	−0.002
	(1.455)	(9.160)	(−8.607)	(−1.413)
El Salvador	−0.002	0.003	−0.011	−0.022
	(−3.491)	(8.460)	(−12.624)	(−18.900)
Ethiopia	−0.003	−0.000	0.009	0.005
	(−6.182)	(−1.112)	(−10.208)	(−3.322)
Greece	0.002	0.000	−0.000	−0.002
	(8.370)	(0.755)	(−1.105)	(−1.622)
Guatemala	0.002	0.003	−0.002	−0.003
	(5.390)	(5.460)	(−5.644)	(−2.479)
Guyana	0.005	0.007	−0.003	−0.020
	(6.389)	(13.481)	(−2.214)	(−9.588)
Honduras	0.002	0.002	−0.002	−0.013
	(5.431)	(4.679)	(−2.169)	(−14.271)
India	0.008	0.008	0.008	0.001
	(20.414)	(4.014)	(12.364)	(1.090)
Israel	0.004	0.012	0.007	−0.010
	(7.101)	(4.781)	(5.504)	(−8.813)
Kenya	0.002	0.001	0.001	0.009
	(8.411)	(1.859)	(0.866)	(8.686)
Korea	0.001	0.009	−0.002	−0.001
	(1.623)	(1.259)	(−3.155)	(−0.686)
Malaysia	0.002	0.002	0.002	−0.006
	(7.433)	(4.452)	(3.309)	(−4.815)
Malta	0.006	0.008	0.003	−0.007
	(14.428)	(16.603)	(3.150)	(−8.638)
Mauritius	0.003	0.005	0.002	0.005
	(15.864)	(9.241)	(5.100)	(3.773)
Mexico	0.003	−0.002	0.006	0.007
	(5.138)	(−8.459)	(4.442)	(1.775)

Table 4.4 (continued)

	1965–1985	1965–1971	1972–1985	1978–1985
Pakistan	0.010	−0.004	−0.001	0.001
	(10.065)	(−6.518)	(−0.557)	(0.656)
Paraguay	0.000	0.003	−0.007	−0.029
	(−0.364)	(3.650)	(−3.784)	(−12.787)
Peru	0.007	0.005	0.008	−0.012
	(11.257)	(3.564)	(5.656)	(−6.604)
Philippines	0.005	0.010	−0.001	−0.006
	(8.293)	(3.955)	(−2.349)	(−3.833)
Singapore	0.001	0.004	0.003	−0.004
	(2.905)	(5.926)	(3.471)	(−3.323)
South Africa	0.003	−0.003	−0.000	−0.010
	(6.550)	(−5.584)	(−0.073)	(−9.582)
Sri Lanka	0.022	0.007	0.032	−0.005
	(20.052)	(6.593)	(14.958)	(−4.562)
Thailand	0.002	0.000	−0.001	−0.010
	(6.077)	(0.482)	(−2.021)	(−12.150)
Tunisia	0.004	−0.003	0.005	0.005
	(13.829)	(5.453)	(11.090)	(6.582)
Turkey	0.007	0.053	0.006	0.016
	(8.288)	(5.441)	(6.518)	(8.233)
Yugoslavia	0.002	0.009	0.001	0.123
	(2.277)	(1.461)	(0.995)	(5.777)
Zambia	0.000	−0.009	−0.000	−0.006
	(0.949)	(−7.495)	(−0.235)	(−3.214)

a. The numbers in parentheses are t-statistics.

mainly used by those nationals who want to spend their vacations abroad and are only allowed a limited quota of foreign exchange at the official rates. In other cases, the coverage of the parallel market is very broad and the parallel market exchange rate is the relevant marginal rate for most transactions. The degree of legality of these parallel markets also varies from case to case. While in some cases they are quasi-legal and accepted by the authorities as a minor nuisance, in others they are strongly repressed, with the authorities severely persecuting those that engage in black market transactions.

By the very nature of these markets—illegal or quasi-illegal—it is not possible to have accurate data on their volume of transactions and of their relative importance. However, there are relatively reliable data on parallel market quotations and parallel market premiums. Generally speaking, the parallel market premium will become higher as exchange controls become more pervasive and generalized and as fewer and fewer transactions are allowed through the official market. In fact, under conditions of generalized exchange controls and rationing, the RER indexes computed using official rates will become more and more irrelevant for a number of transactions— and in particular for imports. In this study data on parallel market quotations were collected for 28 out of the 33 countries in section 4.1 (see table 4.5).[8] These quotations refer to the nominal exchange rate with respect to the U.S. dollar, and were used to construct series on parallel market premiums and on parallel market bilateral (with respect to the United States) real exchange rate indexes.

Figures 4.9–4.15 depict the behavior of the parallel market premium for the 28 countries that have data. As can be seen, the premiums have varied significantly across countries and periods.[9] The cases of Bolivia, Chile, and Pakistan are particularly interesting, showing how the premium can not only become extremely acute, but also exhibit dramatic jumps. As is discussed in great detail in chapter 6, in a vast number of cases the parallel market premium behaves very closely to what our model of chapter 3 predicts, increasing very rapidly in the period immediately preceding a (major) nominal devaluation, and falling quite drastically immediately following the devaluation. Perhaps the most remarkable example of this type of behavior is given by Pakistan. Table 4.5 contains a summary of the most important statistical properties of the parallel market premium for the 28 developing countries.

There is no reason why the parallel market RER index (PMRER) should move closely with the indexes constructed using the official nominal exchange rates. In fact, as pointed out in chapter 3, there are a number of circumstances under which, in a country with pegged nominal official rates, these two RER indexes will tend to move in opposite directions. This will be the case, for example, when there is a massive domestic credit creation under generalized exchange controls and active parallel markets. Under these circumstances, the higher growth of domestic credit will simultaneously generate an appreciation of the official RER index and a depreciation of the parallel market RER. Table 4.6 contains coefficients of correlation between the parallel market RER and official RER bilateral indexes. The parallel market index was constructed as

$$PMRER1_t = (PM)_t \frac{WPI^{US}}{CPI},\tag{4.5}$$

where $(PM)_t$ is an index of the parallel market bilateral nominal exchange rate with respect to the U.S. dollar, WPI^{US} is the U.S. wholesale price index,

Table 4.5
Basic statistical properties of black market premium (quarterly data 1965–1983)[a]

	Mean	Standard deviation	Coefficient of variation	Maximum	Minimum
Bolivia	40.40	73.30	181.41	444.96	4.58
Brazil	19.35	17.53	90.62	79.95	−15.00
Chile	190.50	498.85	261.85	2934.18	1.87
Colombia	13.47	16.29	120.99	87.40	−1.27
Cyprus	4.23	5.63	133.24	29.79	−2.82
Dominican Republic	30.79	14.78	48.00	78.33	−9.66
Ecuador	19.93	24.75	124.13	119.18	0.06
El Salvador	36.62	36.04	98.40	146.66	4.66
Ethiopia	56.15	43.24	77.01	175.84	1.77
Greece	5.08	3.14	61.95	16.43	1.49
India	34.40	26.07	75.80	124.00	6.10
Israel	16.12	18.13	112.33	72.27	−10.66
Kenya	22.12	13.62	61.59	65.89	1.11
Korea	9.76	11.31	115.95	60.70	−5.23
Malaysia	0.71	0.99	138.93	3.61	−1.40
Mexico	5.24	13.75	262.15	86.39	−0.10
Pakistan	54.52	42.28	77.55	171.95	2.58
Paraguay	27.29	40.97	150.10	224.07	5.29
Peru	26.77	28.52	106.52	82.60	−0.27
Philippines	8.70	8.96	102.95	55.85	0.17
Singapore	0.28	0.67	237.97	2.59	−0.80
South Africa	11.97	10.01	83.61	49.88	−19.73
Sri Lanka	89.80	58.96	65.65	220.25	1.70
Thailand	0.09	1.85	187.90	6.37	−5.19
Tunisia	17.37	18.02	103.74	80.31	−7.14
Turkey	21.98	19.13	87.02	74.12	−4.82
Yugoslavia	8.40	7.07	84.15	26.02	−6.41
Zambia	93.19	50.54	54.23	201.66	29.08

Source: based on raw data obtained from various issues of *Pick's Currency Yearbook* and *World Currency Yearbook*.
a. In some countries the time period is slightly shorter, due to data limitations.

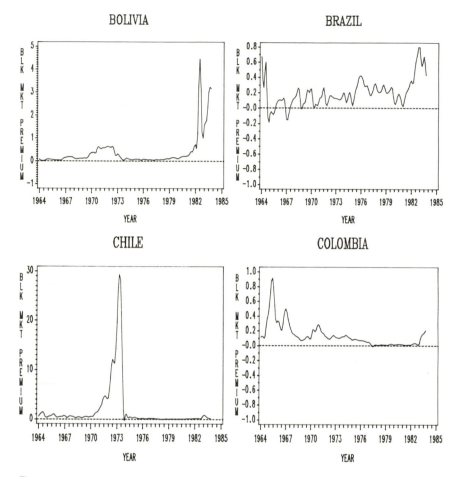

Figure 4.9
Black market premium. Source: constructed from raw data obtained from *Pick's Currency Yearbook*.

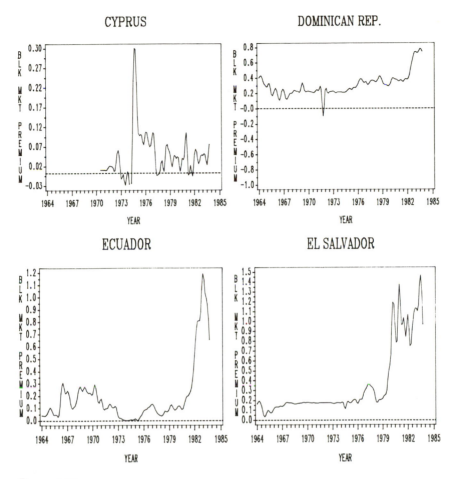

Figure 4.10
Black market premium. Source: constructed from raw data obtained from *Pick's Currency Yearbook*.

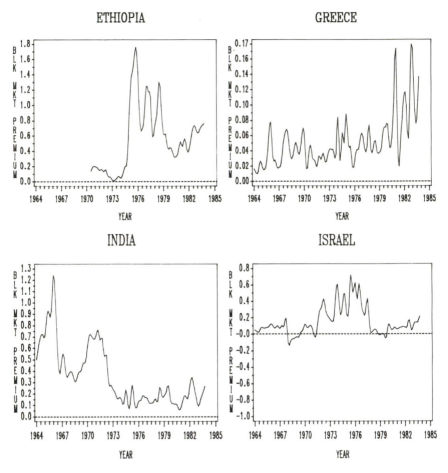

Figure 4.11
Black market premium. Source: constructed from raw data obtained from *Pick's Currency Yearbook*.

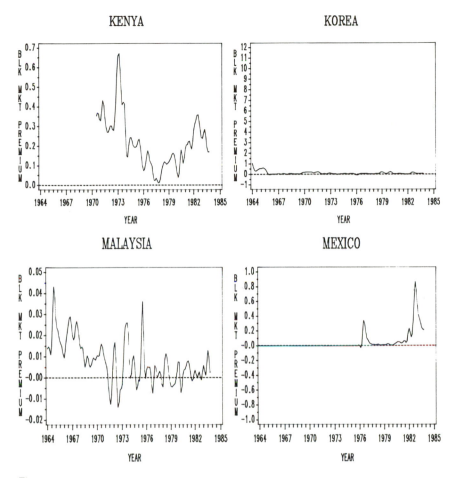

Figure 4.12
Black market premium. Source: constructed from raw data obtained from *Pick's Currency Yearbook*.

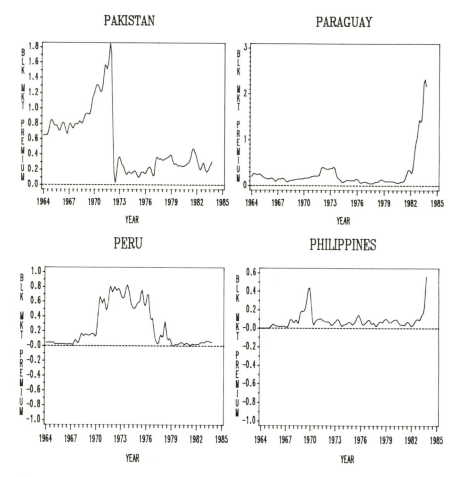

Figure 4.13
Black market premium. Source: constructed from raw data obtained from *Pick's Currency Yearbook*.

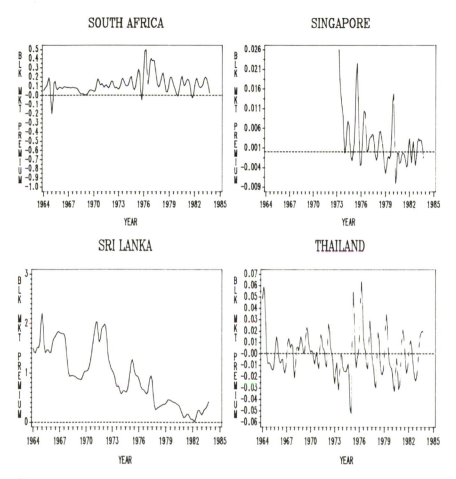

Figure 4.14
Black market premium. Source: constructed from raw data obtained from *Pick's Currency Yearbook*.

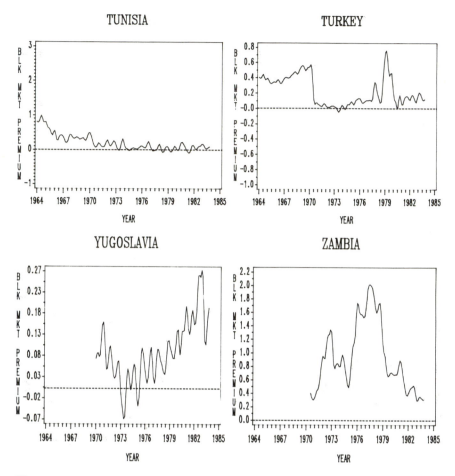

Figure 4.15
Black market premium. Source: constructed from raw data obtained from *Pick's Currency Yearbook*.

Table 4.6
Coefficient of correlation of bilateral real exchange rate indexes constructed using official and parallel nominal exchange rates

	Coefficient of correlation
Bolivia	−0.180
Brazil	0.642
Chile	−0.776
Colombia	0.337
Cyprus	0.124
Dominican Republic	0.422
Ecuador	0.230
El Salvador	0.434
Ethiopia	0.312
Greece	−0.436
India	−0.215
Israel	0.317
Kenya	0.217
Korea	−0.142
Malaysia	−0.053
Mexico	0.726
Pakistan	−0.007
Paraguay	−0.416
Peru	0.293
Philippines	0.620
Singapore	0.875
South Africa	0.326
Sri Lanka	−0.044
Thailand	−0.419
Tunisia	−0.688
Turkey	−0.347
Yugoslavia	0.477
Zambia	−0.091

Source: See text.

and CPI is the domestic country consumer price index. PMRER1, then, is the bilateral parallel index equivalent to BRER1 in section 4.1.[10] The coefficients of correlation in table 4.6 clearly capture the fact that the parallel and official RER index indeed behave very differently. In fact, in 13 out of the 28 cases the coefficients of correlation turned out to be negative. Table 4.7 contains a summary of the basic statistics for the parallel market RER index PMRER1.

4.3 Deviations from PPP and Stationarity of Real Exchange Rates in Selected Developing Countries

An important question, and one that has recently received increased attention in the industrial countries (Frankel and Meese, 1987), is whether the real exchange rate series have behaved according to the purchasing power parity (PPP) theory of real exchange rates. According to the strict absolute version of PPP, the log of the real exchange rate is characterized by a white noise process. That is, any deviation of the log of the RER from its constant equilibrium level should be completely random. This question has important implications for the analysis of real exchange rate misalignments. If the RER indeed behaves as suggested by the PPP theory, any (large) deviations of the actual RER from its PPP level will reflect misalignment.

In order to test the PPP proposition a time-series procedure was used. Autocorrelation functions were estimated for detrended series of the log of MRER1 and PMRER1, for the period 1965–1985, using 24 lags. Table 4.8 contains estimates of the first 6 lags for the (log of the) detrended official multilateral index MRER1; table 4.9, on the other hand, contain the equivalent estimates for the parallel market index PMRER1. These tables also contain the value of the Box-Pierce statistic with 18 degrees of freedom for each country. The null hypothesis is that the log of these real exchange rate indexes can be characterized as a white noise process.[11] As can be seen from these tables, in all cases the null hypothesis that (the log of) the real exchange rate can be characterized by a white noise is strongly rejected. This provides strong evidence indicating that in all cases the observed variability of the real effective exchange rate index around its mean or around its trend cannot be described as a white noise process; as in previous analyses on industrial countries' data, the strong absolute version of PPP fails miserably.

An important related question refers to whether the time series of real exchange rates have unit roots and thus are nonstationary.[12] Whether RERs are stationary has a number of important implications. First, under

Table 4.7
Basic statistical properties of black market real exchange rate index
(quarterly data 1965–1985)

	Mean	Standard deviation	Coefficient of variation	Maximum	Minimum
Bolivia	131.11	47.81	36.47	318.54	90.88
Brazil	89.92	25.36	28.20	188.98	60.50
Chile	195.24	251.32	128.72	1473.40	94.13
Colombia	118.96	14.98	12.59	156.03	94.77
Cyprus	110.08	14.10	12.81	148.12	85.19
Dominican Republic	99.64	7.75	7.78	122.05	70.60
Ecuador	117.09	22.00	18.79	197.67	93.80
El Salvador	77.04	12.72	16.51	124.02	57.07
Ethiopia	128.82	39.36	30.55	265.86	91.21
Greece	107.73	8.84	8.21	141.76	96.02
India	109.12	13.38	12.26	137.84	77.74
Israel	103.26	14.04	13.59	138.44	76.97
Kenya	133.30	22.80	17.10	198.95	98.56
Korea	102.51	7.30	7.12	116.44	90.53
Malaysia	98.53	5.34	5.42	108.53	83.19
Mexico	122.99	29.81	26.38	246.98	86.57
Pakistan	105.24	13.72	13.04	148.03	84.65
Paraguay	141.84	26.39	18.60	241.07	99.82
Peru	102.56	19.54	19.05	142.47	65.61
Philippines	105.24	17.73	16.84	206.32	78.74
Singapore	96.05	6.17	6.42	103.48	80.90
South Africa	110.35	13.96	12.65	165.86	78.14
Sri Lanka	74.98	20.78	27.72	120.61	48.93
Thailand	107.16	3.71	3.46	115.85	100.00
Tunisia	107.45	18.32	17.05	160.82	75.64
Turkey	103.45	18.31	17.69	149.52	80.84
Yugoslavia	110.25	22.08	20.03	190.18	86.72
Zambia	120.21	30.13	25.06	183.79	82.00

Source: See text.

Table 4.8
Autocorrelation coefficients of detrended MRER1 (quarterly data 1965–1985)

	Lag						
	1	2	3	4	5	6	Q(18)
Bolivia	0.665	0.409	2.402	0.366	0.291	0.185	86.5
Brazil	0.827	0.659	0.441	0.316	0.167	0.106	78.5
Colombia	0.897	0.757	0.688	0.679	0.635	0.577	260.0
Cyprus	0.891	0.794	0.717	0.652	0.570	0.465	247.1
Dominican Rep.	0.756	0.538	0.366	0.252	0.191	0.159	94.1
Ecuador	0.903	0.797	0.717	0.620	0.523	0.448	239.8
El Salvador	0.941	0.880	0.815	0.747	0.679	0.611	316.9
Ethiopia	0.878	0.748	0.640	0.539	0.450	0.363	191.2
Greece	0.708	0.608	0.492	0.519	0.393	0.409	144.9
Guatemala	0.865	0.778	0.706	0.643	0.583	0.519	244.7
Guyana	0.936	0.878	0.826	0.749	0.670	0.591	310.7
Honduras	0.937	0.866	0.793	0.723	0.657	0.581	302.2
India	0.814	0.534	0.311	0.142	−0.005	−0.090	89.7
Israel	0.858	0.705	0.549	0.428	0.317	0.242	158.5
Kenya	0.810	0.644	0.588	0.535	0.449	0.314	169.9
Korea	0.885	0.732	0.583	0.463	0.366	0.271	134.4
Malaysia	0.914	0.787	0.672	0.509	0.468	0.353	218.3
Malta	0.957	0.903	0.843	0.777	0.711	0.641	337.8
Mauritius	0.670	0.533	0.364	0.236	0.166	0.227	84.3
Mexico	0.848	0.639	0.390	0.180	−0.005	−0.150	111.7
Pakistan	0.926	0.788	0.656	0.528	0.406	0.308	207.0
Paraguay	0.923	0.813	0.718	0.637	0.567	0.492	254.8
Peru	0.880	0.755	0.647	0.508	0.400	0.265	190.5
Philippines	0.906	0.782	0.657	0.546	0.455	0.391	213.6
Singapore	0.926	0.804	0.684	0.569	0.447	0.317	209.2
South Africa	0.900	0.772	0.664	0.553	0.460	0.407	214.5
Sri Lanka	0.923	0.807	0.714	0.645	0.502	0.515	258.1
Thailand	0.927	0.825	0.747	0.684	0.598	0.497	269.7
Tunisia	0.857	0.667	0.508	0.364	0.208	0.092	136.3
Turkey	0.782	0.582	0.391	0.245	0.143	0.068	80.7
Yugoslavia	0.615	0.156	0.069	0.066	0.023	−0.009	34.3
Zambia	0.821	0.663	0.489	0.324	0.208	0.095	126.9

Source: See text.

Table 4.9
Autocorrelation coefficients of detrended PRER1 (quarterly data 1965–1985)

	Lag						
	1	2	3	4	5	6	Q(18)
Bolivia	0.882	0.780	0.612	0.437	0.292	0.130	164.9
Brazil	0.796	0.606	0.435	0.256	0.126	0.041	101.8
Chile	0.808	0.486	0.215	0.037	−0.046	−0.048	46.6
Colombia	0.821	0.610	0.490	0.431	0.400	0.343	141.3
Cyprus	0.744	0.517	0.419	0.320	0.182	0.089	66.2
Dominican Rep.	0.423	0.189	0.048	0.003	−0.103	−0.083	18.7
Ecuador	0.919	0.777	0.624	0.471	0.344	0.234	179.5
El Salvador	0.681	0.593	0.428	0.218	−0.017	−0.146	85.7
Ethiopia	0.860	0.655	0.468	0.342	0.275	0.202	94.4
Greece	0.757	0.659	0.533	0.416	0.287	0.261	130.0
India	0.843	0.690	0.593	0.445	0.259	0.115	146.9
Israel	0.668	0.429	0.387	0.301	0.135	0.153	73.3
Kenya	0.880	0.748	0.613	0.492	0.408	0.340	131.2
Korea	0.525	0.101	0.053	0.145	0.147	0.072	20.0
Malaysia	0.868	0.705	0.575	0.525	0.457	0.355	177.0
Mexico	0.860	0.637	0.389	0.157	−0.026	−0.148	107.1
Pakistan	0.874	0.740	0.681	0.640	0.562	0.467	220.5
Paraguay	0.865	0.697	0.564	0.411	0.252	0.105	144.1
Peru	0.905	0.796	0.676	0.607	0.546	0.492	228.4
Philippines	0.754	0.612	0.484	0.402	0.303	0.214	118.9
Singapore	0.653	0.449	0.318	0.264	0.189	−0.018	39.4
South Africa	0.578	0.398	0.477	0.417	0.229	0.105	77.2
Sri Lanka	0.878	0.741	0.602	0.459	0.311	0.135	161.4
Thailand	0.632	0.500	0.341	0.220	−0.063	−0.046	65.6
Tunisia	0.778	0.606	0.588	0.566	0.432	0.364	158.6
Turkey	0.834	0.707	0.635	0.561	0.474	0.376	148.0
Yugoslavia	0.855	0.732	0.678	0.386	0.456	0.374	147.3
Zambia	0.900	0.763	0.618	0.499	0.391	0.288	132.4

Source: See text.

nonstationarity there are serious problems with interpreting standard regressions that attempt to explain the behavior of the (log of the) real exchange rate. In this case the standard errors of the estimated parameters are meaningless. Second, if the log of RER is a random walk, the variance of forecast of log(RER) into the future would be infinite; in a way the system would not be anchored. As can be seen from tables 4.8 and 4.9, the one-lag autocorrelation coefficients are in most cases high, and in some instances even higher than 0.9. These high autocorrelation coefficients, of course, do not necessarily reflect nonstationarity—they can indeed capture slowly convergent mean reverting processes. In fact, when these implicit quarterly speeds of adjustment (one minus the first-order autocorrelation coefficient) are translated into annual terms, they do not appear to be that high. For example, a value of 0.92 for the coefficient of a quarterly autoregressive process of order one (AR1) corresponds in annual terms to 0.732. Unfortunately, the existing tests for unit roots have limited power. In the case of our series the use of the Box-Pierce statistic indicates that in the majority of our cases—in 19 out of the 33 countries—we can reject the hypothesis of a random walk process. When the more powerful augmented Dickey-Fuller test is used, we cannot reject nonstationarity for a larger number of these cases. However, if moving average components are allowed into the analysis, the hypothesis of no random walk cannot be rejected for most of our countries. For example, for 25 of the countries in the sample it is not possible to reject the hypothesis that the detrended log of the multilateral real exchange rate follows an autoregressive-moving average process of order one [i.e., ARMA(1, 1)]. For these 25 countries the value of the $\chi^2(15)$-statistic ranged from 4.2 to 21.6. The critical value of the χ^2 with 15 degrees of freedom and at the 10% level of significance is 22.3. Although there are strong indications of slow mean reverting processes, these tests do not allow us to resolve fully the stationarity issue for every country.[13]

4.4 Summary

The purpose of this chapter has been to provide a broad and preliminary look at real exchange rates in a large group of developing countries. The chapter started by constructing two multilateral and two bilateral RER indexes using data on official nominal rates for 33 countries. The evolution of these indexes through time was analyzed, and it was found that while for most countries the two alternative indexes of multilateral real rates had

moved closely together, they had behaved significantly differently from
the bilateral indexes.

Some important statistical properties of the time series of the "official"
multilateral real exchange rate indexes were also analyzed in section 4.1.
The main findings of that analysis can be summarized as follows: First, in a
large number of countries real effective exchange rates have exhibited no
significant long-run trends. Over the more recent period, however, some
strong evidence of generalized real exchange rate appreciation could be
detected. Second, the multilateral real exchange rate indexes have been
quite volatile throughout the period. In addition, this variability has been
very different across countries; the ratio of the highest to lowest coefficients of variation of the real effective rate was almost equal to nine. Third,
the degree of RER variability has increased significantly through time,
being much larger in recent years than during the Bretton Woods period.

Section 4.2 dealt with parallel markets for nominal exchange rates and
RER indexes. Data on nominal exchange rate quotations on parallel markets for 28 countries were used to construct alternative RER indexes. It was
found that in many of these countries the "official" and "parallel" RER
indexes have moved very differently and even in opposite directions. This
is an important result, since it introduces an important degree of skepticism
regarding the relevance of conventional computations of RERs. These
results indicate that since for many transactions the relevant marginal
exchange rate is the parallel market one, analysts and policymakers should
usually look closely at the parallel market spread and at the parallel market
real rate when undertaking economic decisions.

In section 4.3 the results from a univarite time series analysis of the
logarithm of the official multilateral RER index MRER1 and of the parallel
bilateral index PMRER1 for all countries are reported. The results obtained
clearly showed that, contrary to the traditional PPP theory of RER behavior,
these time series could not be characterized as a white noise process.

These findings generate a number of important questions, some of which
will be tackled in the chapters that follow. Among the more important ones
it is possible to mention the following: (1) If the (log of the) real exchange
rate cannot be represented as a white noise process, how can we explain
RER behavior? (2) Is it possible to explain the wide movements of the real
effective rate index by the behavior of the fundamental determinants derived
in the theoretical analysis of part I? (3) Is it possible to explain the observed
differences across countries in the degree of variability of the real exchange
rate by some characteristics specific to each country? (4) Is it possible to

relate some of the more acute movements of the real exchange rate to changes in the nominal exchange rate and other policy variables?

Appendix: Trade Weights Used in the Construction of Real Effective Exchange Rate Indexes for Selected Developing Countries

Note that the figures in parentheses are percentages of trade weights in 1975. Trade partner countries are based on the 10 largest trading partners whose price indexes are available. Source: International Monetary Fund, *Directions of Trade*.

1. *Bolivia:* U.S. (32.3), U.K. (7.3), Japan (11.5), Belgium (1.9), W. Germany (6.6), Netherlands (1.9), Switzerland (3.0), Argentina (23.2), Brazil (10.6), Chile (1.8).

2. *Brazil:* U.S. (35.3), U.K. (5.3), Japan (14.4), France (4.7), W. Germany (16.2), Italy (7.4), Netherlands (5.8), Spain (3.6), Argentina (4.7), Belgium (2.8).

3. *Chile:* U.S. (27.1), U.K. (8.5), Japan (12.1), Belgium (3.5), France (4.8), W. Germany (16.7), Italy (4.8), Netherlands (5.7), Spain (4.5), Argentina (12.5).

4. *Colombia:* U.S. (49.3), U.K. (4.2), Canada (2.5), Japan (6.9), France (4.4), W. Germany (15.4), Italy (3.4), Netherlands (5.2), Spain (3.9), Venezuela (4.8).

5. *Cyprus:* U.S. (4.0), U.K. (41.5), Japan (4.4), Austria (2.1), France (8.3), W. Germany (8.4), Italy (8.5), Netherlands (4.5), Greece (16.2), Spain (2.2).

6. *Dominican Republic:* U.S. (69.9), U.K. (2.0), Canada (2.5), Japan (4.4), Belgium (1.7), W. Germany (1.8), Italy (2.8), Netherlands (4.4), Switzerland (2.6), Venezuela (7.8).

7. *Ecuador:* U.S. (58.2), U.K. (2.9), Japan (11.0), France (1.8), W. Germany (8.5), Italy (3.3), Netherlands (2.1), Argentina (6.3), Colombia (4.4), Spain (1.5).

8. *El Salvador:* U.S. (35.6), U.K. (3.0), Japan (11.0), Belgium (2.6), W. Germany (10.9), Italy (2.1), Netherlands (5.3), Costa Rica (6.6), Guatemala (17.8), Venezuela (5.1).

9. *Ethiopia:* U.S. (19.6), U.K. (8.6), Japan (16.1), France (5.5), W. Germany (16.7), Italy (12.5), Netherlands (4.4), Iran (7.8), Israel (3.2), Egypt (5.8).

10. *Greece:* U.S. (11.0), U.K. (7.9), Japan (10.4), Belgium (4.2), France (10.5), W. Germany (28.6), Italy (13.5), Netherlands (7.4), Spain (3.3), Tunisia (3.3).

11. *Guatemala:* U.S. (37.4), U.K. (7.0), Japan (9.2), Canada (2.2), W. Germany (11.1), Italy (4.9), Netherlands (3.1), Costa Rica (5.1), El Salvador (12.7), Venezuela (7.3).

12. *Guyana:* U.S. (39.2), U.K. (37.0), Canada (5.6), Japan (4.5), Denmark (1.6), France (2.4), W. Germany (3.6), Italy (1.4), Netherlands (2.7), Norway (2.1).

13. *Honduras:* U.S. (55.7), U.K. (2.1), Japan (6.5), Belgium (2.3), W. Germany (8.0), Netherlands (3.1), Costa Rica (3.5), Guatemala (6.1), Mexico (1.5), Venezuela (11.3).

14. *India:* U.S. (30.1), U.K. (11.9), Canada (4.6), Japan (15.6), Australia (3.3), France (5.1), W. Germany (9.4), Italy (3.0), Belgium (3.0), Iran (13.9).

15. *Israel:* U.S. (30.7), U.K. (17.6), Japan (4.4), France (6.3), W. Germany (14.0), Italy (6.2), Netherlands (7.3), Belgium (5.6), Switzerland (4.9), Iran (2.9).

16. *Kenya:* U.S. (10.4), U.K. (28.9), Japan (10.7), France (3.5), W. Germany (14.5), Italy (5.7), Netherlands (4.5), Canada (3.3), Australia (2.2), Iran (16.3).

17. *Korea:* U.S. (37.6), U.K. (3.1), Canada (3.8), Japan (41.0), Australia (2.9), France (2.0), W. Germany (5.6), Italy (0.8), Netherlands (1.6), Iran (1.6).

18. *Malaysia:* U.S. (22.5), U.K. (13.3), Australia (8.0), Japan (28.5), France (2.9), W. Germany (7.8), Italy (2.7), Netherlands (8.0), Philippines (1.9), Thailand (4.5).

19. *Malta:* U.S. (7.6), U.K. (33.7), Japan (2.7), Belgium (5.4), Denmark (2.8), France (4.8), W. Germany (16.5), Italy (19.1), Netherlands (5.9), Canada (1.5).

20. *Mauritius:* U.S. (6.5), U.K. (54.3), Canada (2.6), Japan (4.9), Australia (3.9), Belgium (1.7), France (8.7), W. Germany (5.2), S. Africa (6.9), Iran (5.5).

21. *Mexico:* U.S. (71.5), U.K. (2.7), Canada (2.3), Japan (5.0), France (2.5), W. Germany (7.0), Italy (1.9), Switzerland (1.6), Argentina (3.1), Brazil (2.3).

22. *Pakistan:* U.S. (20.7), U.K. (13.1), Canada (5.5), Japan (23.0), Australia (8.6), Belgium (3.3), France (5.2), W. Germany (11.6), Italy (6.3), Netherlands (2.7).

23. *Paraguay:* U.S. (13.0), U.K. (11.7), Japan (4.3), Belgium (1.9), France (3.5), W. Germany (12.4), Netherlands (5.3), Switzerland (4.7), Argentina (28.0), Brazil (15.3).

24. *Peru:* U.S. (41.7), U.K. (5.3), Japan (14.1), France (3.2), W. Germany (13.1), Italy (3.4), Netherlands (5.2), Brazil (4.5), Chile (4.5), Venezuela (5.2).

25. *Philippines:* U.S. (33.1), U.K. (4.9), Canada (2.0), Japan (41.7), Australia (3.9), France (2.1), W. Germany (4.6), Italy (0.9), Netherlands (5.1), Iran (1.7).

26. *Singapore:* U.S. (29.4), U.K. (9.2), Japan (26.7), Australia (7.9), France (3.0), W. Germany (6.8), Italy (2.1), Netherlands (3.2), Iran (6.6), Thailand (5.2).

27. *South Africa:* U.S. (18.7), U.K. (26.2), Canada (2.7), Japan (14.4), Belgium (2.9), France (4.7), W. Germany (19.5), Italy (3.9), Netherlands (3.0), Switzerland (4.0).

28. *Sri Lanka:* U.S. (12.3), U.K. (11.9), Canada (3.5), Japan (13.9), Australia (12.0), France (10.5), W. Germany (8.2), Iran (7.4), Pakistan (12.5), Thailand (7.9).

29. *Thailand:* U.S. (21.1), U.K. (5.2), Japan (48.4), France (2.9), W. Germany (6.7), Italy (2.1), Netherlands (7.6), Australia (2.8), Switzerland (1.8), India (1.5).

30. *Tunisia:* U.S. (10.7), U.K. (4.6), Belgium (2.8), France (38.1), W. Germany (10.8), Italy (16.2), Netherlands (3.2), Greece (9.1), Spain (2.8), Brazil (1.8).

31. *Turkey:* U.S. (13.7), U.K. (9.9), Japan (5.7), Belgium (3.8), France (8.1), W. Germany (32.6), Italy (10.5), Netherlands (4.5), Switzerland (9.0), Austria (2.0).

32. *Yugoslavia:* U.S. (12.3), U.K. (5.4), Japan (3.4), Austria (7.1). France (7.9), W. Germany (31.7), Italy (22.4), Netherlands (3.1), Switzerland (4.4), Belgium (2.2).

33. *Zambia:* U.S. (9.5), U.K. (28.7), Japan (17.4), Belgium (3.7), France (6.4), W. Germany (14.2), Italy (10.8), Netherlands (2.5), S. Africa (5.4), India (1.4).

Notes

1. For a review of the literature on RER measurement problems see Edwards (1985c) and Edwards and Ng (1985). See also Wood (1987) and Dornbusch and Helmers (1988).

2. See Edwards (1985c).

3. The partners and weights used for constructing the multilateral indexes are given in the appendix to this chapter.

4. The possibility of having the bilateral and multilateral real exchange rates moving in opposite directions can be easily seen by using the triangular arbitrage condition for nominal exchange rates to rewrite the MRER index as

$$\text{MRER} = \frac{E_{\text{US}}}{P}\{\sum \alpha_i E_{\text{US},i} P_i^*\}, \tag{4.4}$$

where E_{US} is an index of the bilateral nominal rate between the country in question and the United States, and where $E_{\text{US},i}$ is the bilateral nominal exchange rate between the United States and the ith partner. It is clear from this expression that even if this country pegs with respect to the dollar (i.e., E_{US} is fixed), the fact that the U.S. dollar is floating against other major currencies ($E_{\text{US},i}$ moves) will affect the MRER.

5. As noted, the real multilateral exchange rate indexes were constructed using trade weights for 1975 and each country's 10 largest trade partners. An important question is, How different will these indexes behave if other weighting schemes and a larger number of partners are used in the computation? In theory the effective indexes constructed using a different number of partners and weighting schemes can be quite different. From a practical perspective, however, once a large enough number of partners is used (say, 8–10) and a fairly normal year is taken as the base, the addition of other countries or the use of other weighting schemes will generate little variation in the index. In order to illustrate this point, 19 indexes of the effective real exchange rate were constructed for some of these countries and their behavior was compared between 1960 and 1983. The alternative indexes considered 20 partner countries (instead of 10) and used, alternatively, trade, export and import weights. Also, the weights were taken from averages for 1975–1980 (instead of 1975 only). The results obtained strongly support the claim that further refinements would not add much to the indexes constructed for this study. For instance, for the case of Colombia, the correlation coefficient between the MRER1 index, constructed with 10 partners and 1975 trade weights, and the index constructed using average 1975–1980 import weights and 20 partners was 0.999. When the MRER1 index was compared with other more complete indexes, the resulting coefficients of correlation had similar magnitudes.

6. The countries were Greece, Turkey, Yugoslavia, Colombia, Ecuador, El Salvador, Guatemala, Mexico, Israel, India, Korea, Pakistan, and Singapore. The data on wages were obtained from various issues of the *ILO Labor Market Yearbook*.

7. Remember, however, that in those countries with multiple official rates the "most common" rate was used.

8. For the other five countries—Guatemala, Guyana, Honduras, Malta, and Mauritius—it was not possible to find data on parallel market quotations.

9. Notice that these diagrams show that in some countries with no exchange controls the premium has even been briefly negative. This can be a reflection of either poor quality data or the fact that during some periods the central bank did not buy all the foreign exchange, causing the freely determined parallel rate to be below the official rate. In other cases the negative premium may be reflecting the fact that, at times, foreign exchange remittances from illegal activities (e.g., drugs) generated gluts in the foreign exchange market. In most cases, however, the premium has been positive and significantly so.

10. Unfortunately, since there are only quotations of the parallel market rate with respect to the U.S. dollar, it is not possible to construct multilateral parallel market rates directly.

11. To be rigorous, r_k refers to the first K autocorrelations from an ARIMA (p, d, s) process and n is the number of observations (x minus d). In the present case, however, the log of the real exchange rate is supposed to follow an ARIMA $(0, 0, 0)$ process.

12. For a good discussion on nonstationarity and real exchange rates in the industrialized countries see Kaminsky (1987).

13. Most studies on real exchange rates in industrial countries during the floating period have not been able to reject nonstationarity. For longer periods of time, however, the evidence is consistent with (slow) mean reverting processes for real exchange rates. For example, in their recent massive study Frankel and Meese (1987) argue that "the evidence for a unit root in real exchange rates is much less convincing than the evidence for a unit root in nominal exchange rates...."

5   Real and Nominal Determinants of Real Exchange Rates: The Empirical Evidence

According to the theoretical models of chapters 2 and 3, long-run equilibrium RERs depend on real variables only—the "fundamentals." In the short run, however, both real and nominal variables exercise an influence on actual RERs. In chapter 3 it was argued that unsustainable macroeconomic policies will generate conditions of real exchange rate overvaluation that will usually end up in balance of payments crises and devaluations.

The cross-country empirical evidence presented in chapter 4 showed that RERs in LDCs have indeed exhibited a behavior significantly different from what the traditional purchasing power parity (PPP) theory has suggested; independently of whether multilateral official or bilateral parallel exchange rates were used, for all 33 countries analyzed, deviations from PPP differed significantly from *white noise*. The purpose of this chapter is to analyze empirically the relative importance of nominal and real variables in explaining RER movements in a number of developing countries. This analysis not only serves as a test of the main implications of the models of chapters 2 and 3, but—and this is more important—it sheds light on the crucial question of disentangling equilibrium from disequilibrium real exchange rates. Because only some countries have long enough time series of (at least some of the) "fundamentals," the analysis presented in this chapter is limited to a smaller number of countries than those analyzed in chapter 4.

The chapter is organized in the following way: We start in section 5.1 with two descriptive country "stories"—Chile and Colombia—where simple inspection allows us to illustrate how some major real structural changes have affected the equilibrium real exchange rates in these two countries. In section 5.2 an empirical equation for RER dynamics is developed. Section 5.3 contains results from regression analyses using annual data for 12 countries. In these regressions an effort is made to isolate the roles of real factors, nominal exchange rate changes, and monetary and fiscal policies. In order to capture some of the intertemporal implications of the theoretical models, a distinction is made between temporary and permanent changes in the fundamentals. In section 5.4 we use the results from the regression analysis to analyze briefly the way in which equilibrium RER evoled in some of these countries. Finally, in section 5.5 some conclusions are presented.

5.1 Changes in Fundamentals and Equilibrium Real Exchange Rates: Some Simple Illustrations

In this section we provide two simple illustrations of how structural changes in fundamentals can severely affect equilibrium RERs. The discussion is carried out at a fairly informal level, and serves as an introduction to the econometric analysis presented below. Although these examples—Chile and Colombia—are quite extreme, they still provide a clear sense of the difficulties associated with disentangling equilibrium from disequilibrium real exchange rates movements.

Chile

Figure 5.1 contains the evolution of the RER in Chile. As can be seen, between 1965 and 1970 there was a slow and steady real depreciation, which broadly corresponds to the mild trade liberalization undertaken by the Frei administration. During this period a crawling peg nominal exchange rate helped to achieve and maintain this depreciating real exchange rate (see Corbo, 1985). The period 1970–1973 corresponds to the socialist government of Dr. Salvador Allende, where expansive macropolicies and

Figure 5.1
Real exchange rate for Chile. Source: constructed from raw data obtained from the *IFS*.

the massive imposition of exchange controls resulted in forces that appreciated the real rate by almost 50%. With respect to other "fundamentals," during this period the terms of trade fluctuated without exhibiting a definitive trend (Corbo, 1985). This suggests, then, that during this period Chile's RER became severely overvalued.

The years 1974–1984 correspond to the first decade of the Pinochet regime. The first thing that stands out from the diagram is that between the periods 1965–1973 and 1974–1984 there is a clear structural break in the real exchange rate behavior in Chile. Throughout 1974–1984, in spite of broad fluctuations, the real exchange rate was at all times significantly higher than at any time during the previous 10 years. Two main "real" events that greatly affected the behavior of "fundamentals" are behind the major real depreciation that took place between 1965–1973 and 1979: First, there was a drastic liberalization of international trade, which eliminated all quantitative restrictions and reduced import tariffs from an average of more than 100% to a uniform 10% level (Edwards and Cox-Edwards, 1987). Second, there was a steep, and apparently permanent, deterioration of Chile's terms of trade; during 1975–1979 the average real price of Chile's main export, copper, was 41% below its 1965–1973 average. This casual comparison of the pre- and post-1974 real exchange rates in Chile forcefully suggests that in Chile tariffs reductions and terms of trade worsening "required" a real depreciation to maintain external equilibrium. These indeed were the types of reaction that, according to our discussions of chapter 2, were more likely to occur.

Between mid-1979 and mid-1982 the by-now much discussed real appreciation of the Chilean peso taok place (Corbo, 1985; Edwards, 1985a). This appreciation can in principle be attributed to two interconnected factors related to both nominal and real variables: (1) Between 1979 and 1981 capital controls were greatly relaxed, allowing a massive inflow of foreign funds. As suggested by the model of chapter 2, the opening up of the capital account generated important forces toward an equilibrium real appreciation. (2) The fixing of the nominal exchange rate in June of 1979 as a way to bring down inflation also contributed to the observed real appreciation. Almost every observer of the Chilean scene has pointed out that this loss in competitiveness after mid-1979 was one of the main forces that generated the collapse of the Chilean economy in 1982–1983. What is fascinating is to notice that although during this period the RER declined by 30%, it was still almost 70% higher than its peak during 1965–1973! This, of course, provides a vivid illustration of how changes in fundamentals can greatly change the equilibrium value of the real exchange rate.

A RER that would have been excessively "high" in the 1970s, before the tariff liberalization and structural worsening of the terms of trade, was fatally low in the early 1980s.

A regression analysis for Chile's real exchange rate using quarterly data for 1977–1982 confirms our discussion regarding the roles of capital flows and terms of trade. Unfortunately, the lack of a complete time series on import tariffs and other restrictions did not allow the incorporation of that variable (the numbers in parentheses are t-statistics):[1]

$$\log \text{RER}_t = 0.016 - 0.076 \log(\text{net capital flows})_{t-1}$$
$$(3.973)(-3.521)$$

$$- 0.218 \log(\text{terms of trade})_{t-1} + 0.271 \, \text{growth}_t$$
$$(-1.935) \qquad\qquad\qquad\qquad (1.250)$$

$$+ 0.005 (\text{devaluation dummy})$$
$$(0.194)$$

$$+ 0.964 \log \text{RER}_{t-1} \qquad (\text{DW} = 1.753, \, R^2 = 0.946). \qquad (5.1)$$
$$(7.889)$$

These results, then, support the view that an increase in net capital flows is associated with a real appreciation. Moreover, for the case of Chile, Morandé (1986) has shown that the causality indeed went from capital flows to real exchange rate. The results in equation (5.1) also indicate that, as expected, a deterioration of the terms of trade—that is, a decline in log(terms of trade)—will result in a real depreciation.

Colombia

Figure 5.2 contains the evolution of Colombia's multilateral real exchange rate. Between 1967 and 1975 Colombia embarked on a steady trade liberalization process, where quantitative import restrictions were slowly lowered and import tariffs were reduced (see Diaz-Alejandro, 1976). As can be seen from the figure, during this period a steady real depreciation took place. By 1975 Colombia's real multilateral exchange rate was 43% higher than in 1967. Throughout the period a very successful crawling nominal exchange rate policy was followed, where government authorities frequently devalued the nominal rate, using a set of indicators that included the price of coffee, domestic inflation, foreign inflation, and the level of protection (Urrutia, 1981).

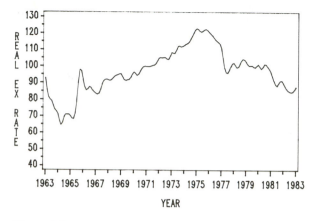

Figure 5.2
Real exchange rate for Colombia. Source: constructed from raw data obtained from the *IFS*.

Between 1967 and 1975 the real price of coffee fluctuated somewhat. In late 1975, however, a major coffee "boom," which continued until 1979, took place. By 1977 the real price of coffee was 170% above its 1975 level. This period was also characterized by an escalation in illegal drug traffic, which resulted in massive inflows of (illegal) foreign funds. As can be seen from figure 5.2, starting in late 1975, and as expected, a process of real appreciation of the Colombian currency began. This quasi-equilibrium real appreciation was partially accommodated by the authorities by slowing down the rate of devaluation of the crawl. However, given the temporary nature of the coffee "boom"—it stemmed from a frost in Brazil that damaged most of that country's coffee trees—the authorities tried to avoid some of the real appreciation by engaging in sterilization and other policies (see Edwards, 1986c).

The Chile and Colombia "stories" presented above serve a double purpose. First, they have illustrated quite vividly that under some circumstances the analyst can detect broad movements in real exchange rates that have been associated with major structural changes in real fundamentals. Second, they have shown that understanding RER movements, and in particular disentangling changes induced by real and monetary shocks, can indeed be very difficult. In the next two sections, results obtained from the estimation of a dynamic equation aimed at explaining real exchange rate movements are presented. The analysis is based on the models of chapters 2 and 3. It uses annual data from 1965–1984 for a group of 12 LDCs, and its main purpose is to separate the effects of real from monetary determinants of RERs.[2]

5.2 An Empirical Equation for Real Exchange Rate Dynamics

The theoretical models of chapters 2 and 3 made the following basic points with respect to the dynamics of RER behavior: First, in the long run, equilibrium real exchange rate movements depend on real variables only. Second, temporary and permanent changes in fundamentals will usually have different effects on the equilibrium RER. Third, under a predetermined nominal exchange rate regime inconsistent macroeconomic policies will generate, in the short run, real exchange rate misalignment. Fourth, if the system is left on its own, the convergence of the actual to the equilibrium RER will usually take some time. The speed at which this convergence will actually take place will depend on the model's parameters, and on the extent of capital mobility. Fifth, nominal devaluations will only have a lasting effect on the equilibrium real exchange rate if they are undertaken from a situation of real exchange rate misalignment and if they are accompanied by "appropriate" macroeconomic policies.[3] Nominal devaluations are neutral in the long run. In addition, the model of chapter 2 provided a complete list of the relevant real "fundamentals" to be incorporated in the estimation of a RER equation.

The following equation for the dynamics of RER behavior captures the main implications of the theoretical analysis:[4]

$$\Delta \log e_t = \theta \{\log e_t^* - \log e_{t-1}\} - \lambda \{Z_t - Z_t^*\} + \phi \{\log E_t - \log E_{t-1}\}, \quad (5.2)$$

where e is the actual real exchange rate; e^* is the equilibrium real exchange rate, which is in turn a function of the fundamentals; Z_t is an index of macroeconomic policies (i.e., the rate of growth of domestic credit); Z_t^* is the sustainable level of macroeconomic policies to be defined more precisely later; E_t is the nominal exchange rate; and θ, λ, and ϕ are positive parameters that capture the most important dynamic aspects of the adjustment process.

Equation (5.2) establishes that actual movements of the real exchange rate respond to three forces. First, there will be an autonomous tendency for the actual real exchange rate to correct existing misalignments. This force is represented by the partial adjustment term $\theta \{\log e_t^* - \log e_{t-1}\}$. With all other things as given, this self-correcting process tends to take place, under pegged nominal rates, through reductions in the price of nontradable goods. The speed at which this self-adjustment takes place is captured in equation (5.2) by the parameter θ. A value of θ of 1 means that in one period any deviation of $\log e$ from its long-run equilibrium value will be completely eliminated. The smaller is θ (i.e., the closer it is to zero), the slower will be the speed at which real exchange rate misalignments will be corrected. Theoretically, the value of θ will depend on a number of institutional factors, including the extent of capital mobility and the existence of wage indexation rules. Since in most cases nominal prices and wages are (somewhat) inflexible downward, this self-correcting process can be very slow and costly in terms of lost real output and increased unemployment.

According to equation (5.2) the second determinant of real exchange rate movements is related to macropolicies and is given by $-\lambda\{Z_t - Z_t^*\}$. This term states that if the macroeconomic policies are unsustainable in the medium-to-longer run and are inconsistent with a pegged rate (i.e., $Z_t > Z_t^*$), there will be pressures toward a real appreciation—that is, if $(Z_t - Z_t^*) > 0$, with other things as given, $\Delta \log e < 0$. Notice that if the macroeconomic disequilibrium and/or λ are large enough, these forces can easily dominate the self-correcting term, generating an increasing degree of overvaluation through time.

Finally, the third determinant of RER movements is related to nominal devaluations and is given by the term $\phi\{\log E_t - \log E_{t-1}\}$. According to this, a nominal devaluation will have a positive effect on the real exchange rate on *impact*, generating a short-run real depreciation; the actual magnitude of this real depreciation will depend on parameter ϕ, itself a function of the structural and institutional characteristics of the economy in question. The larger is ϕ, the larger the instantaneous impact of the nominal devaluation on the real exchange rate. Typically, as discussed in chapter 3, this impact coefficient will be smaller than one. An important property of equation (5.2) is that it captures the fact that, although nominal devaluations will have an effect on the real exchange rate in the *short run*, this effect will not necessarily last through time. In fact, whether the nominal devaluation will have any impact over the medium-to-longer run will depend on the other two terms of equation (5.2), or, more precisely, on the initial conditions captured by $(\log e_t^* - \log e_{t-1})$ and on the accompanying macropolicies, captured by $(Z_t - Z_t^*)$. As the model of chapter 3 indicated, nominal devaluations will help the adjustment process only to the extent that the initial condition is one of disequilibrium and if they are accompanied by consistent macropolicies. An important characteristic of equation (5.2) is that by allowing three different forces to interact, we can, in principle, obtain estimated movements in the RER that resemble their observed fluctuations.

In order to estimate the equation for real exchange rate dynamics (5.2), it is first necessary to specify an empirical equation for the equilibrium real exchange rate ($\log e^*$), and to define the macroeconomic disequilibrium term $(Z_t - Z_t^*)$. This is done below, where on the basis of the insights provided by the models of chapters 2 and 3, an equation for $\log e^*$ is presented, and the empirical definitions of the indexes of macroeconomic disequilibrium are provided.

The Equilibrium Real Exchange Rate

According to the model of equilibrium real exchange rates developed in chapter 2, the most important "fundamentals" in determining the behavior of equilibrium RERs are (1) external terms of trade, (2) level and composition of government consumption, (3) controls on capital flows, (4) exchange and trade controls (i.e., import tariffs), (5) technological progress, and (6) capital accumulation. The simplest possible way of writing down the equilibrium real exchange rate is[5]

$$\log e_t^* = \beta_0 + \beta_1 \log(\text{TOT})_t + \beta_2 \log(\text{GCN})_t$$

$$+ \beta_3 \log(\text{CAPCONTROLS})_t + \beta_4 \log(\text{EXCHCONTROLS})_t$$

$$+ \beta_5 \log(\text{TECHPRO})_t + \beta_6 \log(\text{INVGDP})_t + u_t, \qquad (5.3)$$

where the following notation has been used:

e^*:	equilibrium real exchange rate,
TOT:	external terms of trade, defined at (P_X^*/P_M^*),
GCN:	goverment consumption on nontradables,
CAPCONTROLS:	measure of extent of controls over capital flows,
EXCHCONTROLS:	index of the severity of trade restrictions and exchange controls,
TECHPRO:	measure of technological progress,
INVGDP:	ratio of investment of GDP,
u:	error term.

Before actually estimating the RER equation, a number of issues related to the data have to be resolved. One of the more serious obstacles encountered refers to data availability. In fact, the only fundamentals for which we have reliable time series data are the external terms of trade (TOT) and the investment ratio. This means that in the estimation of the RER equation the other fundamentals either have to be omitted or, alternatively, proxies for them have to be found. In this investigation we followed the two approaches, estimating real exchange rate equations under alternative specifications that either omitted variables or used proxies for those that did not have data.

The following proxies were used—technological progress was proxied by the rate of growth of real GDP. This type of proxy has been used in a number of empirical investigations dealing with the Ricardo-Balassa effect. In the case of capital controls, it was not possible to find time series for an appropriate proxy. For this reason CAPCONTROL was replaced by the lagged ratio of net capital flows to GDP. As discussed in chapter 2, changes in the extent of capital controls will also affect the flow of capital moving in and out of the country. In principle, a hike in capital controls will reduce capital flows and vice versa. It is expected, then, that an increase (decline) in capital inflows will appreciate (depreciate) the equilibrium real exchange rate. With respect to exchange and trade controls (EXCHCONTROLS), two proxies were used. First, we computed implicit import tariffs as the ratio of tariff revenues to imports. This proxy, however, has a number of limitations.[6] First, it is only available for a few years for each country; and second, it ignores the role of nontariff barriers. For this reason a more comprehensive proxy that captures the extent of controls in a broad sense was sought. The spread between the parallel and official rates in the foreign exchange market is a variable that captures in a broad sense the extent and severity of exchange controls, and was thus used as a proxy in the regressions reported here. It should be noted, however, that although the spread has all the characteristics of a good proxy for the extent of trade, exchange, and capital controls, it may also capture other forces. In fact, according to the model in chapter 3, the (actual) real exchange rate and the parallel market spread are jointly determined. Naturally, in the estimation, instruments have to be found for this variable. Finally, there are no data on government consumption on nontradables. For this reason GCN was proxied by the ratio of total government consumption over GDP (GCGDP). However, since this is admittedly not a very good proxy, the results obtained should be interpreted with care.

A limitation of equation (5.3) is that it does not provide an explicit distinction between permanent and temporary movements in the fundamentals. However, this distinction turned out to be an important one in the theoretical analysis of ERERs. To the extent that intertemporal substitution is an important transmission channel from fundamentals to the ERER, we would expect that temporary shocks would play an important role in the observed movements of the ERER. In order to overcome this limitation, in some of the estimated equations the time series of the fundamentals were broken into a permanent component and a temporary (or cyclical) component. This decomposition was done following the methodology suggested by Beveridge and Nelson (1981).

Macroeconomic Policies

In the RER dynamics equation (5.2), the term $-\lambda\{Z_t - Z_t^*\}$ measures the role of macroeconomic policies in real exchange rate behavior. According to the model developed in chapter 3, with other things as given, if macro-economic policies are "inconsistent," the RER will become overvalued. In the estimation the following components of $\{Z_t - Z_t^*\}$ were used:

1. Excess supply for domestic credit (EXCRE) measured as the rate of growth of domestic credit minus the lagged rate of growth of real GDP:

$$\text{EXCRE}_t = \{d\log(\text{domestic credit})_t - d\log(\text{GDP})_{t-1}\};$$

this assumes that the demand for domestic credit has a unitary elasticity with respect to real income.

2. Also, we incorporated the ratio of fiscal deficit to lagged high powered money (DEH) as a measure of fiscal policies.

3. Finally, instead of our measure for the excess supply of domestic credit, in a number of equations we included the rate of growth of domestic credit (DCRE).

5.3 Econometric Results

After replacing the equation for $\log e_t^*$ and the expressions for $\{Z_t - Z_t^*\}$ in (5.2), we obtain an equation that can be estimated using conventional methods. For example, when EXCRE and DEH are the elements of the macroeconomic policies vector $\{Z_t - Z_t^*\}$, the equation to be estimated is

$$\log e_t = \gamma_1 \log(\text{TOT})_t + \gamma_2 \log(\text{GCGDP})_t$$
$$+ \gamma_3 \log(\text{CAPCONTROLS})_t + \gamma_4 \log(\text{EXCHCONTROLS})$$
$$+ \gamma_5 \log(\text{TECHPRO})_t + \gamma_6 \log(\text{INVGDP})_t + (1 - \theta)\log e_{t-1}$$
$$- \lambda_1 \text{EXCRE}_t - \lambda_2 \text{DEH}_t + \phi \text{NOMDEV}_t + u_t, \qquad (5.4)$$

where NOMDEV stands for nominal devaluation, and where the γ's are combinations of the β's and θ.

Several versions of equation (5.4), including a number of equations that decomposed the "fundamentals" into temporary and permanent series, were estimated using pooled data for a group of 12 developing countries: Brazil, Colombia, El Salvador, Greece, India, Israel, Malaysia, the Philippines, South Africa, Sri Lanka, Thailand, and Yugoslavia. These countries were chosen because of data availability. They were the only ones with continuous time series for all the relevant variables (except the proxies for exchange and trade controls) for 1962–1984. The length of the series varied slightly from country to country. Throughout the period all of these countries had predetermined nominal exchange rate regimes—either pegged or crawling. Moreover all of them, except El Salvador, experienced substantial nominal devaluations during the period under analysis. The decision to estimate these regressions using pooled data was based on the fact that there are very few time series observations for most of these variables. In order to test the robustness of the results, the group was broken into two subgroups: one included the middle income countries, and the other the poorer countries.[7]

The estimation was performed using a fixed-effect procedure, with country specific dummy variables included in each regression.[8] Ordinary least squares and instrumental variables (IV) techniques were used.[9] Both indexes of bilateral and multilateral real exchange rates were employed as dependent variables.[10]

Table 5.1 contains a summary of the results obtained from IV estimation of six different variants of the basic equation (5.4); here no distinction is made between temporary and permanent components of the fundamentals. Results obtained when these distinctions are made are discussed below. In this table the χ^2-statistic tests for the significance of all the real variables as a group. The results are satisfactory and provide support for the view that short-run movements in real exchange rates respond to both real and nominal variables.

In all the regressions the measures of macroeconomic policy—the excess supply of domestic credit (EXCRE), the fiscal deficit ratio (DEH), and the rate of growth of domestic credit (DCRE)—affect negatively the RER, and in most of them significantly so. This indicates that as these policies became increasingly expansive in these countries—higher deficits or increased excess supply of credit—the real exchange rate *appreciated*. Naturally, starting from RER equilibrium, if other things, including the fundamentals, remain constant, this appreciation will reflect a mounting disequilibrium or RER overvaluation. For the excess supply for credit (EXCRE)

Table 5.1
Real exchange rate equations (instrumental variables)[a]

Dependent variable	Equation number					
	(5.4.1) RER	(5.4.2) RER	(5.4.3) RER	(5.4.4) REER	(5.4.5) REER	(5.4.6) REER
EXCRE	—	−0.118 (−4.210)	−0.131 (−4.527)	—	—	−0.082 (−2.195)
DEH	−0.016 (−1.837)	−0.012 (−1.531)	−0.014 (−2.100)	—	−0.004 (−0.321)	−0.016 (−1.934)
DCRE	−0.116 (−2.995)	—	—	−0.055 (−2.128)	−0.085 (−2.122)	—
NOMDEV	0.677 (13.436)	0.573 (15.580)	0.634 (17.908)	0.536 (8.439)	0.497 (10.612)	0.489 (10.567)
log TOT	−0.057 (−2.283)	−0.022 (−1.217)	−0.038 (−1.826)	−0.043 (−2.371)	−0.271 (−0.955)	−0.007 (−0.727)
log GCGDP	0.025 (0.909)	−0.018 (−1.968)	−0.030 (−1.528)	0.054 (1.712)	−0.062 (−2.530)	−0.010 (−1.444)
log INVGNP	—	0.073 (1.304)	—	—	0.148 (1.589)	—
log EXCONT	—	−0.162 (−5.795)	—	−0.255 (−2.682)	—	−0.167 (−4.798)
CAPFLO$_{-1}$	—	—	−0.152 (−2.104)	−0.231 (−1.406)	−0.198 (−1.956)	—
GROWTH	0.146 (4.808)	0.062 (0.541)	0.474 (4.365)	0.997 (2.257)	—	0.279 (1.934)
log e_{t-1}	0.941 (30.512)	0.790 (23.518)	0.900 (39.590)	0.739 (8.947)	0.896 (30.572)	0.811 (20.152)
N	226	201	207	226	207	213
Root MSE	0.047	0.048	0.049	0.073	0.061	0.069
R^2	0.99	0.99	0.99	0.99	0.99	0.99
χ^2	51.4	49.2	53.7	52.1	49.7	54.3

a. Numbers in parentheses are t-statistics. N is the number of observations. MSE is the mean square error. R^2 is the coefficient of determination. All regressions included country-specific dummy variables. χ^2 is a chi-square test for the joint significance of the real variables (the "fundamentals").

the estimated coefficients ranged from -0.131 to -0.082. Although these coefficients appear somewhat small, they do imply that inconsistent domestic credit policies maintained for periods of 3–4 years can generate very substantial disequilibria. Consider, for example, the case of equation (5.4.3) with a coefficient for EXCRE of -0.131; if domestic credit grows at a rate of 25% per year and income at 2%, after three years there will be an accumulated real appreciation of approximately 7%. In this sense, the estimates for the coefficients of the macro variables strongly support the view that in these countries inconsistent macroeconomic policies resulted in growing pressures that eventually generated situations of real exchange rate disequilibrium.

The results in table 5.1 show that real variables (the "fundamentals") have also influenced RER behavior in these countries. The χ^2-statistics reported at the bottom of the table show that in all regressions the fundamentals as a group were significantly different from zero. In all regressions the coefficients of the (log of the) terms of trade is negative, and significant at conventional levels in a number of them. This negative sign gives support to the popular views discussed in chapter 2 that suggest that improvements in the terms of trade—an increase in $\log(TOT)$—will result in an equilibrium real appreciation. In a way, this result provides an empirical resolution to the undetermined theoretical response of ERER to terms of trade disturbances discussed in chapter 2.

Due to the lack of data on the composition of government consumption, the ratio of government expenditures to GDP ($\log GCGDP$) is the only real variable related to government behavior incorporated in the analysis. In four of the equations this coefficient was negative, and in a number of them it was statistically significant at the conventional levels. In those regressions where it was included, the coefficient of the (log of the) investment ratio was positive, indicating that in these countries increases in investment resulted in equilibrium real depreciation. Recall that the model in chapter 2 indicated that the effect of investment on the equilibrium RER would depend on factor intensities and, consequently, on whether it took place in the tradables or nontradables goods sectors.

The index proxying exchange and trade controls (the parallel market premium) was significantly negative in all the regressions where it was included, indicating that—at least for these countries during this period— a relaxation of the extent of impediments to international trade resulted in equilibrium real exchange rate depreciation. As was discussed at some length in chapter 2, this has indeed been the contention of the policy literature on trade liberalization reforms. When this index was replaced by the ratio of the revenue from import tariffs to imports, the coefficient was still negative.

With respect to (lagged) capital flows, the coefficient is negative and in most regressions significant. This indicates that when a country has to make a (net) transfer of resources to the rest of the world, an equilibrium real depreciation will be required. This has important implications for the developing countries in the aftermath of the debt crisis. The coefficient of real growth, however, turned out to be positive in all regressions and significant in a number of them. To the extent that growth is considered to be a measure of technological progress, this result seems to contradict the Ricardo-Balassa hypothesis discussed in chapter 2. There are a number of reasons, however, why this estimated coefficient may not be negative as suggested in chapter 2. First, growth is admittedly not a very good proxy for technological progress; and second, this coefficient may be picking up, in part, the effects of growth in the (flow) demand for credit on the behavior of RERs.

The estimated coefficients of nominal devaluation (NOMDEV) and lagged RERs provide the last two elements of analysis for the dynamics of RERs. The coefficient of NOMDEV is always significantly positive, ranging from 0.489 to 0.677. This indicates that even with all other things as given, a nominal devaluation has been transferred in a less than one-to-one real devaluation in the first year. The size of this coefficient is, however, quite large, and provides evidence in support of the view that nominal devaluations can indeed be a quite powerful device for *reestablishing real exchange rate equilibrium*. If, for instance, as in our prior example, the real exchange rate becomes overvalued by 7%, a nominal devaluation of approximately 12% will help regain equilibrium.[11] Naturally, for the nominal devaluation to have a lasting effect, it is necessary that the sources of the original disequilibrium—the positive EXCRE and DEH—be eliminated. If this is not the case, soon after the devaluation the RER will again become overvalued.

The coefficients of lagged RER are quite high in all regressions. In a way this is not too surprising in light of the analysis of the time series properties of RERs discussed in chapter 4.[12] From an economic perspective these high values for the coefficients imply that in the absence of other intervention, actual real exchange rates converge very slowly toward their long-run equilibrium level.

Table 5.2 contains the estimated adjustment coefficients for two of the regressions. As can be seen, in both cases the θ coefficient is in the neighborhood of 0.2, implying that with other things as given, in one year approximately one-fifth of a given discrepancy between the (log of the)

Table 5.2
Estimated coefficients of real exchange rate dynamics equations (selected estimates)[a]

	(5.4.2) RER	(5.4.6) REER
θ	0.210	0.189
λ_1	0.118	0.082
λ_2	0.012	0.016
ϕ	0.573	0.489

Source: table 5.1.
a. $\Delta \log e_t = \theta\{\log e_t^* - \log e_{t-1}\} - \lambda_1 \text{EXCRE} - \lambda_2 \text{DEH} + \phi \Delta \log E_t$.

real exchange rate and its equilibrium value will be corrected. This slow endogenous adjustment provides solid empirical support for the hypothesis that devaluation policies are helpful in speeding up the adjustment process (recall the theoretical analysis of chapter 3).

Permanent and Temporary Changes in Fundamentals

The results presented above did not distinguish between permanent and temporary changes in fundamentals. In order to investigate whether this distinction was empirically important, the method suggested by Beveridge and Nelson (1981) was used to decompose the time series of the fundamentals into a "permanent" and a "temporary" component.[13] This method was applied to each country individually, and the resulting time series for permanent and temporary components were pooled for the 12 countries. The fundamentals decomposed were the terms of trade, the ratio of government consumption to GDP, the exchange controls proxy, and the capital flows. In the appendix to this chapter we report the estimated ARIMA models used to perform this decomposition.

Table 5.3 contains the results obtained from the IV estimation of two alternative equations that distinguished between permanent (P) and temporary (T) shocks to fundamentals. These results are quite interesting. First, they show that for the terms of trade (TOT) and exchange and trade controls (EXCONT) variables the distinction between temporary and permanent was relevant. For both of these variables only changes in the permanent component are significant; they also have the expected sign. Moreover, for these two variables tests for the equality of the permanent and temporary coefficients resulted in strong rejection of the null hypothesis. In the case of GCGDP the distinction between P and T appears to not be empirically important; the test for equality of coefficients indicates that the null hypothesis cannot be rejected. Notice, however, that in both

Table 5.3
Temporary and permanent shocks to fundamentals and real exchange rate dynamics (instrumental variables)[a]

Dependent variable	log TOT		log GCGDP		log EXCONT		CAPFLO	
	P	T	P	T	P	T	P	T
REER	-0.060	-0.201	0.093	0.053	-0.303	0.139	-0.122	0.296
	(-1.980)	(-1.499)	(2.246)	(0.852)	(-3.667)	(1.346)	(-0.747)	(1.214)
RER	-0.059	-0.152	0.069	0.057	-0.373	0.203	0.099	0.041
	(-2.119)	(-1.242)	(1.838)	(0.861)	(-4.372)	(1.640)	(0.672)	(0.179)

Dependent variable	GROWTH	EXCRE	DCRE	NOMDEV	$\log e_{-1}$	R^2
REER	0.083	—	-0.047	0.508	0.698	0.958
	(2.100)		(-0.954)	(8.227)	(9.354)	
RER	0.045	-0.083	—	0.562	0.607	0.998
	(1.274)	(-1.981)		(9.424)	(7.454)	

a. The number of observations was 221. P refers to the permanent component, while T refers to the temporary component. The proxy for technical progress (growth) was not decomposed since the theoretical model of chapter 2 does not suggest that the distinction between permanent and temporary is important for that variable. The numbers in parentheses are t-statistics.

equations the signs do not correspond to what was expected. The coefficients of the capital inflows variables turned out to be nonsignificant in all of the equations.

The coefficients of the macroeconomic variables have the correct signs, but now the degree of significance is lower than in table 5.1. An interesting characteristic of the results in table 5.3 is that the coefficients of the lagged dependent variable are now quite a bit lower than in table 5.1. However, the absolute value of this coefficient remains quite high, still indicating that if the system is left on its own, the return of the actual real exchange rate to its long-run equilibrium value may take a substantial amount of time.

In sum, the results reported in table 5.3 indicate that at least for some of the fundamentals—the terms of trade and exchange and trade controls— the distinction between permanent and temporary changes is an important one. Also, the apparently small role played by temporary shocks seems to cast some doubt on the importance of the intertemporal channels developed in chapter 2 for explaining the dynamic process of RER behavior.[14] These results, however, should be considered as tentative and preliminary. A more definitive analysis along these lines will require longer time series and the development of more powerful econometric techniques.

Nominal Devaluations and the Real Exchange Rate: Country-Specific Estimates

The pooled estimates reported above indicate that, for these 12 countries as a group, the nominal devaluations have had an important impact effect on the real exchange rate. In the longer run, however, devaluations are neutral. Table 5.4 presents, for 11 of the countries, the results obtained when the coefficients for NOMDEV were not restricted to be equal across countries.[15] As can be seen, the estimated value of this coefficient exhibits important differences across countries. These differences may be capturing institutional characteristics of each of these countries that have not been explicitly incorporated into the analysis. Possibly the most important of those institutions refers to the labor markets, including the existence of indexation and other sources of wage rigidities.

Anticipated and Unanticipated Shocks

A limitation of the analysis up to now is that there has been no explicit distinction between expected and unexpected shocks. In order to get around this problem, and in particular to include the role of expectations, a number of steps were taken. First, series on expected and unexpected monetary

Table 5.4
Impact effect of a nominal devaluation on
the real exchange rate by country[a]

	NOMDEV
Brazil	0.491
	(7.426)
Colombia	0.645
	(3.000)
Greece	0.659
	(4.825)
India	0.677
	(3.764)
Israel	0.466
	(5.519)
Malaysia	1.034
	(3.353)
Philippines	0.680
	(5.902)
South Africa	0.704
	(4.789)
Sri Lanka	1.039
	(9.092)
Thailand	0.763
	(1.081)
Yugoslavia	0.819
	(11.295)

a. The numbers in parentheses are t-statistics.

variables were constructed, and estimated domestic credit surprises were incorporated in the regression analysis.[16] The introduction of this measure of unanticipated policies did not affect our results, nor were its estimated coefficients significant. The following equation is an example of this type of regression, where DDCU refers to unexpected growth in domestic credit:

$$\log RER_t = -0.034 \log(GCGDP)_t - 0.023 \log(TOT)_t$$
$$ (-1.726) (-1.157)$$

$$+ 0.450(GROWTH)_t - 0.132 \, DDCRE_t - 0.017 \, DEH_t$$
$$ (4.417) (-3.932) (-2.376)$$

$$+ 0.035 \, DDCU_t + 0.621 \, NOMDEV_t$$
$$ (1.567) (11.189)$$

$$+ 0.907 \log RER_{t-1} (N = 220, \, MSE = 0.053).$$
$$ (38.705)$$

The second procedure for analyzing the role of innovations of nominal and real variables consisted in using quarterly data for a reduced number of countries—those that had long enough series—to estimate (for one country at a time) vector autoregressions (VARs). A limitation of this analysis, however, is that for a number of the important variables, such as GDP, fiscal deficit, and government consumption, there are no quarterly data. The results obtained from these VARs should then be taken as being merely suggestive. The estimated correlation matrix of residuals from the VARs indicates that, in general, the role of innovations does not seem to have played an important role in explaining real exchange rate behavior in these countries.

The Parallel Market Spread

The model derived in chapter 3 also provided a number of insights regarding the determination of the spread in the parallel market. Regressions performed for this group of 12 countries provide some support for the implications of the model. For instance, when an IV procedure was used, the following result was obtained:[17]

$$spread_t = 0.123\,EXCRE_t - 0.121\log E_{t-1} + 0.251\log GCGDP_t$$
$$(1.090)\qquad\quad(-2.933)\qquad\qquad(3.315)$$

$$- 0.198\,GROWTH_t + 0.230\log TOT_t\ (R^2 = 0.741, N = 216).$$
$$(-4.615)\qquad\qquad(3.221)$$

These results indicate that, with other things as given, expansive macropolicies will result in a higher spread, while nominal devaluations will generate a reduction in the spread. These results, then, suggest that the model derived in chapter 3 provides promising leads toward the understanding of parallel market behavior. More definitive analyses, however, should be sought to use monthly, or at most quarterly, data. The reason, of course, is that parallel market spreads are very sensitive to developments in the monetary sector. By using annual data a significant quantity of information is being lost.

5.4 Estimated Equilibrium Real Exchange Rates

The real exchange rate equations reported above can be used to generate *estimated* series of long-run equilibrium real exchange rates. In order to obtain these ERERs we have to consider a long-run situation where the monetary sector is in equilibrium, and only the "fundamentals" influence the ERER. In terms of our equations this means that we impose EXCRE = 0, DEH = 0, and DCRE = 0. Next we compute the estimated long-run coefficients ($\hat{\beta}_i$) for the equilibrium real exchange rate equation as $\hat{\gamma}_i/(1 - \hat{\theta})$, where the $\hat{\gamma}_i$ are the estimated coefficients of the fundamentals in the RER equation (5.4), and where $\hat{\theta}$ is the estimated coefficient of the endogenous speed of adjustment in equation (5.2).

Once the long-run coefficients for the equilibrium real exchange rate equation are computed, we can find the estimate of the long-run equilibrium real exchange rate log $\hat{e}_t^*$. In order to do this, however, we first have to decide what values of the fundamentals actually use in this equation. Here there are several possible ways to proceed. The simplest, and not very satisfactory, solution is to use *actual* values of log TOT, log GCGDP, and so on. A problem with this, however, is that, as discussed in chapter 2, the concept of ERER refers to sustainable values of the fundamentals, rather than to actual values. A second alternative is to choose values for these series of fundamentals arbitrarily, perhaps based on some historical pattern. A third alternative is to use some kind of averaging procedure to smooth the series of the RER fundamentals. In many ways this third procedure is closer to the theoretical concept of ERER.

There are at least two possible ways to "smooth" the series of the fundamentals before using them in the construction of series for ERER. One way consists in using the permanent component of the series obtained from the Beveridge-Nelson decomposition. A second method consists in constructing a moving average of the actual fundamentals. In this section this latter procedure was used; 5 years moving averages were computed in order to construct time series for the "sustainable" values of the ERER fundamentals.

Figure 5.3 contains the evolution of the estimated index of equilibrium real exchange rate for eight countries for the period 1965–1980. In the computation of these indexes we used the estimated coefficients from equation (5.4.3) reported in table 5.1. Naturally, instead of this equation any of the other reported in that table can be used to generate series of equilibrium real exchange rates. The most important characteristic of these indexes of ERERs is that they exhibit nontrivial variations throughout the 15 years. These movements, of course, are a reflection of changing *real structural* conditions in these economies, and do *not* constitute a disequilibrium situation.[18]

It is interesting to notice that in spite of the fact that the estimated ERERs depicted in figure 5.3 move through time, the amplitude of these

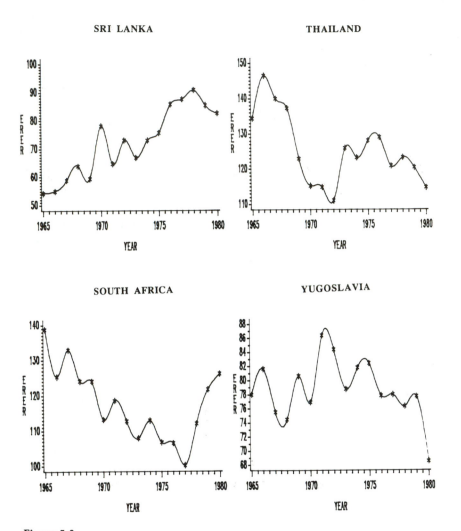

Figure 5.3
Estimated equilibrium real exchange rates for Sri Lanka, Thailand, South Africa,
Yugoslavia, India, Malaysia, Brazil, and the Philippines.

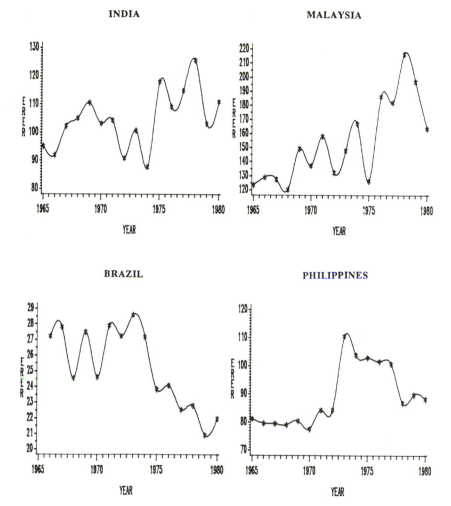

Figure 5.3 (continued)

movements can only explain a small fraction of the observed RER variations for these countries during the years under study. This provides some
preliminary evidence that suggests that, at least for these specific cases, the
dominant force behind observed real exchange rate movements has been
financial and macroeconomic instability, and not structural real changes.

5.5 Summary

In this chapter we have empirically investigated the process of real exchange rate determination in a group of developing countries. In particular,
we have analyzed whether, as our theoretical models suggest, real exchange rate movements have historically responded to both real and nominal disturbances. In order to carry out the analysis, an augmented partial
adjustment equation for real exchange rate dynamics was postulated. This
equation captures in a simple and yet powerful way the most important
features of our theoretical analysis: (1) Discrepancies between actual and
equilibrium real exchange rates will tend to disappear slowly if left on their
own. (2) Nominal devaluations are neutral in the long run, but can be
potentially helpful in speeding up the restoration of real exchange rate
equilibrium. (3) Macroeconomic disequilibria affect the real exchange rate
in the short run. (4) The long-run equilibrium real exchange rate responds
to changes in fundamentals. (5) Temporary and permanent changes in the
fundamentals will affect the equilibrium real exchange rate in different
ways.

   This dynamic equation was estimated using pooled data for a group of
12 countries. The estimation was done using two-stage least squares on a
fixed effect procedure with country- and time-specific fixed terms, and the
results obtained provide support for the broad implications derived from
the models of chapters 2 and 3. In these countries short-run real exchange
rate movements have responded to both nominal and real disturbances. In
particular, expansive and inconsistent macroeconomic policies have inevi-
tably generated forces toward real overvaluation. Moreover, our analysis
suggests that, at least for these countries, macroeconomic instability has
been the major force behind observed real exchange rate fluctuations.

   The estimation also indicates that the autonomous forces that move the
RER back to equilibrium operate fairly slowly, keeping the country out of
equilibrium for a long period of time. Also, these results show that if a
country is indeed in disequilibrium, nominal devaluations can greatly help
to speed up the real exchange rate realignment. If, however, we start from
a situation of equilibrium, a nominal devaluation will be neutral. The esti-

mated coefficients from the real exchange rate equations were used to generate a series of *estimated long-run real exchange rates*. In Edwards (1989e) the estimated series for equilibrium RER were used to construct indexes of real exchange rate misalignment for this group of developing countries. These indexes were then used to test whether there has been any relation between the extent of real exchange rate misalignment and economic performance. It was found that countries with persistent misalignment were systematically outperformed by those countries that manage to maintain their RERs closer to equilibrium.

Appendix

In this appendix ARIMA estimates of the terms of trade, government consumption ratio, capital flows, and parallel market premium for each individual country are reported. These estimates were then used to decompose these time series into permanent and temporary components according to the procedure suggested by Beveridge and Nelson (1981). $Q(x)$ is the Box-Pierce statistic, which is distributed χ^2 with x degrees of freedom. B is the lag operator, and n is the number of observations.

Table 5A

	Estimated process	Estimates	Q, n
A. log TOT			
Greece	ARIMA(2, 1, 0)	$(1 + 0.22217B + 0.2235B^2)(1 - B)X_t = \varepsilon_t$ $\qquad\quad(1.28)\qquad\quad(1.26)$	$Q(9) = 6.4$ $n = 35$
Yugoslavia	ARIMA(3, 1, 0)	$(1 + 0.3901B + 0.2755B^2 + 0.2213B^3)(1 - B)X_t = \varepsilon_t$ $\qquad\quad(2.23)\qquad\ \ (1.50)\qquad\ \ (1.25)$	$Q(8) = 5.6$ $n = 35$
South Africa	ARIMA(2, 1, 0)	$(1 - 0.0925B + 0.1123B^2)(1 - B)X_t = \varepsilon_t$ $\qquad\quad(0.53)\qquad\ \ (0.64)$	$Q(9) = 4.4$ $n = 36$
Brazil	ARIMA(2, 1, 0)	$(1 - 0.2127B + 0.3335B^2)(1 - B)X_t = \varepsilon_t$ $\qquad\quad(0.99)\qquad\ \ (1.55)$	$Q(9) = 7.5$ $n = 23$
Colombia	ARIMA(3, 1, 0)	$(1 - 0.0658B + 0.3074B^2 - 0.3002B^3)(1 - B)X_t = \varepsilon_t$ $\qquad\quad(0.35)\qquad\ \ (1.69)\qquad\ \ (1.57)$	$Q(8) = 11.3$ $n = 29$
El Salvador	ARIMA(3, 1, 0)	$(1 - 0.0739B + 0.1462B^2 - 0.1108B^3)(1 - B)X_t = \varepsilon_t$ $\qquad\quad(0.38)\qquad\ \ (0.76)\qquad\ \ (0.56)$	$Q(8) = 4.5$ $n = 31$
Israel	ARIMA(3, 1, 0)	$(1 + 0.2951B + 0.2956B^2 + 0.3365B^3)(1 - B)X_t = \varepsilon_t$ $\qquad\quad(0.16)\qquad\ \ (1.70)\qquad\ \ (1.83)$	$Q(8) = 3.2$ $n = 31$
Sri Lanka	ARIMA(3, 1, 0)	$(1 - 0.2059B + 0.3446B^2 + 0.1853B^3)(1 - B)X_t = \varepsilon_t$ $\qquad\quad(1.18)\qquad\ \ (2.0)\qquad\ \ (1.02)$	$Q(8) = 3.5$ $n = 36$
India	ARIMA(3, 1, 0)	$(1 - 0.0453B + 0.4629B^2 + 0.2925B^3)(1 - B)X_t = \varepsilon_t$ $\qquad\quad(0.24)\qquad\ \ (2.63)\qquad\ \ (1.48)$	$Q(8) = 2.7$ $n = 31$
Malaysia	ARIMA(2, 1, 0)	$(1 + 0.0296B + 0.4156B^2)(1 - B)X_t = \varepsilon_t$ $\qquad\quad(0.16)\qquad\ \ (2.30)$	$Q(9) = 5.4$ $n = 29$
Philippines	ARIMA(2, 1, 0)	$(1 + 0.2065B + 0.4196B^2)(1 - B)X_t = \varepsilon_t$ $\qquad\quad(1.32)\qquad\ \ (2.65)$	$Q(9) = 9.4$ $n = 37$
Thailand	ARIMA(2, 1, 0)	$(1 - 0.1926B + 0.5282B^2)(1 - B)X_t = \varepsilon_t$ $\qquad\quad(1.21)\qquad\ \ (3.33)$	$Q(9) = 9.3$ $n = 32$

B. Capital Inflows over GDP

Country	Model	Equation	Statistics
Greece	ARMA(1, 1)	$(1 + 0.3025B)X_t = (1 + 0.6416B)\varepsilon_t$ (0.56) (1.50)	$Q(9) = 5.22$ $n = 23$
Yugoslavia	ARMA(1, 1)	$(1 + 0.5369B)X_t = (1 + 0.9910B)\varepsilon_t$ (2.46) (14.14)	$Q(9) = 3.61$ $n = 22$
South Africa	AR(3)	$(1 - 0.3972B + 0.3450B^2 + 0.1803B^3)X_t = \varepsilon_t$ (1.76) (1.48) (0.78)	$Q(8) = 6.26$ $n = 23$
Brazil	AR(1)	$(1 - 0.5185B)X_t = \varepsilon_t$ (2.61)	$Q(10) = 16.42$ $n = 22$
Colombia	AR(1)	$(1 - 0.4972B)X_t = \varepsilon_t$ (2.63)	$Q(10) = 7.80$ $n = 23$
El Salvador	AR(2)	$(1 + 0.2310B + 0.6486B^2)X_t = \varepsilon_t$ (1.24) (3.46)	$Q(9) = 7.21$ $n = 22$
Israel	AR(2)	$(1 - 0.4112B + 0.6572B^2)X_t = \varepsilon_t$ (2.42) (3.84)	$Q(9) = 5.46$ $n = 23$
Sri Lanka	AR(1)	$(1 - 0.4432B)X_t = \varepsilon_t$ (2.13)	$Q(10) = 7.85$ $n = 23$
India	AR(1)	$(1 - 0.7587B)X_t = \varepsilon_t$ (5.12)	$Q(10) = 11.20$ $n = 22$
Malaysia	AR(1)	$(1 - 0.4426B)X_t = \varepsilon_t$ (2.26)	$Q(10) = 11.29$ $n = 23$
Philippines	ARMA(1, 1)	$(1 - 0.3711B)X_t = (1 + 0.5388B)\varepsilon_t$ (1.35) (2.16)	$Q(9) = 10.35$ $n = 23$
Thailand	AR(3)	$(1 - 0.4357B + 0.6272B^2 + 0.5561B^3)X_t = \varepsilon_t$ (2.16) (2.92) (2.40)	$Q(8) = 7.51$ $n = 23$

Table 5A (continued)

	Estimated process	Estimates	Q, n
C. log GCGDP			
Greece	ARIMA(1, 1, 0)	$(1 + 0.1861B)(1 - B)X_t = \varepsilon_t$ (1.12)	$Q(10) = 6.02$ $n = 37$
Yugoslavia	AR(3)	$(1 - 0.6941B + 0.3796B^2 + 0.1069B^3)X_t = \varepsilon_t$ (2.99)　(1.44)　(0.45)	$Q(8) = 2.91$ $n = 24$
South Africa	ARIMA(3, 1, 0)	$(1 + 0.0174B + 0.2557B^2 + 0.3679B^3)(1 - B)X_t = \varepsilon_t$ (0.11)　(1.63)　(2.25)	$Q(8) = 4.63$ $n = 37$
Brazil	ARIMA(3, 1, 0)	$(1 + 0.0586B - 0.3251B^2 - 0.0574B^3)(1 - B)X_t = \varepsilon_t$ (0.25)　(1.40)　(0.23)	$Q(8) = 1.47$ $n = 22$
Colombia	ARIMA(3, 1, 0)	$(1 - 0.2477B + 0.1454B^2 + 0.1247B^3)(1 - B)X_t = \varepsilon_t$ (1.36)　(0.78)　(0.68)	$Q(8) = 22.82$ $n = 34$
El Salvador	ARIMA(3, 1, 0)	$(1 + 0.0151B - 0.0683B^2 + 0.0683B^3)(1 - B)X_t = \varepsilon_t$ (0.08)　(0.36)　(0.35)	$Q(8) = 8.17$ $n = 34$
Israel	ARIMA(1, 1, 0)	$(1 + 0.2141B)(1 - B)X_t = \varepsilon_t$ (0.79)	$Q(4) = 1.91$ $n = 15$
Sri Lanka	ARIMA(1, 1, 0)	$(1 + 0.2382B)(1 - B)X_t = \varepsilon_t$ (1.38)	$Q(10) = 8.34$ $n = 34$
India	ARIMA(3, 1, 0)	$(1 + 0.2426B + 0.3364B^2 - 0.2291B^3)(1 - B)X_t = \varepsilon_t$ (1.29)　(0.85)　(0.12)	$Q(8) = 6.27$ $n = 33$
Malaysia	AR(1)	$(1 - 0.6057B)X_t = \varepsilon_t$ (4.02)	$Q(10) = 7.86$ $n = 31$
Philippines	ARIMA(1, 1, 0)	$(1 + 0.5153B)(1 - B)X_t = \varepsilon_t$ (3.50)	$Q(10) = 6.65$ $n = 36$
Thailand	ARIMA(3, 1, 0)	$(1 - 0.0581B + 0.2084B^2 + 0.0918B^3)(1 - B)X_t = \varepsilon_t$ (0.32)　(1.19)　(0.51)	$Q(8) = 12.53$ $n = 35$

D. Parallel Market Spread

Greece	ARIMA(1, 1, 0)	$(1 - 0.2593B)(1 - B)X_t = \varepsilon_t$ $\quad\quad(1.13)$	$Q(10) = 8.08$ $n = 21$
Yugoslavia	AR(1)	$(1 - 0.8776B)X_t = \varepsilon_t$ $\quad\quad(5.21)$	$Q(10) = 11.74$ $n = 14$
South Africa	ARIMA(2, 1, 0)	$(1 + 0.2411B + 0.2940B^2)(1 - B)X_t = \varepsilon_t$ $\quad\quad(1.07)\quad\quad(1.30)$	$Q(9) = 8.33$ $n = 21$
Brazil	ARIMA(1, 1, 0)	$(1 + 0.414B)(1 - B)X_t = \varepsilon_t$ $\quad\quad(1.91)$	$Q(10) = 4.03$ $n = 20$
Colombia	ARIMA(2, 1, 0)	$(1 + 0.4493B + 0.3196B^2)(1 - B)X_t = \varepsilon_t$ $\quad\quad(1.96)\quad\quad(1.40)$	$Q(9) = 5.68$ $n = 21$
El Salvador	ARIMA(2, 1, 0)	$(1 - 0.2336B + 0.3193B^2)(1 - B)X_t = \varepsilon_t$ $\quad\quad(0.98)\quad\quad(1.31)$	$Q(8) = 6.68$ $n = 21$
Israel	AR(3)	$(1 - 0.8401B + 0.0149B^2 + 0.2596B^3)X_t = \varepsilon_t$ $\quad\quad(3.68)\quad\quad(0.15)\quad\quad(1.13)$	$Q(8) = 7.87$ $n = 22$
Sri Lanka	ARIMA(2, 1, 0)	$(1 - 0.0961B + 0.3987B^2)(1 - B)X_t = \varepsilon_t$ $\quad\quad(0.44)\quad\quad(1.83)$	$Q(8) = 9.71$ $n = 21$
India	ARIMA(2, 1, 0)	$(1 - 0.5129B + 0.7251B^2)(1 - B)X_t = \varepsilon_t$ $\quad\quad(3.01)\quad\quad(4.17)$	$Q(9) = 4.81$ $n = 21$
Malaysia	AR(2)	$(1 - 0.4167B - 0.2629B^2)X_t = \varepsilon_t$ $\quad\quad(1.88)\quad\quad(1.16)$	$Q(9) = 12.27$ $n = 22$
Philippines	AR(1)	$(1 - 0.4907B)X_t = \varepsilon_t$ $\quad\quad(1.94)$	$Q(10) = 3.49$ $n = 22$
Thailand	AR(1)	$(1 - 0.2779B)X_t = \varepsilon_t$ $\quad\quad(1.29)$	$Q(10) = 12.80$ $n = 22$

Notes

1. This regression was run using OLS. The devaluation dummy takes a value of 1 for June 1979 and March 1982 and zero otherwise. For further details see Edwards and Cox-Edwards (1987).

2. The length of the series varies from country to country depending on data availability. The earliest year is 1962 and the latest 1985. Given the lack of appropriate series for all the important variables, a number of compromises had to be made during the estimation process. However, in spite of these shortcomings, the results are highly revealing, providing broad empirical support to the theoretical analysis of part I of this book.

3. Notice that, theoretically, a devaluation that accompanies a trade liberalization with no macroeconomic disequilibrium is still undertaken from a situation of misalignment. When the level of trade restrictions is reduced, the old RER will (under most cases) be below its new equilibrium level and, thus, *overvalued*.

4. It should be stated at the outset that the empirical analysis reported here does not attempt to provide *direct* tests of the theories developed in chapters 2 and 3, in the sense of testing a precise equation derived from those models. What this analysis does, however, is to use a dynamic equation for the real exchange rate to test the more salient *implications* of those theories. Since all economic models are extremely simplified representations of reality, strict testing of any model will always lead, if well done, to rejection of the theory.

5. The investment ratio term (INVGDP) has been included in order to capture the role of capital accumulation. Remember that most of the analysis in chapters 2 and 3 proceeded under the assumption of no investment (see, however, the last part of section 2.3).

6. The data on import tariff revenues were obtained from the IMF *Yearbook of Government Finances*.

7. The results obtained from this analysis were less precise than those for the whole group. The main conclusions, however, were not altered in a significant way. Test statistics (χ^2) used to test the appropriateness of pooling the two groups suggested that such a procedure was not always fully warranted. For this reason, in a number of runs some of the parameters were allowed to differ across countries (see below).

8. In a first run both country- and time-specific dummies were included. Tests for the significance of each group were then performed. The time-specific variables were never significant, and, thus were dropeed in the final estimation. When a random effect technique was used (the Fuller-Battesse procedure), the results obtained were not significantly different from those reported below. On deciding whether to use a fixed or a random effect methodology for estimating pooled models see Judge et al. (1980).

9. In the IV estimation, choosing the instruments is not trivial. The reason, of course, is that equation (5.4) includes a lagged dependent variable. As a consequence, lagged endogenous variables are not adequate instruments. A serious, and well known, problem is that by ruling out lagged dependent variables, we are left with instruments that are only poorly correlated with the endogenous variables. In the results reported here, different sets of instruments were used. In a few regressions lagged dependent variables were also included. Most of the regressions, however, used the following instru-ments: $EXCRE_t$, $EXCRE_{t-1}$, $EXCRE_{t-2}$; time-specific country dummies; $\log TOT$, $\log TOT_{t-1}$, $\log TOT_{t-2}$, $\log TOT_{t-3}$; $DCRE$, $DCRE_{t-1}$, $DCRE_{t-2}$ lagged, twice lagged, and thrice lagged real exchange rates; lagged, twice lagged, and thrice lagged domestic credit innovations; DEH, DEH_{t-1}; $NOMDEV$, $NOMDEV_{t-1}$, $\log GCGDP_t$, $\log GCGDP_{t-1}$, $\log GCGDP_{t-2}$; nominal exchange rate, lagged, twice lagged, and thrice lagged nominal exchange rates; country-specific dummy variables; money surprises (as defined in chapter 8); investment ratio; and output growth.

10. The issue of stationarity of the real exchange rate series also has to be addressed before estimating equation (5.4). As shown in chapter 4, due to the little power that the currently available tests have, the evidence regarding this issue is not completely clear.

11. This is obtained using a coefficient of NOMDEV of 0.634, corresponding to equation (5.4.3). This result assumes that there have been no changes in fundamentals.

12. Obviously, a relatively high value of lagged RER brings up the issue of possible nonstationarity of the real exchange rate. Our discussion of chapter 4, however, indicates that it is not possible to determine accurately, in a meaningful enough way, whether these series are stationary and mean revert slowly or are nonstationary. In the analysis of that chapter, however, we came to the conclusion that for the majority of the sample countries there is evidence that makes us comfortable in rejecting the unit-root hypothesis. For nonstationary series, as seems to be the case of RERs in the developed countries, the implications of our theory can be tested using *cointegration* analysis (see Kaminsky, 1987). Frequency domain techniques can also be used to analyze any differences between short- and long-run effects of different disturbances (Huizinga, 1986).

13. On easier ways to implement this method see Cuddington and Winters (1987) and Miller (1988).

14. Naturally, this is by no means a definitive and direct test of the importance of intertemporal substitution in consumption. One possible way of performing such a test is by directly testing the restrictions embodied in the first-order conditions of the theoretical intertemporal model. This approach has recently been persued by, among others, Eckstein and Leiderman (1988) within the context of intertemporal models of consumption and money.

15. These coefficients were obtained from the estimation of a RER equation that included terms of trade (permanent and transitory), $\log GCGDP$ (permanent and

transitory), technological progress, capital flows (permanent and transitory), DCRE, a lagged dependent variable, and country-specific dummies. The estimation did not include El Salvador since the (official) nominal exchange rate did not change in that country during the period under study.

16. These series were computed by first estimating domestic credit and money supply equations. The monetary surprises were computed as the innovations from these equations. The domestic credit and money equations were constructed with lagged, twice lagged, and thrice lagged dependent variables *plus* a fiscal deficit measure. On this procedure see, for example, Edwards (1986a).

17. For a list of the instruments used see note 9.

18. It is important to notice that although these estimated series provide important information regarding the behavior of equilibrium real exchange rates, they have a somewhat limited use in directly computing RER misalignments. The problem, of course, is that we have to "anchor" the actual RER at some point in the past. Only if we are willing to assume that the actual and equilibrium rates were equal some X years back can we talk about RER misalignment.

III

**Devaluations, Real
Exchange Rate
Realignment, and
Adjustment**

6

Real Exchange Rates, Exchange Controls, and Devaluation Crises

In this and the following two chapters we analyze empirically the effectiveness of nominal devaluations as policy measures, and in particular their ability to affect real exchange rates. In an effort to understand the economics surrounding the causes and consequences of devaluations, 39 devaluation episodes that took place between 1962 and 1982 are investigated in detail. The discussion also focuses on (1) the relation between (inconsistent) macroeconomic policies and exchange rate crises, (2) the relation between the devaluation episodes and the external environment as summarized by terms of trade behavior, (3) the role of real exchange rate "overvaluation" in the precipitation of balance of payment crises under predetermined nominal exchange rates, (4) the role of exchange controls, multiple exchange rates, and black markets in the period preceding devaluations, and (5) the balance of payments and output effects of devaluations. This chapter deals with points (1)–(4), which refer mainly to the causes of devaluation crises; chapter 7 analyzes the period immediately following the balance of payments crises, emphasizing the real exchange rate effects of the devaluation; and chapter 8 concentrates on the real output and income distribution ramifications of devaluations.

The approach followed in these three chapters is predominantly empirical; however, it is rooted in the theoretical framework provided in part I of this book that is captured by the macroeconomic model of chapter 3. We have followed an empirical approach that combines nonparametric tests with more traditional regression analysis. An important aspect of this study consists in analyzing in detail the evolution of a number of key variables during the three years preceding and the three years following the 39 devaluation episodes. In doing this, an effort is made to detect regularities across countries that allow us to infer some general rules related to the causes and effects of devaluations. At the same time care is taken to point out peculiarities that help us to understand better the exchange rate history of a particular country. A *control group* consisting of 24 developing nations that maintained a fixed nominal exchange rate for at least 10 years was constructed and its behavior compared with that of the devaluing countries, using a battery of nonparametric tests.[1]

Although the episodic strategy for empirical inquiry used in this part of the book departs from the current practice of using almost exclusively different regression techniques, it has modern precedents in Cooper's (1971a) well known article on devaluation and, more recently, in Harberger and Edwards's (1982) study on balance of payments crises.[2] The episodic approach adopted in this part of the book has both advantages and drawbacks. On the positive side it allows us to look at individual cases, thereby detecting peculiarities and regularities. It also permits us to deal with issues that are very difficult to quantify accurately and, thus, include in any type of regression analysis, such as the evolution of exchange controls and quantitative restrictions. On the other hand, a well known drawback of this empirical strategy is that by focusing on "before" and "after," it is not always easy to detect causality among variables. For this reason, and in order to shed additional light on the problem at hand, the episodic approach is supplemented with some more traditional statistical procedures, including regressions.

6.1 Macroeconomic Policies and Devaluation

Table 6.1 contains the list of the 39 devaluation episodes considered in this part of the book. All of these countries devalued their currencies by at least 15% after having maintained a fixed (official) exchange rate with respect to the U.S. dollar for 2 or more years. Twenty-nine of them implemented a stepwise devaluation, where after the nominal exchange rate adjustment they attempted once again to fix the parity (part A of table 6.1).[3] Many of them did not succeed and experienced recurrent devaluations. Ten of the countries adopted a crawling exchange rate after devaluing (part B). This table also contains data on the amount of each nominal devaluation measured as the percentage change of the *official* exchange rate with respect to the U.S. dollar. Later in the chapter, however, we look in detail at the behavior of the parallel market exchange rate and at the multilateral real exchange rate. A number of these devaluations were taken in conjunction with adjustment programs sponsored by the IMF. In appendix A to this chapter a list of IMF programs in these countries is provided.

Under fixed nominal exchange rates, macroeconomic policies determine

Table 6.1
Devaluation crises in selected developing countries: rate of devaluation (percentage)[a]

Country	Year of devaluation crisis	Percentage of devaluation			
		Year of devaluation	1 year after devaluation	2 years after	3 years after
A. Stepwise Devaluations					
Argentina	1970	25.0	0.0	0.0	0.0
Bolivia	1972	66.6	0.0	0.0	0.0
Bolivia	1979	25.0	0.0	0.0	684.0
Colombia	1962	34.3	0.0	0.0	50.0
Colombia	1965	50.0	0.0	16.7	7.1
Costa Rica	1974	28.8	0.0	0.0	0.0
Cyprus	1967	16.6	0.0	0.0	0.0
Ecuador	1961	20.0	0.0	0.0	0.0
Ecuador	1970	38.8	0.0	0.0	0.0
Egypt	1962	23.9	0.0	0.0	0.0
Egypt	1979	78.8	0.0	0.0	0.0
Guyana	1967	15.9	0.9	0.6	0.2
India	1966	58.6	−0.3	1.0	−0.9
Indonesia	1978	50.6	0.3	0.0	2.7
Israel	1962	66.6	0.0	0.0	0.0
Israel	1967	16.6	0.0	0.0	0.0
Israel	1971	20.0	0.0	0.0	7.1
Jamaica	1967	15.9	0.9	−0.6	0.2
Jamaica	1978	86.4	5.1	0.0	0.0
Malta	1967	16.6	0.0	0.0	0.0
Nicaragua	1979	43.0	0.0	0.0	0.0
Pakistan	1972	130.1	−10.2	0.0	0.0
Peru	1967	44.4	0.0	0.0	0.0
Philippines	1962	94.0	0.2	0.0	0.0
Philippines	1970	63.7	0.0	5.3	−0.7
Sri Lanka	1967	24.1	0.0	0.5	0.0
Trinidad	1967	15.9	0.9	−0.6	0.2
Venezuela	1964	38.1	0.0	0.0	0.0
Yugoslavia	1965	66.6	0.0	0.0	0.0
B. Devaluations Followed by Crawling Peg					
Bolivia	1982	684.0	155.1	1,700.0	—
Chile	1982	88.2	19.2	46.5	43.3

Table 6.1 (continued)

| | | Percentage of devaluation | | | |
Country	Year of devaluation crisis	Year of devaluation	1 year after devaluation	2 years after	3 years after
Colombia	1967	16.7	7.1	5.7	6.9
Ecuador	1982	32.6	63.1	24.1	42.5
Kenya	1981	35.9	23.7	8.4	14.3
Korea	1980	36.3	6.1	6.9	6.2
Mexico	1976	59.6	13.9	−0.0	0.3
Mexico	1982	267.8	49.1	33.7	93.0
Pakistan	1982	29.6	5.1	13.7	4.0
Peru	1975	16.2	54.2	87.9	50.4

Source: International Financial Statistics.
a. Devaluation of the official rate with respect to the U.S. dollar. In the case of multiple rates the *IFS* reports the "most common" of them. Table 6.10 contains data on the evolution of the number of official rates as well as on the parallel market premiums.

whether the exchange rate chosen by the authorities can be sustained in the longer run. As the model of chapter 3 indicates and the results in chapter 5 showed, under most circumstances, if macroeconomic policies become "inconsistent," international reserves will be eroded, the real exchange rate will experience an appreciation (i.e., it will become overvalued), and an exchange rate crises, including a devaluation, will eventually occur. From an empirical point of view it is not trivial to determine whether, for a particular country at a particular time, macroeconomic policies have indeed become inconsistent with the fixed peg. In this section we tackle this issue by comparing the evolution of macroeconomic policy in the devaluing countries with that of the control group of fixed exchange rate countries.[4]

Table 6.2 summarizes the behavior of five indicators of domestic credit and fiscal policies for the devaluing countries and for the control group: (1) rate of growth of domestic credit (part A), (2) rate of growth of domestic credit to the public sector (part B), (3) percentage of credit received by the public sector as proportion of total domestic credit (part C), (4) fiscal deficit as proportion of GDP (part D), and (5) growth of domestic credit to the public sector as a proportion of GNP (part E). All these indicators have been constructed using data from various issues of the *International Financial Statistics* as well as several *IFS* tapes.[5] For the devaluing countries these indicators are reported for 3 years, 2 years, and 1 year prior to the devalu-

Table 6.2
Indicators of macroeconomic policy in devaluing countries during year of devaluation and 3 years preceding devaluation: comparison with control group of fixers

	3 years prior to devaluation	2 years prior to devaluation	1 year prior to devaluation	Year of devaluation	Control group
A. Annual Rate of Growth of Domestic Credit (Percentage)					
First quartile	10.7	11.6	11.9	13.1	14.4
Median	20.3	17.5	17.7	21.9	17.4
Third quartile	34.9	31.9	29.7	38.3	29.9
Mean	21.7	21.3	20.5	26.8	19.3
B. Annual Rate of Growth of Domestic Credit to Public Sector (Percentage)					
First quartile	4.8	<0	0	10.9	<0
Median	19.9	16.5	18.5	29.7	22.7
Third quartile	57.9	51.0	48.9	63.6	33.2
Mean	38.0	25.4	29.3	53.2	5.7
C. Ratio of Domestic Credit to Public Sector to Total Domestic Credit (Ratio × 100)					
First quartile	9.7	10.7	8.8	7.7	<0
Median	25.4	21.1	24.5	24.9	11.4
Third quartile	39.8	44.1	45.9	48.2	27.9
Mean	25.4	24.8	24.8	25.3	14.0
D. Fiscal Deficit as Percentage of GDP (Percentage)					
First quartile	0.44	0.26	0.01	0.01	0.7
Median	2.01	1.53	2.40	4.14	1.6
Third quartile	5.57	5.35	5.01	6.45	2.7
Mean	2.8	3.1	2.8	4.4	1.9
E. Growth of Credit to Public Sector as Proportion of GDP (Percentage)					
First quartile	0.17	−0.22	−0.51	0.02	0.03
Median	0.95	0.78	0.73	1.6	0.76
Third quartile	1.9	2.2	2.4	3.4	1.6
Mean	1.8	1.2	1.9	2.6	.75

Source: See text.

ation as well as for the year of the devaluation. While part A deals with monetary (or domestic credit) policy, the rest of the parts take us beyond the monetary realm and into the fiscal side of the economy. Indeed, these parts provide four different ways of looking at fiscal pressures.

A number of revealing facts emerge from this table. First, macroeconomic policies became increasingly expansive in the devaluing countries as the year of the devaluation drew nearer. Indeed, when we compare 3 years before the crises with 1 year prior to them, we can detect some shift to the right of all five distributions, with the extent of these shifts varying across indicators. Second, the devaluing countries as a group behaved quite differently from the control group. This is particularly clear for the fiscal policy indicators. For example, in the year prior to the crisis half of the devaluing countries allocated one-quarter or more of total domestic credit to the public sector; the median for the control group countries, on the other hand, was only slightly over 10%. Formal χ^2 tests indicate that the probability of these policy indicators for the devaluing countries coming from the same population than that of the control group is very low. For 2 years prior to the devaluation the value of these $\chi^2(2)$ were 7.0 (level of probability 0.02) for the rate of growth of domestic credit, 1.3 (level of probability 0.5) for the rate of growth of domestic credit to the public sector, 6.9 (level of probability 0.04) for the fraction of total credit that goes to the public sector, and 5.4 for the ratio of the fiscal deficit to GDP (level of probability 0.05). Moreover, these χ^2 tests suggest quite clearly that as the crisis date approached, the devaluing countries' macropolicies tended to become more and more inconsistent with the goal of maintaining a fixed exchange rate. For instance, in the year of the devaluation the $\chi^2(2)$ statistic was 13.5 for the growth of domestic credit (level of probability 0.001), 4.8 for the rate of growth of domestic credit to the public sector (level of probability 0.1), 8.4 for the ratio of public sector credit to total credit (level of probability 0.015), and 16.9 for the fiscal deficit ratio (level of probability 0.001). Table 6.3 contains a summary of the χ^2-statistics used to test the null hypothesis that devaluers and the control group come from the same population.

Although not all devaluing countries behaved differently from the control group—Venezuela, Israel in 1962, and the Commonwealth nations being the main exceptions—the nonparametric tests reported here provide broad and strong support to the hypothesis that in the period preceding the crisis, the devaluing countries' macroeconomic policies were significantly more expansive than those of the control group of countries that

Table 6.3
χ^2 tests comparing devaluing countries with control group of fixers[a]

	3 years before devaluation	Year of devaluation
Growth of domestic credit	9.0 (0.011)	13.5 (0.001)
Growth of domestic credit to public sector	4.6 (0.100)	4.8 (0.09)
Ratio of domestic credit to public sector to total domestic credit	8.4 (0.015)	8.4 (0.015)
Ratio of fiscal deficit to GNP	1.3 (0.533)	16.9 (0.000)
Growth of credit to public sector as proportion of GDP	7.3 (0.026)	13.8 (0.001)

a. This test is distributed χ^2 with 2 degrees of freedom. The numbers in parentheses are the levels of probability. These χ^2-statistics are computed as $\sum (O - E)^2/E$, where O is the observed count and E is the expected count. These χ^2 were estimated using the ProcFreq procedure of the SAS computer package.

successfully maintained a pegged nominal exchange rate for a long period of time.

An important question is whether these devaluation episodes and related balance of payments crises have been, at least partially, caused by exogenous deteriorations of the external environment. Table 6.4 contains information on the evolution of the external terms of trade for those countries that have data. Although this table shows a variety of individual country experiences, it indicates that for the stepwise devaluers as a group (part A) there was no significant worsening of the terms of trade in the period immediately preceding the crisis. However, the situation is very different for the group of crawling countries. As can be seen, these countries as a group were subject to massive negative terms of trade shocks; in some cases the deterioration of the terms of trade exceeded 30% in 3 years. It is interesting to note that the cases of large negative terms of trade shocks correspond predominantly to more recent devaluations episodes. Even though the information in this table clearly suggests that terms of trade deterioration have not been the overwhelming cause of these crises, in a number of cases the crisis may have had its origins in exogenous deterioration of the external environment. It should be noticed that in some episodes, in addition to these negative shocks, and sometimes even in response to them, these countries pursued inconsistent macroeconomic policies.[6]

Table 6.4
Terms of trade in period preceding devaluation crises

Country	Year of devaluation crisis	3 years prior to devaluation	1 year prior to devaluation	Year of crisis
A. Stepwise Devaluation				
Colombia	1962	100.0	100.9	94.8
Colombia	1965	100.0	109.3	111.4
India	1966	100.0	99.6	103.2
Indonesia	1978	100.0	117.6	119.1
Israel	1962	100.0	100.9	103.0
Israel	1967	100.0	106.1	104.0
Israel	1971	100.0	97.2	99.2
Malta	1967	100.0[a]	100.1	90.6
Nicaragua	1979	100.0	104.9	100.7
Pakistan	1972	100.0[a]	86.9	95.9
Philippines	1962	100.0	87.3	86.8
Philippines	1970	100.0	95.9	93.9
Sri Lanka	1967	100.0	102.3	95.5
Trinidad	1967	100.0[a]	100.1	103.9
Yugoslavia	1965	100.0	100.9	100.7
Average		100.0	100.7	100.2
B. Devaluation Followed by Crawling Peg				
Chile	1982	100.0	77.4	69.8
Colombia	1967	100.0	80.9	95.2
Kenya	1981	100.0	84.5	72.4
Korea	1980	100.0	102.6	88.9
Pakistan	1982	100.0	77.3	75.0
Average		100.0	84.5	80.3

Source: International Financial Statistics.
a. This number refers to 2, rather than to 3, years prior to the devaluation.

6.2 Real Exchange Rates, the External Sector, and Devaluations

According to the model in chapter 3, inconsistent macroeconomic policies will result in (a) real exchange rate appreciations (i.e., overvaluations), (b) current account deficits, and (c) losses of international reserves. Table 6.5 contains data for the 39 episodes on the evolution of: (1) the index of the bilateral real exchange rate with respect to the U.S. dollar and (2) the index of multilateral real exchange rates. Table 6.6, on the other hand, contains data on the ratio of net foreign assets of the monetary system to money, and the ratio of the current account over GDP during the 3 years preceding the crises. The main differences between table 6.2 and tables 6.5 and 6.6 is that in the former we have summarized the behavior of five key *exogenous* policy variables, while tables 6.5 and 6.6 deal with *endogenous* variables whose behavior responds to policy measures and other shocks.

Table 6.5 shows that in 29 out of the 38 countries with relevant data, the bilateral real exchange rate experienced a real appreciation in the 3 years prior to the devaluation; in 24 out of the 38 cases there also was a real appreciation of the multilateral RER during the period immediately preceding the crisis. For those countries experiencing an appreciation, the average decline in the real bilateral exchange rate during the 3 years preceding the devaluation crisis was almost 9.1%, while the real multilateral appreciation was 11.1%. Notice that the extent of real exchange rate appreciation before the crisis not only varied across countries but also was more marked in recent years. This has been particularly the case for the countries that after the devaluation became crawlers; starting with the mid-1970s devaluing countries experienced real appreciations of almost 17%.[7]

Naturally, these real appreciations were the result of domestic rates of inflation that increasingly exceeded the world rate of inflation. A set of χ^2 tests, in fact, indicates that as the crisis date became closer, the rate of CPI inflation in the devaluing countries became more distinct from that of the fixed exchange rate control group. While the $\chi^2(2)$ was 3.1 3 years prior to the crisis (level of probability 0.21), it was 15.2 1 year before the crisis, reflecting a probability of less than 0.001% of the null hypothesis being accepted.

The behavior of RERs shows some important differences across countries. While some of them, such as Colombia in 1965, Peru in 1967, Mexico in 1982, Chile in 1982, and Yugoslavia in 1965, went through major dete-

Table 6.5
Evolution of real exchange rate indexes during 3 years prior to devaluation
(index = 100 in year prior to devaluation)

Country	Year	Bilateral real exchange rate		Multilateral real exchange rate	
		3 years before devaluation	1 year before devaluation	3 years before devaluation	1 year before devaluation
Argentina	1970	102.8	100	100.4	100
Bolivia	1972	97.8	100	98.7	100
Bolivia	1979	103.2	100	100.1	100
Colombia	1962	108.1	100	105.7	100
Colombia	1965	155.7	100	123.8	100
Costa Rica	1974	101.6	100	93.9	100
Cyprus	1967	95.8	100	97.2	100
Ecuador	1961	101.5	100	102.7	100
Ecuador	1970	104.3	100	103.9	100
Egypt	1962	101.3	100	98.1	100
Egypt	1979	109.4	100	96.4	100
Guyana	1967	99.7	100	100.1	100
India	1966	121.2	100	119.7	100
Indonesia	1978	120.5	100	105.9	100
Israel	1962	105.9	100	108.4	100
Israel	1967	107.0	100	112.0	100
Israel	1971	102.5	100	104.8	100
Jamaica	1967	99.7	100	100.0	100
Jamaica	1978	110.6	100	107.4	100
Malta	1967	97.2	100	99.6	100
Nicaragua	1979	101.9	100	95.3	100
Pakistan	1972	105.1	100	97.9	100
Peru	1967	119.5	100	115.7	100
Philippines	1962	106.6	100	103.6	100
Philippines	1970	97.9	100	98.2	100
Sri Lanka	1967	95.2	100	92.2	100
Trinidad	1967	100.7	100	100.8	100
Venezuela	1964	100.5	100	98.0	100
Yugoslavia	1965	117.7	100	120.5	100
Bolivia	1982	129.9	100	144.8	100
Chile	1982	129.9	100	140.6	100
Colombia[a]	1967	(78.7)	100	(83.1)	100

Table 6.5 (continued)

Country	Year	Bilateral real exchange rate		Multilateral real exchange rate	
		3 years before devaluation	1 year before devaluation	3 years before devaluation	1 year before devaluation
Ecuador	1982	105.6	100	115.3	100
Kenya	1981	93.5	100	93.1	100
Korea	1980	111.6	100	112.9	100
Mexico	1976	109.2	100	108.6	100
Mexico	1982	112.9	100	128.2	100
Pakistan	1982	100.6	100	115.2	100
Peru	1975	95.3	100	91.5	100

Source: real exchange rates indexes constructed as described in chapter 4.
a. Colombia devalued in 1965. This explains the evolution of the RER index before 1967.

Table 6.6
Evolution of net foreign assets and current account in period preceding devaluation

Country	Year	Ratio of net foreign assets[a]		(Current account/GDP)	
		3 years before devaluation	1 year before devaluation	3 years before devaluation	1 year before devaluation
Argentina	1970	7.3	6.3	0.006	−0.010
Bolivia	1972	12.0	8.6	−0.056	−0.044
Bolivia	1979	26.0	2.9	−0.039	−0.099
Colombia	1962	1.2	−1.8	0.016	−0.030
Colombia	1965	−10.7	−11.6	−0.022	−0.030
Costa Rica	1974	12.8	16.7	−0.119	−0.091
Cyprus	1967	49.8	55.0	−0.134	−0.072
Ecuador	1961	18.9	16.4	−0.009	−0.025
Ecuador	1970	19.1	11.2	−0.057	−0.079
Egypt	1962	12.0	4.1	−0.000	−0.011
Egypt	1979	−27.5	−36.6	−0.092	−0.044
Guyana	1967	62.6	33.0	−0.063	−0.142
India	1966	2.3	1.2	−0.025	−0.029
Indonesia	1978	−13.6	12.1	−0.039	−0.001
Israel	1962	20.7	30.6	−0.180	−0.179
Israel	1967	42.3	34.3	−0.236	−0.145
Israel	1971	29.4	3.5	−0.195	−0.259

Table 6.6 (continued)

Country	Year	Ratio of net[a] foreign assets		(Current account/GDP)	
		3 years before devaluation	1 year before devaluation	3 years before devaluation	1 year before devaluation
Jamaica	1967	16.8	25.5	−0.100	−0.147
Jamaica	1978	−1.1	−22.3	−0.095	−0.049
Malta	1967	83.3	83.0	−0.247	−0.182
Nicaragua	1979	16.8	−35.5	−0.028	−0.009
Pakistan	1972	7.5	3.9	−0.028	−0.029
Peru	1967	23.9	17.9	0.003	−0.036
Philippines	1962	9.5	4.7	−0.006	−0.022
Philippines	1970	1.0	−5.9	−0.028	−0.043
Sri Lanka	1967	5.2	−0.5	−0.025	−0.039
Trinidad	1967	31.4	21.3	−0.084	−0.061
Venezuela	1964	28.4	33.9	0.068	0.091
Yugoslavia	1965	2.3	−0.9	−0.017	−0.031
Bolivia	1982	−10.5	−23.3	−0.101	−0.104
Chile	1982	24.2	16.4	−0.062	−0.155
Colombia	1967	−11.6	−8.8	−0.030	−0.047
Ecuador	1982	26.6	17.0	−0.038	−0.044
Kenya	1981	13.4	10.2	−0.156	−0.246
Korea	1980	13.2	1.8	−0.019	−0.072
Mexico	1976	14.3	9.5	−0.025	−0.044
Mexico	1982	7.5	6.8	−0.038	−0.052
Pakistan	1982	4.3	2.1	−0.030	−0.012
Peru	1975	18.0	18.9	−0.000	−0.062
Average % change			−38.4%		−15%

Source: Constructed from data obtained from the *IFS*.
a. Ratio of net foreign assets to the sum of net foreign assets plus domestic credit × 100 (lines 31N over the sum of lines 31N + 32 of *IFS*).

riorations in competitiveness, others (e.g., Venezuela in 1964) only experienced an insignificant change in the real exchange rate index, while still others (such as Cyprus and Sri Lanka) experienced a real depreciation in the period preceding the devaluation. In many cases, however, the recorded average real appreciation during the period leading to the crisis provides an underestimation of the magnitude of the disequilibrium. This is because in many countries, in the period prior to the devaluation, price controls became quite pervasive, rendering official CPIs somewhat inadequate to construct RER indexes.

The evolution of net foreign assets and of the current account balance, presented in table 6.6, clearly captures the effect of the inconsistent macropolicies on the external accounts. In 32 out of the 39 countries the ratio of net foreign assets experienced a decline during this 2-year period, confirming the view that devaluation crises are usually preceded by an important rundown of international reserves (recall the model in chapter 3). On average, for these 39 countries, the net foreign assets ratio declined in more than 38% during 2 years prior to the devaluation. The year before the crisis the median of this indicator was 6.9%, significantly below the median for the control group, 20.1%. Also, in 26 of the 39 countries the current account ratio experienced a decline in the 2 year before the crisis, with the average deterioration amounting to 15%. The year before the devaluation the median of the current account deficit was 4.5% of GDP, about a full percentage point higher than the 3.6% for the control group. Moreover, in some of these episodes the current account to GDP ratio reached remarkable levels. In Kenya and Israel in 1971 the current account *deficit* was approximately equal to one-fourth of GDP!

In addition to the deterioration of the current account, capital flight is a crucial force underlying the weakening position of countries with external payments difficulties. Naturally, since by their own nature these capital movements are semiillegal, there are no official data on capital "flight." Table 6.7, however, contains estimates of capital flight for 38 of the devaluation episodes. For those countries that had the appropriate data, capital "flight" was proxied by the sum of "net errors and omissions" and "other short-term capital" from the *International Financial Statistics* balance of payments summary. For those countries that lacked data on "other short-term capital movements," "errors and omissions" only were used. Although due to the lack of comparable data these proxies are somewhat rough, they do provide a very revealing picture of the behavior of volatile capital movements.[8] In 21 out of 38 episodes there was an increase in the

Table 6.7
Estimates of capital "flight" in devaluing countries in period prior to crisis
(millions of U.S. $)

Country	Year	3 years before devaluation	1 year before devaluation
Argentina[a]	1970	−315	−28
Bolivia[a]	1972	6	68
Bolivia[a]	1979	106	33
Colombia[b]	1962	4	8
Colombia[b]	1965	−33	132
Costa Rica[a]	1974	−63	−46
Ecuador[b]	1961	−7	2
Ecuador[a]	1970	−18	−23
Egypt[b]	1962	−13	31
Egypt[a]	1979	303	564
Guyana[b]	1967	−1	6
India[b]	1966	81	−102
Indonesia[a]	1978	1,986	445
Israel[a]	1962	−17	21
Israel[a]	1967	−125[c]	72
Israel[a]	1971	121	114
Jamaica[a]	1967	−8[c]	30
Jamaica[a]	1978	−2	71
Malta[a]	1967	4[c]	2
Nicaragua[a]	1979	9	184
Pakistan[a]	1972	28	35
Peru[b]	1967	29	−12
Philippines[a]	1962	57	39
Philippines[a]	1970	20	−19
Sri Lanka[b]	1967	2	−2
Trinidad[b]	1967	0	4
Venezuela[b]	1964	76	−33
Yugoslavia[b]	1965	−21	16
Bolivia[a]	1982	−9	−384
Chile[a]	1982	−455	−1,220
Colombia[a]	1967	40	−140
Ecuador[a]	1982	39	442
Kenya[a]	1981	−26	−136
Korea[a]	1980	42	−1,954

Table 6.7 (continued)

Country	Year	3 years before devaluation	1 year before devaluation
Mexico[a]	1976	246	421
Mexico[a]	1982	−596	8,976
Pakistan[a]	1982	−325	−160
Peru[a]	1975	−79	−409

Source: Only those countries with data are listed here. A positive sign means that there was capital flight from the country. This table was constructed from raw data obtained from *International Financial Statistics*.
a. Capital "flight" proxied by the sum of the *IFS* balance of payments items "net errors and omissions" (line 77ed) and "other short term capital" (line 77dd).
b. When the proxy [a] was not available, capital "flight" was proxied by "net errors and omission" only.
c. Two years prior to devaluation.

extent of capital "flight" in the period preceding the crisis. Of these the most notable is Mexico in 1982, where the year prior to the devaluation capital flight reached almost U.S. $9 billion. As expected, in those episodes where the devaluation was not associated with major macroeconomic disequilibria—Venezuela and Indonesia, for example—there was no increase in capital "flight" in the period prior to the devaluation itself.

The data in these tables clearly highlight the fact that although one can identify a dominating pattern among these devaluation episodes, there are nontrivial differences across countries. In the majority of them the devaluation responded to the simultaneous depletion of international reserves and loss in competitiveness (i.e., real exchange appreciation). In a small number of cases, however, it is not possible to detect any of these symptoms in the years prior to the crisis, while in still other episodes only one of the symptoms related to the crisis was present. This is the case, for example, of the Indonesian devaluation of 1978, which basically responded to the decision of the Indonesian authorities to attack early on what they saw as the negative effects of a Dutch Disease type of situation (Woo and Nasution, 1987). In other cases—of which the 1964 Venezuelan devaluation is the primer example—the exchange rate adjustment amounted to an important corrective measure, with the devaluation really being an elimination of the lowest of three official exchange rates. Finally, as already pointed out, for many of the Commonwealth countries the devaluation of 1967 reflects the adjustment of the pound sterling in that year. However, some of these countries, such as Guyana, were independently suffering some of the symptoms of a substantial disequilibrium of the external sector.

Devaluation Crisis and Real Exchange Rate Overvaluation

Table 6.5 clearly shows a generalized pattern toward an appreciation of the (official) real exchange rate in the period preceding the crisis. This, however, is not in itself an indication of real exchange rate misalignment. As has been pointed out in the previous chapters, in order to determine whether or not misalignment has taken place, it is first necessary to analyze the actual behavior—as well as the expected behavior—of the real exchange rate fundamental determinants, and of the equilibrium real exchange rate. A partial analysis—limited by data availability—provides evidence suggesting that these RER movements were indeed a disequilibrium phenomenon. For example, the data on terms of trade behavior in table 6.4 indicate that in a number of countries—Colombia in 1962, Malta in 1967, Pakistan in 1972, Sri Lanka in 1967, the Philippines in 1962, the Philippines in 1970, Pakistan in 1982, Chile in 1982, Colombia in 1967, Korea in 1980, and Kenya in 1981—there was a strong terms of trade deterioration, and thus a movement toward a higher (depreciated) equilibrium RER, in the years preceding the devaluation. Also, capital inflows tended to drop in most of these countries prior to the crisis, suggesting again that, if anything, the equilibrium real exchange rate should have moved toward an equilibrium real depreciation, rather than toward an appreciation. By and large, then, this (impressionistic) evidence suggests that the real exchange rate appreciation observed in many of these countries prior to the crisis did not respond to an equilibrium change, but can be characterized rather as an overvaluation situation.

For a few episodes it is possible to use the series on estimated equilibrium real exchange rates reported in chapter 5 to analyze the directions in which ERERs moved in the period immediately preceding the crisis. Table 6.8 contains data for Colombia, Israel, the Philippines, and Sri Lanka. As can be seen in three of these cases, the period preceding the devaluations were characterized by equilibrium real depreciations, which in the case of Sri Lanka was quite significant—8.4%. This means that while the *actual* real exchange rate was declining prior to the devaluation, the *equilibrium* real exchange rate was increasing. These results underscore, at least for these countries, the notion that these devaluations indeed took place under conditions of growing real exchange rate disequilibrium.

Table 6.8
Evolution of estimated equilibrium real exchange rates in period preceding devaluation: selected countries[a]

	Change in equilibrium RER 3 years prior to crisis (%)
Colombia, 1967[b]	3.9
Israel, 1971	1.8
Philippines, 1970	-2.4
Sri Lanka, 1967	8.4

a. Computed from the estimated equilibrium real exchange rates series reported in chapter 5 (section 5.3). In each case the percentage change was computed by comparing the estimated ERER the year of the devaluation with its value 3 years prior to the crisis. A positive number indicates an equilibrium real depreciation, whereas a negative number denotes an equilibrium real appreciation.
b. Refers to 2 years before crisis.

6.3 Exchange Controls and Devaluations

Table 6.9 contains data on the evolution of exchange controls and trade impediments in the period leading to these 39 devaluations. These data have been classified according to the IMF practice and distinguish between[9] (a) payments restrictions on current transactions, such as licenses, prior approvals, multiple rates, prohibitions, and so on, (b) tariffs, duties, and price related measures, and (c) restrictions on capital movements in the form of either licenses or taxes. In this table we have tried to convey information on the conditions prevailing 2 years prior to the devaluation and on any changes implemented in the degree of controls in the year immediately prior to the abandonment of the fixed peg. Given the nature of the information available, it is very difficult to have quantitative idea of the extent to which impediments have evolved. For this reason, in this book we have decided to analyze the evolution of exchange controls qualitatively, without making an attempt to construct a subjective *index* of trade restrictions. Indexes of trade controls have a number of problems and limitations. First, although they are purely subjective, by attaching numbers they sometimes give the false impression of a more or less precise measure. Second, these indexes cannot be compared across countries. Appendix C to this chapter contains a much more detailed description of the evolution of these exchange and trade controls both before and after the devaluations. Table 6.9 reveals that in the great majority of the cases the devaluation was preceded by an important piling up of exchange controls and restrictions. In a small number of episodes, such as Colombia in 1962 and 1967, Ecuador in 1961,

Table 6.9
Evolution of exchange controls and trade restrictions in the 2 years preceding devaluation

Episode	Payments restrictions on current transactions	Tariffs, duties, and cost related measures	Restrictions on capital transactions
Argentina (1970)	• Increasing restrictions on capital goods. • Public sector payments monitored. • All foreign exchange transactions suspended for 10 days prior to devaluation.	• Advance deposits of 40% for 180 days. • Taxes on traditional exports. • Special regimes and exceptions abolished.	• No restrictions, and no changes prior to devaluation.
Bolivia (1972)	• Public sector payments highly controlled. • QRs on foodstuffs, cattle, and cotton. • Between May and Aug. a number of imports are prohibited (1972).	• Custom charge of 15% is in place in 1970. • 20% tax on exports imposed.	• Restrictive initial conditions. No changes prior to devaluation.
Bolivia (1979)	• Payments restrictions were increased for a number of items the year before. • Exchange transactions suspended for 8 days prior to devaluation.	• In 1977 most imports subject to 5–25% advance deposit. • Exceptions for duty payments eliminated for essentials (Feb.). • 500% advance deposit imposed on 600 items.	• All capital movements required authorization. • Ceiling set on new foreign borrowing.
Bolivia (1982)	• Imports of industrial goods produced locally are prohibited. • All sales of foreign exchange subject to authorization.	• In 1980 advance deposits of 5–25% were introduced. • 1981: Advance deposits reduced; import duties reduced.	• Jul. 1982, payments restrictions tightened.
Chile (1982)	• Payments highly liberalized. No restrictions imposed.	• Flat import tariff of 10% not altered prior to devaluation.	• Some restrictions on capital movements were in place preceding devaluation. No changes prior to abandonment of peg.

Chapter 6

Table 6.9 (continued)

Episode	Payments restrictions on current transactions	Tariffs, duties, and cost related measures	Restrictions on capital transactions
Colombia (1962)	• Initial conditions highly restrictive. • Large number of goods moved into prior license list during 1961. • All but 11 items in free list moved to prior license (Aug.). • Many items moved to prohibited list (Nov. 1962).	• 1960: Advance deposits ranging from 1% to 130%. • 1961: Many advance deposits reduced during first half of year. • 1962 (Apr.): Advance deposits raised.	• Dual exchange rates plus active parallel market. No changes prior to crisis.
Colombia (1965)	• Dec. 1964: Import free list suspended. 95% advanced deposit imposed. • 1965: Many goods passed to prior licensing. • Dual rates imposed (Sep.).	• Sep. 1964: 5% advance deposit imposed. • Dec. 1964: 95% advance deposit imposed on selected items. • 1965: More goods subject to advance deposits.	• Oct. 1964: Banco de la Republica ceased operations in free market. • Slight increase in tightness.
Colombia (1967)	• Highly restrictive payments structure.	• Jan. 1967: All advance deposits increased by 50%. • Feb.: Advance deposits further increased.	• Starting from controls, slight increase in degree of restrictions.
Costa Rica (1974)	• Dual exchange rates (1972). • Most imports channeled at higher rate during 1973. • Process continued in 1974 prior to devaluation.	• Mild restrictions on trade, not increased.	• Some restrictions in place (10–15% tax on remittances to rest of world).
Cyprus (1967)	• System of open general licenses for imports and exports, except some 50 items that required individual licenses to be imported. • No major changes prior to devaluation.	• No changes in year prior to devaluation.	• Transactions in foreign securities required prior approval. • Restrictions to foreign investment. • No major changes prior to devaluation

Table 6.9 (continued)

Episode	Payments restrictions on current transactions	Tariffs, duties, and cost related measures	Restrictions on capital transactions
Ecuador (1961)	• 1959: Multiple rates; all imports subject to licenses. • 1960: Proceeds from nontraditional exports moved to free rate. • Prior to devaluation, tightening of controls. Many items passed to restrictive list.	• Highly restrictive system, became tighter year prior to devaluation. • Aug. 1962: Advance deposits increased to 100% for list 2 imports.	• Capital movements should be registered.
Ecuador (1970)	• Two types of import lists with different degrees of restrictions. • Jan.–Jul. 1970: Increased restrictions including $400 quota on travelers.	• 1968: List 1 subject to 15% duties; list 2 subject to 70% duty. • 1969: Import surcharges hiked. • Jan. 1970: Duties raised to 40% for list 1 and 80% for list 2. • May: Further increases in surcharges.	• June 1970: Increased restrictions. Banks and residents required to sell all foreign exchange holdings to central bank at the free market exchange rate.
Ecuador (1982)	• Same list 1/list 2 structure. Multiple rates • 1981: Increased restrictions.	• Feb. 1981: Increase in coverage and rates of advance deposits. • June: Import tariffs raised on 500 items.	• Slight increase in restrictions.
Egypt (1962)	• Dual exchange rates. • Several imports were prohibited and all the others required individual licenses. • QRs on invisible payments. • The import trade was almost monopolized by the government the year prior to devaluation.	• Some imports subject to a 20% premium and some exports to a 20% tax • On most previously premium exempted imports a 10% premium was imposed in the year prior to devaluation.	• Severe restrictions on capital flows. • Royalties and dividends were subject to QRs. • No major changes prior to devaluation.

Table 6.9 (continued)

Episode	Payments restrictions on current transactions	Tariffs, duties, and cost related measures	Restrictions on capital transactions
Egypt (1979)	• Dual exchange rates. • Official foreign exchange allocated to "essential" imports on a yearly basis. • Some "essential" imports and most invisible transactions were shifted to the parallel market 6 months before the devaluation.	• No changes in year prior to devaluation.	• Outward capital transfers were restricted, with specific limits on each type of transaction. • Foreign currency accounts were available only for some residents. • Supervision of the central bank on all public foreign debt was required in the year prior to devaluation.
Guyana (1967)	• Individual licenses on imports of domestically produced goods and prohibitions on some other imports. • QRs on invisible payments. • In the 15 months preceding the devaluation, a number of items were added to the list of goods subject to specific license.	• An advance deposit requirement on imports' letters of credit was introduced 1 year before the devaluation.	• Flows of capital to or from outside the Sterling Area were not normally permitted. • No major change prior to devaluation.
India (1966)	• Highly restrictive system; most imports required individual licenses, which were usually denied to nonessential imports. • Payments for invisibles required approval on an individual basis. • No major change the year prior to devaluation.	• Feb. 1965: Custom surcharge of 10% ad-valorem was introduced on all imports. • July 1965: All private imports required a 25% advance deposit. • Aug. 1965: The custom surcharge and the prior deposit requirements were abolished.	• Almost complete capital mobility except for foreign investment, which required prior approval.

Table 6.9 (continued)

Episode	Payments restrictions on current transactions	Tariffs, duties, and cost related measures	Restrictions on capital transactions
Indonesia (1978)	• Prohibition on imports of vehicles and durable consumer goods. • Imports of food-stuffs and industrial inputs could only be made by the public sector. • No major change in the year prior to devaluation.	• Sales taxes of 5%, 10%, and 20% were levied on most imports. • Jan. 1977: A system of 100% advance deposits, 100% financial guarantee, and 100% advance payments of duties was introduced on some imports. • Exemptions on import duties and sales taxes were granted for some items during the 8 months preceding devaluation. • Sep. 1978: Tariff reductions were announced on 138 items imported from ASEAN countries.	• Stringent regulation on foreign borrowing and foreign investment. • No restrictions on flows of foreign currency and securities. • No change in the year prior to devaluation.
Israel (1962)	• Most imports and invisible payments required individual licenses. • No major change prior to devaluation.	• No changes in year prior to devaluation.	• Specific regulations on repayment and amortization of foreign debt and other remittances. • Foreign currency time deposits were allowed. • No change in year prior to devaluation.
Israel (1967)	• 50% of all imports were subject to individual licenses; the other half was free of all restrictions. • A process of relaxation of import restrictions began to take place 18 months before the devaluation.	• No changes in the year prior to devaluation.	• Same regulations in force as those of the previous episode.

Table 6.9 (continued)

Episode	Payments restrictions on current transactions	Tariffs, duties, and cost related measures	Restrictions on capital transactions
Israel (1971)	• Two types of import lists with different degree of restrictiveness. • In the 18 months preceding devaluation a number of import items were transferred to the less restrictive list.	• Jan. 1970: A 5-year program seeking to reduce the maximum tariff to 35% was announced. • An import deposit scheme of 50% of the CIF value was introduced. • Aug. 1970: An import surcharge of 20% of CIF value was introduced. • Jan. 1971: Some reductions in tariffs and a 10% reduction in the advance deposit rate.	• Stringent regulation on foreign investment. • Foreign currency deposits were allowed, but transfers of capital abroad was restricted. • The banking system suspended foreign exchange dealings 1 week before the devaluation.
Jamaica (1967)	• Open general license system for all imports except 150 items that required individual licenses. • Since Jan. 1966 a great number of imports were required to have specific licenses. • Stringent controls on all other payments.	• Consumption tax on imports of 2.5%. • Sep. 1967: The consumption tax on imports was raised to 5%.	• Restrictions on foreign investment and foreign debt. • Oct. 1967: Banks were prohibited from selling foreign exchange for personal transfers.
Jamaica (1978)	• Highly restrictive structure; most imports required specific licenses, payments for invisible subject to QRs • Dec. 1976: The foreign exchange market was closed and reopened on a limited basis on Jan. 1977. • Feb. 1977: 128 items were included in the list of prohibited imports. • Apr. 1977: Dual exchange market was created.	• No change took place in period prior to devaluation.	• Stringent capital controls. • Apr. 1977: With the creation of dual markets, all capital transactions were made at a depreciated rate. Some payments were temporarily suspended.

Table 6.9 (continued)

Episode	Payments restrictions on current transactions	Tariffs, duties, and cost related measures	Restrictions on capital transactions
Kenya (1981)	• Multiple exchange rates. • Imports classified into 4 lists for the provision of licenses. • June 1980: Prohibition on certain imports was lifted.	• Some imports subject to a 3-month advance deposit ranging from 10% to 100% of the CIF value of imports. • June 1980: Surcharge of 10% in all imports; custom duties for consumer goods were increased by 100%. • June 1981: Tariffs were further raised.	• Stringent capital controls. • Mar. 1981: Repatriation of assets held abroad was required to be completed by Dec.
Korea (1980)	• All imports required licenses, but 30% of the universe of imports were prohibited items. • QRs on invisible payments. • 18 months before devaluation a process of relaxation of licensing requirements began to take place.	• Advance deposit scheme on all imports with rates ranging from 10% to 20% of CIF value.	• Mild regulations on capital flows, which were progressively relaxed.
Mexico (1976)	• Import licenses required for almost all imports. • Public imports severely restricted.	• Nonessential imports made subject to a 10% ad-valorem surcharge. • The 10% surcharge was eliminated in Jan. 1975, but in Aug. of that year the average import duty was increased from 15% to 20%.	• Foreign investment severely restricted. • Borrowing abroad of public and private sector was subject to approval from ministry. • Foreign currency time deposits were permitted.
Mexico (1982)	• Initial conditions: import licensing and import quotas. • 1981: Import licensing requirements greatly increased.	• May 1981: Duties increased on 374 items. • July: Further increases in duties levels. • Nov.: Duties hiked for 120 items.	• No change in capital controls in period preceding devaluation.

Table 6.9 (continued)

Episode	Payments restrictions on current transactions	Tariffs, duties, and cost related measures	Restrictions on capital transactions
Nicaragua (1979)	• 2 groups of imports. • Sales of foreign exchange at official rate restricted. • Licenses hiked in 1978/1979. • Multiple rates imposed (Apr. 1979).	• Nov. 1979: Weekly foreign exchange allocation for imports was imposed.	• Increased restrictions.
Pakistan (1972)	• Multiple rates. • 4 lists of permitted imports with different degree of restrictive-ness regarding the issuance of licenses. • Payments for invisibles subject to QRs. • 1971: Licenses hiked and prohibitions increased.	• Imports from 2 of the 4 lists were subject to advance deposits.	• Transfers of capital and purchase of foreign securities were rarely allowed. • Jan. 1972: All citizens were required to repatriate assets held abroad. • May 1972: A partial moratorium on external debt service was declared.
Pakistan (1982)	• 2 lists of permitted imports; both of them required licenses. • Payments for invisibles and some exports were subject to QRs. • Aug. 1981: Some export goods were exempted from quota restrictions.	• 1981: Increase in import duties of several items throughout the year.	• Transfers of capital and purchase of foreign securities were rarely permitted. • No changes in year prior to devaluation.
Peru (1967)	• Initial conditions (1965)—no licenses required (except for 12 items). • In 1967 a number of restrictions were imposed. Exports required licenses (Oct.). Exports proceeds surrendered for certificates.	• Aug. 1966: Most imports were made subject to surcharge. • June 1967: Generalized hike in import duties.	• Mild initial restrictions. • Sept. 1967: A moratorium on payments of foreign debt is declared. Lifted after 16 days. • Slight increase in degree of restrictions.

Table 6.9 (continued)

Episode	Payments restrictions on current transactions	Tariffs, duties, and cost related measures	Restrictions on capital transactions
Peru (1975)	• Initial conditions (1973)—severe restrictions. Multiple exchange rates. Licenses or prior approval required for almost every item. • No major changes during year prior to devaluation.	• Restrictive initial conditions. During 1974 degree of restrictiveness is increased. • Jan. 1975: 12% surcharge on all imports	• Very restrictive initial conditions. • No changes during year prior to devaluation.
Philippines (1962)	• Dual exchange rates • "Decontrol" program aimed at withdrawing all restrictions on foreign exchange payments (accomplished by Jan. 1962).	• Advance deposits scheme with rates ranging from 50% to 150% of CIF value. • Requirement was not removed despite the "decontrol" program.	• Mild restrictions on capital movements, which were completely withdrawn by Jan. 1962.
Philippines (1970)	• Import prohibitions were in force and most imports required individual licenses. • Payments for invisibles subject to QRs. • Increased restrictions prior to devaluation.	• Advance deposits scheme with rates ranging from 25% to 175%. • 1969: Import duties on many commodities were raised.	• Stringent regulations on foreign securities purchases, foreign debt, and capital transfers. • Aug. 1969: Profit remittances from foreign firms were requested to be reduced. • Nov. 1969: Contracting in foreign currency was prohibited.
Sri Lanka (1967)	• All private imports required individual licenses and were divided into 3 groups, 2 of them subject to QRs and the others highly restricted. • QRs on payments for invisibles. • Nov. 1966: Payments restrictions increased.	• Most imports made subject to a 10% custom duty surcharge. • July 1966: The average and dispersion of the tariff structure was reduced, setting the maximum tariff at 150%. • The fees payable on import licenses and on surcharges increased steadily until the devaluation.	• Capital remittances of residents were limited. • The moratorium on transfers of dividends, profits, and interest established in 1964 was relaxed in July 1966. • No change took place until the devaluation.

Table 6.9 (continued)

Episode	Payments restrictions on current transactions	Tariffs, duties, and cost related measures	Restrictions on capital transactions
Trinidad-Tobago (1967)	• Regulations included prohibitions, individual import licensing, and state trading. • In 1966–1967 an increasing number of imports became subject to individual licenses.	• No change took place prior to devaluation.	• Restrictions placed on all imports and exports of securities. • Sep. 1966: A 30% tax was imposed on dividends remittances.
Venezuela (1964)	• Multiple rates. • Some restrictions initially, with licenses required on some items. • No changes in year prior to devaluation.	• No changes in year prior to devaluation.	• Almost complete capital mobility, which is maintained throughout the episode.
Yugoslavia (1965)	• 75% of imports were free of quantitative restrictions but subject to licenses; 25% of imports were subject to QRs. • Feb. 1964: Relaxation of import controls.	• No change took place prior to devaluation.	• Stringent capital controls and low degree of capital mobility. • No change before devaluation.

Source: See text.

and Peru in 1975, the initial conditions (2 years prior to the crisis) were already extremely restrictive, and became even tighter as the erosion of reserves became severe and/or real exchange rate appreciation increased. In other cases, however—Venezuela in 1964 and Chile in 1982, for example—the period preceding the devaluation was characterized by a fairly free environment, with little restrictions and no attempts by the authorities to impose any additional controls.[10] Furthermore, in the case of Indonesia in 1978, Israel in 1967 and 1971, and Korea in 1980, the period leading to the devaluation was accompanied by a liberalization of commodity trade.

Table 6.9 is supplemented by table 6.10, which shows that in the majority of these episodes the period preceding the devaluation was characterized by the existence of multiple official exchange rates. In fact, only 13 out of 34 cases had a unified official exchange rate 1 year prior to the crisis,

Table 6.10
Multiple exchange rates and parallel market premium in period prior to devaluations

Country	Year	Number of official exchange rates (years before devaluation)		Parallel market premium (percentage) (before devaluation)			
		−3	−1	3 years	9 months	3 months	1 month
Argentina	1970	1	1	0	0.3	0.0	0.0
Bolivia	1972	2	2	31.2	64.0	67.1	60.0
Bolivia	1979	1	1	6.6	10.0	17.5	17.5
Colombia	1962	3	3	11.1	33.4	34.7	58.0
Colombia	1965	3	3	37.5	42.8	110.6	114.4
Costa Rica	1974	8	5	0.5	42.2	34.7	30.2
Ecuador	1961	2	2	37.6	21.9	23.3	66.7
Ecuador	1970	2	2	11.1	22.5	23.9	55.6
Egypt	1962	2	2	3.3	91.4	125.7	128.6
Egypt	1979	3	3	94.4	87.2	84.6	92.3
India	1966	1	1	51.9	77.5	131.1	134.2
Indonesia	1978	4	4	0.0	2.7	0.5	1.2
Israel	1962	1	1	−0.6	36.3	46.9	50.8
Israel	1967	1	1	7.8	5.6	13.9	9.9
Israel	1971	1	1	−5.0	26.9	7.7	6.9
Jamaica	1978	1	2	n.a.	n.a.	n.a.	n.a.
Nicaragua	1979	1	2	0.2	27.1	78.6	92.9
Pakistan	1972	1	2	112.2	152.1	157.3	134.2
Peru	1967	1	1	5.2	2.2	2.2	43.6
Philippines	1962	1	2	43.2	85.0	106.0	126.0
Philippines	1970	1	1	8.9	15.4	44.9	59.0
Sri Lanka	1967	1	1	163.2	180.3	173.1	152.1
Venezuela	1964	3	3	0	35.5	35.5	35.5
Yugoslavia	1965	2	2	n.a.	39.5	41.9	54.7
Bolivia	1982	2	2	n.a.	25.0	502.3	434.1
Chile	1982	1	1	n.a.	10.3	12.8	17.9
Colombia	1967	3	4	35.9	19.2	46.3	48.1
Ecuador	1982	3	3	n.a.	25.0	45.0	74.1
Kenya	1981	3	3	n.a.	0.7	10.7	19.8
Korea	1980	2	2	4.4	14.0	19.2	42.3
Mexico	1976	1	1	0.0	0.0	0.0	0.0

Table 6.10 (continued)

Country	Year	Number of official exchange rates (years before devaluation)		Parallel market premium (percentage) (before devaluation)			
		−3	−1	3 years	9 months	3 months	1 month
Mexico	1982	1	1	0.0	5.4	11.7	12.5
Pakistan	1982	1	1	n.a.	33.8	48.5	40.9
Peru	1975	4	4	77.8	52.5	56.3	75.7

Source: *Pick's Currency Yearbook, World's Currency Yearbook*, and *IFS* (various issues).

Interestingly enough, however, in most instances the multiple rates were in place at least 3 years before the crisis, and in most countries there was no increase in the number of official rates as the devaluation date approached. Only in Jamaica in 1978, Nicaragua in 1979, Pakistan in 1972, Colombia in 1967, and the Philippines in 1962 was there an increase in the number of official nominal exchange rates during the 3-year period preceding the crisis.

The data on parallel market premiums in table 6.10 are particularly revealing.[11] In 28 out of the 33 devaluation episodes that have data, there was a significant increase in the black market premium during the 3 years preceding the crisis. Moreover, the parallel market spread increased very quickly as the crisis approached, reaching in many countries very significant levels just 1 month prior to the crisis. This behavior of the spread closely traces the predictions of the model of chapter 3, and reflects three interrelated forces. First, in the presence of a freely fluctuating parallel market rate, expansive domestic credit policies will usually be reflected in a depreciation of the free rate, at the same time as the domestic rate of inflation increases and international reserves are eroded. Second, this hike in the premium captures the public's reaction to the movement toward greater exchange controls. And third, it also reflects the generalized expectations that the situation is increasingly unsustainable and will result in an eventual devaluation.

As the data on net foreign assets and on the current account in table 6.6 show, the imposition of these exchange controls and payments restrictions did not succeed in putting an end to the erosion of foreign exchange; nor did they succeed in halting the deteriorating situation in the country's degree of international competitiveness. At most one can argue that these heightened impediments to trade managed to slow down the unavoidable balance of payments crisis unleashed by the inconsistent macroeconomic policies.[12] An important side effect of these trade restrictions and exchange controls is that they introduced serious distortions that had an impact on the economic performance of the country. Data on the evolution of real growth of GDP show that already 1 year prior to the devaluation crisis countries were performing significantly worse than the control group. χ^2 tests indicated that the null hypothesis that the devaluing and the control groups come from the same population is strongly rejected. This finding, which has important consequences for the *"contractionary devaluation"* controversy, is discussed in great detail in chapter 8.

6.4 International Liquidity, Real Exchange Rates, and the Probability of Devaluation: Econometric Estimates

The empirical analysis of the preceding sections has provided a comprehensive picture of the circumstances surrounding the 39 devaluation episodes. The methodological approach was based on the inspection of key variables in the period preceding the devaluation, and on the use of nonparametric tests to compare their behavior to that of a control group. In this section we use a probit regression analysis to investigate the effects of changes in the levels of international liquidity, real exchange rates, fiscal policy, and parallel market premiums on the probability of occurrence of a devaluation.

According to the model of chapter 3, devaluations will be preceded by (a) severe depletions of foreign assets held by the central bank and the monetary system, (b) real exchange rate appreciation (i.e., overvaluation), and (c) increases in the parallel market premium. While the loss of foreign assets and the real exchange rate overvaluation are the proximate factors triggering most devaluations, the ultimate causes of these exchange rate crises are related to inconsistent macro and especially fiscal policies.

The probit analysis reported here inquired into the role of both the proximate and ultimate causes of devaluation. Pooled quarterly data were used, and every regression was estimated with country-specific dummy variables. Since not every country had long enough quarterly time series, the number of countries included in the analysis had to be greatly reduced. Those regressions that did not include the parallel market premium as an explanatory variable covered 17 countries, while those that included it

Table 6.11
Probit estimates of devaluation[a]

	(Eq. 1)	(Eq. 2)	(Eq. 3)	(Eq. 4)	(Eq. 5)	(Eq. 6)
$FARE_{-1}$	—	−0.944	−0.800	—	—	—
		(−2.917)	(−2.304)			
$NFAM_{-1}$	—	—	—	−0.259	−0.784	−0.230
				(−0.404)	(−1.571)	(−2.384)
$PSCRE_{-1}$	1.456	—	0.597	1.257	—	—
	(2.206)		(0.760)	(1.530)		
RER_{-1}	−0.142	−0.126	−0.189	−0.135	−0.132	−0.030
	(−4.610)	(−4.636)	(−2.304)	(−4.446)	(−4.804)	(−0.772)
$BMPR_{-1}$	—	—	—	—	—	1.110
						(2.824)
N	758	794	751	758	708	435
log likelihood	32.4	41.8	46.9	32.0	33.6	33.6

a. The numbers in parentheses are t-statistics, and N refers to the number of observations. All explanatory variables were lagged one period.

dealt with 7 countries only.[13] The reason why these regressions were run on pooled data is that there are very few (discrete) devaluations for any one country, and country-by-country regressions would then have very few (one or two) "ones" and many "zeros."

The results obtained from different specifications of these probit regressions are reported in table 6.11, where the dependent variable took a value of one when there was a devaluation and zero otherwise. The following notation for the explanatory variables has been used:

FARE: Ratio of foreign assets of the central bank to base money. This is a measure of international liquidity.

NFAM: Ratio of *net* foreign assets of the monetary sector to the quantity of money (M1). This is an alternative measure of international liquidity.

PSCRE: Ratio of domestic credit to the public sector to total domestic credit.

RER: Real (bilateral) exchange rate index.

BMPR: Parallel market premium.

Broadly speaking these estimates confirm the implications of the model developed in chapter 3 and provide further support to the nonparametric tests reported in section 6.2 The main results in table 6.11 can be summarized as follows: (1) Real exchange rate appreciations significantly increases the probability of devaluation. (2) A worsening in the foreign assets position of either the central bank or the monetary system as a whole increases the probability of devaluation. (3) More expansive fiscal policies—characterized here by increases in the ratio of public sector credit—increase the probability of devaluation. (4) Higher parallel market premiums also reflect a significant increase in this probability.[14] Although in light of the exhaustive data analysis of the previous sections these results are not too surprising, they clearly reflect the robustness of our findings. Not only do our results hold from a qualitative point of view (an aspect captured by the nonparametric tests), but they are confirmed when more strict parametric tests are used.

6.5 Summary

In this chapter we have analyzed in detail the anatomy of devaluation crises in the developing countries. This was done by scrutinizing 39 major devaluation episodes that took place between 1962 and 1982. The analysis was carried out using two different methodologies: First, non-parametric tests were used to compare the behavior of the devaluers with that of a control group of fixers. Second, limited dependent variable econometric techniques were used to analyze how different variables—such as the real exchange rate—have been connected to exchange rate crises and devaluations.

Throughout the empirical investigation, the macroeconomic model of chapter 3 provided the analytical framework. As suggested by that model, most of the devaluation episodes were the result of inconsistent macroeconomic—and, in particular, fiscal—policies. As a consequence of these policies, in the vast majority of the cases current account balances deteriorated, the stock of international reserves was depleted, the parallel market spread shot up, and the real exchange rate experienced a massive appreciation, becoming overvalued. In fact, the probit analysis indicates that the evolution of reserves, the real exchange rate, and a fiscal policy indicator trace closely the probability of devaluation.

It was also found that in the majority of cases, the authorities imposed a number of payments and trade controls in an effort to stop the drainage of reserves. These measures, however, were to a large extent ineffective, being unable to stop the deterioration of the external accounts. In fact, the data on capital "flight" show quite clearly that as the devaluation date approached, these countries' nationals were able to "smuggle" increasing amounts of funds out of the country. These data provide a very consistent picture of the ineffectiveness of capital controls. If the ultimate sources of the disequilibria—the inconsistent domestic credit and fiscal policies—are not altered, capital controls are unable to stop an unavoidable collapse of the external sector. Under most circumstances, and as suggested by our model in chapter 3, this collapse comes in the form of a large devaluation and a stabilization package, many times administered by the IMF. The purpose of the next chapter is to investigate in detail, for the same 39 devaluation episodes, the effectiveness of devaluations as a policy tool for restoring RER equilibrium.

Appendix A

IMF programs in countries in devaluation sample

Country	Year of devaluation crisis	Standby agreement Date[a]	Amount[b]	External fund facility Date[a]	Amount[b]
Argentina	1970	1968(4/15)	$125.00	—	—
Bolivia	1972	1973(1/17)	27.30	—	—
Bolivia	1979	1981(2/1)	66.38	—	—
Bolivia	1982	—	—	—	—
Chile	1982	1983(1/10)	500.00	—	—
Colombia	1962	1962(1/1) 1963(1/14)	$10.00 $52.50	— —	— —
Colombia	1965	1964(2/14) 1967(4/15)	$10.00 $60.00	— —	— —
Colombia	1967	1967(4/15) 1968(4/19)	$46.00 $60.00	— —	— —
Costa Rica	1974	—	—	—	—
Cyprus	1967	—	—	—	—
Ecuador	1961	1963(7/1)	$6.00	—	—
Ecuador	1970	1970(9/14)	$22.00	—	—
Ecuador	1982	1983(7/25)	157.50	—	—
Egypt	1962	—	—	—	—
Egypt	1979	—	—	1978(7/28)	600.00
Guyana	1967	1967(2/15) 1968(2/15)	$7.50 $4.00	— —	— —
India	1966	1965(3/22)	$100.00	—	—
Indonesia	1978	—	—	—	—
Israel	1962	—	—	—	—

IMF programs in countries in devaluation sample (continued)

Country	Year of devaluation crisis	Standby agreement		External fund facility	
		Date[a]	Amount[b]	Date[a]	Amount[b]
Israel	1967	—	—	—	—
Israel	1971	—	—	—	—
Jamaica	1967	—	—	—	—
Jamaica	1978	—	—	—	—
Kenya	1981	1979(8/20)	122.48	—	—
		1980(10/15)	241.50	—	—
Korea	1980	1980(3/3)	640.00	—	—
		1981(2/13)	576.00	—	—
Malta	1967	—	—	—	—
Mexico	1976	—	—	1977(1/1)	518.00
Mexico	1982	—	—	1983(1/1)	3410.63
Nicaragua	1979	1979(5/14)	34.00	—	—
Pakistan	1972	1972(5/18)	9.00	—	—
Peru	1967	1967(8/18)	$42.50	—	—
Peru	1975	—	—	—	—
Philippines	1962	1964(4/12)	$40.40	—	—
Philippines	1970	1970(2/20)	27.50	—	—
		1971(3/16)	45.00		
		1972(5/11)	45.00		
Sri Lanka	1967	—	—	—	—
Trinidad	1967	—	—	—	—
Venezuela	1964	—	—	—	—
Yugoslavia	1965	1967(1/1)	$45.00	—	—

Source: International Monetary Fund.
a. Numbers in parentheses refer to the month and date in which the agreement was signed.
b. Millions of SDRs or dollars $.

Appendix B

Control group countries

Country	IFS country code	Years of study
Cote d'Ivoire	662	1965–1977
Dominican Republic	243	1960–1980
Ecuador	248	1971–1980
Egypt	469	1960–1971
El Salvador	253	1960–1980
Ethiopia	644	1960–1970
Greece	174	1960–1973
Guatemala	258	1960–1980
Honduras	268	1960–1980
Iran	429	1960–1971
Iraq	433	1960–1971
Jordan	439	1960–1971
Malaysia	548	1960–1970
Mexico	273	1960–1974
Nicaragua	278	1960–1977
Nigeria	694	1960–1970
Panama	283	1960–1980
Paraguay	288	1960–1982
Singapore	576	1960–1970
Sudan	732	1960–1976
Thailand	578	1960–1971
Tunisia	744	1960–1970
Venezuela	299	1965–1971
Zambia	754	1960–1971

Appendix C: Exchange Controls and Trade Restrictions in Devaluation Episodes

This appendix contains information on the evolution of exchange controls and trade restrictions before and after 38 of the 39 devaluation episodes analyzed in this study. (No information for Malta was available.) The information reported here has been obtained from various issues of the IMF's *Annual Report on Exchange Arrangements and Payments Restrictions* and *Pick's Currency Yearbook*.

Broadly following the IMF's methodology, this appendix considers three types of exchange controls and trade impediments: (a) payments restrictions on current transactions, (b) tariffs, duties, and cost-related measures, and (c) restrictions on capital transactions. The first type of impediments comprise (I) all the measures related to the availability of foreign exchange for import payments, such as licenses, prior approvals, priority lists, multiple exchange rates, and prohibitions, (II) all quotas and quantitative restrictions placed on payments for invisibles not related to capital movements, such as tourism allowances and ceilings on private transfers, and (III) the existing regulations concerning the handling of export proceeds.

All the measures that, directly or indirectly, affect the effective cost of foreign goods for domestic importers are included in the second category of impediments. Thus, this category comprises all the available information regarding changes in the tariff structure, the imposition of import surcharges and of taxes on current transactions on foreign exchange, and the evolution of advance deposit requirements. Finally, the third category describes the special arrangements or limitations attached to international capital movements and domestic capital transactions in foreign exchange. Regulations on foreign investment and on profits and dividends remittances, special procedures for the acquisition and service of foreign debt, and restrictions on the holding of foreign currency by domestic residents and institutions are included in this type of impediments.

As said before, the information reported in these tables is of a qualitative nature. Thus, special attention should be paid to the institutional arrangements preexisting in each country before extracting any conclusion regarding the relative restrictiveness of the exchange controls and impediments in the period surrounding each devaluation episode.

The exact dates of the 39 devaluation episodes are the following:

Episode	Year	Date
Stepwise Devaluations		
Argentina	1970	June 18, 1970
Bolivia	1972	October 27, 1972
Bolivia	1979	November 30, 1979
Colombia	1962	November 20, 1962
Colombia	1965	September 2, 1965
Costa Rica	1974	April 25, 1974

Episode	Year	Date
Cyprus	1967	November 20, 1967
Ecuador	1961	July 14, 1961
Ecuador	1970	August 17, 1970
Egypt	1962	May 7, 1962
Egypt	1979	January 1, 1979
Guyana	1967	November 20, 1967
India	1966	June 6, 1966
Indonesia	1978	November 16, 1978
Israel	1962	February 9, 1962
Israel	1967	November 19, 1967
Israel	1971	August 21, 1971
Jamaica	1967	November 21, 1967
Jamaica	1978	May 9, 1978
Malta	1967	November 20, 1967
Nicaragua	1979	April 6, 1979
Pakistan	1972	May 11, 1972
Peru	1967	October 9, 1967
Philippines	1962	January 22, 1962
Philippines	1970	May 1, 1970
Sri Lanka	1967	November 22, 1967
Trinidad-Tobago	1967	November 23, 1967
Venezuela	1964	January 18, 1964
Yugoslavia	1965	July 26, 1965
Devaluation Followed by Crawling Peg		
Bolivia	1982	February 5, 1982
Chile	1982	June 15, 1982
Colombia	1967	March 22, 1967
Ecuador	1982	March 3, 1982
Kenya	1981	September 21, 1981
Korea	1980	January 12, 1980
Mexico	1976	September 1, 1976
Mexico	1982	August 5, 1982
Pakistan	1982	January 8, 1982
Peru	1975	September 26, 1975

I Evolution of payments restrictions on current transactions

Situation at December (t − 2)	Previous year (t − 1)	Devaluation year (t)	Following year (t + 1)
		1. ARGENTINA (1970)	
• Prohibition on imports of some vehicles, tractors, and engines.	**1/21** The value beyond which imports of capital goods were subject to special financement was raised to $20,000.	**5/23** Imports of synthetic fertilizers were prohibited.	**1/25** Exchange agencies resumed their operations.
• Some capital goods over $10,000 must be paid in a period from 2–5 years.	**3/13** An institution to monitor all import applications of the public sector was created.	**6/9** All exchange transactions were suspended (until the devaluation 6/18).	**3/23** Exchange market was closed except for trade transactions.
• No restrictions on invisible payments.		**10/15** The exchange market was closed again.	**3/29** Exchange sales for travel abroad were permitted. Allowances: $200–1,000.
• Imports free of any kind of licensing.		**10/19–12/12** 6 telephone communications allowed 3 increasing broader resumptions of exchange transactions.	**4/16, 5/10** Exchange sales were resumed for additional purposes (family transfers, health).
+ Only traditional exports must be surrendered to the central bank.			**5/27** The exchange market was reopened 5/29.
			6/30 Imports of many "nonessential" commodities were prohibited for 1 year.
			7/30 Travel allocations were reduced to $150–500. Family remittances restricted to $100/month.
			9/19 Almost all imports were prohibited until 10/31.
			9/20 Dual exchange market was reintroduced.
			11/1 All imports of the public sector were prohibited. Restrictions on "nonessential" goods were maintained.

- Public sector imports of goods available in Bolivia are prohibited.
- Private imports of cigarettes, cement, and other locally produced goods are prohibited.
- Private imports of live cattle, cotton, foodstuff, and petroleum subject to quotas.
+ Export proceeds must be surrendered.

2. BOLIVIA (1972)

- Progressive travel tax was introduced.

5/30 Imports on alcoholic beverages were prohibited.
8/25 Imports of beef and cattle were temporarily prohibited.

11/30 Imports of certain agricultural products were prohibited.

3. BOLIVIA (1979)

- Same general structure as in 1970–1973.

1/25 Import prohibitions of liquors were removed (with some exceptions).
1/27 Imports of acrylic fiber thread became subject to specific authorization.
6/22 Imports of dry batteries and wooden furniture were no longer prohibited.

11/12 The central bank suspended all purchases of foreign exchange, these were resumed after the devaluations of 11/30.

2/15 Imports of diesel vehicles and second-hand equipment were prohibited.
5/16 Prohibitions for automobiles imports were waived.
5/25 Some exceptions on the prohibition of diesel vehicles were granted.
7/17 The import of cement was prohibited.

I (continued)

Situation at December ($t - 2$)	Previous year ($t - 1$)	Devaluation year (t)	Following year ($t + 1$)
	4. BOLIVIA (1982)		
• Departing from the same general framework described in the previous episode (including the abolition of the fixed exchange rate).	**7/30** All sales of foreign exchange were made subject to central bank authorization; all imports would require approval of the Ministry of Finance and would depend on the foreign exchange budget. **9/11** Prohibition of imports of manufactured goods that could be produced locally was extended from public sector agents to all importers.	**11/5** All import payments required being covered by letters of credit drawn on foreign banks. • The importation of 600 "inessential" products was temporarily prohibited.	**1/5** A restrictive system of foreign exchange budgets for the public and private sectors was implemented. • Nonprohibited imports were allowed to be made with the importers' own foreign exchange. • Individuals were only allowed to request foreign exchange up to the limit of their disposable annual incomes. • Quotas for services' payments were reduced significantly.
	5. CHILE (1982)		
• Imports receive foreign exchange as soon as a paper formality is filled and the shipping documents are received. • Central bank authorization is required when the payments for invisibles exceed the (high) established limits ($10,000/month for most categories) + Export proceeds must be surrendered after 300 days of shipment.	**1/2** The requirement for an import registration for imports exceeding $10,000 was replaced by a simpler "informe de importacion." **8/18** All goods that remained on the list of prohibited imports were removed from there.	**9/21** 12/3 the exchange quotas for services' payments were reduced substantially. **9/29** The range of transactions handled by foreign exchange houses was curtailed. **10/28** The "Informe de importacion" became mandatory and was used as an import license.	**3/14** Quotas for services' payments become even more restrictive and required central bank's authorization.

6. COLOMBIA (1962)

• 3 lists of imports: (a) prohibited, (b) subject to license, (c) freely imported.

• *All* transactions require prior approval.

• Basic foodstuff may only be imported by the public sector.

+ Export proceeds of coffee, bananas (subject to minimum price of surrender), and metals must be surrendered at a lower rate.

5/24, 8/2, 9/9 A lot of products were transferred from the prohibited and freely imported goods lists into the prior license list.

3/18 With the exception of 11 items, all merchandise on the import free list was transferred to the list of goods subject to licensing.

11/17 Merchandise included in the import free list and the prior licensing goods was temporarily transferred to the list of prohibited imports.

11/20 Devaluation.

12/6 Some items were transferred from the prohibited imports to the import free list.

12/17 522 items were transferred from the prohibited to the prior licensing list.

6/5 Export quotas for sugar were reduced by 60%.

7/6 Exports of sugar were prohibited.

10/16 Chassis for trucks and cars were taken off the prohibited list.

I (continued)

Situation at December ($t-2$)	Previous year ($t-1$)	Devaluation year (t)	Following year ($t+1$)
• Departing from the same general framework described in the previous episode.	**7/17** The Board of Trade and the Superintendency of Foreign Trade were created. **12/1** The import free list was suspended for 90 days; during that period all goods required a prior license. **12/28** Prior exchange registration for imports ceased to be automatically accepted. A 95% advance deposit was required 20 days before the application for foreign exchange.	**7. COLOMBIA (1965)** **1/1, 3/24** New items were included in the list of goods subject to license. **5/5** *All* imports required a license. **7/7** The export proceeds other than from coffee and bananas had also to be surrendered 90 days after the registration. **9/2** The structure of the foreign exchange market was changed; a preferential and an intermediate rate were created. **9/7** The exchange rate to be applied to each category of imports was determined. **12/1** Priorities in the allocation of foreign exchange were established for the intermediate and preferential markets.	**1/21, 2/22, 2/28, 3/17, 7/29** Lists of imports that did not require a license if imported at the intermediate rate but require it if imported at the preferential rate were issued. **7/1** A Col. 500 travel tax was introduced. **8/21** All imports payments were to be made at the intermediate rate. **11/29** Operations in the free exchange market were suspended. *All* imports required again import licenses.

8. COLOMBIA (1967)

- Departing from the framework described in the previous episode.
- See last year of precedent episode.

3/22 The exchange rates in the capital and certificate markets were fixed (after devaluation).

5/7 Tourists were allowed to buy up to $60 on leaving the country.

5/9 Products from 150 tariff positions were exempted from import licensing and included in the (by then insignificant) import list.

6/5 The 95% advance deposit for foreign exchange applications was lifted for some payments.

7/10 The advance deposit for foreign exchange applications for travel purposes was increased to 100%.

9. COSTA RICA (1974)

- Dual exchange market.
- No import licensing, but stringent division between imports that apply for each exchange rate.
+ Most proceeds (invisibles and exports) must be surrendered although at different rates.

1/26 Transfers of foreign exchange from the free market to the official market to speed up transactions on the latter.

8/23 The central bank tightened the conditions under which official rate could be available for capital goods imports.

3/13 The only import payments that remained eligible for the official rate were basic cereals and pharmaceutical products.

4/25 Unification of exchange market. All restrictions on payments at the official rate were lifted. The period for surrendering export proceeds was reduced from 60 to 25 days.

9/30 The travel allowance of foreign exchange was raised from $1,000 to $3,000.

1/15 All imports in excess of $300 became subject to prior registration with the central bank before the foreign exchange could be obtained.

11/25 The total travel allowance became subject to central bank's approval and limited to twice a year.

I (continued)

Situation at December (t − 2)	Previous year (t − 1)	Devaluation year (t)	Following year (t + 1)
10. CYPRUS (1967)			
• Member of Sterling Area. • Most imports may be made freely under an open general license; except for some 50 items subject to individual licenses that can be denied. • Certain invisible payments are subject to quotas. + All exports are subject to licenses and the proceeds must be surrendered.	3/24 Imports from South Africa were prohibited.	5/4 The open general license ceased to be applied to imports from North Korea, North Vietnam, and Tibet. 11/20 The par value was changed.	5/24 Unrestricted importation of almost all goods from the permitted countries previously under the open general license was allowed.
11. ECUADOR (1961)			
• Multiple currency practices. • Prior licenses required for all imports. • Imports divided into 2 categories: list 1—essential and semiessential goods; list 2—nonessential and luxury goods. Goods not included in lists are prohibited. + Almost all exports require licenses to ensure the surrendering of proceeds.	• Proceeds from various types of exports were allowed to be sold in the "free market" during the year.	2/1 The central bank suspended the sales of foreign exchange for prepayment of list 1 imports. 2/20 Cocoa exports were converted at the (lower) official rate. 3/8 Payments in advance or by letter of credit were prohibited for list 2 imports. 3/14 Some imports were transferred from list 1 to list 2. 5/23 Imports of network and displayed metals were prohibited. 7/14 Devaluation and foreign exchange market reform.	• On various dates, certain items were shifted between the 2 import lists. Others were deleted or added. No clear pattern of the measures.

12. ECUADOR (1970)

5/13 Imports of cotton were suspended.

5/6 Increase of the travel tax.

1/20 The importation of dairy products was restricted (whenever domestic production was affected).

6/22 All foreign exchange transactions were placed under the supervision of the central bank. Both exchange markets were closed.

7/3 Sales of exchange for some invisibles were restricted; $400 yearly per person for travel purposes and 50% deposit for medical payments.

8/17 Unification of the foreign exchange market (devaluation).

8/28 Quotas for travels, medical payments, and study were increased ($1,350/year, $2,000/year, $400/month). All other invisibles did not have limit for allowance.

11/22 A secondary free exchange market was reintroduced (mainly for capital and private sector transactions).

• Same official/free markets.
• Same list 1/list 2 imports structure.
• Some invisibles had to be sold in the official market.
+ Licenses required to ensure the full surrender of export proceeds.
• Minimum surrender price for banana exports.

13. ECUADOR (1982)

2/13 The central bank was prohibited from authorizing exchange at the official rate for making advance payments for imports.

Feb.–Mar. Several changes in the import lists were made.

5/15 The central bank was allowed to extend its intervention in the free market.

12/8 Imports of some vehicles were prohibited.

11/17 About 100 items of list 1 and over 500 items of list 2 were prohibited.

12/27 Exemptions of the suspension of imports of some capital goods were granted to importers with long-term financing.

• Throughout the year, several exemptions to the import prohibitions regulations were granted.

• Same official/free markets.
• Same list 1/list 2 imports structure.
• Prior import licenses are required for all permitted imports.
• Some private payments for invisibles can be made at the official rate, if the prefixed quota is exceeded the exchange can be obtained in the free market.
+ All exports require licenses and must be surrendered.

I (continued)

Situation at December ($t-2$)	Previous year ($t-1$)	Devaluation year (t)	Following year ($t+1$)
		14. EGYPT (1962)	
• Dual exchange market (the official and a 20% higher exchange rate).	**7/1** The import trade was largely monopolized by the government; besides some industrial firms, private importers were prohibited from importing.	**5/7** A single (25% devalued) rate was applied to almost all transactions.	**8/28** Private imports of any kind were no longer permitted.
• Several import items and all imports from Israel are prohibited.			
• All other imports require individual licenses issued under the framework of an import budget.			
• Certain invisible payments require central bank approval and are subject to quotas.			
+ Besides exports to Israel, all goods may be exported without license, but the proceeds must be surrendered.			
		15. EGYPT (1979)	
• Dual exchange market (official and parallel).	**7/1** Imports of tea and oil were shifted from the official to the parallel market.	**1/1** The unification of the exchange market at the previously prevailing parallel rate was completed.	**2/29** The laws boycotting Israel were abolished.
• Imports from Israel and South Africa were prohibited.	**7/2** Almost all invisible transactions were shifted to the parallel market.		
• No official exchange was allocated for nonessential imports.			
• Imports are regulated more by exchange allocations determined by an annual budget than by licenses.			
+ Export proceeds must be surrendered.			

16. GUYANA (1967)

- Member of the Sterling Area.
- Imports of a few commodities are prohibited; other luxury and domestically produced goods are subject to individual licensing. The rest of the goods are imported under open general license.
- Invisible payments are subject to limits.

+ Exports are free of licensing but must be surrendered.

• In March and July some items were added to the "negative list" of goods subject to specific import licensing.

• During the year a number of commodities were added to the "negative list."

11/20　The par value was changed.

1/1　The import of certain goods included in the "negative list" was prohibited.

17. INDIA (1966)

- Member of the Sterling Area.
- Practically all imports require individual licenses.
- Licensing priority to foodstuff, capital goods, and raw materials; all other imports are severely limited; licenses are given on an annual basis.
• Payments for invisibles require approval on an individual basis; no foreign exchange for tourists' travels.

+ Most goods may be exported without a license. A few are subject to quotas or license. All proceeds must be surrendered.

• From September to December: emergency measures regarding transactions with Pakistan.

10/20　The National Defense Remittance Scheme favoring repatriation or inward flow of invisibles was introduced.

5/27　The suspension of transactions with Pakistan was rescinded.

5/31　The National Defense Scheme was terminated.

6/6　The par value for the rupee changed. 59 priority industries were allowed to import at full capacity for 6 months.

• Quotas for certain imports were increased.

6/23　Restrictions on raw materials imports were relaxed substantially.

10/24　Some machine tools imports were prohibited.

5/1　Import restrictions on the 59 priority industries were removed, but prohibitions of imports of 80 more items were introduced.

9/8　Import licenses for the production of some exportables were granted more liberally.

I (continued)

Situation at December ($t-2$)	Previous year ($t-1$)	Devaluation year (t)	Following year ($t+1$)
		18. INDONESIA (1978)	
• Single exchange rate. • Registry of authorized importers requires an initial deposit. • Importation of vehicles and durable consumer goods are prohibited. • Other imports are restricted to public enterprises (foodstuffs, inputs). • Proceeds and payments from invisibles are not restricted and do not need to be surrendered. **+** Some goods cannot be exported; all export proceeds must be surrendered.	• (No measure of this type was taken.)	**1/26** The export of 14 species of timber was banned. **11/16** The rupiah was devalued by 34%. **12/11** Exports of certain commodities were made subject to quotas.	• (No measure of this type was taken.)
		19. ISRAEL (1962)	
• Most imports require individual licenses, and so do most payments abroad for invisibles. **+** Export licenses are required for most products, and export proceeds must be surrendered.	• (No measure of this type was taken.)	**2/9** Major reform and unification of the exchange system. **3/14** The travel allocation was increased from \$150/year to \$250/year. **5/7** The export licensing requirement was eliminated for most industrial exports. **5/28** The travel allocation was increased from \$250/year to \$400/year. **6/1** Some 400 import items were freed from all licensing and other restrictions. Previously prohibited items were allowed to be imported under individual licenses.	**1/18** Some 300 import items were transferred to the "Free Import Orders." In Mar., Jun., and Nov., some 100 import items hitherto prohibited were added to the Automatic Approval List. **7/1** The travel allocation was increased from \$400 to \$500 per travel.

20. ISRAEL (1967)

- Unified exchange rate.
- Few imports are prohibited.
- 50% of all imports are free of all licensing and restrictions; the others are subject to individual licenses.
- Most payments abroad require individual licenses and some are subject to quotas.

+ Most exports do not require licenses, but the proceeds must be surrendered.

- On various dates import restrictions were relaxed, freeing some articles from licensing requirements and restrictions and deleting commodities from the list of prohibited imports.

- The import liberalization process continued throughout the year. Besides this:

2/1 The travel allocation was reduced from $500 to $350/travel.

2/21 Foreign exchange was granted for membership fees.

11/19 The par value was changed.

- Import restrictions were further relaxed throughout the year.

5/30 The travel allocation was increased from $350 to $375 per travel.

6/19 The amount allowed for remittance in support of relatives was increased.

21. ISRAEL (1971)

- Single exchange rate.
- Few imports are prohibited. All imports not liberalized are included in the "Negative List," formed by the Automatic Approval List and the Restricted List.
- Most payments for invisibles require individual licensing, and some of them are subject to quotas.

+ Most exports do not require licenses and the proceeds must either be surrendered or held in a special type of foreign currency account.

2/1 Goods in 7 tariff classifications were transferred from the Restrictions List to the Automatic Approval List.

3/1 Goods in 5 Tariff classifications were shifted from the Restricted to the Automatic Approval List.

3/2 Exchange allowances for travel were reduced from $375 to $250 per travel.

- During the year further import items were added to the Free Import List or shifted to the Automatic Approval List.

8/21 The par value was changed.

12/5 Exchange allowance for travel was increased from $250 to $450 per travel. Other quotas for invisibles payments were also increased.

I (continued)

Situation at December $(t-2)$	Previous year $(t-1)$	Devaluation year (t)	Following year $(t+1)$
		22. JAMAICA (1967)	
• Member of the Sterling Area. • Most goods might be imported freely under an open general license. • Some 150 tariff items and imports from some countries require industrial licenses issued according to some "essential criteria." • Payments of invisibles outside the Sterling Area require previous approval and are subject to quotas. + Exports outside Sterling Area require a license and the proceeds must be surrendered within 6 months.	**1/5** Imports of refrigerators require a specific license. **4/4** Imports of irons require a specific license.	• During the year, many imports were required to have a specific license (restrictive tendency). **9/20** The foreign exchange allowance for foreign travel purposes was restricted. **11/18** The exchange control was extended to transactions within the Sterling Area. **11/21** The Jamaican pound was devalued. **12/6** The exchange control was no longer applied to the Sterling Area. **12/7** Restrictions on imports from Japan were relaxed.	• During the year, many imports were excluded from the open general license scheme and became subject to specific licenses. **8/8** Exports to some socialist countries were prohibited.

23. JAMAICA (1978)

• A few goods can be freely imported under an open general license. All other imports require a specific license to be allowed the foreign exchange.

• Payments for invisibles require approval from the authorities and are subject to specific quotas and compulsory waiting periods.

+ A large number of exports do not require a license, but the proceeds must be surrendered.

• The foreign exchange market was closed as of early December.

1/6 The foreign exchange market was reopened on a limited basis for outstanding import and debt payments, but remained closed for other transactions.

1/19 New exchange control guidelines came into force, centralizing foreign exchange transactions.

2/9 128 items were included in the list of banned imports (which already included cars, consumer goods, and foodstuffs).

4/21 A dual exchange market was implemented and the allowance for travel was slightly increased.

10/21 The "spread" between rates was increased and the allowance for travel was slightly increased again.

1/13 Both the "basic" and the "special" rates were devalued.

5/9 The exchange market was reunified at a further devalued exchange rate. The allowances for travel were further increased.

6/8 A devaluation schedule was announced for the next 12 months.

5/30 The exchange allocation for tourism and business travels was increased.

I (continued)

Situation at December ($t - 2$)	Previous year ($t - 1$)	Devaluation year (t)	Following year ($t + 1$)
		24. KENYA (1981)	
• Several "effective" exchange rates. • Some imports are prohibited; many goods may be freely imported under general open license, but others require a specific license. Imports are classified into 4 categories for the provision of licenses. • Payments for invisibles have no restrictive quotas (education, travel). + Exports of certain foodstuffs require licenses, while most other exports do not. Export proceeds must be surrendered within 3 months of the shipment.	**6/20** Some privileges of protected industries that allowed them to determine the prohibition of certain imports were abolished.	**11/10** New import system replaced the 4 categories and the open general licenses by 3 schedules with an explicit list of import items.	• (No change took place.)

25. KOREA (1980)

- All imports require licenses, some of them issued upon application.
- 2 categories of imports: those paid with Korean foreign exchange and those paid with foreign funds.
- Restricted items list (328 out of 1,010 items) are seldom imported.
- All payments for invisibles require individual licenses, but most of them are automatically granted. Large quotas for standard payments.
+ Certain exports require individual licenses; the export proceeds may be either surrendered or deposited in foreign exchange accounts.

2/1 21 import items were transferred from the Restricted to the Automatic Approval List.
7/1 34 import items were transferred to the Automatic Approval List by then covering 67.5% of the universe of imports.
12/1 14 items were transferred from the Automatic Approval List to the Restricted List.

7/1 33 import items were transferred to the Automatic Approval List, raising the proportion of this type of imports to 68.6% of the total.
10/15 Foreign exchange control regulations were simplified (period for receiving export proceeds was extended, and transactions eligible for foreign exchange were expanded.)

1/5 Import quotas were established on 64 import items (foodstuff, chemicals).
5/30 396 categories were shifted to the Automatic Approval List, by then accounting for 74.7% of all basic items.
6/20 The maximum foreign exchange allowance for emigrants was set at $100,000.
7/22 Temporary quotas were introduced on 62 import items.
8/1 The list of invisibles eligible for automatic approval was extended.

26. MEXICO (1976)

- Few imports are prohibited.
- Import licenses from the Ministry of Trade are required for almost all imports, and these may be subject to qualitative restrictions or a validity period.
- Public imports are not permitted if a domestic equivalent is available at 15–20% price differential.
- No exchange control is in force for payments or proceeds from invisibles.
+ No exchange control requirement is applied to export proceeds.

• Increasing restrictiveness in the issuance of import licenses. In July most imports licenses were cut by half the amount allowed in 1974.
• In Aug., an announcement was made that import licenses would continue to be required until Dec. 1977 for "basic products."
• In Sept., 430 tariff items were exempted from import licensing.

1/1 More stringent import licensing requirements for 3,535 items (although 4,286 items were exempted from 1975 measure).
1/29 Import licensing requirement was eliminated for additional commodities.
9/1 Devaluation; the peso was allowed to float, and it was announced that no exchange control will be imposed.
9/15 The import licensing requirement was eliminated for 683 tariff items, and it was reconfirmed that no exchange controls would be introduced.

4/1 The import licensing requirement was eliminated for 400 items.
12/28 It was announced that the import licensing requirement would be eliminated with effect on Jan 1, 1978, for 1,920 tariff items.

I (continued)

Situation at December ($t-2$)	Previous year ($t-1$)	Devaluation year (t)	Following year ($t+1$)
		27. MEXICO (1982)	
• A small number of imports are prohibited; most imports require licenses. + Certain exports are prohibited and some others require licenses, but no exchange control applies to export proceeds.	**3/24** Import licensing requirements were introduced for 63 tariff items (luxury goods). **6/26** Import licensing requirements were introduced in 861 tariffs items (metal-mechanical industry). **11/2** Import licensing. **12/30** requirements were introduced in 202 and 828 tariff items covering dairy products and foodstuffs.	**9/1** A stringent exchange control system was established. Almost all imports became subject to prior licensing. Quotas on most services' payments were introduced.	**5/6** Imports of inputs for export production were exempted from prior licensing. **12/22** The number of items exempted from prior import licensing was increased to 1,703.
		28. NICARAGUA (1979)	
• 2 categories of importers: one allowed to import any kind of merchandise, the other allowed to import only for industrial needs. • All sales of foreign exchange at the official rate must be authorized by the central bank and are subject to quotas. + Some exports require specific authorization, and others general authorization, while still others can be freely made. Almost all the proceeds must be surrendered.	**11/1** The surrender period for exports was reduced from 120 to 30 days. **11/14** Import and invisible payments were classified in terms of priorities. The central bank would allocate the foreign exchange on this basis weekly (very restrictive).	**2/19** Payments for all imports and most invisibles were made subject to a minimum waiting period of 7 days; the quotas for travel and medical expenses were reduced. **4/6** A multiple exchange rate system was introduced. **8/30** The multiple exchange system was abolished, but the parallel market continued. All sales of foreign exchange were temporarily prohibited.	**7/11** The parallel market was officially closed from July 12 to July 20. **3/8** A number of nonessential imports were excluded from the official market.

29. PAKISTAN (1972)

• Several "effective" exchange rates.

• 4 lists of permitted imports: a free list, a licensable list, an export bonus list, and a cash cum bonus list. All imports except those on the "free list" require licenses; the latter 2 lists are subject to deposits and administrative delay.

• All payments for invisibles are subject to approval, and some items (tourism) have no quota assignment.

+ Exports of most goods are allowed freely (except 24 items that require licenses); the proceeds must be surrendered within 6 mths.

1/1 In the import program for the first half of 1971, no provision was made for certain nonessential consumer goods.

4/24 The import of 46 items was prohibited and 28 items were shifted from the licensable list to the cash cum bonus list.

11/24 Prohibitions on some metal manufacturers and foodstuff imports were introduced.

4/21 The opening of letters of credit for the import of raw material for the pharmaceutical industry under the free list was no longer permitted.

5/11 Unification of the exchange market.

5/14 The existent licensing lists were consolidated into 2: 23 items on a tied list (foreign aid) and 327 items without quantitative restrictions or licenses.

7/5 Some quotas for invisibles were increased, and the exchange allocation for tourism was permitted.

• During the year a number of previously prohibited items were added to the free list of imports. Private banks were allowed to carry out more transactions.

6/7, 8/6, 9/7 Exports of some food products were prohibited.

10/15 Some import items were transferred from the free list to the tied list.

30. PAKISTAN (1982)

• 2 lists of permitted imports: a free list and a tied list (procured only from tied sources). All imports require licenses, except for those made by the government, and their validity is 1 year.

• Payments for invisibles require prior approval, and some items are subject to annual quotas (travel: $500 per trip).

+ Exports of some goods are prohibited (foodstuff, metals); most others may be made freely, but the proceeds must be surrendered within 4 months after the shipment.

2/21 The limit on the value of machinery imports by non-restricted industries was increased. All

7/1 Some shifts and changes in the import lists were made.

8/16, 11/21 Export prohibitions were lifted for 21 agricultural products. Other goods were exempted from quota restrictions.

6/1 The quotas for most services' payments were increased.

1/7 Mild liberalization of import restrictions. 148 tariff items were made freely importable.

11/22 Quotas for most services payments were increased further.

I (continued)

Situation at December (t − 2)	Previous year (t − 1)	Devaluation year (t)	Following year (t + 1)
		31. PERU (1967)	
• All imports, except a dozen items, were permitted freely. • No restrictions on payments or proceeds of invisibles. + Besides exports of fishmeal and coffee, exports are not subject to license, and no control was exercised over export proceeds.	• (No measure of this type was taken.)	3/10 Imports of corn and its substitutes were made subject to license. 9/4 The central bank suspended its operations in the foreign exchange market. 10/5 All exports required licenses, and all export proceeds had to be surrendered again into negotiable exchange certificates. All payments not eligible for certificates could be made through a free exchange market.	2/26 The validity of the exchange certificates were reduced from 5 to 3 days. 3/1 Temporary (3-month) prohibition on nonessential imports. 5/29 This list of prohibited imports was reduced to 90 items. 6/24 A new list of imports prohibited, covering about 250 items, was introduced.
		32. PERU (1975)	
• Dual exchange market. • Imports of some "nonessential" goods are prohibited, and imports of a large number of manufactured goods are seldom granted. • Private sector imports require the approval of the competent ministry, and almost all must be made on a letter of credit basis. • The central bank stringently classified the exchange rate that applies to each category of invisibles, some of which are subject to quotas (travel $1,200/year). + All exports are subject to licenses to assure the surrendering of the procedures to the certificate market.	9/24 The basic exchange allocation for tourism was raised from $30 to about $40 per day for up to 30 days.	9/26 The exchange rates were unified, but the dual exchange market was maintained. The documentary letter of credit required for private imports was abolished. 11/21 Exports of fishmeal and fish oil were suspended. 12/17 The exchange allocation for expenditures abroad was reduced to $25/day.	9/1 A system of import licenses was announced. 2/25 All applications for the purchase of exchange for travel were forced to be made 48 hours in advance. 5/18 A list of permitted imports within a National Import Program was published. 6/28 The sol was devalued in both markets. 7/15 The quotas for student remittances and business travel expenditures were increased. 9/22 A system of periodic devaluations was adopted. 11/22 The National Import Program and the Import Exchange Budget for 1977 were announced.

• (No significant changes took place.)

33. PHILIPPINES (1962)

1/22 The final phase of the "decontrol" program was put into effect. All restrictions on foreign trade and payments were withdrawn.

3/2 Third phase of "decontrol" program was put into effect, determining the items affected by each exchange rate (official and fluctuating).

10/16 Exchange allowances granted for travel and studies abroad were curtailed.

10/20 All purchases of exchange for imports were made subject to prior approval of the central bank.

• A fluctuating rate applies to almost all transactions.

• No quantitative restrictions on imports or in the exchange allocation (except for a few items).

• No restrictions or exchange quotas on payments for invisibles.

+ Some "strategic" exports cannot be made and the export proceeds must be surrendered.

34. PHILIPPINES (1970)

2/21 Major exchange reform: adoption of a fluctuating rate and relaxation on restrictions on trade and payments. Some import categories and limits to invisibles were maintained.

3/10 Exporters were required to receive their proceeds at most 30 days after the shipment.

5/1 All exchange transactions were forced to be carried at the free market rate (including exports).

4/29 The supervision measures on the foreign exchange allocation for travel purposes were tightened.

6/9 Opening of import letters of credit was suspended.

6/19 The opening of letters of credit was resumed, but restricted to 4 categories of goods.

11/24 Foreign exchange allowances for travel purposes were reduced.

11/26 All imports other than the 4 categories mentioned above received the approval of the central bank, as well as all the invisibles payments. The surrendering period was reduced to 1 business day.

7/28 The central bank eliminated the provisions requiring its approval for importation in excess of $50,000 on some capital goods.

9/6 Certain consumer goods for which letters of credit could not be opened were allowed to be imported.

• Imports of certain agricultural goods were prohibited, and those of cars, textiles, and liquors were "voluntarily" restrained.

• Almost all imports should be covered by a letter of credit.

• All payments for invisibles required central bank approval and were subject to quotas.

+ Some "strategic" products cannot be exported, and the export proceeds must be surrendered.

I (continued)

35. SRI LANKA (1967)

Situation at December (t − 2)	Previous year (t − 1)	Devaluation year (t)	Following year (t + 1)
• Member of the Sterling Area. • Annual import program in force. • All private imports require individual licenses and are divided into 3 groups: essential, less essential, and nonessential goods. The first 2 groups are subject to quotas, and the last one is highly restricted. • All payments for invisibles require individual permits and are subject to quotas. + All exports require 2 types of licenses.	11/27 It was announced that the foreign exchange budget for 1967 would be much lower than the 1966 one due to a terms of trade shock.	11/22 The par value was changed.	5/6 A foreign exchange certificate scheme was introduced. Imports were divided into 2 groups, both requiring licenses; but one of them also required the surrendering of certificates. 5/31 The open general license import list was expanded by 35 groups of commodities. 7/15 The export of 13 items was banned and that of 18 other items was made subject to export licenses.

36. TRINIDAD-TOBAGO (1967)

Situation at December (t − 2)	Previous year (t − 1)	Devaluation year (t)	Following year (t + 1)
• Member of the Sterling Area. • For import controls countries are divided into 2 groups: (a) Soviet countries and China (discriminated) and (b) all other countries, except U.K. • Regulations include prohibitions, state trading, individual licensing, and open general license. • Payments of invisibles outside the Sterling Area require specific approval, supporting documents and are subject to quotas. + Exports of certain goods (foodstuff, petroleum) require individual licenses and all proceeds must be surrendered.	• During the year, the import of a number of goods became subject to individual import licenses.	• During the year an increasing number of imports became subject to individual licenses (4/6, 4/27, 5/5, 10/12). 11/23 The par value was changed.	3/19 Some authorized banks were allowed to deal in foreign exchange. 10/10 It was announced that licenses would not be granted for the importation of motorcars and cosmetics.

37. VENEZUELA (1964)

- Multiple exchange rate system.
- Some goods are prohibited, and others may be imported only by the government. A number of items require specific licenses. All imports (27 tariff items) at the special subsidy rate require special permit.
- No restrictions on invisibles.
+ Some products require a special license to be exported. Petroleum and iron ore proceeds must be surrendered to the central bank, other proceeds to the banking system.

- No significant change took place.

1/18 Major exchange reform toward the unification of the different exchange rates and relaxation of controls.

3/24 Imports of fertilizers and chemicals require a license.
5/21 Imports of most consumer durable goods require a license.
7/27 Import licensing restrictions on textiles under 178 tariff items imposed for 60 days.
9/29 Almost all of the above measures became permanent.

38. YUGOSLAVIA (1965)

- Single fixed exchange rate.
- 89 groups of commodities (raw material) may be imported without quantative restriction.
- Import licenses are issued freely for the other 12 groups of commodities.
- For 28 other groups and capital goods a system of quotas is in force.
- Payments for trade related invisibles are treated similarly to imports. Tourism exchange allowance: $20/year.
+ All proceeds from exports must be surrendered within 30 days. Some exports are subject to individual licenses, and others to quotas.

2/13 A less restrictive structure of the import and export lists was introduced.
10/30 The travel exchange allowance was increased slightly.

7/26 New par value of the dinar.

3/17 A more liberal use of the foreign exchange proceeds was allowed.
7/21 The access to foreign trade was made easier to more economic institutions.

II Evolution of tariffs, duties, and cost related import restrictions

Situation at December ($t-2$)	Previous year ($t-1$)	Devaluation year (t)	Following year ($t+1$)
		1. ARGENTINA (1970)	
• All imports subject to a 4% tax on the freight, consular fee 1.5%, and statistical taxes (0.3–1.5%). • Import duties range: 5%–140% (exceptions on machinery). • Advance deposits of 40% of CIF value in pesos, refunded after 180 days (exception for public sector imports and basic input imports). + Taxes on traditional exports.	**3/14** Fertilizers, formerly exempted, were charged 20% and 40% import duties.	**2/6** Most of the special regimes and exceptions from the custom tariff were abolished. **6/15** Import duty concessions were given to some energy and steel industry inputs. **7/11** New import duties—those of 15% were reduced to 0% and higher rates were reduced by 15 to 30 points. **7/15** Taxes on exports up to 35% were introduced. **12/4** New import duties of 200% on 160 items; some concessions were rescinded, and others increased.	**8/25 +** The export taxes were raised up to 45%. **10/25** All settlements of imports and exports took place at a mixed exchange rate. **12/20 +** Export taxes on traditional exports were eliminated.
		2. BOLIVIA (1972)	
• Custom surcharge of 15% ad valorem is in force. + Taxes on traditional exports. • No advance deposit requirements.	**3/17** Reduction in export tax to copper.	**10/20** A 20% tax on traditional exports was introduced as well as a 15% tax on the net value of all other exports. **11/15** The custom surcharge of 15% was abolished.	**12/1** New (more protective) custom tariff came into effect.

3. BOLIVIA (1979)

• Most private sector imports subject to an advance deposit of 5%, 10%, or 25% of the CIF value that must be lodged 120 days prior to the release from customs.

• Custom tax of 1%, "additional tax" 3%, and 8% tax on services rendered.

+ Taxes on traditional exports.

1/5 Advance deposit requirements were waived from Andean Pact imports.

1/27 Imports of acrylic fiber thread became subject to a specific duty.

3/7 Certain minerals were exempted from export taxes.

6/22 Custom tariff on textiles, paper, vehicles, and other goods were adjusted.

2/1 Exemptions of "essential goods" from custom duties and tariffs and prior deposit requirements were extended.

2/16 Public imports were required to pay all custom duties and tariffs.

7/25, 6/28, 8/20 Military supplies and armaments were exempted from the requirement of paying custom duties and tariffs.

9/18 A 180 days 500% advance deposit was introduced for about 600 tariff positions.

11/30 Devaluation of the peso and abolishment of the 500% prior deposit requirement (return to 25%, 10%, 5% scheme).

1/18 Some deductions of required taxes and duties for certain imports were granted.

6/23 A 10% additional tax on textile exports to Europe was introduced.

4. BOLIVIA (1982)

• Advance deposit requirement of 25% for private imports (also 10% and 5% rates).

1/12 The 25% advance deposit requirement was terminated.

2/20 Certain import duty rates were reduced.

2/5 The dispersion of the tariff structure was reduced, but a tax of 1.8% on all foreign exchange sales was introduced.

7/13 Free market transactions were exempted from the 1.8% tax.

• (No change took place.)

5. CHILE (1982)

• Import duties for most items are at a 10% uniform rate. A value added tax on 20% is levied on the sum of the CIF value and the import duty.

• No advance deposits requirements.

3/25 Special duties on milk derivatives were eliminated or reduced.

5/9 Duties were raised on imports of most dairy products.

11/12 Temporary tariff increases, averaging 17 percentage points, were imposed on 12 products.

3/23 A 12% tax was levied on foreign exchange's purchases for the financing of imports.

• The 10% uniform import tariff was raised to 20% until December 1985.

II (continued)

Situation at December ($t - 2$)	Previous year ($t - 1$)	Devaluation year (t)	Following year ($t + 1$)
		6. COLOMBIA (1962)	
• Advance deposits of 1%, 5%, 20%, 50%, 75%, and 130% were discriminatorily and discretionarily requested on different import categories. Returned 90 days after the imports are cleared.	• Advance deposit requirements (new): **3/1** on tractors and automobiles: reduced from 130% to 20%; **4/19** on plastic products: from 130% to 65%; **5/24** on iron and steel: from 130% to 100%; **6/21** of automobiles and other vehicles: reduction to a 5% rates; other products were uniformly set at 20%.	**4/5** Advance deposits to 5 categories of imports were increased: from 5% to 20%, 20% to 50%, 50% to 150%, 75% to 180%, and 100% to 200%. **7/1** Advance deposits of the same 5 categories were reduced: from 20% to 15%, 50% to 40%, 150% to 110%, 180% to 150%, and 200% to 170%. **8/1** The advance deposits were further reduced from 170% to 150%, 150% to 120%, 110% to 90%, 40% to 30%, and 15% to 10%. **9/1** Advance deposits of 3 categories were reduced: from 150% to 120%, 120% to 90%, and 90% to 65%.	**2/28** Advance deposits on 2 categories of imports were reduced to 1%. **3/11** Raw materials for export products were exempted from duties and advance deposit requirements. **4/4** Advance deposits on 4 categories were reduced to 10%. **5/2** Advance deposits on 2 categories were reduced to 10% and to 30% in another category.
		7. COLOMBIA (1965)	
• Departing from the advance deposit requirements described in the last year of the previous episode.	**9/2** A 5% advance deposit for imports of basic industry machinery was introduced. **12/28** a 95% advance deposit was required for the application for foreign exchange.	**1/20** Advance deposit requirements were announced for some items. **7/10** A 100% peso deposit guarantee was required from all exporters. **10/1** Advance deposit for imports that could only be imported at the (higher) intermediate rate was reduced by 5% of the rate in force. Further 5% monthly reductions for a 20-month period were announced.	• (No change in advance deposits requirements.)

8. COLOMBIA (1967)

- See last year of preceding episode.

1/25 All advance deposit requirements were increased by 50%.

2/15 The advance deposit requirements were restored to their 1965 levels. Rates of 70%, 95%, and 130% were introduced.

4/6 The prior import deposit for certain capital goods was fixed at 5%.

- During the year the advance deposit requirements were reduced on numerous occasions.

6/5 The 95% advance deposit for foreign exchange applications in some transactions was eliminated.

11/28 Some imports made by nonprofit institutions were exempted from the prior deposit requirement.

9. COSTA RICA (1974)

- In addition to custom duties: 5% ad valorem sales tax and selective 10–50% ad valorem consumption tax on imports coming from outside Central America.

- No advance deposit requirements for imports.

+ Export taxes on bananas, coffees, sugar.

4/25 + Ad valorem taxes ranging from 1% to 18% were introduced on some exports.

- (No change took place.)

12/27 A temporary import surcharge of 10–50% for many goods was applied.

10. CYPRUS (1967)

- No advance deposit requirements.

- (No change took place.)

- (No change took place.)

- (No change took place.)

II (continued)

Situation at December ($t - 2$)	Previous year ($t - 1$)	Devaluation year (t)	Following year ($t + 1$)
		11. ECUADOR (1961)	
• Advance deposit requirements up to 50% for certain imports on list 2 and 25% on list 1.	**4/1** Advance deposits for certain list 2 imports were reduced from 50% to 20%. **12/15** Advance deposits for certain list 2 imports were abolished.	**3/7** Advance deposits were reintroduced on all private imports (25% on list 1 imports and 50% on list 2 imports). **4/14** An import tax of 2.25% on the CIF value of all imports was introduced. **8/17** Advance deposits were increased to 100% on most list 2 imports (except some 100 items still at 50%).	• Certain items were shifted between the 2 import lists during the year.
		12. ECUADOR (1970)	
• Advance deposit requirements apply to most public and private imports financed with official exchange. Numerous different rates. • Import surcharge of 10% on list 1 items and 20% of list 2. • 15% of custom duties must be prepaid by list 1 imports and 70% by list 2 imports.	**2/4** Increases in all the categories of the advance deposit scheme took place. **5/27** Further increase in the advance deposit requirements for list 2 imports. Only the portion of the deposit exceeding 100% of the import value would be released on the date of arrival—the remaining, 90 days later. **10/23** Increase in the import surcharge to 11% on list 1 and 22% on list 2. The advance deposit scheme was changed; 385 possible rates ranging from 0% to 700% were created.	**1/23** The proportion of prepaid custom duties was raised to 40% on list 1 imports and 80% on list 2. **3/5** The range and dispersion of advance deposits rates was increased. **4/1** The rates for advance deposits were further raised. **5/12** The import surcharges were increased. **8/17** With the unification of the exchange market, some import surcharges were reduced and all restrictions on current payments were abolished. **9/21** Some list 2 imports were exempted from the additional 20% ad valorem duty.	**1/1** New advance import deposits ranging from 2% to 30% were introduced. **2/4** Public imports were exempted from the 20% ad valorem duty. **4/1** New, reduced, advance deposits were announced for April, May, and June. **6/16** The advance deposit requirements were abolished for list 1 imports. **11/22** Advance import deposits were reintroduced for list 1 imports and increased for list 2 imports.

13. ECUADOR (1982)

- Most imports are subject to advance deposit requirements that range from 15% to 50% of the CIF value for a period of 180 or 270 days.
+ Certain exports are subject to taxes—others receive tax credit subsidy.

2/13 The advance deposit imports scheme was made more restrictive (increase in rates and retention period).
2/18 Tariffs on automobiles were raised by up to 100 percentage points.
6/29 Import duties were increased on items of about 500 tariff categories.
9/23 + Export taxes on cocoa and coffee were reduced.

10/11 The advance deposit rates for imports were increased 80% on average.

3/17 A tax surcharge ranging from 5% to 15% was imposed on all imports.

14. EGYPT (1962)

- No advance deposit requirements.
- Some imports are made at a 20% premium.
+ Some exports are subject to a 20% tax.

9/1 Previously premium exempted imports were made subject to a 10% premium.

• (No change took place.)

15. EGYPT (1979)

- No official exchange allocated for nonessential imports; they should be acquired with foreign exchange from the free market.
- No advance deposits requirement.

• (No change took place.)

9/1 Custom duties on certain goods became effectively payable in foreign currency.

16. GUYANA (1967)

- No advance deposit requirement on imports.

11/16 An advance deposit requirement on imports' letters of credit was introduced.

• (No change took place.)

5/10 Import duties were abolished or reduced in several import items (agricultural, capital goods, food).
6/4 An advance deposit scheme was introduced and the requirement of paying custom duties in foreign currency was abolished.

• (No change took place.)

II (continued)

Situation at December ($t-2$)	Previous year ($t-1$)	Devaluation year (t)	Following year ($t+1$)
		17. INDIA (1966)	
• No advance deposit requirement on imports. + Export taxes on some products.	**2/17** Custom surcharge of 10% ad valorem was introduced on all imports. **7/1** Almost all private imports require a 25% advance deposit. **8/20** The 10% surcharge and the prior deposit requirement were abolished.	• (No change took place.)	**5/26 +** Reduction in export duties on some products.
		18. INDONESIA (1978)	
• System of advance deposits in force. • Sales taxes on 5%, 10%, and 20% are levied on most CIF value of imports.	**1/1** A system of 100% advance deposit, 100% financial guarantee, and 100% advance payments of duties was introduced for some imports.	**1/1** Preferential 20% duty for imports coming from ASEAN countries. **2/25** 50% reduction of import duties and sales tax on imports of a few goods. **5/23** Higher import duty on imports of aluminum and cigarette paper. **6/2** Exemptions on import duties and sales tax for a few items. **9/1** Tariff reductions were announced on 138 imports from ASEAN countries. **11/16** 50% reduction in import duties and sales taxes for imports of intermediate inputs (100% if used in manufactured exports). **12/13** The special 100%-100%-100% system was reduced for textiles and other imports.	**Apr.** Exemptions from import duties and sales taxes were granted for a number of imports. **9/26** Custom duties were reduced on 334 categories of raw materials and intermediate goods, reducing the range from (5–40%) to (5–10%).

19. ISRAEL (1962)

- (No change took place.)

- (No change took place.)

- The method of payment of each import is specified on the required individual license.

20. ISRAEL (1967)

6/1 Some 400 items were freed from all restrictions.

- During the year import licensing requirements were relaxed.

- The method of payment of each import is specified on the required individual license.

10/1 Import duties on some 400 commodities were reduced by 10–16%.

11/19 Custom duties were reduced by 12.5% to maintain constant their domestic currency value at predevaluation levels.

21. ISRAEL (1971)

1/1 The advance deposit requirement was reduced from 40% to 30% of the CIF values. Tariff reductions related with the Kennedy Round concessions were implemented.
4/15 Custom duties were reduced on average 5% on imports of 420 commodities.
6/1 Further tariff reductions of up to 10% were announced for imports of 1,350 items.
8/1 Custom duties reductions ranging from 20% to 30% were put into effect for some consumer goods.

1/1 The advance deposit rate was reduced from 50% to 40% of the CIF value. More reductions in import duties were announced as part of the 5-year plan. The 20% import surcharge was extended to March 31, 1972.

1/1 Reduction in import duties on a wide range of domestically produced goods was announced as part of a 5-year program seeking to reduce the maximum level of tariff protection to 35%.
1/11 An import deposit scheme of 50% of the CIF value for a 6-month period earning a 6% interest was introduced.
2/8 Increases in tax rates for certain imported "luxury" goods were announced.
8/17 An import surcharge of 20% of the CIF value was introduced (foodstuff and fuel imports were exempted).

- No advance deposit requirement for imports.

22. JAMAICA (1967)

8/1 Imports of many industrial raw material were admitted free of duty.

6/9 The consumption tax was raised to 5%, and the universe of goods subject to it was widened.

- (No change took place.)

- No advance deposit requirement for imports.
- Consumption tax (on imports) of 2.6%.

II (continued)

Situation at December ($t - 2$)	Previous year ($t - 1$)	Devaluation year (t)	Following year ($t + 1$)
23. JAMAICA (1978)			
• The foreign exchange market was closed since early December. • No advance deposit requirement was in effect.	• (No change took place.)	• (No change took place.)	• (No change took place.)
24. KENYA (1981)			
• Some imports are subject to a 3 months advance deposit ranging from 100% to 10% of the CIF value of imports that bears no interest.	6/20 A surcharge of 10% was introduced in all import items, and custom duties for a wide variety of consumer goods were increased by up to 100%.	6/13 As part of an import reform, tariffs were raised on over 1,400 import items. 11/10 The retention period for the advance deposits was reduced to 1 month for most goods.	• (No change took place.)
25. KOREA (1980)			
• Advance deposit scheme on all imports. Rates ranging from 10 to 20% of CIF value. • Customs tariff system defined as "flexible" (can be changed at any time).	1/1 Tariffs on most imports were reduced, driving down the unweighted average level of tariffs from 36% to 25%. The advance deposit scheme was only retained for private imports on a deferred payment basis. 3/29 The advance deposit rate was reduced from 20% to 10% for the imports still subject to this scheme.	7/19 Import tariffs on some "luxury" items were raised from an average of 52% to one of 71% until December 31.	1/5 Tariff rates on imports subject to quotas were reduced, on average, from 19.5% to 9.2%.

26. MEXICO (1976)

• Import licenses for certain goods are subject to the payment of a fee of usually between 1% and 6% of the value of import transactions.

• Many nonessential imports are subject to an import surcharge of 10% ad valorem.

Jan. The 10% import surcharge levied on 2,408 items was eliminated.

Aug. The number of tariff items exempt from export duties was increased, and import duties were increased on 5,845 tariff items (excluding "basic" goods). The average import duty was thus increased from 15% to 20%.

• The import surcharge applicable to all imports was increased from 1% to 2% ad valorem.

9/8 Export taxes were increased and export incentives were abolished.

9/8 Import duties were widely reduced to a range of (2–75%). It was officially estimated that the average tariff rate fell from 20% to 9%.

10/6 Export taxes were substantially reduced.

May Subsidies of up to 40% of import duties were granted to imports of machinery and equipment for some "basic" industries.

27. MEXICO (1982)

• The issuance of the required import licenses may require payments between 1% and 17% of the import value.

1/8 Firms and producers of capital goods were given exceptions of up to 100% of import duties of raw material.

5/13 Import duties were modified on 374 tariff items (foodstuff, textiles, and machinery).

3/4 Import duties on 1,517 items were reduced to their level of May 1981.

1/39 The import duty rates for essential imports were reduced on average by 10 percentage points.

28. NICARAGUA (1979)

• No advance deposit requirement on imports.

• Most imports are subject to an import surcharge of 30% of the import duty.

11/14 Weekly foreign exchange allocation for import payments.

• (No change took place.)

• (No change took place.)

29. PAKISTAN (1972)

• Imports from 2 of the 4 existing lists (bonus import list and cash cum bonus list) are subject to advance deposit requirements and administrative delay.

5/14 Import reform: the 4 lists were consolidated into 2 and the advance deposit requirement was abolished.

• (No change took place.)

9/15 Import duties were increased and a 25% flood relief surcharge was levied on all dutiable imports.

II (continued)

Situation at December (t − 2)	Previous year (t − 1)	Devaluation year (t)	Following year (t + 1)
	30. PAKISTAN (1982)		
• The 12-month valid license required for all private imports is subject to a 2% fee. • Irrevocable letters of credit must be opened for all commercial imports.	**1/1** Import duties ranging from 25% to 45% were imposed on 11 basic raw material items. **3/28 +** An ad valorem export duty of 30% was levied on onyx blocks. **7/1** Increases in protective duties ranging from 10% to 50% were introduced on 8 items and from 12% to 85% on 13 raw material items.	**7/1** An across-the-board import surcharge of 5% was levied on all imports.	• (No change took place.)
	31. PERU (1967)		
• No advance deposit scheme for imports was in force.	**8/10** Most imports were made subject to a 1.5% surcharge. **10/28** All commodities listed in Peru's GATT schedule were exempted from the 1.5% surcharge. **11/9 +** A tax of 10% on the FOB value of most exports was introduced until March 31, 1969.	**6/7** Import duties on a wide range of commodities were increased substantially. The scope of import duty concessions granted under the Industrial Promotional Law was reduced. **7/31** A list of minimum CIF prices on which import duties would be based was issued.	**3/1** Sales tax of 10–35% was introduced in nonessential imported goods. **5/29** A 15% surtax was introduced on most imports on which payments were made with exchange certificates. **9/13 +** Exports of agricultural products were exempted from the 10% sales tax.

32. PERU (1975)

• Virtually all private sector imports must be made on a letter of credit basis.

• For imports of capital goods valued over $10,000, at least 80% must be financed abroad.

• No advance deposit scheme in force.

+ Traditional exports subject to taxes and nontraditional exports to tax credit (15–30% of FOB value).

1/15 + A 10% special tax on traditional exports was introduced temporarily.

5/11 A 180-day foreign financing requirement on goods other than capital goods was introduced.

10/30 The 180-day foreign financing requirement, the letter of credit, and the guarantee letter requirements were abolished.

1/1 New general customs law introduced a 10% surcharge tax and a 2% statistical tax on all imports.

4/22 + The tax surcharge of 10% on exports was extended indefinitely.

5/18 A national import program was announced.

6/28 + The tax on traditional exports was increased from 10% to 15%.

6/30 Many import duties were increased.

8/31 Imports of agricultural goods and inputs were exempted from import duties until the end of 1976.

33. PHILIPPINES (1962)

• Advance deposit scheme ranging from 50% to 150% (according to the nature of the import); the funds were kept as time deposits on banks for 120 days.

• (No change took place.)

1/22 Although the decontrol program ended, the advance deposit requirement was not removed.

5/22 The range of rates of the advance deposit requirement was reduced to 25–100%. Imports of raw material by domestic industries were exempted from this requirement.

• (No change took place.)

II (continued)

Situation at December (t − 2)	Previous year (t − 1)	Devaluation year (t)	Following year (t + 1)
		34. PHILIPPINES (1970)	
• Advance deposits in the form of cash margin deposits are required on the obligatory opening of letters of credit with rates ranging from 25% to 175% of the import value, and they are held for 90 or 120 days.	**4/1** Extended the advance deposit requirement for imports. **2/2** Import duties on petroleum and derivatives were raised. **4/16** The period for which the advance import deposits were to be held was reduced to 90 days for some goods and eliminated for others. **9/1** Import duties on many commodities were raised retroactively.	**2/21** Major exchange reform accompanied by relaxation of restrictions. **5/1** A stabilization tax of 8–10% was introduced on some exports.	**7/1** The rates of the export taxes were reduced 2 percentage points.
		35. SRI LANKA (1967)	
• Most imports subject to a 10% custom surcharge on the import duty rate (others to 5% or 20%). • No advance deposit scheme was in force.	**3/25** Textiles imports became subject to maximum retail prices (they were already subject to maximum import and wholesale prices). **7/29** A substantial revision of import duties became effective, lowering the average and the dispersion of the tariff structure and setting the maximum tariff on consumer goods at 150%. **11/1** A 10% fee on the CIF value of textile imports was introduced.	**5/11** Custom duties were reduced on some "essential" raw materials and capital goods. **7/26** The fees payable on import licenses were increased. **8/9** The fees payable on import licenses were further modified.	**5/6** Custom duties on imports under open general license were revised downward. **8/2** The tariff structure was adjusted, reducing duties on "essential" items and raising them on "nonessential" ones.

36. TRINIDAD-TOBAGO (1967)

- (No change took place.)

- (No change took place.)

- (No change took place.)

- No advance deposit scheme was in force (restrictions were more in the form of licenses and exchange availability).

37. VENEZUELA (1964)

- (No change took place.)

1/18 Unification of the exchange market; the subsidized rate was maintained.

12/30 25 custom classifications were no longer eligible for the subsidized rate; this only remained for milk and wheat.

- (No change took place.)

- No advance deposit scheme was in force for imports.
- 27 custom classifications: imports were eligible for a subsidized exchange rate upon permit.

38. YUGOSLAVIA (1965)

- (No change took place.)

10/14 Yugoslavia applied for full membership in the GATT.

8/25 Yugoslavia became a full contracting party of the GATT (duties adjusted downwards in some sectors).

- No advance deposit scheme was in force for imports.

III **Payments restrictions on capital transactions**

Situation at December ($t − 2$)	Previous year ($t − 1$)	Devaluation year (t)	Following year ($t + 1$)
		1. ARGENTINA (1970)	
• No limitation on inward or outward capital transfers by residents and nonresidents. • No restrictions on invisible payments.	**6/15** The forward discount of U.S. dollars was moved from 4% to 8%.	**10/19** The central bank reduced the premium on forward exchange from 8% to 6%. **10/21** Within the partial reopening of the exchange market the central bank's approval was required for sales of exchange connected with foreign investments or deposits. Profits and dividend remittances were kept restricted.	**3/29** In another reopening of the exchange market the services of foreign loans were permitted. **5/10** Within the partial reopening process remittances of profit and dividends remain suspended. **7.29** External dollar bonds could be issued to encourage repatriation of resident owned capital. **7/31** New foreign investment law permitted remittances after the first year of operation. **9/16** Remittances of profits, dividends, and royalties were only permitted through the purchase of negotiable 5-year U.S. $ denominated bonds issued by the government. **9/20** Within the created dual exchange market all financial transactions were to be carried out at the floating rate.

2. BOLIVIA (1972)

- Outward capital transfers were free of controls. Inward capital transfers could be done through the free market, but public sector receipts should be surrendered to the central bank.
- Invisible payments may be made freely through the free market.

- (No change took place.)

- (No change took place.)

- (No change took place.)

3. BOLIVIA (1979)

- Same general framework as in 1971, but foreign loans were subject to the authorization of the National Council for Planning and Economy and had to be registered.

8/17 A ceiling on short-term indebtedness of Bolivian and foreign financial institutions was set at the level existing June 30, 1978.

11/30 With the new exchange regime, new ceilings on short-term and medium-term foreign exchange liabilities of the banking system were adopted.

- (No change took place.)

4. BOLIVIA (1982)

- Same general framework as in previous episode.

7/30 All sales of foreign exchange required the authorization of the central bank.

2/5 Devaluation date. Dealings in the parallel market were declared illegal.

3/11 A dual exchange market was created. The official exchange rate was available only for public sector's transactions. All other transactions were conducted at the free rate.

11/3 The exchange rate system was unified and dollar denominated contracts were prohibited.

1/5 Foreign borrowing through the official market became highly regulated.

III (continued)

Situation at December ($t-2$)	Previous year ($t-1$)	Devaluation year (t)	Following year ($t+1$)
		5. CHILE (1982)	
• Capital inflows are generally free but outflows are restricted. • Most new foreign borrowing or refinancing of existent credits require prior approval of the central bank. • Incentives to foreign direct investment are in force. • Central bank's approval is required for invisible payments in excess of some (high) predetermined limits.	**3/25** Chilean banks were permitted to contract lines of credit of up to 1 year maturity with foreign banks without central bank's approval. **4/29** Permission was granted for individuals to maintain deposits in foreign banks. **12/23** Commerical banks were permitted to contract short-term credits abroad for relending up to a limit determined by a bank's capital and reserves.	**5/5** The minimum average of maturity of 24 months for foreign borrowing was abolished. A reserve deposit requirement of 20% was imposed on short term borrowing. **8/5** It was announced that the exchange rate would be freely determined in the market. **9/3** A preferential exchange rate was established for the service of foreign debt. **9/26** A crawling peg system with daily adjustments was adopted.	**2/1** A 90-day moratorium was placed on amortization payments of foreign loans guaranteed by official agencies. **3/14** Transfer of profits and dividends and payments of foreign debt were made subject to authorization of the central bank. **7/15** An exchange guarantee to refinance foreign debt payments of private firms was introduced.
		6. COLOMBIA (1962)	
• Capital imported for the petroleum and metal extracting industries must be sold to the central bank at the fixed rate. Other capital inflows and outflows subject to a dual system. Capital imported before 6/17/57 pay amortization and profits at auction rate, capital imported afterward may enter and remit freely through the parallel market. • Payments of official debt were made at the (lower) certificate rate.	• (No change took place.)	• (No change took place.)	**1/19** The conversion rate of official foreign loans was devalued.

7. COLOMBIA (1965)

10/25 The Bank of the Republic ceased its operations in the free market.

11/19 Operations in the free market were suspended. All Colombian residents who possessed foreign exchange were required to communicate the amounts held and were prohibited to use the funds without previous authorization.

12/1 A capital market replaced the free market and those transactions could take place only through the Bank of the Republic.

• Banks were required to maintain 100% reserves against their foreign currency liabilities.

12/13 An Exchange Control Prefecture was created to enforce the controls on invisibles and capital transactions.

3/10 The exchange rate for petroleum companies proceeds was devalued.

7/7 The administrative requirements for capital flows were tightened.

7/15 Debt contracts abroad had to be registered.

• Except for the petroleum industry, capital may be brought in either through the free market or through the intermediate market, but all amortization and payments must be made through the *same* market.

• All capital inflows and outflows must be recorded at the Superintendency of Foreign Trade.

8. COLOMBIA (1967)

• See last year of previous episode.

3/22 The capital market rate was fixed. The remittance tax on certain transfers was abolished. The holding of foreign currency deposits was abolished.

5/9 A limit of 10% on the net value of the foreign investment was set for the allowed repatriation.

6/12 The surrendering of all the proceeds from profits and interests was made obligatory.

3/12 The limit to the transfer of foreign capital was raised from 10% to 14%.

6/1 The capital exchange market was abolished.

• Departing from the general framework described in the previous episode.

III (continued)

Situation at December (t − 2)	Previous year (t − 1)	Devaluation year (t)	Following year (t + 1)
9. COSTA RICA (1974)			
• Most public debt and services payments were made at a lower exchange rate. • Taxes of 15% and 10% were levied on remittances abroad of debt payments and interest. • Transfers of capital may be made freely through the free market. • Foreign capital entering through the official market must be registered at the central bank to ensure access to that market for the related transfer.	• (No change took place.)	**4/25** Unification of the dual market; all existing restrictions on transactions at the official rate were lifted. **9/30** Restrictions on outflows of resident owned capital were introduced: the central bank denied transfers of capital without actual obligation abroad or when the amount was considered unjustified. **10/1** Various measures to stimulate capital inflows came into force: higher interest rates on foreign currency deposits (different for residents and nonresidents).	• (No change took place.)
10. CYPRUS (1967)			
• Capital inflows from non-Sterling Area countries must be surrendered; payments in those currencies require prior approval. • Foreign investment is permitted if its participation in domestic industries is smaller than 50%. • Transactions with foreign securities require prior approval.	• (No change took place.)	• (No change took place.)	**2/2** Commercial banks were required to transfer their foreign assets to the central bank gradually.

11. ECUADOR (1961)

• (No change took place.)

5/22 Despite the reorganization in the exchange market, most nontrade and capital transactions remained in the free market.
7/14 A higher exchange rate (official) was to be applied to registered capital and debt operations.

• (No change took place.)

• Unregistered capital is free to enter through the free market in unlimited quantities.
• Foreign capital may enter at the official rate if it was registered with the central bank for approved purposes.
• Invisible payments at the official rate require a license.

12. ECUADOR (1970)

8/2 Branches of foreign banks could not accept savings or fixed term deposits of Ecuadorian residents.
11/22 With the reintroduction of a free market, private (including foreign branches) banks were allowed to maintain deposits in foreign currency.

6/29 Bank and nonbank residents were required to sell to the central bank all foreign currency they held at home or abroad at the free market exchange rate.
8/17 Unification of the exchange markets.
10/29 Official agencies and foreign institutions were allowed to maintain accounts in foreign currency in the banking system.
12/23 Any person receiving a payment in foreign currency had to surrender the exchange within 10 days.

• (No change took place.)

• Voluntary registration of inward capital flows in the central bank to have the right to access to the official state.

• Government receipts of invisibles must be channeled through the official market.

III (continued)

Situation at December (t − 2)	Previous year (t − 1)	Devaluation year (t)	Following year (t + 1)
		13. ECUADOR (1982)	
• Capital may freely enter or leave the country through the free market. Most borrowing from abroad is subject to an exchange tax ranging from 0.5% to 2%. • All foreign investment and public debt must be registered at the central bank to have the right to access to the official market rate. • Foreign securities or real estate abroad cannot be purchased with official exchange.	**5/15** The central bank was allowed to sell foreign exchange for private loans repayments.	**3/3** A "free market" exchange rate for the payment of some imports and refinancing of foreign debt was established. **5/13** The surrender of foreign exchange from private sector's loans approved by the central bank was made mandatory.	**2/6** Foreign exchange was authorized to be sold at the official rate for the service of private sector's foreign debts. **4/5** Foreign loans to the private sector maturing in 1985 were authorized under the condition of surrendering the foreign exchange to the central bank.
		14. EGYPT (1962)	
• The import and export of securities and similar items require licenses that are seldom granted. • Some transfers of capital can be made through a system of blocked accounts in foreign currency. • Royalties and dividends are subject to specific quotas.	**12/31** The import of Egyptian bank notes by travelers was prohibited.	• (No change took place.)	• (No change took place.)

15. EGYPT (1979)

- Residents who have deposited foreign currency in Egyptian banks may use those funds for any purpose, including transfers abroad.
- Otherwise, outward capital transfers are restricted, with specific limits to each kind of transfer.
- Some foreign exchange accounts are available for residents that receive transfers from abroad.

7/2 Public debt services were exempted from the shift of all invisibles to the parallel market.
8/29 All public debt in foreign currency required the supervision of the central bank.

1/1 Unification of the exchange markets.

7/1 Foreign banks were required to ensure that 15% of their foreign currency deposits could be made available on call by the central bank.

16. GUYANA (1967)

- Residents of the Sterling Area may freely invest and repatriate their capital at any time; nonresidents must obtain "approved status."
- The export of capital to non-Sterling Area countries is not normally allowed.

- (No change took place.)

- (No change took place.)

17. INDIA (1966)

- Intricate system of nonresident accounts in domestic and foreign currency.
- The inward movement of capital is practically free, except when it is part of an investment that requires prior approval.
- Foreign securities can be imported and held.
- No restrictions on the remittance of profits, dividends, and interest to nonresidents.

10/20 The National Defense Remittance Scheme, which favored repatriation of capital and inward flow of invisibles, was implemented.
5/31 The National Defense Remittance Scheme was terminated.

- (No change took place.)

III (continued)

Situation at December ($t - 2$)	Previous year ($t - 1$)	Devaluation year (t)	Following year ($t + 1$)
18. INDONESIA (1978)			
• Stringent regulation of foreign investment. • Foreign currency deposits and securities can be held and transferred freely by residents and nonresidents, but certain foreign borrowing is subject to approval.	**2/15** A list of 4 categories of foreign investment priorities was announced.	• (No change took place.)	• (No change took place.)
19. ISRAEL (1962)			
• Incoming capital had to be surrendered at the official rate. • Repayment and amortization of capital are subject to specific regulations according to its maturity. • Exchange proceeds from invisibles or capital may be held in foreign currency time deposits or sold at a premium over the official rate.	• (No change took place.)	• (No change took place.)	• (No change took place.)
20. ISRAEL (1967)			
• Similar framework as in previous episode. • Two types of foreign currency deposits: TAMAM and NATAD. • Most payments of invisibles required individual licenses.	• (No change took place.)	**2/21** The quota of foreign exchange for patent rights was reduced to $250/year.	**2/9** Purchases of foreign securities were restricted to those assets listed on the London, Zurich, or N.Y. exchanges. **6/23** Regulations on capital transactions were eased. **10/18** The purchase of foreign securities from a larger number of countries was permitted.

21. ISRAEL (1971)

- Foreign currency deposits may be held by residents and non-residents under different regulations.
- Stringent regulations for foreign investment.
- Residents cannot maintain money, securities, or income from property outside Israel.
- Transfers of capital abroad by residents is not generally permitted.
- Owners of TAMAM accounts are the only ones allowed to purchase foreign securities.

- (No change took place.)

8/16 At the request of the central bank, the banking system suspended foreign exchange dealings except in U.S. dollars.

12/15 Banks were free to establish their own rates of interest on foreign currency accounts.

22. JAMAICA (1967)

- Previous approval is required for investing in non-Sterling Area securities as well as for direct foreign investments (and its remittances) and foreign debt over a certain limit.
- The Bank of Jamaica is allowed to charge up to 0.75% on inward and outward transfers.

8/29 The commission charged on outward transfers was raised from 3/8% to $1\frac{1}{2}$%.

3/17 The commission charged on inward transfers was reduced from 3/16% to 1/8%.

9/18 The blocking of the sterling assets of migrators was lifted.

10/12 Banks were prohibited from facilitating foreign exchange for personal transfers of capital.

11/22 Commission charges on outward transfers was increased from 0.5% to 0.75%, while that on inward transfers was reduced from 1/8% to 1/16%.

11/28 The free convertibility into sterling of the Jamaican pound was limited to dealings with commercial banks.

9/22 The commission on outward transfers was reduced from 0.75% to 0.5%.

III (continued)

Situation at December ($t-2$)	Previous year ($t-1$)	Devaluation year (t)	Following year ($t+1$)
23. JAMAICA (1978)			
• Foreign currency accounts are only allowed for nonresidents. • Outflows of resident owned capital are totally restricted. • Foreign exchange transfers are prohibited. • Stringent controls on direct foreign investment (some repatriation facilities) and on foreign debt payments.	**1/19** Payments for royalties and trademarks were to be blocked for some period. Restrictions on profits, dividends, interest, and amortization payments. **4/27** With the creation of a dual market, all capital transactions were effected at a depreciated rate.	**5/9** Reunification of the exchange market. **6/26** All entrants to Jamaica were required to declare the foreign exchange brought in and taken out.	• (No change took place.)
24. KENYA (1981)			
• Capital transfers to all countries are restricted. • Foreign investment is not restricted, but is subject to registration. • All flows of securities require approval, and residents are not normally granted it.	• (No change took place.)	**3/17** Repatriation of assets held abroad was required to be completed by Dec. 31.	• (No change took place.)
25. KOREA (1980)			
• All capital remittances require approval. • Loans from abroad are officially guaranteed if the authorization is granted (obligatory to request for loans larger than $200,000).	**1/1** Residents were allowed to hold foreign currency accounts up to a ceiling of $3,000. Restrictions on holding foreign securities were removed. **1/4** The maximum permissible spread over LIBOR for foreign loans was reduced.	**6/10** Foreign banks' activities (with residents) were permitted. **9/5** Measures regarding foreigners' shares and repatriation of profits were taken as an incentive to foreign investment. **10/15** The remaining regulations for purchasing foreign securities were relaxed.	**7/29** New regulations to promote direct foreign investment were announced. **8/1** Some capital related invisible payments became eligible for automatic approval.

26. MEXICO (1976)

• No significant change took place.

• No exchange control requirement on capital receipts and payments by residents or nonresidents.

• New foreign investment in banking and insurance companies was prohibited.

• Investment in most types of activities is reserved exclusively for Mexican individuals and corporations (some exclusively public).

• Borrowing abroad by public sector subject to ministry's approval, while for private sector was subject to Bank of Mexico's approval.

• Some U.S. $ deposits are allowed (and their interest rate is controlled) for residents of the northern border area.

3/22 Foreign currency time deposits (3 or 6 months) were authorized for residents from any part of Mexico.

9/29 The Bank of Mexico established a special credit line to enable banks to support firms with large foreign currency liabilities.

10/26 The Bank of Mexico ceased to intervene in the foreign exchange market. The maximum spread between buying or selling rates for financial institutions was set at 1%.

11/9 Short-term foreign loans contracted before Sep. were allowed immediate renewal.

11/22 Banks were instructed to refrain temporarily from buying and selling foreign exchange to the public.

12/1 The incoming president announced that the free convertibility of the peso would be maintained and that minting of silver coins will be resumed.

12/20 Banks were allowed again to buy and sell foreign currency at freely determined rates.

3/22 Net yields on U.S. $ deposits were pegged at 1 point above LIBOR. Only investment banks were allowed to hold dollar denominated deposits.

8/1 The legal reserve requirement on dollar denominated deposits was raised from 30% to 75%.

8/30 A rediscount facility was introduced to secure for Mexican borrowers credit in pesos against compensatory foreign deposits.

III (continued)

Situation at December ($t - 2$)	Previous year ($t - 1$)	Devaluation year (t)	Following year ($t + 1$)

27. MEXICO (1982)

• No exchange control requirements are imposed on capital receipts or payments by residents or nonresidents. • New foreign investment in banking, insurance, and petroleum is banned, and the foreigners' share of Mexican industries is regulated. • Private and public borrowing abroad requires prior approval.	• (No change took place.)	**8/5** A two-tier exchange rate was established. The preferential rate was applied to foreign debt's payments and some priority imports. **8/13** The foreign-currency deposits were frozen. The foreign exchange market closed for 6 days. **9/1** Private banking institutions were nationalized. **10/11** Payments on royalties and profit remittances were limited to 15% of the value of equity.	• Throughout the year the short-run obligations with foreign creditors were rescheduled several times.

28. NICARAGUA (1979)

• Domestic and foreign currencies may be freely exported and imported. • Proceeds from loans and investments should be channeled through the official market. • Only those funds converted at the official rate are allowed access to the official market for repatriation purposes (interests, profits, etc.)	**11/14** The invisible payments were classified in terms of priorities; most capital related items stayed in the official market.	**2/10** Most invisibles were subject to a minimum waiting period of 7 days. **7/26** Foreign banks were nationalized and were not allowed to service savings accounts. **8/30** All sales of foreign exchange were prohibited temporarily.	**6/17** All 17 financial institutions of Nicaragua were consolidated into 5 banks. **7/11** The parallel market was closed from July 12 to July 20.

29. PAKISTAN (1972)

- Incentives to direct foreign investment and repatriation facilities were in force.
- Transfers of capital abroad are, in general, not permitted, and the purchase of foreign securities is rarely allowed.
- Exports of securities are also subject to approval.

• (No change took place.)

1/3 All citizens were required to declare and surrender all assets held abroad unless they had specific permission of the state bank.

1/13 A 45% tax-free bonus was extended to repatriated foreign exchange.

5/1 Pakistan declared a partial moratorium on its external debt obligations.

8/25 Residents and nonresidents were allowed to hold foreign currency accounts in Pakistan.

• (No change took place.)

30. PAKISTAN (1982)

- Incentives to direct foreign investment and repatriation facilities.
- Transfers of resident owned capital or purchase of securities are, in general, not permitted.

• (No change took place.)

1/10 Forward sales of foreign exchange were suspended, except for foreign currency accounts.

6/29 Nonresidents were allowed to repatriate proceeds from domestic securities and foreign currency deposits.

III (continued)

31. PERU (1967)

Situation at December (t − 2)	Previous year (t − 1)	Devaluation year (t)	Following year (t + 1)
• No exchange controls were imposed on capital receipts and payments made by residents or nonresidents. • Foreign investments should be registered and approved.	7/14 Foreign firms selling securities in Peru were required to register and to maintain detailed records.	9/4 A moratorium on payments of credit instruments in foreign currency held by banks was declared. 9/20 The moratorium was lifted. 10/5 A dual exchange market was created. 11/11 All public entities had to declare their outstanding obligations in foreign currency. 11/17 Amortization payments on foreign loans could only be made through the certificate market up to the amount sold to the central bank by the debtors.	1/23 The use of exchange certificates for the service of private debt required a specific ministerial resolution. 2/9 An institution to monitor public borrowing was created. 2/29 The sale of securities by foreign companies and banks was prohibited. 6/24 Foreign exchange for payments of interest higher than 9% a year was not provided. 6/28 A 1% tax was applied to almost all payments of invisibles.

32. PERU (1975)

- All outward capital transfers required prior approval.
- Government capital payments and certain private capital payments could be made at the lowest certificate rate.
- Foreign currency deposits were prohibited for residents and nonresidents.
- Very stringent regulations are imposed on foreign investment (companies should transform into national companies in a 15-year period)—concessions for mining and petroleum.
- A limit on profit remittances of 14%/year was in force.

7/30 The government admitted the need for refinancing the external debt.

- (No change took place.)

10/30 The limit on profit remittances was raised from 14%/year to 20%/year.

33. PHILIPPINES (1962)

- No restrictions on capital movements, but all exchange purchases for capital purposes must be registered.
- No restrictions on invisibles payments.

11/21 A limit of 50% over total sales was set to the remittances of foreign exchange for dividends and profits purposes.

1/22 All remaining restrictions on capital movements were withdrawn.

- (No change took place.)

III (continued)

Situation at December ($t-2$)	Previous year ($t-1$)	Devaluation year (t)	Following year ($t+1$)
		34. PHILIPPINES (1970)	
• No restrictions on inward capital movements, but they had to be surrendered within 1 business day. • Detailed regulations concerning foreign securities and foreign debt are in force. • Outward capital transfers must be supported with evidence. • Restrictions on foreign investment.	**8/29** The central bank requested foreign firms to reduce voluntarily their profits remittances. **11/26** Free contracting in foreign currency was prohibited.	**7/13** Remittances of profits and dividends was permitted without restrictions. **7/21** Foreign currency deposits were allowed in the banking system with a 100% reserve requirement. **11/9** Foreign borrowing was made subject to the central bank's approval.	**8/4** Banks were required to hold a reserve requirement of 15% of all marginal deposits against letters of credit (and to increase the rate to 30% in November).
		35. SRI LANKA (1967)	
• Foreign investment is strictly regulated. • Foreign securities owners must be registered. • Capital remittances of residents are limited to specific cases. • The transfer of dividends, profits, and interest is subject to a moratorium since 1964.	**3/25, 7/29** The moratorium on dividends, profits, and interest was suspended.	• (No change took place.)	• (No change took place.)

36. TRINIDAD-TOBAGO (1967)

- Capital transfers inside the Sterling Area are freely permitted, but those outside it are closely regulated.
- Restrictions placed on almost all imports and exports of securities.
- No discrimination against foreign direct investment.

9/27 A withholding tax of 30% was imposed on dividends.

• (No change took place.)

4/13 Sterling Area currencies ceased to be considered foreign currencies.

37. VENEZUELA (1965)

- No registration procedure is in force for incoming capital.
- Capital transfers are freely permitted.

• (No change took place.)

• (No change took place.)

• (No change took place.)

38. YUGOSLAVIA (1965)

- All capital transfers require an individual license.
- Foreign direct investment is highly restricted.
- Residents are not usually allowed to hold foreign exchange.

• (No change took place.)

• (No change took place.)

1/1 Less restrictive regulations concerning the opening of foreign currency accounts for residents were implemented.

Notes

1. A word of caution should be said regarding the use of the *control group* methodology for cross-country comparisons. In order for the nonparametric tests performed (χ^2 tests) to be unbiased, the selection of the control group should not be affected by the definition of the "treatment" group (i.e., the devaluers). The clearest case where this requirement is violated refers to selectivity bias. Goldstein and Montiel (1986) have persuasively argued that a number of recent studies— and in particular those comparing the performance of countries with IMF programs with those without IMF programs— do not meet this criterion. The current study, however, is not subject to this *selectivity bias* problem. This is because we are basically comparing the behavior of *policy instruments* for a number of years prior to the crisis. A more subtle potential problem with this analysis based on a control group refers to possible cross-country policy interdependence. If, for example, domestic credit policy in a control group country depends on credit policy in a devaluing country—via some policy reaction function—then the nonparametric test will be biased. Although it is not possible to know exactly the extent of policy interdependence across these small countries, the great variety of nations and years involved in the analysis strongly suggests that this is not a serious problem.

2. Cooper (1971a), however, did not deal with the period preceding the devaluations. Moreover, contrary to this study, and to Harberger and Edwards (1982), Cooper did not use a control group for comparison. Recently, Edwards (1985c) and Kamin (1985) have also used the episodic approach, as have some of the studies that have analyzed the effectiveness of IMF programs.

3. Notice that five of the episodes—Guyana in 1967, Cyprus in 1967, Jamaica in 1967, Malta in 1967, and Trinidad in 1967—correspond to Commonwealth nations that pegged their exchange rates to the pound sterling. When the pound was devalued in 1967, so were these countries' currencies. A question that this analysis will address, then, is whether these episodes are significantly different from the rest of the devaluations investigated here.

4. This, of course, assumes that the policies followed by the fixers are consistent and sustainable. This is not a very farfetched assumption. See appendix B to this chapter for a list of countries in the control group.

5. In order to avoid the influence of extreme outliers in the analysis we have summarized the data by means of the first, second (median), and third quartiles. Outliers can indeed distort the analysis if, for example, averages are used. In our case, the Bolivian devaluation of 1982, for example, is a major outlier. For the sake of completeness the means are also reported for each variable.

6. It may be argued, however, that if the countries fail to adapt their macroeconomic policy to the new international environment, the ultimate cause of the crisis is still an inconsistent macroeconomic regime.

7. The amount of real appreciation in the years preceding devaluation is relatively small on average. This can be partially explained by measurement error. In most

countries as the crisis unravels, price controls are imposed, distorting the official CPI.

8. As a consequence of the 1982 debt crisis the definition and measurement of capital "flight" has become a much discussed subject. See, for example, Cumby and Levich (1987). The measures used in this chapter are among the simplest, and thus the easiest to calculate of those suggested in this literature. Notice that given the indirect way, of computing it, for some countries capital "flight" is positive. What we care about, however, is the change in our proxy as the crisis date approaches.

9. See IMF's *Annual Report on Exchange Arrangements and Payments Restrictions*. The information summarized in table 6.8 was obtained from various issues of this yearbook. More detailed information on the imposition of these controls is reported in appendix C of this chapter.

10. In the case of Venezuela, however, the existence of a multiple exchange rate system introduced some restrictions.

11. Depending on the country, these figures refer either to the black market for foreign exchange or to the fluctuating rate in the "free segment."

12. On the ineffectiveness of capital controls see Edwards (1989a).

13. The 17 countries are Bolivia, Colombia, Costa Rica, Ecuador, Indonesia, Egypt, Guyana, Yugoslavia, India, Israel, Jamaica, Nicaragua, Pakistan, Peru, the Philippines, Sri Lanka, and Trinidad. The 7 countries included in the regressions with parallel market premium data are Colombia, Ecuador, Sri Lanka, India, Pakistan, the Philippines, and Yugoslavia.

14. Regressions were also estimated using the right-hand-side variables in logs. A problem with those estimates is that since some observations had negative values, we lost a number of data points. The results, obtained with these reduced samples, however, confirmed our findings ($N = 481$):

$$DEV_t = -0.820 \log FARE_{t-1} - 0.411 \log RER_{t-1} + 0.879 \log PSCRE_{t-1}.$$
$$(-2.421) \qquad\qquad (-3.727) \qquad\qquad (0.795)$$

Devaluations, Real Exchange Rates, and the External Sector

For many years, much of the controversy surrounding the IMF and the so-called orthodox adjustment programs has been centered on the effectiveness of nominal devaluations. The IMF critics have persistently argued that devaluations and their accompanying policies fail in one respect or another.[1] In this chapter we use data on the 39 devaluations episodes of chapter 6 to investigate the way in which these devaluations affected the external sector in these countries. An important objective of this analysis is to determine whether these devaluations have "worked," and to find out why some devaluations seem to succeed while others seem to fail. The empirical analysis of chapter 6 showed that in the vast majority of the 39 episodes the devaluations took place as a result of unsustainable pressures accumulated after a long period of severe macroeconomic disequilibrium. According to the theoretical discussion of chapter 3, it is precisely under these initial disequilibrium conditions that a nominal devaluation may indeed be very effective. This chapter deals exclusively with the effects of devaluations on variables related to the external sector—the real exchange rate, the current account, the parallel market premium, and the accumulation of net foreign assets, among others—with special emphasis being placed on the ability of nominal devaluations to generate a real exchange realignment. The analysis of the effects of devaluations on some of the most important real variables, including real output, employment, real wages, and income distribution, is relegated to chapter 8.

Various possible criteria can be used to evaluate the "effectiveness" of a devaluation. However, the most convenient single *indicator* of the effectiveness of a nominal devaluation is its impact on the real exchange rate. It is, indeed, through this channel that nominal devaluations seek to affect the external sector balance. If a nominal devaluation generates and sustains a real devaluation, there will be forces at work that will tend to improve the current account and the balance of payments (recall the model in chapter 3). If, on the contrary, a nominal devaluation fails to affect the RER, an important—indeed, crucial—channel will disappear. Although the RER effect is the most important indicator of the effectiveness of nominal devaluations, it is not a goal in itself; the ultimate targets are the external sector accounts.[2] For this reason the empirical analysis in this chapter concentrates on a number of variables—including net foreign assets, inflation, capital flight, and RERs. This analysis places special emphasis on investigating the role of accompanying macroeconomic policies in determining the degree of effectiveness of a devaluation.

7.1 Nominal Devaluations and Real Devaluations

In this section we investigate the reaction of real exchange rates in the period immediately following the 39 devaluation episodes of chapter 6. In table 7.1 the index of the bilateral (with respect to the U.S. dollar) real exchange rate 1 year before the devaluation, the year of the devaluation, and 1, 2, and 3 years after the devaluation is presented. (In the appendix to this chapter, table 7A1 contains data on a multilateral index of real exchange rates during the same period.) Table 7.2 presents data on the ratio of the cumulative ex post elasticity of the real exchange rate with respect to the nominal exchange rate for the year of the devaluation, and 1, 2, and 3 years after the devaluation. These elasticities can be interpreted as an "effectiveness" index of devaluation. They are computed in the following form:

$$\text{effectiveness index}_k = \frac{\widehat{\text{RER}}_k}{\hat{E}_k}, \tag{7.1}$$

where k refers to the year of the devaluation, and 1, 2, and 3 years after the devaluation. $\widehat{\text{RER}}_k$ is the percentage change in the real exchange rate between the year prior to the devaluation and k years after the devaluation ($k = 0, 1, 2, 3$). $\hat{E}_k$ is the percentage change in the nominal exchange rate during the same period. This elasticity, then, provides an index of the degree of *erosion* experienced by the real exchange rate during the three years after the devaluation. A value of one means that the nominal exchange rate adjustment has been fully transferred into a one-to-one *real* devaluation. A negative value of the index, on the other hand, indicates that more than 100% of the nominal devaluation has been eroded and that, at that particular point, the real exchange rate is below its value 1 year before the crisis.

The value of this ex post elasticity index measures in a very broad sense what percentage of the nominal devaluation has been "effective," in the

Table 7.1
Evolution of bilateral real exchange rate index after devaluation[a]

Country	Year	Year prior to devaluation	Year of devaluation	1 year after	2 years after	3 years after
Argentina	1970	100	114.2	87.5	57.7	40.4
Bolivia	1972	100	108.2	134.5	90.5	90.2
Bolivia	1979	100	96.6	90.1	74.3	86.0
Colombia	1962	100	131.4	99.2	84.4	(125.0)[b]
Colombia	1965	100	148.2	127.1	(138.0)[b]	(142.6)[b]
Costa Rica	1974	100	117.6	110.2	110.6	112.8
Cyprus	1967	100	116.5	114.6	116.8	118.1
Ecuador	1961	100	115.0	112.0	105.7	101.1
Ecuador	1970	100	136.9	130.7	126.6	126.6
Egypt	1962	100	127.7	126.5	122.2	108.9
Egypt	1979	100	183.2	173.3	171.3	152.2
Guyana	1967	100	113.2	113.2	115.6	116.3
India	1966	100	146.8	129.5	130.1	131.9
Indonesia	1978	100	150.1	140.6	135.4	135.2
Israel	1962	100	151.2	143.9	131.9	129.5
Israel	1967	100	113.1	115.5	116.2	112.7
Israel	1971	100	109.8	102.9	96.6	88.9
Jamaica	1967	100	113.2	110.2	107.4	103.6
Jamaica	1978	100	148.9	136.5	122.4	118.5
Malta	1967	100	116.6	116.7	118.7	118.8
Nicaragua	1979	100	108.7	91.7	80.8	66.0
Pakistan	1972	100	228.6	188.6	176.8	160.7
Peru	1967	100	131.7	113.5	111.4	109.0
Philippines	1962	100	184.8	174.1	160.5	160.3
Philippines	1970	100	149.1	133.9	133.8	131.9
Sri Lanka	1967	100	122.1	117.8	114.9	112.5
Trinidad	1967	100	114.3	108.6	109.7	111.3
Venezuela	1964	100	135.1	135.9	137.3	138.1
Yugoslavia	1965	100	127.8	194.3	87.4	95.9
Average		100	167.6	126.7	116.0	114.0
Bolivia	1982	100	115.8	131.9	n.a.	n.a.
Chile	1982	100	174.7	165.7	207.4	295.6
Colombia	1967	100	108.5	112.2	112.3	116.4
Ecuador	1982	100	116.4	129.6	125.5	181.6

Table 7.1 (continued)

Country	Year	Year prior to devaluation	Year of devaluation	1 year after	2 years after	3 years after
Kenya	1981	100	132.6	138.9	136.8	145.5
Korea	1980	100	120.9	115.5	117.3	122.1
Mexico	1976	100	143.4	134.6	123.3	118.0
Mexico	1982	100	236.1	176.7	146.3	232.5
Pakistan	1982	100	124.9	125.3	136.9	174.8
Peru	1975	100	103.2	124.4	179.6	184.6
Average		100	137.8	135.5	142.8	174.6

Source: See text.
a. An increase in the index denotes a real devaluation.
b. Means that a new devaluation took place that year; consequently the value of the index reported in parentheses is not relevant to the evaluation of the effectiveness of the devaluation.

Table 7.2
Index of effectiveness of nominal devaluations: ex post real exchange rate elasticities of official nominal devaluation

Country	Year	(A) Year of devaluation	(B) 1 year after devaluation	(C) 2 years after	(D) 3 years after	(E) Ratio of RER 3 years after to 3 years prior
Argentina	1970	0.57	<0	<0	<0	0.39
Bolivia	1972	0.12	0.52	<0	−0.14	0.92
Bolivia	1979	<0	<0	<0	−0.01	0.83
Colombia	1962	0.91	0.52	0.46	(0.24)	—
Colombia	1965	0.96	0.54	(0.50)	(0.48)	—
Costa Rica	1974	0.61	0.35	0.37	0.44	1.11
Cyprus	1967	0.90	0.87	1.00	1.08	1.23
Ecuador	1961	0.75	0.60	0.29	0.08	1.00
Ecuador	1970	0.95	0.79	0.68	0.68	1.21
Egypt	1962	1.16	1.10	0.93	0.37	1.07
Egypt	1979	1.05	0.93	0.90	0.66	1.39
Guyana	1967	0.82	0.78	0.96	0.98	1.16
India	1966	0.80	0.50	0.50	0.54	1.08
Indonesia	1978	0.99	0.79	0.69	0.63	1.12
Israel	1962	0.77	0.66	0.48	0.44	1.22

Table 7.2 (continued)

Country	Year	(A) Year of devaluation	(B) 1 year after devaluation	(C) 2 years after	(D) 3 years after	(E) Ratio of RER 3 years after to 3 years prior
Israel	1967	0.79	0.93	0.98	0.76	1.05
Israel	1971	0.49	0.14	−0.17	−0.38	0.86
Jamaica	1967	0.83	0.60	0.45	0.22	1.03
Jamaica	1978	0.57	0.38	−0.23	0.19	1.07
Malta	1967	0.99	0.99	1.12	1.12	1.22
Nicaragua	1979	0.20	−0.19	−0.45	−0.78	0.64
Pakistan	1972	0.99	0.83	0.72	0.56	1.52
Peru	1967	0.71	0.30	0.26	0.20	0.91
Philippines	1962	0.90	0.79	0.65	0.64	1.50
Philippines	1970	0.77	0.53	0.47	0.44	1.34
Sri Lanka	1967	0.91	0.74	0.60	0.50	1.18
Trinidad	1967	0.90	0.50	0.60	0.68	1.10
Venezuela	1964	0.92	0.94	0.98	0.99	1.37
Yugoslavia	1965	0.42	0.06	−0.02	−0.06	0.81
Bolivia	1982	0.02	0.02	n.a.	n.a.	n.a.
Chile	1982	0.85	0.53	0.47	0.52	2.27
Colombia	1967	0.51	0.49	0.38	0.39	1.48
Ecuador	1982	0.50	0.25	0.15	0.28	1.71
Kenya	1981	0.91	0.57	0.45	0.41	1.55
Korea	1980	0.58	0.35	0.32	0.34	1.09
Mexico	1976	0.73	0.42	0.28	0.21	1.08
Mexico	1982	0.51	0.17	0.07	0.10	2.05
Pakistan	1982	0.84	0.70	0.67	1.21	1.73
Peru	1975	0.20	0.31	0.34	0.20	1.93

Source: See text.

sense of being translated into a real devaluation. The main reason why it is only a broad and somewhat inaccurate measure of "effectiveness" is that it is based on a "before" and "after" analysis, without maintaining other relevant variables constant. In section 7.5, however, we report the results from an analysis that makes an explicit effort to control for other variables, such as domestic credit policy, fiscal policy, and foreign shocks. The last column in table 7.2 includes the ratio of the real exchange rate index 3 years after the devaluation to 3 years prior to the devaluation and provides further information on how effective these nominal devaluations have actually been.

These tables are very revealing, and provide a useful start for our analysis. Let us first focus on the cases of stepwise devaluation. The data in table 7.1 show that in 8 of the 29 episodes—Argentina in 1970, Bolivia in 1972 and 1979, Colombia in 1962 and 1965, Israel in 1971, Nicaragua in 1979, and Yugoslavia in 1965—3 years after the devaluation the real exchange rate index was below its value 1 year before the crisis. In all of these cases, in less than 3 years the real effect of the nominal devaluation had more than fully eroded, and in some of the cases the erosion was very rapid. For example, in Argentina in 1970, Bolivia in 1979, Colombia in 1962, and Nicaragua in 1979, it took *less than a year* for the effect of the nominal devaluation to be completely wiped out.

Table 7.2 shows that in 12 of the 29 episodes the index of effectiveness was below 1/3 after 3 years—Argentina in 1970; Bolivia in 1972 and 1979, Colombia in 1962 and 1965, Ecuador in 1961, Israel in 1971, Jamaica in 1967 and 1978, Nicaragua in 1979, Peru in 1967, and Yugoslavia in 1965. These countries—with Latin American nations predominant—were unable to sustain a significant real devaluation following the nominal adjustment of the peg. While columns (A)–(D) in table 7.2 use the year prior to the devaluation as the benchmark for comparison, column (E) looks at the value of the RER index *3 years* prior to the devaluation. As can be seen, in many of these episodes the ratio of RER index 3 years after to 3 years before the crisis is above one, indicating that even though there has been significant real exchange rate erosion, some correction with respect to 3 years prior to the crisis was achieved.

The data on the crawling peg countries present a different picture. In the 9 cases for which there are data, 3 years after the devaluation the RER index was higher—and in most cases significantly higher—than for the year before the devaluation. Naturally, this was achieved by "fighting off" the real exchange rate erosion with additional devaluations in the following years. Typically, under crawling peg regimes the authorities further devalue the currency in magnitudes approximately equal to the domestic rate of inflation. Of course, a potential problem with this policy is that it can lead to an explosive (nonconvergent) process, where the devaluation generates inflation, which partially erodes the effect of the devaluation; this leads to a higher devaluation and an even higher inflation and so on, ad infinitum. This would be the case, for example, if an unsustainable fiscal policy is maintained in our model of chapter 3. An alternative scenario for the crawlers is one where the process is stabilized at some mild rate of inflation, as in Chile in the recent period, Colombia since 1967, Korea since 1980, and Pakistan after 1982.

Given the inflationary proclivity of a crawling peg regime, it is particularly useful to look at the effectiveness indexes of table 7.2 when evaluating the successfulness of having adopted this regime. As can be seen from the table, in 4 out of 9 crawling peg episodes, the effectiveness index was below 1/3—our "arbitrary" threshold for success. This means that whatever real devaluations were obtained in these countries were achieved at the cost of important increases in inflation. Of the crawling peg countries, only in Chile, Colombia (1967), Kenya, Korea, and Pakistan (1982) was the rate of inflation 3 years after the crisis below its level 3 years before the devaluation, as reported in table 7.3. Also, these data indicate that among the crawlers in Bolivia, Peru, and Mexico (1982), the higher real exchange rate was sustained at the cost of substantial medium-to-longer-term increase in the rate of inflation.

Parallel Markets and Real Exchange Rates

The real exchange rate data in table 7.1 were constructed using indexes on official nominal rates. However, as noted throughout this book, in these countries parallel markets of varying degrees of importance have traditionally existed. Data on nominal exchange rates in parallel markets were used to construct parallel market real exchange rate indexes. Table 7A2 in the appendix to this chapter contains these indexes. Naturally, the behavior of the parallel market real rates varied across countries, depending to a large extent on the way in which the parallel market spread reacted to the devaluation. Table 7.4 contains information on parallel market spreads and on the evolution of multiple exchange rate practices during the period following the devaluations. As can be seen, in most cases—25 out of 35 episodes—the parallel market spread declined rapidly during the months immediately following the crisis (i.e., 3 months after the crisis). In a number of epi-

Table 7.3
Inflation rates in devaluing countries

Country	Year of devaluation	Inflation rates (%)			
		3 years before	1 year before	1 year after	3 years after
Argentina	1970	29.41	7.65	34.79	61.21
Bolivia	1972	2.22	3.69	31.49	7.88
Bolivia	1979	4.50	10.36	47.23	133.33
Colombia	1962	7.22	8.71	31.96	3.53
Colombia	1965	2.46	17.65	19.85	5.84
Costa Rica	1974	3.08	15.21	17.37	4.17
Cyprus	1967	−0.30	0.51	3.80	2.45
Ecuador	1961	1.34	1.68	2.87	4.03
Ecuador	1970	3.82	6.33	8.38	13.01
Egypt	1962	0.33	0.69	0.71	14.87
Egypt	1979	10.28	11.08	20.66	14.82
Guyana	1967	0.35	2.07	3.03	3.37
India	1966	3.08	9.21	13.59	1.72
Indonesia	1978	19.07	11.02	20.59	12.24
Israel	1962	4.40	6.71	6.57	7.70
Israel	1967	5.15	7.99	2.09	6.10
Israel	1971	2.09	6.10	12.88	39.71
Jamaica	1967	1.82	1.99	5.91	7.73
Jamaica	1978	17.38	11.19	29.08	12.74
Malta	1967	2.27	0.55	2.07	3.70
Nicaragua	1979	2.81	4.56	35.30	24.79
Pakistan	1972	1.21	7.73	23.07	20.90
Peru	1967	9.92	8.96	18.97	5.00
Philippines	1962	1.10	1.27	5.74	2.42
Philippines	1970	6.41	1.91	15.06	14.00
Sri Lanka	1967	3.13	−0.18	5.84	5.90
Trinidad	1967	0.83	4.15	8.23	2.52
Venezuela	1964	2.65	1.15	1.71	0.00
Yugoslavia	1965	10.47	10.89	26.17	5.00
Bolivia	1982	19.73	28.57	269.05	1.2×10^4
Chile	1982	33.36	19.69	27.26	30.70
Colombia	1967	17.65	19.85	5.84	6.84
Ecuador	1982	10.27	16.39	48.43	27.98

Table 7.3 (continued)

Country	Year of devaluation	Inflation rates (%)			
		3 years before	1 year before	1 year after	3 years after
Kenya	1981	16.89	13.80	20.40	10.18
Korea	1980	10.17	18.26	21.26	3.42
Mexico	1976	12.04	15.15	29.00	18.17
Mexico	1982	18.17	27.93	101.76	57.75
Pakistan	1982	8.27	11.88	6.15	5.83
Peru	1975	7.16	16.90	33.49	57.83

Source: International Monetary Fund.

Table 7.4
Multiple rate practices and parallel market spreads following devaluation

Country	Year	Number of official rates				Parallel market spread		
		Year prior	Year of deval-uation	1 year after	3 years after	Month prior	3 months after	9 months after
Argentina	1970	1	1	5	5	0	0.5	9.0
Bolivia	1972	2	1	1	1	60.0	32.5	5.0
Bolivia	1979	1	2	2	1	17.5	15.0	20.0
Colombia	1962	3	3	3	4	57.8	11.0	14.4
Colombia	1965	3	4	4	2	114.4	35.9	19.3
Costa Rica	1974	5	3	3	3	30.2	3.5	15.2
Cyprus	1967	1	1	1	1	n.a.	n.a.	n.a.
Ecuador	1961	2	2	2	2	66.7	30.8	57.3
Ecuador	1970	2	1	2	3	55.6	16.0	9.2
Egypt	1962	2	2	1	1	128.6	93.0	79.1
Egypt	1979	3	4	5	5	92.3	7.1	4.3
India	1966	1	1	1	1	134.2	53.3	54.7
Indonesia	1978	4	5	2	2	1.2	1.8	1.3
Israel	1962	1	1	1	1	50.8	9.2	13.9
Israel	1967	1	1	1	1	9.9	2.0	8.9
Israel	1971	1	1	1	1	6.9	28.8	36.0
Jamaica	1978	2	2	2	2	n.a.	n.a.	n.a.
Nicaragua	1979	2	5	3	6	92.9	97.0	47.8
Pakistan	1972	2	1	1	1	134.2	1.9	40.9
Peru	1967	1	2	3	4	43.6	1.6	13.7
Philippines	1962	2	2	2	1	126.0	5.4	7.6

Table 7.4 (continued)

| Country | Year | Number of official rates | | | | Parallel market spread | | |
		Year prior	Year of deval-uation	1 year after	3 years after	Month prior	3 months after	9 months after
Philippines	1970	1	2	2	2	59.0	19.1	7.3
Sri Lanka	1967	1	1	2	2	152.1	97.5	95.0
Venezuela	1964	3	2	2	2	35.2	0	0
Yugoslavia	1965	2	1	1	1	54.7	22.4	15.2
Bolivia	1982	2	1	1	n.a.	434.0	180.0	300.0
Chile	1982	1	2	3	n.a.	17.9	2.4	10.6
Colombia	1967	4	3	2	2	48.1	30.7	15.4
Ecuador	1982	3	4	4	n.a.	74.4	76.4	118.7
Kenya	1981	3	3	4	n.a.	19.8	23.2	17.9
Korea	1980	2	1	1	1	42.3	5.3	7.0
Mexico	1976	1	1	1	1	0.0	0.0	0.0
Mexico	1982	1	2	2	n.a.	12.3	82.9	33.5
Pakistan	1982	1	1	1	n.a.	40.9	23.5	23.5
Peru	1975	4	5	5	4	75.7	55.6	77.8

Source: Various issues of *Pick's Currency Yearbook* and *World Currency Yearbook*.

sodes, however—14 out of the 25—this decline was short-lived, and after 9 months the premium had once again increased. This evolution of the premiums provides some important information, and is in broad agreement with the model developed in chapter 3 and with the regression results of chapter 5. In most instances, a large nominal devaluation of the official rate will, on impact, tend to reduce the gap between the freely determined parallel rate and the predetermined (i.e., fixed) official rate. As time passes, however, and other forces are unleashed, the freely determined black market rates starts responding to these forces and to expectations.

Table 7.4 shows that only a handful of these official devaluations were coupled with an exchange rate unification at a single higher official rate— Bolivia in 1972, Ecuador in 1970, Pakistan in 1972, Yugoslavia in 1965, Bolivia in 1982, and Korea in 1980; in the case of Ecuador, however, this unification was very short-lived. In a few other episodes the number of multiple rates was reduced—Costa Rica in 1974, Venezuela in 1964, and Colombia in 1967—but multiple-rate practices were not eliminated. Interestingly enough, and contrary to popular belief, instead of leading to unification, many of these devaluations were actually followed by a more generalized use of multiple rates, either during the year of the devaluation or in the subsequent 2 years.

7.2 Devaluations and Macroeconomic Policies

In theory, and in particular according to the model in chapter 3, whether nominal devaluations succeed or not in helping a country regain international competitiveness will largely depend on the accompanying macroeconomic policies. If the economic authorities do not put a check on the ultimate causes of the crisis—that is, the inconsistent and unsustainable macroeconomic policies—the effects of the exchange rate adjustment will indeed be very short-lived. In this section we analyze the role played by macroeconomic policies in the outcome of the 39 devaluation episodes.

Table 7.5 contains data on three of the indicators of domestic credit and fiscal policies considered in chapter 6 (table 6.2): (a) rate of growth of domestic credit, (b) rate of growth of domestic credit to the public sector, and (c) proportion of total domestic credit received by the public sector. If we consider the control group policies as a broad characterization of those policies "consistent" with maintaining a fixed rate, a comparison between the data in table 7.5 and the control group can shed additional light on what is behind the degree of success of a devaluation.

One way of organizing this discussion is by assuming that the median values of these indicators for the control group provide an approximate (and conservative) measure of a policy consistent with maintaining a pegged rate. The median values of the control group are 17.4% for the rate of growth of domestic credit, 22.7% for the rate of growth of domestic credit to the public sector, and 0.114 for the ratio of credit to the public sector to total domestic credit. In table 7.5 we have used an asterisk to denote those indicators with a value below the control group median. As can be seen in 29 of the 39 devaluation episodes, the rate of growth of domestic credit was lower than the median for the control group (17.4%) *either* 1 or 3 years after the devaluation. However, in only 8 of the episodes was this indicator below the control group median *both* 1 and 3 years after the devaluation— Ecuador in 1961, Ecuador in 1970, India in 1966, Peru in 1967, the Philippines in 1970, Sri Lanka in 1967, Venezuela in 1964, and (the only crawler) Colombia in 1967.

The analysis of the rate of growth of credit to the public sector shows in an even starker way the inability of some of these countries to impose fiscal discipline. In 14 out of the 29 stepwise devaluers this indicator exceeded (3 years after the devaluation) the level of the third quartile (33.2%)

Table 7.5
Macroeconomic policies in the period following devaluation[a]

Country	Year of deval-uation	Rate of growth of Domestic credit (years after)		Rate of growth of domestic credit to public sector (years after)		Fraction of total credit to public sector (years after)	
		1	3	1	3	1	3
Argentina	1970	41.9	94.7	14.3*	133.3	2.1*	4.8*
Bolivia	1972	31.2	38.5	4.1*	185.5	45.8	23.2
Bolivia	1979	38.1	343.2	62.5*	411.7	44.8	53.0
Colombia	1962	16.7*	22.9	12.6	45.6	24.0	31.3
Colombia	1965	17.9	16.4*	−6.1*	−1.5*	24.9	21.5
Costa Rica	1974	45.2	30.9	161.5	126.5	14.1	21.4
Cyprus	1967	19.2	3.2*	−6.2*	−19.5*	−57.0*	−56.5*
Ecuador	1961	1.9*	10.8*	3.3*	−40.9*	10.9*	4.7*
Ecuador	1970	12.9*	7.7*	18.7*	−31.9*	27.7	16.0
Egypt	1962	20.4	7.3*	35.1	12.0*	52.1	57.5
Egypt	1979	42.1	23.1	13.9*	33.5	58.6	51.7
Guyana	1967	30.5	17.7	46.2	12.6*	27.9	30.5
India	1966	8.7*	9.7*	6.3*	3.9*	57.8	52.5
Indonesia	1978	4.4*	35.6	n.a.	−18.5*	−26.1*	−52.8*
Israel	1962	34.1	18.4	438.9	17.9*	12.7	13.1
Israel	1967	37.8	28.1	111.4	35.4	29.0	40.7
Israel	1971	12.5*	74.6	−5.5*	96.6	35.8	31.4
Jamaica	1967	22.5	20.2	29.5	394.1	6.7*	7.9*
Jamaica	1978	45.6	43.3	68.3	52.7	62.5	59.3
Malta	1967	44.5	29.9	382.7	60.9	5.9*	18.9
Nicaragua	1979	n.a.	31.5	n.a.	54.9	34.2	34.7
Pakistan	1972	9.0*	29.9	2.6*	41.1	46.2	48.4
Peru	1967	12.1*	13.2*	18.5*	−12.8*	36.2	25.0
Philippines	1962	25.3	6.2*	17.8*	−23.0*	12.2*	8.1*
Philippines	1970	11.9*	12.9*	5.0*	−47.7*	14.4	5.8*
Sri Lanka	1967	13.6*	10.0*	6.1*	9.6*	63.6	61.2
Trinidad	1967	17.3*	27.4	62.3	61.3	22.0	17.6
Venezuela	1964	10.7*	8.8*	20.7*	14.7*	−13.3*	−11.7*
Yugoslavia	1965	25.2	16.3	22.4*	−10.7*	9.4*	6.4*
Bolivia	1982	171.3	5126.4	217.2	n.a.	62.0	n.a.
Chile	1982	10.9*	n.a.	36.7	n.a.	9.3*	n.a.
Colombia	1967	16.4*	17.2*	−1.5*	−6.3*	21.5	14.2
Ecuador	1982	59.2	n.a.	n.a.	n.a.	−6.5*	n.a.

Table 7.5 (continued)

Country	Year of deval- uation	Rate of growth of Domestic credit (years after)		Rate of growth of domestic credit to public sector (years after)		Fraction of total credit to public sector (years after)	
		1	3	1	3	1	3
Kenya	1981	28.6	10.3*	58.0	9.8*	41.0	33.4
Korea	1980	31.0	16.0*	84.9	2.3*	10.9*	9.6*
Mexico	1976	142.1	34.9	94.7	33.0	50.5	46.1
Mexico	1982	49.4	67.9	47.4	87.0	57.4	55.0
Pakistan	1982	14.5*	17.5	8.9*	4.4*	45.8	39.7
Peru	1975	54.3	54.1	113.9	55.4	32.5	35.2

a. These indicators were constructed from raw data obtained from the *International Financial Statistics*. An asterisk means that the value is less or equal to the median of the same variable for the control group of fixers.

for the control group, suggesting a greater tendency to maintain the unsustainable fiscal policy that got these countries into trouble in the first place. This tendency appears to be particularly common among the Latin American stepwise episodes—in Argentina in 1970, Bolivia in 1972 and 1979, Colombia in 1962, Costa Rica in 1974, and Nicaragua in 1979, the rate of growth of domestic credit to the public sector exceeded the third quartile value for the control group of fixers.

A comparison of table 7.5 on fiscal policy with tables 7.1 and 7.2 on the evolution of the real exchange rate after the devaluation is particularly revealing. In 8 out of the 12 episodes where there was a rapid and significant erosion of the real devaluation, the macroeconomic indicator shows highly "inconsistent" fiscal policies—with the exceptions being Colombia in 1965, Ecuador in 1961, Peru in 1967, and Yugoslavia in 1965. This link is extraordinarily strong, providing persuasive preliminary evidence on the crucial role of accompanying fiscal policies in devaluation episodes.

Cross-Episode Regressions

A limitation of the analysis up to this point is that we have not attempted to separate the effects of the nominal devaluations from those of other policies or exogenous disturbances. In order to investigate more formally the way in which macroeconomic policies and devaluations interacted during the 29 stepwise devaluation episodes included in this part of the study, a number of cross-section regressions were estimated. These equations took each devaluation episode as the observation unit, and considered the rate of change of the real exchange rate as the dependent variable. The independent variable included the nominal devaluation, the rate of growth of domestic credit, the change in the rate of growth of domestic credit to the public sector, and the change in the ratio of the fiscal deficit to GDP. The equations estimated were of the following form:

$$\widehat{RER}_k = \alpha_1 \hat{E}_k + \alpha_2 \hat{C} + \alpha_3 \widehat{FIS}_k + u, \tag{7.2}$$

where $\widehat{RER}_k$ is the cumulative percentage change in the real exchange rate between the year prior to the devaluation and k years after the devaluation (for $k = 0, 1, 2, 3$ years), for episode n. $\hat{E}_k$ is the percentage change of the nominal exchange rate during the same period, for country n. Given the nature of the data set used, in most stepwise devaluation cases $\hat{E}_1 = \hat{E}_2 = \hat{E}_3 = \hat{E} =$ initial devaluation. $\hat{C}_k$ is the rate of growth of domestic credit between year k and the year prior to the devaluation. $\widehat{FIS}_k$ is the change in an index of fiscal policy. The following indexes of fiscal policy were actually used: rate of growth of domestic credit to the public sector ($\widehat{CPS}_k$), growth in ratio of public sector to total domestic credit ($\widehat{RPSCR}_k$), and change in fiscal deficit ratio ($\widehat{DEF}_k$). The estimation of this equation allow us to have an idea of the *average* effects of our 29 stepwise nominal devaluation episodes on RERs, (most) other things kept constant.[3] It should be stressed that the purpose of these regressions is only to have a better understanding of the average effect of the 29 stepwise nominal devaluations, and not to undertake a thorough analysis of the process of RER determination. The lack of adequate data on the most important variables, as well as the cross-episode nature of these regressions, dictates the more modest objective of this exercise. In particular, the absence of any "fundamentals" in equation (7.2) means that it cannot be interpreted as providing a full depiction of the process of RER determination; by concentrating on the role of macroeconomic variables only, the current analysis is clearly of a short-run nature. Remember, however, that the econometric investigation of chapter 5 does provide a thorough analysis of RER determination based on the theoretical models of chapters 2 and 3. In spite of the more modest claim made in this chapter, in the discussion that follows an effort is made to relate, when appropriate, the cross-episode results to the time series-cross section analysis of chapter 5.

The results obtained are presented in table 7.6; A, B, C, and D refer to regressions for the year of the devaluation (A), 1 year after the nominal devaluation (B), 2 years after the devaluation (C), and 3 years after the devaluation (D). The coefficients of $\hat{E}_k$, for $k = 0, 1, 2,$ and 3, should

Table 7.6
Nominal and real devaluations: cross-section results for stepwise episodes (OLS)[a]

$\widehat{E}_k$	$\widehat{C}_k$	$\widehat{CPS}$	$\widehat{RPSCR}_k$	$\widehat{DEF}_k$	$\bar{R}^2$
A: $k = 0$ years					
0.863	—	—	−0.030	−0.006	0.967
(23.451)			(−0.624)	(−3.346)	
0.857	−0.107	—	—	−0.003	0.914
(36.457)	(−5.647)			(−0.641)	
0.816	—	−0.014	—	−0.002	0.893
(32.628)		(−0.717)	—	(−2.134)	
B: $k = 1$ year					
0.601	—	—	−0.119	−0.014	0.839
(9.701)			(−1.917)	(−2.471)	
0.722	−0.127	—	—	−0.007	0.843
(25.603)	(−7.600)			(−1.710)	
0.622	—	−0.005	—	−0.015	0.769
(20.491)		(−0.512)		(−1.974)	
C: $k = 2$ years					
0.445	—	—	−0.035	−0.001	0.623
(5.438)			(−0.809)	(−0.651)	
0.602	−0.114	—	—	0.028	0.748
(19.101)	(−7.569)			(0.250)	
0.475	—	−0.002	—	−0.013	0.633
(14.776)		(−0.978)		(−0.107)	
D: $k = 3$ years					
0.366	—	—	−0.049	−0.004	0.567
(4.720)			(−1.938)	(−1.030)	
0.554	−0.092	—	—	−0.006	0.693
(16.551)	(−7.684)			(−0.380)	
0.408	—	−0.008	—	−0.014	0.542
(12.136)		(−0.946)		(−0.798)	

a. Ordinary least squares. Numbers in parentheses are t-statistics.

be interpreted as providing a measure of the percentage of the nominal devaluation that, with (some of) the macroeconomic variables given, has been translated on average into a real depreciation 0, 1, 2, and 3 years after the devaluation. In all but one of the regressions in table 7.6, the coefficients had the expected signs, confirming for these episodes that expansive macroeconomic policies resulted in an erosion of the real exchange rate effect of the devaluation. The coefficient of the nominal devaluation ($\hat{E}$) declined steadily as we moved away from the year of devaluation; for the year of the devaluation (A) it exceeds 0.8 in all regressions, reaching significantly lower values—ranging from 0.37 to 0.55—3 years after the devaluation (D). This illustrates the fact that, even with macroeconomic polices kept constant, there will be some erosion of the real exchange rate effects of nominal devaluations. The negative coefficients of the macroeconomic policy variables provide a clear support to the hypothesis that unless nominal devaluations are accompanied by demand management policies, they will not have a lasting effect on the real exchange rate. This suggests that when a nominal devaluation fails to generate a sustained real devaluation, it is the whole macroeconomic package, and not only the devaluation, that has failed. Notice, however, that within the macroeconomic variables, the rate of change of domestic credit ($\hat{C}_k$) is capturing most of the effect.

As noted, the regressions reported in table 7.6 have been restricted to the devaluation episodes and have only considered macroeconomic policies as the other determinants of the evolution of RERs. It is interesting, then, to compare these results with those obtained in chapter 5, where a general equation of RER dynamics that allowed a role for both monetary and real variables was performed. The results from that chapter indicated that, with other things given, for the countries in that sample a nominal devaluation of 10% had had an effect on the real exchange rate during the first year of approximately 6%, a magnitude compatible to the estimates in table 7.6 for the effects 1 year after the devaluation ($k = 1$ year).

7.3 Devaluations, Exchange Controls, and Payment Restrictions

As shown in chapter 6, the vast majority of our devaluation episodes were preceded by a massive piling up of exchange controls and trade restrictions. As these efforts to slow down, or halt, the erosion of international reserves failed, the economic authorities were eventually "forced" to devalue and implement some sort of a stabilization program. Table 7.7 contains a summary of the evolution of exchange controls and trade restrictions in the period following these devaluations.[4] As can be seen from table 7.7, in

Table 7.7
Summary of evolution of exchange controls and trade restrictions after the devaluation

Episode	Payment restrictions on current transactions	Tariffs, duties, and cost related measures	Restrictions on capital transactions
Argentina (1970)	• Foreign exchange sales for several transactions were resumed. • One year after the devaluation, imports from the public sector and many "nonessential" imports were prohibited and a dual exchange market was reintroduced.	• Import tariffs were reduced by 15 to 30 points in most items 1 month after the devaluation. • Tariffs were abruptly increased (up to 200%) 5 months later.	• Profits and dividends remittances of foreign firms remain suspended. Services of foreign loans were permitted 9 months after the devaluation. • After 15 months all financial transactions were carried out at the floating dual rate.
Bolivia (1972)	• Restrictions on public sector imports were not lifted, and the import of some agricultural final and intermediate goods was prohibited.	• The 15% custom surcharge was eliminated 1 month after the devaluation, but a substantial increase in tariffs took place 1 year later.	• No significant change; most capital inflows and outflows took place through the "free" market.
Bolivia (1979)	• No significant changes. Prohibitions on automobiles and other vehicles were lifted.	• The advance deposit requirement was reduced from 500% to 25% for most private imports. • Some deductions on paid duties were granted to importers.	• The ceilings on short-term and medium-term foreign exchange liabilities of the banking sector were increased.

Bolivia (1982)	• The new official exchange rate was restricted to wheat and public imports 1 month after the devaluation. • All nonessential imports were prohibited 9 months after the devaluation. • Quotas for invisible payments were reduced drastically.	• The 2% tax on exchange transaction was abolished after the devaluation. • The advance deposit scheme became highly restrictive 3 months later.	• Only public debt service had access to the official exchange rate; all other transactions were made at the "free" rate. • The foreign exchange market was closed for 15 days, 7 months after the devaluation. • The system became highly restrictive 2 months later.
Chile (1982)	• Significant tightening in foreign exchange controls. Quotas for services' payments were progressively reduced starting 3 months after the devaluation. • All imports became subject to prior approval 6 months after the devaluation.	• A 5% advance deposit for all imports was implemented. • Tariffs on imports doubled (from 10% to 20% on average) 7 months after the devaluation, and a 12% tax surcharge on the purchase of foreign exchange was established 2 months later.	• A mechanism to bail out commercial banks' foreign debt was introduced; a special exchange rate was created for that purpose. • Restrictions on new foreign borrowing increased substantially.
Colombia (1962)	• Several items were transferred from the list of prohibited imports to the list of freely imported goods in the year following the devaluation.	• The advance deposit requirement of some import categories was reduced further.	• No significant change; except for public debt service, all capital flows were channeled through the parallel market.
Colombia (1965)	• Imports were divided into two groups. One of them had access to a preferential exchange rate and required a license; the other did not require a license, but was subject to a higher exchange rate.	• Advance deposits for goods imported at the highest exchange rate were reduced by 5% per month.	• One year after the devaluation, commercial banks were required to maintain 100% reserves against their foreign currency liabilities and transactions in foreign exchange by residents were strongly restricted.

Table 7.7 (continued)

Episode	Payment restrictions on current transactions	Tariffs, duties, and cost related measures	Restrictions on capital transactions
Colombia (1967)	• Licensing requirements were eliminated for products from 150 tariffs lines.	• The advance deposits requirements for most imports were progressively reduced.	• The holding of foreign currency deposits was abolished. • Regulations on payments and inflows of dividends and profits were simplified.
Costa Rica (1974)	• Prior registration of imports in the central bank became obligatory.	• A temporary import surcharge of 10–50% was introduced 15 months after the devaluation.	• Several measures to impede capital flight were adopted. Resident owned capital outflows were severely restricted, and the interest rate on domestically held foreign currency deposits was raised.
Cyprus (1967)	• The open general license system was eliminated, and most goods could be imported without restriction.	• No change took place. Advance deposits requirements were not introduced.	• The central bank forced the commercial banks gradually to transfer to it their foreign exchange assets.
Ecuador (1961)	• Several items were continuously shifted between the 2 import lists (essential and nonessential goods). No clear pattern can be detected.	• Advance deposits were increased from 50% to 100% on most list 2 imports 1 month after the devaluation.	• Registered capital transactions were made at a higher (fixed) exchange rate.
Ecuador (1970)	• Quotas on most service payments were eliminated.	• Some list 2 imports and all public imports were exempted from the 20% ad valorem duty. • Advance deposits requirements were significantly reduced, but were increased again 15 months after the devaluation.	• Private banks and residents were allowed to maintain foreign currency deposits 1 year after the devaluation.

Ecuador (1982)	• Significant increase in the degree of restrictiveness. A third exchange rate was created. • The import of 550 items was prohibited, and several other imports were suspended for a year 6 months after the devaluation.	• Tariffs were increased in several final and intermediate goods. • The advance deposit requirement was hiked to 20–80% 6 months after the devaluation.	• Several restrictions on public foreign borrowing were introduced. • Capital controls were severely tightened.
Egypt (1962)	• Private imports were prohibited 14 months after the devaluation.	• No change took place. Some imports were still subject to a 10% tariff premium.	• No change took place. Capital transactions remained strictly regulated.
Egypt (1979)	• The reunification of the exchange rates caused the lifting of all quotas on services and import payments.	• Import duties were reduced, and an advance deposits scheme was introduced 15 months after the devaluation.	• The operations of foreign banks were slightly restricted.
Guyana (1967)	• The import of some items previously on the "negative list" was prohibited.	• No change took place. The advance deposit scheme remained in effect.	• No change took place. Capital transactions remained strictly regulated.
India (1966)	• Quantitative restrictions on intermediate imports were substantially relaxed. • Imports of 80 items were prohibited 1 year after the devaluation.	• No change took place. The advance deposit requirement was not reintroduced.	• No change took place. Capital inflows and outflows remained fairly unrestricted.
Indonesia (1978)	• No change took place. The import of most items remained highly regulated.	• Significant reduction in import duties and sales taxes (especially for intermediate imports).	• No change took place. Except for foreign investment, capital transactions remained fairly unrestricted.
Israel (1962)	• Significant liberalization. Previously prohibited items were allowed to be imported under individual licenses, and several items were exempted from all licensing requirements.	• No change took place. Few items required an advance deposit.	• No change took place. Capital transactions remained fairly regulated.

Table 7.7 (continued)

Episode	Payment restrictions on current transactions	Tariffs, duties, and cost related measures	Restrictions on capital transactions
Israel (1967)	• The process of lifting import restrictions continued after the devaluation. • The quotas for most services' payments were increased.	• Import duties were reduced by the same rate as the devaluation. • One year later they were reduced again by 10–15%.	• Regulations on capital transactions were eased.
Israel (1971)	• The process of reducing the licensing requirements for most imports continued after the devaluation. • The quotas for several services were further increased.	• The advance deposit requirements were progressively reduced. • A preannounced plan for reducing tariffs and import duties was implemented.	• No significant change. Banks were allowed to establish their own interest rates in foreign currency deposits.
Jamaica (1967)	• Slight increase in restrictiveness. Many imports were excluded from the open general license scheme and became subject to specific licenses.	• Duties on some intermediate imports were reduced 9 months after the devaluation.	• No significant change. • The free convertibility into sterling of the Jamaican pound was limited to dealings with commercial banks.
Jamaica (1978)	• The quotas for some services' payments were increased.	• No change took place. No advance deposit scheme was in effect.	• No change took place. Capital transactions remained strictly regulated.
Kenya (1981)	• No significant change. Most foreign exchange transactions continued requiring prior licenses. • The licenses started to be auctioned 1 year after the devaluation.	• The term of the advanced deposits was reduced, and tariffs were lowered in several items. • Advance deposits became more strict 1 year after the devaluation.	• No significant change. Capital transactions remained strictly regulated.
Korea (1980)	• No significant change. The import licensing requirement was maintained, and the quotas for services' payments were increased slightly.	• No change took place. The advance deposit requirement and the 2.5% import surcharge were not removed.	• Restrictions on foreign investment were relaxed significantly. • The Korean financial market was opened to nonresidents, and foreign currency deposits were allowed for some agents.

Mexico (1976)	• The import licensing requirement was progressively eliminated in the year after the devaluation.	• Substantial reduction in tariff rates. The average tariff was reduced from 20% to 9% approximately. • Subsidies of up to 40% of import duties were granted to some "basic" industries.	• Restrictions on capital movements were significantly relaxed. • Investment banks were allowed to hold foreign currency deposits.
Mexico (1982)	• Severe foreign exchange controls were imposed. A three-tier system was established, and most imports were made at the free rate. • Quotas on services' payments were drastically reduced, and some imports were made subject to prior license.	• No significant change took place. No advance deposit requirement was introduced, and only a few tariff rates were raised.	• Abrupt increase in restrictiveness. • Foreign currency deposits were frozen and converted to domestic currency, payments on foreign debt were suspended, and foreign currency holdings were almost banned. • The last 2 restrictions were lifted 5 months later.
Nicaragua (1979)	• Most sales of foreign exchange remained strictly regulated. • Several nonessential imports were excluded from the official market 15 months after the devaluation.	• No change took place. The 30% import surcharge was not removed.	• Significant increase in restrictiveness. Foreign banks were nationalized, and the banking system became strictly regulated.
Pakistan (1972)	• Most imports were progressively exempted from licensing requirements and other types of quantitative restrictions. • Several quotas for services' payments were increased.	• The advance deposit requirement was abolished. • Import duties were increased 15 months after the devaluation.	• Residents were allowed to hold foreign currency deposits.
Pakistan (1982)	• No significant change. The import licensing requirement and the stringent quotas on services' payments were not eased.	• A 5% surcharge was imposed on all imports 6 months after the devaluation. The surcharge was selectively increased 6 months later.	• No significant change. Capital transactions remained strictly regulated.

Table 7.7 (continued)

Episode	Payment restrictions on current transactions	Tariffs, duties, and cost related measures	Restrictions on capital transactions
Peru (1967)	• The number of prohibited imports increased significantly in the year after the devaluation.	• Many import duties were increased 6 months after the devaluation. • A 10–35% sales tax surcharge was imposed on nonessentials imports.	• Significant increase in restrictiveness. Interest payments and other capital transfers became strictly regulated.
Peru (1975)	• The number of permitted imports was increased slightly 9 months after the devaluation. • Some quotas for services' payments were increased marginally.	• Import duties on several items were increased 9 months after the devaluation.	• No significant change. Capital transactions remained strictly regulated.
Philippines (1962)	• The final phase of the "decontrol" program coincided with the devaluation. All remaining restrictions on foreign trade and services' payments were eliminated.	• The advance deposit requirement was reduced from a range of 50–150% to one of 25–100%. Intermediate imports were exempted from this requirement.	• The few remaining restrictions on capital transactions were eliminated.
Philippines (1970)	• A few remaining restrictions on trade payments were eliminated. • Quotas on services' payments remained effective.	• No change took place. The advance deposit scheme was not eliminated.	• Decrease in the degree of restrictiveness. • Remittances of profits and dividends became unregulated. • Residents were allowed to hold foreign currency deposits.

Sri Lanka (1967)	• Import licensing requirements were eased. The coverage of the open general license scheme was extended.	• Tariffs on essential imports were reduced, and those on "nonessential" imports were raised.	• No change took place. Capital transactions remained strictly regulated.
Trinidad-Tobago (1967)	• The system remained highly restrictive. More imports were prohibited 1 year after the devaluation.	• No change took place. No advance deposit scheme was in effect.	• No change took place. Capital transactions remained fairly regulated.
Venezuela (1964)	• Several import licensing requirements were introduced 1 year after the devaluation.	• With the unification of the exchange market, the subsidized rate for 25 tariff lines was eliminated.	• No change took place. Capital transactions remained fairly regulated.
Yugoslavia (1965)	• The allocation of foreign exchange for current transactions became less restrictive and discriminatory for domestic residents.	• Some import duties were reduced as the country became a member of the GATT 1 year after the devaluation.	• Foreign currency deposits were allowed. • Regulations on foreign investment were not eased.

Source: constructed from information obtained from various issues of the IMF's *Annual Report on Exchange Arrangements and Payments Restrictions* and from various issues of *Pick's Yearbook* and *World Currencies Yearbook* (for a more detailed description of the evolution of these policies see appendix C to chapter 6).

21 of the episodes the devaluation was followed by some liberalization of trade restrictions and of controls applied to current account transactions; in 8 of these episodes capital account transactions were also liberalized after the devaluation. In 4 cases, however, we observe a mixed evolution of restrictions where some measures toward liberalizing the current account were undertaken at the same time as capital movement restrictions were hiked.

The general tendency toward liberalizing captured in table 7.7 reflects the fact that in many cases after devaluing, and (somewhat) reestablishing, the degree of international competitiveness of the country, the authorities usually felt that the controls imposed in the few years preceding the crisis were not needed any more. The combination of these trade liberalization programs with the devaluations make the evaluation of the impact of the latter on the trade account somewhat difficult. First, this reduction in the degree of trade restrictions will result in a change—usually an increase— in the *equilibrium* real exchange rate, making the "required" real exchange rate devaluation higher than with the controls. Second, given this policy mix—devaluation with trade liberalization—it is not surprising to find that in a large number of countries real imports grew at very fast rates during the 3 years following the crisis.

In a number of instances (and in particular in the Latin American countries —Argentina in 1970, Bolivia in 1972, and Costa Rica in 1974, for example) the liberalization of trade was short-lived, being reversed after few months. Not too surprisingly, these are some of the countries for which the effect of the devaluation on the real exchange rate eroded fairly rapidly (recall table 7.1), and where fiscal discipline could not be attained after the devaluation. The observations provide some preliminary evidence suggesting that the reversibility of trade liberalization reforms observed so often in the developing world may have its roots in lax fiscal policies. Overly expansive fiscal policies will usually undermine the degree of credibility on the sustainability of the liberalization reforms, generating "perverse" reactions in the private sector.[5] To the extent that the authorities in the devaluing country are unable to impose fiscal discipline, the public will realize that the real exchange rate will soon become again overvalued and thus will not engage in the process of reallocating resources and redirecting production toward the "nontraditional exports" sector.

Table 7.7 shows that in some cases—Peru in 1967, Egypt in 1962, and Nicaragua in 1979—the devaluation was accompanied by a sharp increase in trade and/or capital movements restrictions. This reflects the fact that in some countries, devaluations were in fact implemented in an environment where the authorities saw them as partial remedies, without really intending to implement demand management policies concurrently.

7.4 The Current Account, Foreign Assets, and Devaluation

In this section we investigate how devaluations affect the external sector in the 39 episodes, placing especial emphasis on the current account. Table 7.8 contains data on the evolution of the ratio of the current account balance to GDP and the ratio of net foreign assets to money after the devaluation.[6] These indicators compare the levels of these variables 1 and 3 years after the crisis with their levels 1 year before the devaluation, and refer to absolute changes. This table provides a broad summary of how the external sector of these economies evolved during the years following the abandonment of the peg. A first revealing fact refers to the difference between the behavior in the short run (i.e., 1 year) and that of the medium run (i.e., 3 years). While in a number of countries there was a deterioration in most of these indicators in the short run, the situation changed through time, and after 3 years there was a substantial improvement.

In some countries there was simultaneously a deterioration of the current account and an improvement in the stock of net foreign assets. This apparently puzzling phenomenon is nothing more than a reflection of the fact that capital movements have played an active role in the period following the devaluation. While in some of the earlier episodes the devaluations were accompanied by substantial capital inflows, in the more recent cases capital flight has many times continued after the devaluation itself— especially in those cases where the public deemed the magnitude of the devaluation "insufficient." Moreover, as noted in chapter 6, in a number of the earlier episodes the devaluation was part of an IMF supported adjustment program that allowed the country in question to obtain substantial short- and medium-term resources, both from the international private banks and from the IMF itself.

The data on the ratio of net foreign assets indicate that in a nontrivial number of countries, the external situation in fact deteriorated after the devaluation, over and above the already precarious initial conditions of 1 year before the crisis. Interestingly enough, and not too surprisingly, most of those countries whose external position, measured by the ratio of foreign assets, experienced a deterioration are among those for which the effect of the devaluations on the RER eroded fully before 3 years—

Table 7.8
Behavior of external sector variables 1 and 3 years after devaluation

Country	Year of devaluation	Change in current account ratio (years after)[a]		Change in ratio of net foreign assets (years after)[b]	
		1	3	1	3
Argentina	1970	−0.011	0.025	−0.029	−0.051
Bolivia	1972	0.014	−0.119	−0.036	0.138
Bolivia	1979	0.051	0.018	−0.144	−0.936
Colombia	1962	−0.008	0.025	−0.108	−0.042
Colombia	1965	−0.042	−0.021	0.028	0.060
Costa Rica	1974	0.056	0.011	−0.130	−0.002
Cyprus	1967	−0.005	−0.027	0.021	0.038
Ecuador	1961	0.017	−0.016	0.001	0.038
Ecuador	1970	−0.054	0.048	−0.062	0.213
Egypt	1962	−0.008	0.041	−0.074	−0.104
Egypt	1979	n.a.	0.060	0.270	0.345
Guyana	1967	0.074	0.040	0.005	−0.129
India	1966	0.007	0.006	−0.008	0.036
Indonesia	1978	−0.011	−0.055	0.239	0.359
Israel	1962	0.042	0.047	0.187	0.108
Israel	1967	−0.044	−0.025	−0.049	−0.308
Israel	1971	0.029	0.003	0.216	0.090
Jamaica	1967	−0.018	0.035	0.047	−0.026
Jamaica	1978	−0.052	−0.074	−0.293	−0.314
Malta	1967	−0.039	−0.055	−0.048	−0.203
Nicaragua	1979	−0.321	0.067	−0.019	0.134
Pakistan	1972	0.025	−0.048	0.088	0.001
Peru	1967	0.046	0.021	−0.038	0.094
Philippines	1962	0.035	0.005	0.009	0.007
Philippines	1970	0.001	0.014	−0.001	0.263
Sri Lanka	1967	−0.001	0.020	−0.107	−0.174
Trinidad	1967	0.032	−0.051	0.030	−0.044
Venezuela	1964	−0.028	0.007	0.014	0.008
Yugoslavia	1965	−0.014	−0.002	0.005	0.002
Bolivia	1982	n.a.	n.a.	−0.131	n.a.
Chile	1982	0.040	n.a.	−0.056	n.a.
Colombia	1967	−0.022	0.002	0.031	0.045

Table 7.8 (continued)

Country	Year of devaluation	Change in current account ratio (years after)[a]		Change in ratio of net foreign assets (years after)[b]	
		1	3	1	3
Ecuador	1982	0.068	n.a.	−0.088	n.a.
Kenya	1981	0.077	−0.029	−0.193	−0.115
Korea	1980	0.023	n.a.	−0.125	−0.193
Mexico	1976	0.013	−0.010	−0.030	−0.020
Mexico	1982	0.033	n.a.	0.016	0.001
Pakistan	1982	0.033	−0.011	0.044	−0.068
Peru	1975	0.036	0.050	−0.435	−0.768

a. Change in ratio of current account to GDP with respect to 1 year before devaluation.
b. Change in ratio of net foreign assets to money relative to 1 year before crisis.

Argentina in 1970, Bolivia in 1972, Colombia in 1962, Bolivia in 1979, and Nicaragua in 1979.[7]

The Peruvian episode of 1975 provides a fascinating contrast. As was reported in table 7.1, in this episode the authorities were able to maintain, via successive devaluations and at the cost of a rapid increase in inflation, a relatively high real exchange rate during the 3 years following the crisis. However, as table 7.8 shows, this was of no avail, and the external sector continued to deteriorate to the point that in 1979 the Peruvian government was forced to reschedule its massive foreign debt. This was largely the result of generalized expectations that the policies undertaken by the authorities were not consistent with a return to stability.

A Current Account Equation

In order to investigate further the relation between real exchange rates, macroeconomic policies, and the current account, a number of current account equations were estimated.[8] According to the model in chapter 3 the current account will respond to RER changes as well as to changes in macroeconomic policies—both monetary and fiscal—and to changes in external conditions such as the international terms of trade. Table 7.9 reports the results obtained from the estimation of alternative current account equations of the following general form suggested by Khan and Knight (1983):

Table 7.9
Estimates of current account equations (3SLS)[a]

	Equation number and real exchange rate variable			
	(7.3.1) RER	(7.3.2) RER	(7.3.3) REER	(7.3.4) REER
$\log e_t$	0.095 (3.280)	0.065 (2.363)	0.095 (3.255)	0.067 (2.150)
$\log e_{t-1}$	−0.086 (−3.316)	−0.060 (−2.430)	−0.085 (−3.293)	−0.061 (−2.008)
GROWTH$_t$	−0.015 (−0.237)	0.010 (0.163)	−0.014 (−0.226)	−0.003 (−0.048)
GROWTH$_{t-1}$	−0.113 (−3.510)	−0.186 (−3.095)	−0.194 (−3.231)	−0.167 (−2.743)
$\log$ TOT$_t$	0.052 (4.668)	0.055 (4.882)	0.053 (4.684)	0.057 (4.871)
$\log$ GCGDP$_t$	−0.003 (−0.272)	−0.005 (−0.451)	−0.003 (−0.280)	−0.003 (−0.264)
DEH	−0.005 (−0.860)	−0.001 (−0.198)	0.001 (0.100)	−0.002 (−0.322)
EXCRE	—	−0.051 (−3.359)	−0.054 (−3.449)	—
DCRE	−0.055 (−3.510)	—	—	−0.057 (−3.417)
N	220	220	220	207
R^2	0.976	0.999	0.937	0.928

a. These equations were estimated using a three-stage least squares procedure. The other equations in the system were an RER equation of the form reported in chapter 5 and a parallel market spread equation. The numbers in parentheses are t-statistics. N is the number of observations. When N is 220 observations, a two-equation system consisting of the RER and current account equations was estimated; an N of 207 means that a three-equation system was estimated. R^2 refers to the weighted coefficient of determination of the system as a whole.

$$\left(\frac{CA}{Y}\right)_t = \alpha_0 + \sum_i \alpha_1 \log e_{t-i} + \sum_i \alpha_2 \, EXCRE_{t-i}$$

$$+ \sum_i \alpha_3 DEH_{t-i} + \sum_i \alpha_4 \log GCGDP_t + \sum \alpha_5 \log TOT_{t-i}$$

$$+ \sum \alpha_6 GROWTH_{t-i} + \sum \alpha_7 Q_{t-i} + \delta_t, \qquad (7.3)$$

where, as before, (CA/Y) is the ratio of current account to GDP; e is the real exchange rate, which was alternatively defined as the bilateral or multilateral rate; EXCRE is our measure of excess supply of credit defined in chapter 5; DEH is the ratio of fiscal deficit to lagged high powered money; GCGDP is the ratio of government consumption to GDP; TOT is the international terms of trade index; GROWTH is the rate of growth of real output; Q_t are "other" variables; and δ_t is an error term. The decision of which variables to include in this regression analysis was based on the model developed in chapter 3.

Equation (7.3) was estimated using pooled data for the 12 countries of chapter 5—India, Malaysia, the Philippines, Sri Lanka, Thailand, Greece, Israel, Brazil, Colombia, El Salvador, South Africa, and Yugoslavia. As mentioned in that chapter, these are the only nations that have long enough time series for the relevant variables. These countries are a fairly representative group, accounting among them for 11 devaluation episodes. The results reported in table 7.9 were obtained using a three-stage least squares procedure, where the current account equation was part of a system that included either a RER equation or both a RER and parallel market spread equations of the type discussed in chapter 5.[9] In every case a fixed effect procedure for estimating pooled data was used, where in a first round time- and country-specific dummy variables were used. After testing for the significance of each of these two groups of dummies, in the second round of estimation—which corresponds to the results reported here—only country-specific dummies were included. According to the model developed in chapter 3, we expect that in the estimation of (7.3), $\sum \alpha_1 > 0$, $\sum \alpha_2 < 0$, $\sum \alpha_3 < 0$, $\sum \alpha_4 < 0$, $\sum \alpha_5 \gtrless 0$, and $\sum \alpha_6 \gtrless 0$. In determining the number of lags to include for each right-hand-side variable, an effort was made to maintain parsimony. In the initial steps of the analysis, up to four lags of each variable were included. In second rounds an effort was made to reduce the number of lags by dropping the insignificant coefficients. Broadly speaking, the results reported in table 7.9 confirm our hypotheses. In all equations the coefficient of the contemporaneous real exchange rate was significantly positive while the lagged real exchange rate had a significantly negative coefficient. The sum of e_t and e_{t-1} was in all regressions significantly positive, indicating that, other things being equal, real exchange rate depreciation has had a positive impact on these countries' current accounts. These results also show that even with a constant real exchange rate, expansive domestic credit policies will have a negative effect on the current account balance. Interestingly enough, while the coefficient of DEH has the expected sign in three of the equations, it was never significant. The positive coefficient of log TOT indicates that in these countries terms of trade improvements have generally resulted in current account improvements.

7.5 Successful and Unsuccessful Devaluations

What makes a devaluation "successful"? This has been the main question this chapter has addressed. In this section we pull together the discussion of the previous sections, and we make an attempt to classify formally our 39 episodes as "successful" and "unsuccessful" devaluations. In doing this, we keep in mind the fact that devaluations are usually only one component of broader stabilization packages.

In classifying these episodes as successful and unsuccessful, we have concentrated on the behavior of three key indicators during the period following the devaluations:

1. Real exchange rates. Our focus here is on the behavior of the *effectiveness index* defined in section 7.1 and reported in table 7.2. The most important property of this index is that it allows us to capture the inflationary consequences of the devaluations. This is particularly important for the crawling peg countries since, as noted above, almost by definition a crawler can sustain a real depreciation by continuously increasing the country's rate of inflation.

2. Behavior of net foreign assets of the monetary system.

3. Behavior of the current account ratio.

Given the difficulties associated with classifying some of these episodes in a clear-cut fashion, a three-way classification was used: (1) successful episodes, (2) unsuccessful episodes, and (3) devaluations with a limited degree of success.[10]

In order for an episode to qualify as *successful*, the following two conditions have to be met: (1) 3 years after the devaluation the effectiveness index had to exceed 0.3, *and* (2) 3 years after the devaluation either the current account or net foreign assets indicators had to exhibit an improvement relative to the year before the crisis. The first requirement implies that in order for an episode to be classified as successful, no more than 70% of the devaluation impact on the real exchange rate has to be eroded in 3 years. The second requirement means that a real depreciation per se is not enough for the nominal devaluation to be considered a success; in addition, the external sector accounts have to be improved. An episode was defined as *unsuccessful* if 3 years after the devaluation the real exchange rate was below its value the year before the crisis—that is, the effectiveness index was negative—or if even when the effectiveness index was positive (but still below 0.3), both the net foreign assets *and* current account positions had worsened 1 *and* 3 years after the devaluation. These definitions of success and failure are quite strict and are able to discriminate sharply between countries. A number of episodes, however, sit in between these two extreme groups. We have called them limited success episodes, since in most of them we observe some improvement in the level of the real exchange rate and/or the external sector accounts.

Table 7.10 contains the 39 episodes classified according to this criterion. As can be seen, among the 29 stepwise devaluers, there are 13 clearcut successful cases, 9 clearcut failures, and 7 limited success cases. For the 10 crawlers there are 3 successful episodes, 5 unsuccessful ones, and 2 cases of limited success.

The 13 successful stepwise devaluers (A.1 of table 7.10) were able to sustain substantial real depreciations in the medium term. The average for the *effectiveness index* after 3 years is 0.66, indicating that on average 2/3 of these nominal devaluations had been transmitted into a real devaluation. For these 13 countries as a group, 3 years after the crisis the RER stood on average 26% higher than its value immediately before the devaluations. For the 9 stepwise cases with limited success (A.2 of table 7.10) the average value of the effectiveness index is still an impressive 0.49, while the average ratio of the RER 3 years after to 3 years prior to the crisis is only 1.05. On the whole, then, this evidence strongly shows that for a large number of cases nominal devaluations have been helpful in generating real exchange rate realignments.

Let us now turn to the unsuccessful episodes. For the 9 unsuccessful stepwise episodes the index of devaluation effectiveness had an average of -0.21 3 years after the crisis, indicating that at that time the RER was more then 20% *below* its value immediately prior to the crisis. For these cases, devaluations not only failed to generate a real exchange realignment, but even worse, 3 years after the event the magnitude of the external dis-

Table 7.10
Successful and unsuccessful devaluations

A.	Stepwise Devaluers		
	A.1	Successful Devaluation Episodes	
		Costa Rica	1974
		Cyprus	1967
		Ecuador	1970
		Egypt	1979
		Guyana	1967
		India	1966
		Indonesia	1978
		Israel	1962
		Pakistan	1972
		Philippines	1962
		Philippines	1970
		Sri Lanka	1967
		Venezuela	1964
	A.2	Limited Success Devaluations	
		Egypt	1962
		Ecuador	1961
		Israel	1967
		Jamaica	1967
		Malta	1967
		Peru	1967
		Trinidad	1967
	A.3	Unsuccessful Devaluations	
		Argentina	1970
		Bolivia	1972
		Bolivia	1979
		Colombia	1962
		Colombia	1965
		Israel	1971
		Jamaica	1978
		Nicaragua	1979
		Yugoslavia	1965
B.	Crawlers		
	B.1	Successful Crawlers	
		Chile	1982
		Colombia	1967
		Korea	1980

Table 7.10 (continued)

B.2	Limited Success Crawlers	
	Kenya	1981
	Pakistan	1982
B.3	Unsuccessful Crawlers	
	Bolivia	1982
	Ecuador	1982
	Mexico	1976
	Mexico	1982
	Peru	1975

Source: See text.

equilibrium had greatly increased. In fact, for these countries in the 3 years following the devaluation the net foreign assets ratio declined on average by more than 10%.

Why did devaluations fail so miserably in these countries? According to the model in chapter 3 and our previous analysis, the answer to this issue should be sought in the realm of the macroeconomic policies that accompanied these devaluations. An analysis of macroeconomic indicators for these episodes shows that in all but one of these countries macroeconomic policies where highly inconsistent, in the sense of greatly exceeding (for each indicator) the median or even the third quartile for the control group (see table 7.5). The only exception is Yugoslavia, which on the face of the macroeconomic indicators looks like a reasonably "successful" country.

Discriminant Analysis

Our analysis until now has placed great emphasis on the role of accompanying macroeconomic policies when evaluating the degree of success of a devaluation. In order to check this relation between success and macroeconomic policies formally, a discriminant analysis was performed. The purpose of this analysis was to test whether it is possible to discriminate statistically between successful and unsuccessful groups *based on the behavior of macroeconomic variables only*. That is, we want to find out whether these two groups indeed pursued macroeconomic policies (domestic credit and fiscal policies) that are significantly different from a statistical point of view.

In performing the discriminant analysis, the 13 successful and the 7 limited success stepwise devaluers were lumped into one grand group of

Table 7.11
Discriminant analysis for macroeconomic policies of successful and unsuccessful stepwise devaluers[a]

	Proportion of "successful" classified as such according to macro policies (%)	Proportion of "unsuccessful" classified as such according to macro policies (%)
1 year after	68	100
3 years after	95	67

a. The classification is based on a generalized squared distant function.

"success"; the 9 "unsuccessful" episodes of table 7.10 were taken as the second group. The following four macroeconomic indicators were used to determine whether our 29 episodes were indeed correctly classified as successful or unsuccessful: (1) rate of growth of domestic credit, (2) rate of growth of domestic credit to the public sector, (3) ratio of public sector to total domestic credit, and (4) increase in the ratio of domestic credit to public sector to GNP. The results obtained are reported in table 7.11; they are very satisfactory and indicate that by and large we can indeed statistically discriminate between these two groups on the basis of their *macroeconomic policies* only. According to these results, 3 years after the devaluation only 1 country classified as successful in table 7.10 did not belong to that group: Egypt in 1979. The posterior probability of it belonging to the successful group was only 2%. On the other hand, only 3 countries preliminarily classified as unsuccessful turned out to be misclassified, in the sense that the posterior probability of them belonging to the "success" group exceeded the posterior probability of them belonging to the unsuccessful group. These countries were (with posterior probabilities of belonging to the unsuccessful group in parentheses) Yugoslavia (8%), Colombia in 1962 (14%), and Colombia in 1965 (8%). These results confirm the existence of a strong and statistically significant relation between macroeconomic policies and successful stepwise devaluations. Indeed, the discriminant analysis results indicate that one can safely use macroeconomic performance—as measured by our four indicators—to classify most of our 29 stepwise episodes into "successful" and "unsuccessful" groups.

In classifying the crawlers, special attention was placed on the effectiveness indexes. The 5 episodes classified as "unsuccessful" were characterized by high rates of inflation after the initial devaluation, meaning that they had to devalue significantly the nominal exchange rate to attain a modest adjustment of the real exchange rate. Also, in these "unsuccessful" crawlers the external sector accounts performed poorly.

Another important determinant of the degree of success of nominal devaluations is the wage indexation policy. If, as discussed in more detail in chapter 8, the nominal wage rate is fully indexed to (past) inflation, nominal devaluations will be self-defeating. In this case, the higher nominal exchange rate will be translated into higher wages, and these, in turn, will be reflected as a higher price of nontradables, generating an offset to the devaluation. Unfortunately, the lack of data precludes a detailed systematic cross-country analysis of the role of indexation. However, episodic evidence from countries such as Brazil, Colombia, and Chile strongly suggests that the existence of strict indexation rules has historically conspired to render nominal devaluations ineffective.

Success and Failure: A Diagrammatic Representation

Figures 7.1–7.8 provide a vivid illustration on the performance of four broadly defined successful devaluations—Colombia in 1967, Ecuador in 1970, Kenya in 1981, and the Philippines in 1970—and four unsuccessful ones—Bolivia in 1979, Jamaica in 1978, Mexico in 1976, and Nicaragua in 1979. Each of these figures contains six parts (A–F) that trace the behavior of six key variables during the 7 years surrounding the devaluations. While parts A–C deal with endogenous variables related to the external sector, D–F refer to macroeconomic policy variables. The exact variables depicted in each part are

• A: real exchange rate index (in each case this index has a value of 100 the year before the crisis),

• B: ratio of current account to GNP,

• C: ratio of net foreign assets of the monetary system to money,

• D: increase in domestic credit to public sector as percentage of GNP (in some cases this index has been multiplied by 100),

• E: rate of growth of domestic credit, and

• F: rate of growth of domestic credit to public sector.

Broadly speaking, the four examples of success are characterized by the following: (1) the RER index remained substantially above its predevaluation value; (2) the current account and/or net foreign assets ratios exhibited substantial positive responses following the devaluation, although in some cases, such as Ecuador in 1970, the current account ratio shows a pronounced J curve behavior; and (3) there is a reduction in the rate of growth of the different macroeconomic indicators. The four unsuccessful episodes

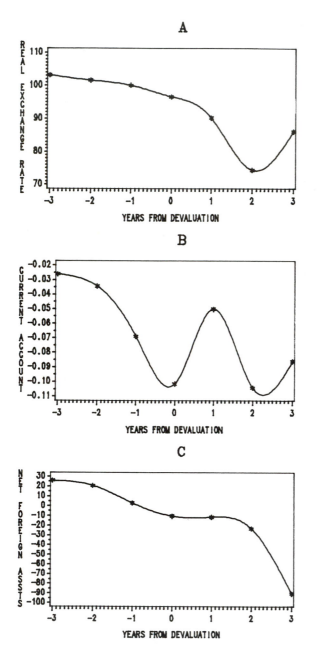

Figure 7.1
Bolivia 1979. Source: constructed from raw data obtained from the *IFS*.

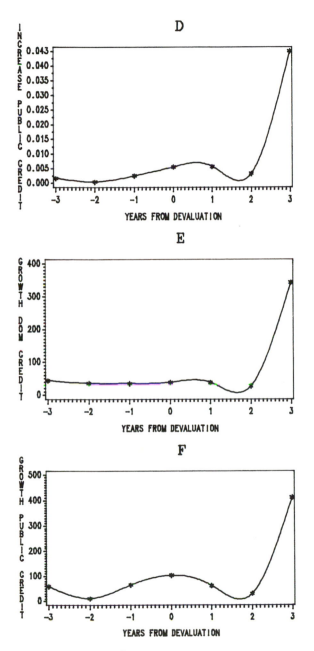

Figure 7.1 (continued)

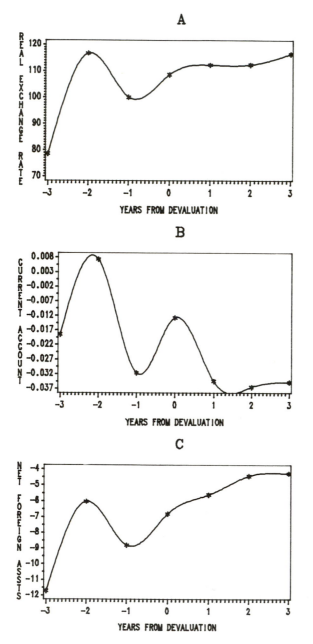

Figure 7.2
Colombia 1967. Source: constructed from raw data obtained from the *IFS*.

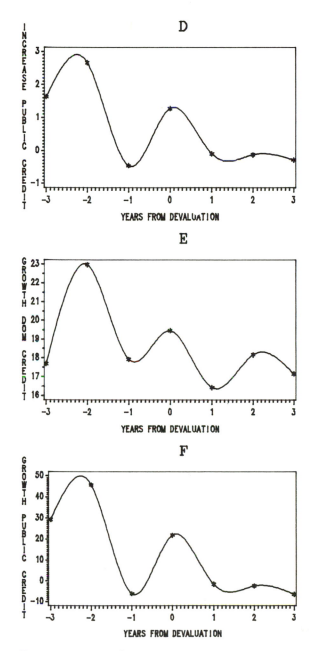

Figure 7.2 (continued)

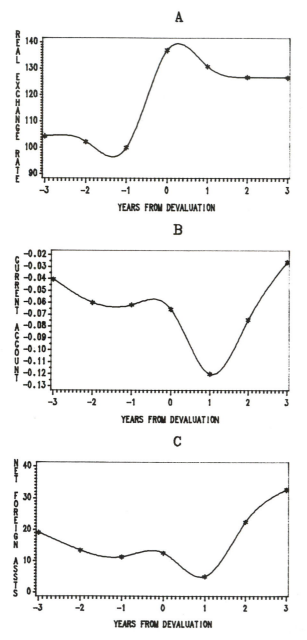

Figure 7.3
Ecuador 1970. Source: constructed from raw data obtained from the *IFS*.

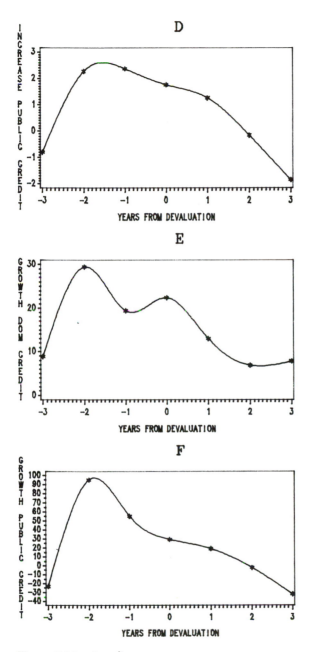

Figure 7.3 (continued)

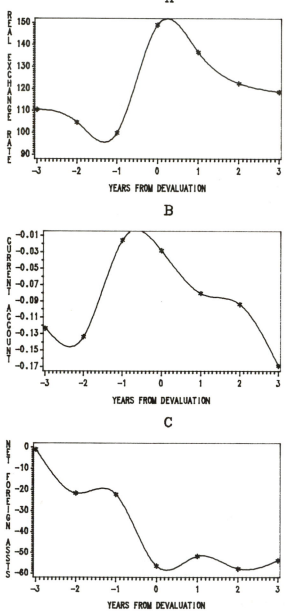

Figure 7.4
Jamaica 1978. Source: constructed from raw data obtained from the *IFS*.

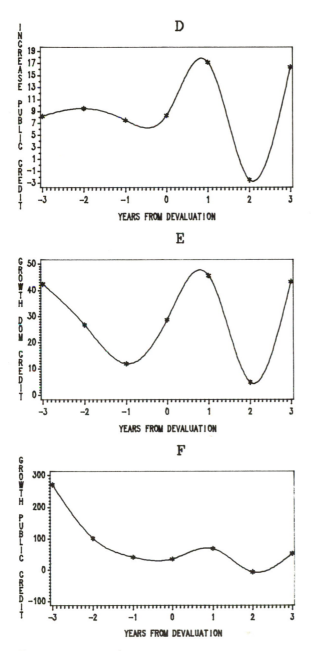

Figure 7.4 (continued)

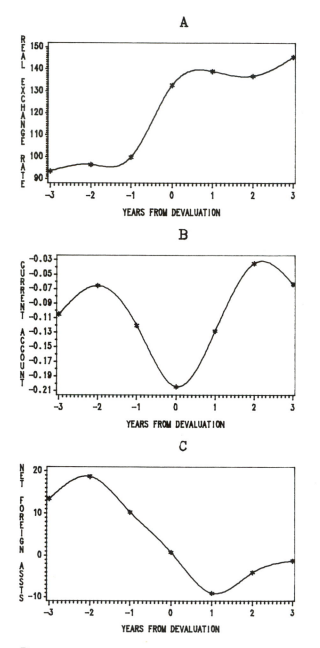

Figure 7.5
Kenya 1981. Source: constructed from raw data obtained from the *IFS*.

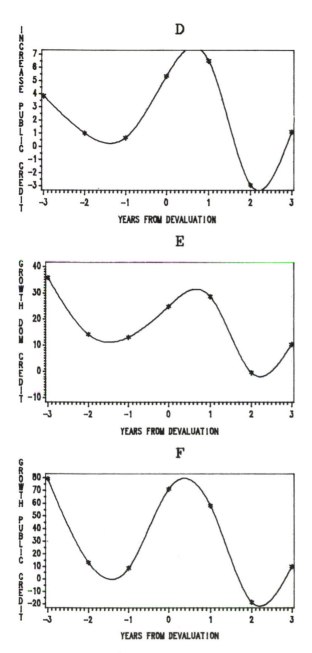

Figure 7.5 (continued)

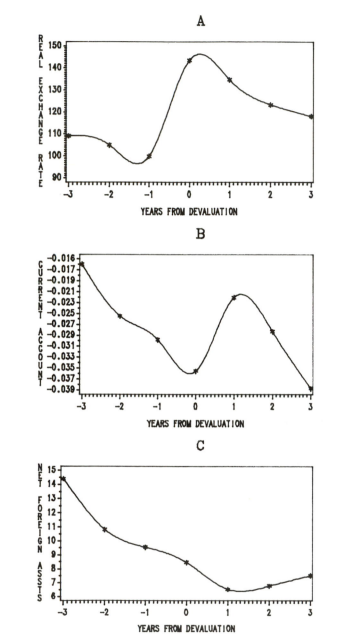

Figure 7.6
Mexico 1976. Source: constructed from raw data obtained from the *IFS*.

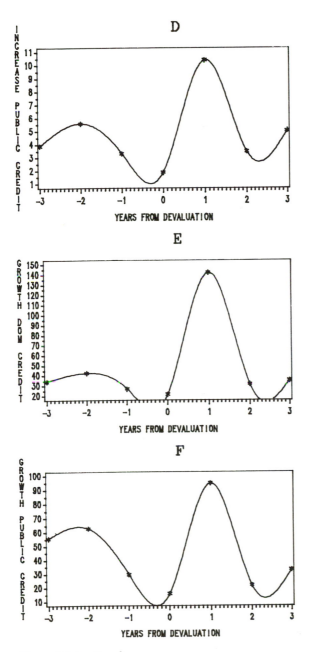

Figure 7.6 (continued)

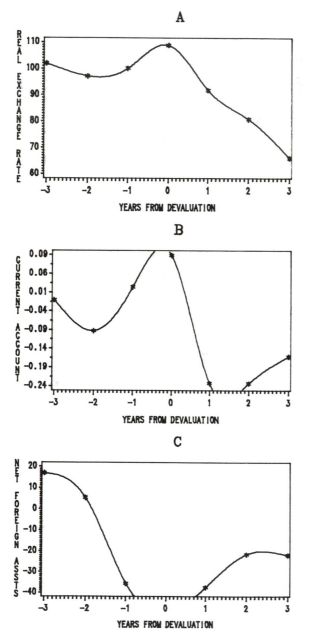

Figure 7.7
Nicaragua 1979. Source: constructed from raw data obtained from the *IFS*.

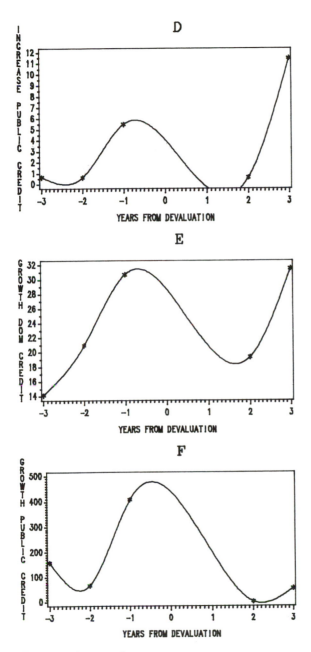

Figure 7.7 (continued)

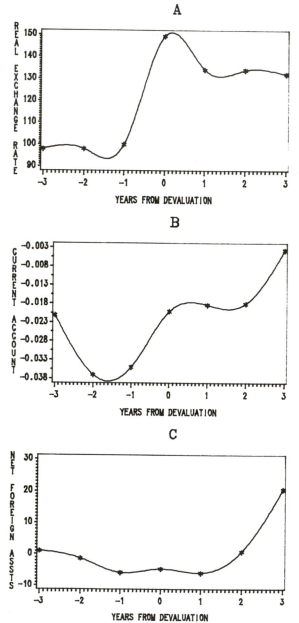

Figure 7.8
Philippines 1970. Source: constructed from raw data obtained from the *IFS*.

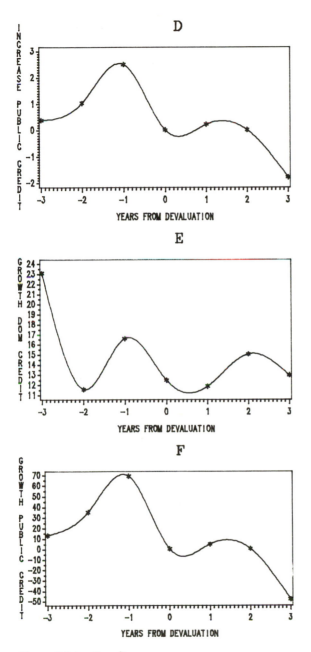

Figure 7.8 (continued)

look very different, Bolivia and Nicaragua providing the most extreme contrasts with the successful cases, because these countries show an almost continuous decline in their real exchange rates. In all four unsuccessful cases, the right-hand-side parts clearly capture the fact that macro, and in particular fiscal, policies either continued to be inconsistent or became even more inconsistent after the devaluation.

Appendix

Table 7A1
Evolution of multilateral real exchange rate index after devaluation[a]

Country	Year	Year prior to devaluation	Year of devaluation	1 year after	2 years after	3 years after
Argentina	1970	100	96.1	90.6	112.1	97.4
Bolivia	1972	100	140.7	138.1	115.1	116.9
Bolivia	1979	100	100.5	95.2	69.4	93.1
Colombia	1962	100	108.2	91.0	87.4	(120.6)*
Colombia	1965	100	138.0	120.3	(129.8)*	(133.8)*
Costa Rica	1974	100	115.9	99.7	109.3	115.6
Cyprus	1967	100	104.2	98.5	99.1	101.7
Ecuador	1961	100	117.8	111.9	108.0	106.4
Ecuador	1970	100	131.1	130.1	129.7	130.9
Egypt	1962	100	130.8	131.2	126.5	112.8
Egypt	1979	100	181.9	167.1	144.7	118.8
Guyana	1967	100	101.4	108.9	111.5	113.6
India	1966	100	142.8	128.6	128.6	133.7
Indonesia	1978	100	141.7	136.2	138.0	127.1
Israel	1962	100	137.8	133.5	130.8	123.7
Israel	1967	100	149.6	133.2	134.6	127.1
Israel	1971	100	95.9	90.3	89.5	90.8
Jamaica	1967	100	101.2	107.4	102.6	100.8
Jamaica	1978	100	139.8	142.1	125.7	119.2
Malta	1967	100	102.7	109.4	111.9	113.4
Nicaragua	1979	100	95.2	86.4	71.4	58.5
Pakistan	1972	100	236.0	193.7	187.1	167.2
Peru	1967	100	120.6	109.1	115.6	111.5
Philippines	1962	100	180.2	170.8	160.7	163.1
Philippines	1970	100	143.1	134.7	147.1	150.3

Table 7A1 (continued)

Country	Year	Year prior to devaluation	Year of devaluation	1 year after	2 years after	3 years after
Sri Lanka	1967	100	103.6	112.7	109.4	108.6
Trinidad	1967	100	102.4	106.6	109.9	110.0
Venezuela	1964	100	131.8	132.7	134.7	135.1
Yugoslavia	1965	100	291.5	273.1	258.2	245.0
Bolivia	1982	100	134.1	87.8	65.7	n.a.
Chile	1982	100	135.9	135.0	149.9	189.8
Colombia	1967	100	107.8	111.3	109.1	116.8
Ecuador	1982	100	104.8	106.3	111.0	103.8
Kenya	1981	100	114.8	104.3	112.4	107.0
Korea	1980	100	117.7	107.6	105.5	113.4
Mexico	1976	100	148.6	135.2	130.8	125.1
Mexico	1982	100	149.9	152.5	127.5	145.4
Pakistan	1982	100	116.8	112.9	115.1	127.8
Peru	1975	100	94.4	105.4	139.1	161.4

Source: See text.
a. Asterisk indicates that a new devaluation took place that year.

Table 7A2
Parallel markets real exchange rate indexes in devaluing countries

Country	Year	3 years before	1 year before	Year of devaluation	1 year after	2 years after	3 years after
Argentina	1970	117.1	100	112.9	196.5	163.7	98.6
Bolivia	1972	79.2	100	108.2	86.2	69.6	66.2
Bolivia	1979	103.0	100	103.2	100.2	96.4	218.4
Colombia	1962	63.6	100	88.5	59.9	70.9	98.9
Colombia	1965	124.8	100	139.4	122.4	113.5	109.0
Costa Rica	1974	112.2	100	99.6	88.6	94.2	86.2
Ecuador	1961	88.1	100	99.8	115.5	92.5	91.3
Ecuador	1970	92.3	100	122.3	115.9	117.4	104.7
Egypt	1962	118.5	100	98.2	102.0	94.8	76.3
Egypt	1979	112.9	100	97.6	89.0	103.2	126.8
India	1966	94.0	100	101.0	91.7	92.0	105.7
Indonesia	1978	126.5	100	136.4	136.4	136.3	133.8
Israel	1962	77.3	100	67.6	63.6	58.6	57.5
Israel	1967	108.9	100	109.9	120.4	134.5	131.4

Table 7A2 (continued)

Country	Year	3 years before	1 year before	Year of devaluation	1 year after	2 years after	3 years after
Israel	1971	91.6	100	107.2	97.4	119.6	109.8
Nicaragua	1979	82.2	100	166.5	115.2	163.5	169.6
Pakistan	1972	80.6	100	109.2	76.0	75.2	67.7
Peru	1967	122.7	100	125.8	130.1	130.0	171.7
Philippines	1962	88.4	100	76.8	71.3	66.8	70.5
Philippines	1970	73.0	100	108.7	98.1	104.3	96.6
Sri Lanka	1967	88.6	100	94.7	80.0	81.2	104.2
Venezuela	1964	104.5	100	96.9	98.3	98.9	99.4
Colombia	1967	81.5	100	92.6	88.9	90.2	108.7
Korea	1980	98.2	100	102.3	94.9	111.2	111.9
Mexico	1976	113.8	100	172.6	135.4	128.8	124.9
Peru	1975	114.8	100	99.1	95.8	103.0	110.8

Source: constructed from data obtained from various issues of *Pick's Currency Yearbook* and *International Financial Statistics*.

Notes

1. See the essays collected in Williamson (1983c).

2. A mistake sometimes made is to think of the RER as an *instrument* and of the balance of payments as a *target*. Instruments are exogenous variables that policy-makers can manipulate. Of course, the RER is an *endogenous* variable. The correct way to think about this is to consider the RER as an *intermediate target*, which turns out to be an excellent indicator of the degree of effectiveness of the policy.

3. These regressions included data on all stepwise devaluations except for Bolivia in 1979. Due to lack of data, those equations where the fiscal deficit ratio was included were restricted to 18 episodes.

4. Appendix C to chapter 6 provides a much more detailed description of the evolution of these policies.

5. See Edwards (1984 and 1989b) for a more detailed discussion of the role of credibility in trade liberalization reforms.

6. If, instead of the ratio of net foreign assets, the *stock* of official international reserves is used, a somewhat different picture emerges. The reason for this is that in growing countries there is a natural tendency to hold more reserves as output and trade grow. On the demand for real international reserves in the developing countries and on the relation between reserves holdings and devaluation crises see Edwards (1983b). Eaton and Gersovitz (1980) develop a model of a central bank

where increases in foreign indebtedness can be used to accumulate more international reserves.

7. Data on estimated capital flight not reported here due to space considerations show that in a large number of the devaluations that took place during the 1982 debt crisis, capital flight continued during the period immediately following the crisis. (These data are available from the author upon request.)

8. Some of the critics of IMF policies have argued that the balance of payments improvement experienced after IMF sponsored programs that include a devaluation are due to the inflow of capital and *not* to an improvement of the current account. For this reason, it is particularly important to inquire how the current account has indeed reacted to devaluations.

9. The following instruments were used: lagged growth; contemporaneous, lagged, and twice-lagged log GCGDP; lagged, twice-lagged, and thrice-lagged real exchange rates; nominal devaluation; lagged and twice-lagged capital inflows; lagged and twice-lagged real output; DEH; EXCRE; lagged and twice-lagged EXCRE; contemporaneous, lagged, and twice-lagged money surprises; log TOT, log TOT_{t-1}, log TOT_{t-2}, and log TOT_{t-3}; contemporaneous and lagged rates of growth of domestic credit; lagged and twice-lagged parallel market premiums; country dummies; time; and contemporaneous, lagged, and twice-lagged domestic credit surprises.

10. As with any attempt to classify individual observations into successful and unsuccessful groups, there is a certain degree of arbitrariness involved. However, by using these three variables we are focusing on the most immediate targets of devaluations and adjustment programs. In chapter 8 we look in detail at the reaction of other variables, including output, real wages, and income distribution.

8   Devaluations, Aggregate Output, and Income Distribution

Even under conditions of severe macroeconomic and real exchange rate disequilibrium, economic authorities in the developing countries many times resist devaluing their currency. Instead, as was shown in chapter 6, in many cases they have tried to impose tariffs, import quotas, and other forms of exchange controls in an effort to avoid the depletion of international reserves that is usually associated with real exchange rate overvaluation.[1] How can we explain this historical regularity? Why do economic authorities in these countries usually prefer to implement highly distortionary controls instead of devaluing? A possible explanation lies in the political consequences of devaluation. In his classical study Richard Cooper (1971a) reported that in the majority of 24 cases he analyzed, the finance minister who had engineered the devaluation had been ousted from office 18 months after the exchange rate realignment.[2] If, indeed, devaluations destroy the political career of their proponents, there is a good reason for politicians to resist them, and to consider them only as a measure of last resort.

This explanation, however, begs the question of why the architects of devaluation are ousted from office so often. In many ways this is a paradoxical result, since according to the traditional theory, devaluation should be highly beneficial for a country with a severe real exchange rate overvaluation and an imminent balance of payments crisis. A possible explanation for this "puzzle" is related to the idea that under some (plausible) circumstances, devaluations are not as beneficial as the traditional theory suggests. In fact, it is possible that although devaluations will help improve the external position of a country, they may result in a reduction of output, increased unemployment, and/or a worsening of income distribution.[3] If indeed devaluations have these negative effects, they may very well result in the firing of those high officials that proposed and backed that measure.

The purpose of this chapter is to analyze the real output and income distribution effects of devaluations. The analysis of the real output effects is done in two ways. First, data for the 39 devaluation episodes identified in chapter 6 are closely scrutinized following the same methodology as the one used in chapters 6 and 7: The behavior of a number of key variables related to aggregate output in the period elapsed between 3 years before the devaluation and 3 years after the devaluation is analyzed. The emphasis is placed on real growth and aggregate gross investment. A limitation of this type of analysis, however, is that it concentrates on the behavior of the key variables "before" and "after" the devaluation, without taking into account the possible role of other policies or external events. This problem is avoided by the second approach taken in this chapter: An equation for aggregate output in an open economy is estimated for a group of countries. In addition to the possible effect of the exchange rate on output, this equation incorporates the role of monetary policy, fiscal policy, and exogenous terms of trade effects.

The analysis of income distribution effects is limited by the availability of data, and concentrates on real wages and on the evolution of factoral distribution of income. The fact that there have been virtually no systematic cross-country empirical studies of devaluation and its effects on income distribution is in part a reflection of the lack of reliable data on income distribution in these countries.[4]

The chapter is organized as follows. In section 8.1 a macroeconomic model of a dependent economy with imported intermediate goods and foreign debt is developed to analyze the way in which devaluations affect aggregate output and employment. In section 8.2 we look at the experience of our 39 devaluation episodes. Once more we use nonparametric tests to compare the behavior of these countries with that of the control group. Section 8.3 presents results from the estimation of the model from section 8.1. Section 8.4 deals with the effects of exchange controls and distortions on real activity. Section 8.5 focuses on income distribution during the period surrounding our 39 devaluation episodes.

8.1 Are Devaluations Contractionary?: A Theoretical Model

Although the theoretical possibility of devaluations being contractionary has been recognized by a number of authors, there has been very limited empirical work related to this issue. Modern theoretical discussions of contractionary devaluation go back at least to Hirschman (1949) and Diaz-Alejandro (1965). Cooper (1971a,b) provided important empirical evidence in his cross-country studies. More recently Krugman and Taylor (1978), Gylfason and Schmid (1983), van Wijnbergen (1986), Buffie (1984), Branson

(1986), and Larrain and Sachs (1986) have provided further theoretical refinements. Empirical studies based on the "before" and "after" approach include Cooper (1971b) and Krueger (1978). Gylfason and Schmid (1983), Gylfason and Risager (1984), and Branson (1986) presented results based on simulation analyses. Edwards (1986a) provides one of the very few regression analyses.

From an analytical point of view, devaluations can affect the real sector of the economy through a number of channels. According to the more traditional views, a devaluation will either have an expansionary effect on aggregate output or, in the worst of cases, will leave aggregate output unaffected. If there is unutilized capacity, a nominal devaluation will be expansionary, and total aggregate output will increase. On the other hand, if the economy is operating under full employment, the nominal devaluation will be translated into equiproportional increases in prices, with the real exchange rate and aggregate output not being affected. This particular aspect of the more traditional approaches has recently been challenged by the neostructuralist critique. Taylor (1983), Katseli (1983), van Wijnbergen (1986) and others have argued that in the less developed countries it is highly plausible that real output will decline after a nominal parity adjustment.

There are several theoretical reasons why, contrary to the traditional views, a devaluation can be contractionary and generate a decline in aggregate real activity, including employment. First, through its effect on the price level, a devaluation will generate a negative real balance effect. This, in turn, will result in lower aggregate demand and, under some circumstances, lower output. Second, a devaluation can generate a redistribution of income from groups with a low marginal propensity to save to groups with a high marginal propensity to save, resulting in a decline in aggregate demand and output. [See, for example, Diaz-Alejandro (1965), see also Krugman and Taylor (1978).] Third, if the price elasticities of imports and exports are sufficiently low, the trade balance expressed in domestic currency may worsen, generating a recessionary effect. And fourth, in addition to these demand related effects, there are a number of supply-side channels through which devaluations can be contractionary. For example, van Wijnbergen (1986) has recently developed a model with intermediate goods and informal (curb) financial markets, where a devaluation results in an increase in the domestic currency price of intermediate inputs, and in an upward shift of the aggregate supply schedule.

In this section a model to analyze the effects of nominal devaluations on aggregate output and employment in a small country is developed.

The model analyzes the case of an economy that produces three goods—importables (M), exportables (X), and nontradables (N)—and uses imported inputs in the production of the nontradables. The model is sufficiently general to include the results of Cooper (1971b), Krugman and Taylor (1978), Hanson (1983), and Branson (1986) as special cases. Although the analysis concentrates on devaluations, the model can easily handle the case of a terms of trade shock. This is indeed done in the empirical section of the chapter.

Although similar in spirit to the model in chapter 3, the model presented here has a number of features that make it particularly suitable for analyzing the aggregate output consequences of devaluation. Specifically, the incorporation of imported intermediate inputs, foreign debt, and wage indexation and the relaxation of the full employment assumption allow us to highlight three important potential channels through which devaluation may affect output. In some ways these new assumptions may be considered to reflect better the characteristics of developing nations. It is important to notice, however, that these new assumptions do not affect in any fundamental way the main results from chapters 2 and 3 regarding equilibrium and disequilibrium real exchange rate behavior. They do, however, introduce in a clear way important interactions between devaluations and real economic activity.[5]

Consider a small country that produces exportables (X), importables (M), and nontradable goods (N). The capital stock is sector specific and fixed during the relevant run discussed here. As in Branson (1986), the production of nontradables requires the use of labor, (specific) capital, and an imported input. To simplify the exposition, it is assumed that exportables and importables are produced using capital and labor only.[6] Moreover, it is assumed that the world prices of X and M do not change. As will be seen below, however, the model can be easily manipulated to analyze effects of changes in the external terms of trade on output and employment. It is also assumed that this country has a stock of foreign debt, whose nominal value in foreign exchange is equal to D^*. As is the case in many developing countries, it is assumed that due to institutional reasons the behavior of nominal wages is governed by an indexation rule that ties changes in wages to changes in the price level. In order to focus on the effects of devaluations on output and employment, the monetary sect rudimentary, almost nonexisting. No distinction is made b pated and unanticipated money changes; nor do we incorpo foreign money. In the empirical implementation of the mod more sophisticated role for money is considered.

The model is given by equations (8.1)–(8.10):

$$y = N^s + \frac{EP_X}{P_N}X^s + \frac{EP_M}{P_N}M^s - \frac{EP_I}{P_N}I - \frac{Ei^*D^*}{P_N}, \tag{8.1}$$

$$N^d = N\left(y, \frac{P_N}{EP_M}, \frac{P_N}{EP_X}, \frac{B}{P_N}\right) + G, \tag{8.2}$$

$$N^s = k[\beta I^{-\rho} + (1 - \beta)V^{-\rho}]^{-1/\rho}, \tag{8.3}$$

$$V = L_N^\gamma \bar{K}_N^{(1-\gamma)}, \tag{8.4}$$

$$X^s = L_X^\theta \bar{K}_X^{(1-\theta)}, \tag{8.5}$$

$$M^s = L_M^\delta \bar{K}_M^{(1-\delta)}, \tag{8.6}$$

$$\hat{W} = \omega\hat{P}, \tag{8.7}$$

$$P = P_N^{a_1}(EP_X)^{a_2}(EP_M)^{(1-a_1-a_2)}, \tag{8.8}$$

$$N^d = N^s, \tag{8.9}$$

$$g = P_0^N N + P_0^X X + P_0^M M - P_0^I I, \tag{8.10}$$

where the following notation is used:

y	= real income in terms of nontradable goods,
N^s, N^d	= supply and demand for nontradables,
X^s	= supply of exportable goods,
M^s	= supply of importable goods,
I	= imported intermediate inputs,
V	= value added in the nontradables goods sector,
P_X, P_M, P_I	= world prices of exportables, importables, and intermediate goods expressed in terms of the foreign currency,
E	= nominal exchange rate, expressed as units of domestic currency per unit of foreign currency,
P_N	= domestic nominal price of nontradable goods,
i^*	= world interest rate,
D^*	= stock of external debt in foreign currency,
B	= nominal stock of base money, assumed to be equal to the nominal stock of money,
G	= real government expenditure in terms of nontradable goods,

L_N, L_X, L_M = labor used in nontradable, exportable, and importable sectors,

$\bar{K}_N, \bar{K}_X, \bar{K}_M$ = (fixed) capital stock in N, X, and M sectors,

P = price level,

W = nominal wage rate, and

g = *real* gross domestic product (GDP) in terms of purchasing power of period 0, where P_0^N, P_0^X, P_0^M, and P_0^I are the base period prices.

Equation (8.1) is real income in terms of nontradable goods. Equation (8.2) is the demand function for nontradables, which is composed of the private sector demand N plus the government's demand G. It is assumed that the private sector demand for N depends on real income, relative prices, and the real stock of money.

Equation (8.3) is the production function for nontradable goods. It is a two-stage Constant Elasticity of Substitution (CES) function with an elasticity of substitution between value added and imported inputs equal to $\sigma = (1 + \rho)^{-1}$. Equation (8.4) specifies that value added in the nontradables sector is produced using Cobb-Douglas technology, and that the capital stock in that sector is fixed. Equations (8.5) and (8.6) are the production functions for X and M, which are assumed to be Cobb-Douglas.

Equation (8.7) is the indexation rule, and establishes that nominal wages are adjusted by a proportion ω of inflation. This equation assumes that due to institutional reasons (unions and other rigidities), the labor market does not clear. If, on the contrary, we assume full flexibility in the labor market, equation (8.7) should be replaced by a labor supply equation. Equation (8.8) is the definition of the price level. From (8.7) and (8.8) we get that nominal wages are adjusted according to the following rule: $\hat{W} = \omega_1 \hat{P}_N + \omega_2 \hat{E}$, where $0 \leq (\omega_1 + \omega_2) \leq 1$. Equation (8.9) establishes that in equilibrium the nontradable goods market clears. Finally, equation (8.10) is real GDP in terms of period 0 purchasing power. The modeling strategy is to find how devaluations—that is, changes in E—affect the level of employment and real economic activity (g).

This model is quite general and differs from previous work in various respects. First, in contrast with Cooper (1971c), Krugman and Taylor (1978), Taylor (1979), and Hanson (1983), who assume a markup pricing in the nontradables good sector, in this model we have a fully specified supply side. Second, unlike Krugman and Taylor (1978), Gylfason and Schmid (1983), Gylfason and Radetzki (1985), Hanson (1983), and Branson (1986), in this model households are allowed to consume all three goods. Third, the current model also incorporates the existence of external debt. In the discussion that follows it will be pointed out how this model can be simplified to generate as special cases the results previously obtained in the literature.

Assuming profit maximization and perfectly competitive firms, we can obtain from equations (8.3), (8.4), (8.5), and (8.6) the demand functions for imported inputs and labor in each sector:

$$I = A_0(P_N/EP_I)^\sigma N, \tag{8.11}$$

$$L_N = A_1(P_N/W)^{1/[1+\gamma(1-\sigma)/\sigma]}N^{1/\sigma[1+\gamma(1-\sigma)/\sigma]}, \tag{8.12}$$

$$L_X = \theta(EP_X/W)X, \tag{8.13}$$

$$L_M = \delta(EP_M/W)M, \tag{8.14}$$

where A_0 and A_1 are constant parameters.

In order to find out how changes in the nominal exchange rate affect total real output and employment, it is first necessary to investigate the way in which devaluations affect the nontradable goods market. From equations (8.1), (8.2), (8.7), and (8.12), and using expressions for the supply functions of X and M obtained from (8.5), (8.6), (8.13), and (8.14), we can derive the following equation for the rate of change of the demand for N [where as customary, $\hat{X} = (dX/dt)(1/X)$]:

$$\hat{N}^d = D_1\hat{E} + D_2\hat{P}_N + D_3\hat{B} + D_4\hat{G}, \tag{8.15}$$

where the D values are given by

$$D_1 = Q[(\lambda_X + \lambda_M) + (\lambda_X\varepsilon_X + \lambda_M\varepsilon_M)(1 - \omega_2) - (\eta_X + \eta_M)/\phi$$
$$- \lambda_I(1 - \sigma) - \lambda_D^*],$$

$$D_2 = -Q[(1 - \lambda_N) + \mu/\phi - (\eta_X + \eta_M)/\phi + \lambda_I\sigma + (\lambda_X\varepsilon_X + \lambda_M\varepsilon_M)\omega_1],$$

$$D_3 = \mu/Q,$$

$$D_4 = G/NQ, \text{ and}$$

$$Q = \phi/[1 - \phi(1 - (\lambda_X + \lambda_M - \lambda_{D^*}))],$$

and where $\phi = (N^p/N)\eta_y$ and (N^p/N) is the ratio of private to total demand for N. η_y is the income elasticity of demand for N; λ_X, λ_M, λ_N, λ_I, and λ_D^* are ratios of exports, imports, nontradables, imported inputs, and debt payments to total income [i.e., $\lambda_X = (EP_XX)/(P_Ny)$]; η_X and η_M are the price elasticities of demand for N with respect to P_N/P_X and P_N/P_M, and consequently are negative. ε_X and ε_M are the price elasticities of supply for X and M [i.e., $\varepsilon_X = \theta/(1 - \theta) > 0$, $\varepsilon_M = \delta/(1 - \delta) > 0$]. μ is the demand elasticity of N with respect to real cash balances, and consequently positive. Stability requires that $Q > 0$.[7]

D_1 captures the effect of a nominal devaluation on the demand for nontradables (with other things given), and its sign is undetermined. The reason is that D_1 combines both an expenditure switching effect—where a higher E will tend to increase the demand for N—and an expenditure reducing effect. The expenditure switching effect is given by $\{(\lambda_X + \lambda_M) + (\lambda_X \varepsilon_X + \lambda_M \varepsilon_M)(1 - \omega_2) - (\eta_X + \eta_M)/\phi\} > 0$. By increasing the relative price of M and X, the devaluation will result in the substitution in consumption away from these goods toward N. The term $(-\lambda_D^*)$ is the pure expenditure reducing effect, which captures the effect of the higher domestic currency value of foreign liabilities (D^*) resulting from the devaluation.

The term $-\lambda_I(1 - \sigma)$ in D_1 captures the effect of the devaluation on intermediate inputs, and its sign depends on the elasticity of substitution between value added and intermediate inputs. If σ is very low (i.e., $\sigma = 0$), a devaluation, by increasing the price of intermediate inputs, will result in a significant backward shift of the supply of N, reducing real income and, consequently, the demand for all goods, including N. If the expenditure reduction effect dominates, then $D_1 < 0$. D_2 is the (total) price elasticity of demand for N and is negative, capturing the fact that, with other things as given, an increase in P_N will result in a reduction of the quantity demanded of nontradable goods. D_3 captures the effect of increases in (real) money balances on the demand for N and is positive. D_4 is also positive and measures the role of higher government consumption on the demand for nontradables.

Note that equation (8.15) is very general and includes, as special cases, a number of previous models. For example, if $\varepsilon_X = \varepsilon_M = \omega_1 = \omega_2 = \lambda_{D^*} = 0$ and $\hat{P}_N = v\hat{E}$ (i.e., there is markup pricing for nontradable goods), equation (8.15) corresponds to Hanson's model. Moreover, if in addition we assume that $\lambda_M = \sigma = 0$, equation (8.15) becomes equivalent to the model by Krugman and Taylor (1978).

Let us now turn to the supply side for nontradable goods. From the first-order conditions (8.11) and (8.12) we obtain expressions for $\hat{I}$ and $\hat{L}_N$. Using the wage indexation equation (8.7) to eliminate $\hat{W}$, we finally obtain the following equation for changes in the supply for nontradable goods:

$$\hat{N}^s = S_1 \hat{P}_N + S_2 \hat{E}, \tag{8.16}$$

where the S coefficients are equal to

$$S_1 = \left(\frac{1}{1-\gamma}\right)\left\{\frac{\pi_1}{\pi_2}(\sigma(1-\gamma)+\gamma)+\gamma(1-\omega_1)\right\} > 0,$$

$$S_2 = -\left\{\frac{\sigma(1-\gamma)+\gamma}{1-\gamma}\right\}[\pi_1/\pi_2 + \gamma\omega_2] < 0,$$

and π_1 and π_2 are the shares of value added and intermediate inputs in the production of N.

From (8.16) it is possible to see that, with other things as given, an increase in P_N generates an increase in the supply of home goods, while a devaluation will shift the aggregate supply curve upward and to the left, tending to reduce the supply of home goods. The channel through which this happens is the effect of the devaluation on the price of the imported intermediate inputs. As the devaluation makes these inputs more expensive, in domestic currency, the marginal cost of producing nontradable goods increases.

Combining (8.15) and (8.16), we can obtain final expressions for $\hat{N}$ and $\hat{P}_N$:

$$\hat{N} = \left\{\frac{D_2 S_2 - D_1 S_1}{D_2 - S_1}\right\}\hat{E} - \left\{\frac{D_3 S_1}{D_2 - S_1}\right\}\hat{B} - \left\{\frac{D_4 S_1}{D_2 - S_1}\right\}G, \tag{8.17}$$

$$\hat{P}_N = \left\{\frac{S_2 - D_1}{D_2 - S_1}\right\}\hat{E} - \left\{\frac{D_3}{D_2 - S_1}\right\}\hat{B} - \left\{\frac{D_4}{D_2 - S_1}\right\}\hat{G}. \tag{8.18}$$

From (8.17) it follows that

$(\hat{N}/\hat{E}) \gtrless 0,$

$(\hat{N}/\hat{B}) > 0,$

$(\hat{N}/\hat{G}) > 0.$

Whether or not a devaluation will reduce the (equilibrium) output of non-tradable goods will depend on whether $(D_2 S_2 - D_1 S_1)$ is positive or negative. A sufficient condition for having a contractionary devaluation is that the devaluation shifts back both demand and supply for N. This will be the case when $D_1 < 0$. However, in the more plausible case where (on the demand side) the expenditure switching effect dominates in (8.15) (i.e., $D_1 > 0$), there will be two forces that will operate in the opposite directions. On one hand, the demand for nontradables will increase as a result of the devaluation, while on the other hand, the higher cost of imported intermediate inputs will contract the supply. In this case, whether a devaluation results in a higher or lower N will be an empirical question. With respect to the price equation (8.18), if the expenditure switching effect dominates in demand $(D_1 > 0)$, then the devaluation will always increase P_N. This is because in this case both supply and demand shift upward. In the rest of this section, and unless otherwise stated, we shall assume that $D_1 > 0$.

The effects of a devaluation on the level of sectoral employment is obtained from equations (8.12), (8.13), (8.14), (8.17), and (8.18):

$$\hat{L}_N/\hat{E} = \left[\frac{1}{\sigma(1-\gamma)+\gamma}\right]\left[\left(\frac{1}{D_2-S_2}\right)(D_2 S_2 - D_1 S_1\right.$$

$$\left. + (1-\omega_1)\sigma(S_2 - D_1) - \omega_2\sigma\right]. \tag{8.19}$$

Again, the sign of this elasticity is ambiguous; the final effect of a devaluation on employment in N will depend on the relative values of the different structural parameters in the model.

From equations (8.5)–(8.8), changes in production of X and M are equal to $\varepsilon_X(\hat{E} - \hat{W})$ and $\varepsilon_M(\hat{E} - \hat{W})$. Thus, as long as the nominal devaluation reduces the real product wage in these two sectors—that is, as long as the nominal devaluation results in a real devaluation—there will be an expansion in their output. A sufficient condition for this is that the weight of P_N in the indexation rule (ω_1) is zero. A necessary condition, on the other hand, is that ω_1 is not "very large." If $\omega_1 \leq (1-\omega_2)[(D_2 - S_1)/(S_2 - D_1)]$, the nominal devaluation will always result in a real devaluation [i.e., $(\hat{E} - \hat{W}) > 0$] and the output of X and M will increase. Notice, however, that even if the nominal devaluation results in a real devaluation, production of home goods can either increase or decrease; that is, the sign of $(\hat{N}/\hat{E})$ is still undetermined. If indeed output of N goes down by a sufficiently large amount, *aggregate* output could be reduced, even if output of X and M increases.

To sum up, the model presented above has clearly indicated that there is a (nontrivial) possibility for devaluations to reduce aggregate output. Whether they do it or not is, in fact, an empirical issue. It is possible to generate testable equations from this model. For example, taking log differences of equation (8.10) and using the expressions for changes in N, X, M, and P_N, it is possible to derive after some simple manipulations the following double-log estimable expression for the log of real GDP:[8]

$$\log g = \text{constant} + a_1 \log E + a_2 \log B + a_3 \log G + u, \tag{8.20}$$

where the parameters a_1, a_2, and a_3 are functions of the different elasticities and structural coefficients, and u is assumed to be an error term with the usual characteristics. a_1 is the elasticity of real GDP with respect to the nominal exchange rate, and can be either positive or negative. In fact, one of the purposes of the empirical analysis in section 8.3 is to use historical data to elucidate the sign of a_1. The coefficient a_2 captures the response of real GDP to changes in the quantity of money, and it is expected that it will be greater than or equal to zero. Finally, a_3 measures the effect of fiscal policy—in our case government demand for N—on real GDP and is expected to be greater than or equal to zero. In section 8.3 alternative versions of equation (8.20) are estimated using data for a group of developing countries.

8.2 Devaluations and Economic Activity in the 39 Devaluation Episodes

This section provides a preliminary empirical analysis of the contractionary devaluation issue. We analyze the evolution of two measures of real economic activity in the period surrounding the 39 devaluations episodes of chapter 6. Table 8.1 summarizes the distribution of the *rate of growth* of real GDP in our devaluation episodes during the period extending from 3 years prior to the devaluation to 3 years after the devaluations. As can be seen, 3 years prior to the devaluation the distribution for the devaluing countries

Table 8.1
Growth of real GDP in devaluing and control group countries (%)

		First quartile	Median	Third quartile
A.	39 Devaluation Episodes			
	3 years before	4.7	6.0	7.4
	2 years before	3.6	6.1	8.4
	1 year before	2.3	5.4	7.3
	Year of Devaluation	1.2	4.2	6.1
	1 year after	3.1	4.7	6.4
	2 years after	3.1	4.7	6.4
	3 years after	3.2	5.8	9.2
B.	Control Group of Nondevaluing Countries			
		4.5	6.4	7.4

Source: See text.

is very similar to that of the control group. In fact, the value of the $\chi^2(2)$ statistic is 0.036 (level of probability 0.98), which indicates that the null hypothesis of both distributions being equal cannot be rejected.

However, things look increasingly different as we move toward the devaluation year. More specifically, notice that in the year of the devaluation, the median for crisis countries (4.2%) is *below* the first quartile for the control group (4.5%), and that the third quartile for the devaluers (6.1%) is below the median for the countries with a fixed exchange rate (6.4%). In fact, for this year the $\chi^2(2)$ has a value of 6.5 (level of probability 0.04), indicating that the null hypothesis of both distributions being equal during that year is rejected at conventional significance levels. As can be seen in the table, the crisis countries exhibit a fairly rapid recovery during the 3 years that follow the devaluation. However, this recovery process is uneven, with the top 25% of the countries doing exceedingly well—the third quartile for the crisis ratios greatly exceeds the control group 3 years after the devaluation—while for the rest of the devaluing countries, growth still lags the behavior from the period preceding the devaluation. For the group as a whole the $\chi^2(2)$ are 3.07 and 6.31 2 and 3 years after the devaluations (levels of probability 0.2 and 0.04), clearly supporting the hypothesis that at that time these nations still behave differently from the control group of fixers.

Table 8.2 contains the list of those countries that had a particularly poor performance in terms of growth of real GDP in the year of the devaluation or during any of the 3 years that followed. In constructing this table the countries in the lowest 25% of the distribution for real GDP growth for each year were included. An asterisk in this table means that for that particular country the rate of growth of real GDP deviates by more than one standard deviation from the average growth for that country during the 8 years prior to the devaluation. The distribution of poor performers is somewhat uniform across geographic regions and across type of devaluers— stepwise or crawlers. Notice however, that in table 8.2 there are a large number of countries that devalued in 1982, in the midst of the international debt crisis. This, of course, suggests that the poor perfromance experienced by these countries during this period may not have been fully the result of the devaluation itself, but of the (exogenous) circumstances surrounding it. In section 8.3 we use regression analysis in an effort to isolate the role of devaluations from that of other factors, including terms of trade disturbances.

Table 8.3 takes us away from the direct sphere of output and looks at the evolution of the investment-GDP ratio before and after the crisis. The reason for looking at this variable is that it has been suggested by some

Table 8.2
Countries with unsatisfactory growth performance in years of devaluation or years following devaluation[a]

			Rate of growth of real GDP (%)
A.	Year of Devaluation		
	India	1966	1.1*
	Jamaica	1978	0.6
	Nicaragua	1979	−26.4*
	Yugoslavia	1965	1.1
	Bolivia	1982	−8.7
	Chile	1982	−14.1
	Ecuador	1982	1.2
	Mexico	1982	−0.6*
	Korea	1980	−2.9*
B.	One Year after Devaluation		
	Bolivia	1979	0.5
	Costa Rica	1974	2.1
	Guyana	1967	0.2
	Jamaica	1978	−1.7
	Peru	1967	0.0*
	Bolivia	1982	−7.7*
	Chile	1982	−0.7
	Ecuador	1982	−2.8*
	Mexico	1982	−5.3*
	Kenya	1981	1.8
C.	Two Years after Devaluation		
	Argentina	1970	2.2
	Bolivia	1979	−0.9
	Egypt	1962	3.0
	India	1966	3.0*
	Jamaica	1978	−5.8*
	Trinidad	1967	0.1
	Venezuela	1964	−1.7
	Yugoslavia	1965	3.0
	Peru	1975	−0.3

Table 8.2 (continued)

			Rate of growth of real GDP (%)
D.	Three Years after Devaluation		
	Bolivia	1979	−8.7*
	Cyprus	1967	3.1
	Egypt	1962	2.9
	Jamaica	1978	2.5
	Nicaragua	1979	−1.2*
	Chile	1982	2.4
	Kenya	1981	0.4*
	Mexico	1982	2.7
	Peru	1975	−1.7*

Source: See text.
a. An asterisk means that the rate of growth of real GDP is below that country's average for the previous 8 years by *more* than one standard deviation.

Table 8.3
Investment ratio in devaluing countries and control group (%)

		First quartile	Median	Third quartile
A.	39 Devaluation Episodes			
	3 years before	22.5	18.0	15.6
	2 years before	23.6	18.1	14.5
	1 year before	22.2	18.3	15.2
	Year of devaluation	21.8	17.6	15.1
	1 year after	20.9	17.3	15.7
	2 years after	21.8	18.0	15.2
	3 years after	24.1	18.4	15.7
B.	Control Group			
		21.8	18.1	15.2

Source: See text.

authors (e.g., Branson, 1986) that investment may be one possible channel through which devaluations negatively affect future economic activity. As can be seen, these distributions look very similar for the devaluers 3 years prior to the crisis and for the control group; the $\chi^2(2)$ was equal to 1.3. However, for the year of the devaluation, and more markedly 1 year after the devaluation, the median and first quartile for the devaluers exhibit an important decline. The $\chi^2(2)$ statistics have values of 4.9 and 6.2, indicating that in fact the probability that these distributions are equal to that of the control group is now greatly reduced.

To sum up, the evidence discussed here regarding the 39 devaluation episodes strongly suggests that in many cases devaluations have historically been associated with declines in the level of economic activity around its trend. These results provide some preliminary evidence tending to support the contractionary devaluation hypothesis. This evidence is only suggestive, however, since it does not distinguish devaluation from other policies and disturbances. This is done in the next section, where the results obtained from a number of regressions based on the model of section 8.1 are reported.

An important characteristic of the distributions of real growth summarized in table 8.1 that should be kept in mind is that, for the devaluers, real GDP growth starts exhibiting a decline *before* the date of the actual devaluation. This finding suggests that the imposition of exchange and trade controls that precede most devaluations introduce important distortions that negatively affect the performance of the economy. Interestingly enough, this possibility has not been addressed by those authors who support the neostructuralist critique of devaluation. This is particularly surprising given the fact that the effect of exchange controls and black markets on the cost of imported inputs will work in these models in *exactly* the same way as a devaluation.

8.3 Regression Analysis

In this section results obtained from a regression analysis based on the model of section 8.1 are reported. These regression results allow us to focus on the effects of devaluation, other factors being kept constant. The following extended version of equation (8.20) is the basis of the estimation:

$$\log g_t = \gamma \, \text{TIME} + \sum \beta_{1i} M_{t-i} + \sum \beta_{2i} \log \text{TOT}_{t-i}$$
$$+ \sum \beta_{3i} \log \text{GCGDP}_{t-i} + \sum \beta_{4i} \log E_{t-i} + u_t, \tag{8.21}$$

where, as before, g_t is real GDP.

In equation (8.21) some modifications have been introduced in relation to the model of section 8.1. First, in (8.21) there is a time trend (γ), and lagged values of the different right-hand-side variables have been included. Second, a general term "money" (M_{t-i}) has been incorporated. This is because two alternative concepts for the monetary variable were used. First, as indicated by the model, actual changes in the log of nominal money—which were denoted ΔM_{t-i}—were included. Second, instead of changes in the actual quantity of money, as in equation (8.20), equation (8.21) also incorporated the role of monetary innovations or *money surprises* (MS_i). This is in the spirit of the rational expectations hypothesis that suggests that only unanticipated changes in money will have effects on real output. In the case where actual money is used, it is expected that $\sum \beta_{1i} = 0$. If, however, the rational expectations' specification is appropriate, it is expected that $\sum \beta_{1i}$ will be positive. Third, the role of changes in the external terms of trade (TOT) was also incorporated. Although this factor did not appear in an explicit way in the solution of the model of section 8.1, it is clear from its structure that a worsening of the terms of trade (i.e., a reduction in TOT) will result in a reduction in real GDP. It is expected, then, that $\sum \beta_{2i}$ will be positive. The coefficients β_{3i} measure the role of fiscal policy, and according to the model it is expected that they will be positive.

The main interest of this analysis lies in the coefficients of the exchange rate—the β_4 values. If devaluations are contractionary, it is expected that they will be significantly negative. If, however, devaluations are expansive, as suggested by the more traditional theories, the β_4 values will be positive. Naturally, it is possible to have a short-run effect that goes in one direction and a long-run effect that goes in the opposite direction. For this reason, in equation (8.21) a number of lags have been incorporated.

Since equation (8.21) is a reduced form based on the model is section 8.1, the exchange rate appearing on the right-hand-side is the *nominal* exchange rate. This is because in deriving (8.20) all endogenous variables—including the real exchange rate—have been solved for. However, in order to investigate more closely the effect of real devaluations on real output, and to be able to compare our results with those of other studies, we also run regressions replacing $\log E_{t-i}$ with $\log e_{t-i}$ (where e is the real exchange rate):

$$\log g_t = \tilde{\gamma} \, \text{TIME} + \sum \tilde{\beta}_{1i} M_{t-i} + \sum \tilde{\beta}_{2i} \log \text{TOT}_{t-i}$$
$$+ \sum \tilde{\beta}_{3i} \log \text{GCGDP}_{t-i} + \sum \tilde{\beta}_{4i} \log e_{t-i} + \varepsilon_t, \tag{8.22}$$

where, as before, M_{t-i} refers either to percentage changes in broadly defined money (ΔM_{t-i}) or to money surprises (MS_{t-i}).

Results

Equations (8.21) and (8.22) were estimated using pooled data for the 12 developing countries of chapter 5—India, Malaysia, the Philippines, Sri Lanka, Thailand, Greece, Israel, Brazil, Colombia, El Salvador, South Africa, and Yugoslavia. As in that chapter, these countries were chosen because of data availability; they were the only developing countries that had long enough time series for all the variables of interest (fiscal deficits and terms of trade are the most difficult data to obtain). The time period, as in chapters 5 and 7, covers 1965–1984 for most countries. As can be seen in chapter 4, all of these countries have experienced important real exchange rate changes (i.e., real devaluations and appreciations) during the period under consideration, and all but El Salvador had also gone through episodes of major nominal devaluations. The exact definition and sources of the data are given in the appendix to this chapter.

Before estimating the rational expectation versions of these equations, which include monetary "surprises," it is necessary to find adequate time series for the unexpected money term MS. In this chapter, as in a number of other studies, this unexpected money growth term is constructed, for each individual country, by taking the differences between actual money growth and the estimated rate of growth of money obtained from a money creation equation.[9] The equation used to generate the expected rate of growth of money should include variables that indeed convey information to the public about central bank behavior. In a large number of developing countries, the printing of money is an important source of fiscal deficit financing (Edwards, 1983a). Consequently, in the money creation equations used in this study, the ratio of the fiscal deficit to lagged high-powered money was used as an explanatory variable. Additionally, the equation included lagged values of $\Delta \log M$.[10] In all cases the residuals were closely examined in order to make sure that they were white noise, and consequently qualified as proxies for money surprises in the estimation of the real output growth equations.

In the estimation of equations (8.21) and (8.22), the γ coefficient was allowed to differ across countries. In this way the differences in trend growth of real output across countries is accounted for. Also, country dummy variables that capture those elements that are specific to each country, such as country size, were included.[11] Those equations that included the RER as an independent variable were estimated using a two-stage least squares procedure.[12]

Table 8.4 contains the results obtained from the estimation of alternative specifications of equations (8.21) and (8.22) for the case of actual money changes. Table 8.5, on the other hand, contains the results obtained when money surprises were included. Details on the estimation technique are provided in the notes to the tables.

Although some of the coefficients are not significant at conventional levels, these results provide support for the view that devaluations have at least a short-run contractionary effect on real output. In all equations the coefficient of the contemporaneous exchange rate variable—either nominal or real—is significantly negative. Moreover, its magnitude is quite large, indicating that, with other things as given, devaluations in these countries have exerted important negative pressures on real output. In all cases the lagged coefficients of the exchange rate variable turned out to be nonsignificant, suggesting that the short-run negative effect of devaluations on real GDP is not reverted as time passes. With respect to the long-run effects of devaluations on real output, the results are somewhat mixed. In two of the regressions—(8.22.1) and (8.22.2) in table 8.4—it is not possible to reject the hypothesis that the sum of the exchange rate coefficients is zero. This suggests that although (real) devaluations have a negative impact effect on output, they are neutral in the long run. However, in the other five regressions the hypothesis that the sum of all exchange rate coefficients is zero was rejected.[13]

Regarding the other variables, these results are also quite revealing. Almost all the coefficients of the change of actual money turned out to be nonsignificant at conventional levels. However, all equations in which at least one of the coefficients of the monetary surprises was included were significantly positive at conventional levels. These results provide some support to the rational expectations view that it is monetary innovations that matters (Hanson, 1980; Edwards, 1983a). It should be noted that when actual money growth was replaced by growth in domestic credit, the results did not change in any significant way.

The terms of trade coefficients are significantly positive and quite large. This indicates that a terms of trade deterioration will result in a reduction of real GDP relative to its trend. This is an important result, since it illustrates the problems related to comparisons based on "before" and "after" analysis only. For example, as was suggested above, the marked declines in real GDP for some countries in the early 1980s can indeed be attributed in part to the deterioration in most of the developing countries' terms of trade during the period. Finally, notice that in all of the equations, the log of GCGDP turned out to be insignificant.

Table 8.4
Devaluations and real GDP in equations with actual money growth (OLS and 2SLS)[a]

	(8.21.1)	(8.22.1)	(8.22.2)
$\log e_t$	—	−0.160 (−3.049)	−0.162 (−3.078)
$\log e_{t-1}$	—	0.074 (1.225)	0.073 (1.192)
$\log e_{t-2}$	—	0.003 (0.056)	0.010 (0.176)
$\log e_{t-3}$	—	0.056 (1.347)	0.052 (1.235)
$\log E_t$	−0.199 (−7.019)	—	—
$\log E_{t-1}$	0.019 (0.445)	—	—
$\log E_{t-2}$	0.032 (0.999)	—	—
ΔM_t	0.086 (1.687)	−0.096 (−1.635)	−0.106 (−1.771)
ΔM_{t-1}	0.021 (0.353)	0.035 (0.455)	0.032 (0.424)
ΔM_{t-2}	0.092 (1.826)	−0.058 (−0.937)	−0.061 (−0.985)
$\log TOT_t$	0.103 (3.340)	0.128 (3.380)	0.132 (3.456)
$\log TOT_{t-1}$	0.019 (0.587)	0.066 (1.662)	0.059 (1.447)
$\log GCGDP_t$	−0.010 (−1.527)	—	−0.005 (−0.185)
$\log GCGDP_{t-1}$	−0.029 (−1.527)	—	−0.031 (−1.313)
N	230	230	230
Root MSE	0.044	0.034	0.054
R^2	0.99	0.99	0.99

a. The equations with nominal exchange rate as an independent variable were estimated using ordinary least squares (OLS). The equations with real exchange rates as independent variables were estimated using two-stage least squares (2SLS). Numbers in parentheses are t-statistics. Root MSE is the root mean square error. All equations were estimated using a fixed effect procedure where country specific dummy variables were included.

Table 8.5
Devaluations and real GDP in equations with money surprises (OLS and 2SLS)[a]

	Equation numbers			
	(8.21.2)	(8.21.3)	(8.22.3)	(8.22.4)
$\log e_t$	—	—	−0.221	−0.222
			(−3.904)	(−3.949)
$\log e_{t-1}$	—	—	0.080	0.083
			(1.330)	(1.393)
$\log e_{t-2}$	—	—	−0.002	−0.025
			(−0.389)	(−0.451)
$\log e_{t-3}$	—	—	0.069	0.070
			(1.546)	(1.586)
$\log E_t$	−0.153	−0.161	—	—
	(−6.173)	(−5.970)		
$\log E_{t-1}$	−0.008	−0.011	—	—
	(−0.211)	(−0.263)		
$\log E_{t-2}$	0.033	0.039	—	—
	(1.074)	(0.997)		
$\log E_{t-3}$	—	−0.007	—	—
		(−0.242)		
MS_t	0.002	0.039	0.024	0.024
	(0.340)	(0.864)	(0.375)	(0.397)
MS_{t-1}	0.046	0.082	0.131	0.132
	(1.008)	(1.790)	(2.316)	(2.351)
MS_{t-2}	0.071	—	0.124	0.127
	(1.565)		(2.197)	(2.255)
$\log TOT_t$	0.100	—	0.129	0.128
	(3.138)		(3.338)	(3.345)
$\log TOT_{t-1}$	0.014	—	0.041	0.040
	(0.420)		(1.005)	(1.017)
$\log GCGDP_t$	−0.007	−0.014	0.007	—
	(−0.349)	(−0.738)	(0.319	
$\log GCGDP_{t-1}$	−0.026	−0.028	−0.010	—
	(−1.363)	(−1.423)	(−0.437)	
N	224	223	220	229
Root MSE	0.044	0.046	0.053	0.053
R^2	0.99	0.99	0.99	0.99

a. Equations (8.22.3) and (8.22.4) with RERs as independent variables were estimated using 2SLS. Equations (8.21.2) and (8.21.3) that used the log of the nominal exchange rate as an independent variable were estimated using OLS. Number in parentheses are t-statistics. Root MSE refers to the root mean square error. All equations were estimated using a fixed-effect procedure where country specific dummy variables were included. Notice tha since lagged money surprises have been used the standard errors reported in this tabl~ subject to the "generated regressor" problem pointed out by Pagan (1984).

A number of alternative specifications were also estimated, without altering the thrust of the results reported in tables 8.4 and 8.5. For example, when the multilateral real exchange rate was used instead of the RER, the estimated contemporaneous coefficient was still significantly negative.

8.4 Distortions, Exchange Controls, and Real Output

Most discussions on contractionary devaluations, including the model of section 8.1, do not specify what are the alternatives to devaluations in conditions of disequilibrium. In reality, however, when faced with adverse external sector conditions, economic authorities face the decision of whether to devalue or to implement other policies. As was shown in chapter 6, in most historical episodes the developing nations have resisted devaluation and have instead imposed exchange and trade controls. An important issue, then, is whether these policies, considered to be alternatives to devaluations, have as well had negative effects on real output. In principle, the model in section 8.1 can be easily amended to incorporate (some) real output effects of trade controls. In fact, in that model import tariffs on imported intermediate inputs will have a contractionary effect similar to that generated by a devaluation. Moreover, in more complete models, distortions will generally have their own negative consequences on output growth.[14]

In order to test the hypothesis that increased trade impediments, exchange controls, and other variables negatively affect real output, equations (8.21) and (8.22) were reestimated adding the black market premium (BMPR) as an additional right-hand-side variable. As discussed in chapter 5, this variable is in fact a good "catchall" proxy for the level of distortions in an open economy.[15] The results for the equation that include the nominal exchange rates were

$$\log y_{nt} = -0.212 \log E_t - 0.056 \log E_{t-1} + 0.107 \log E_{t-2}$$
$$(-6.296) \qquad (-1.090) \qquad\qquad (2.534)$$

$$-0.195 \, \text{BMPR}_t + 0.105 \, \Delta M_t - 0.045 \, \Delta M_{t-1}$$
$$\text{352)} \qquad\qquad (1.935) \qquad (-0.711)$$

$$\text{12} \, \Delta M_{t-2} + 0.073 \log \text{TOT}_t + 0.001 \log \text{TOT}_{t-1}$$
$$\text{55)} \qquad\quad (2.324) \qquad\qquad (0.003)$$

$$\text{3} \log \text{GCGDP}_t - 0.008 \log \text{GCGDP}_{t-1}$$
$$\text{)} \qquad\qquad (-0.419)$$

$$\text{E} = 0.043, N = 207),$$

and when the real exchange rate was used, the following result was obtained:

$$\log y_{nt} = -0.231 \log e_t + 0.045 \log e_{t-2}$$
$$\phantom{\log y_{nt} = } (-3.686) \qquad\quad (0.671)$$

$$-0.002 \log e_{t-2} + 0.114 \log e_{t-3}$$
$$(-0.029) \qquad\qquad (2.205)$$

$$-0.112 \, \mathrm{BMPR}_t - 0.010 \, \mathrm{MS}_t + 0.097 \, \mathrm{MS}_{t-1}$$
$$(-1.958) \qquad\quad (-0.160) \qquad\quad (1.682)$$

$$+0.080 \, \mathrm{MS}_{t-2} + 0.132 \log \mathrm{TOT}_t + 0.034 \log \mathrm{TOT}_{t-1}$$
$$(1.367) \qquad\quad (3.432) \qquad\qquad (0.856)$$

$$+0.017 \log \mathrm{GCGDP}_t + 0.006 \log \mathrm{GCGDP}_{t-1}$$
$$(0.739) \qquad\qquad (0.249)$$

(root MSE $= 0.051$, $N = 207$).

As can be seen, the coefficient of BMPR turned out to be significantly negative at conventional levels. These results then provide evidence supporting the idea that increased distortions in these economies have historically resulted in declines in real output relative to trend. Moreover, these estimates confirm our suspicion that in most of these countries, exchange controls are at least partially responsible for the observed deterioration in real output *before* the devaluation.

8.5 Devaluation, Real Wages, and Income Distribution

In this section some of the income distribution ramifications of devaluations are investigated for the 39 episodes followed in this study. First, the relation between devaluations and real wages is analyzed. Next, we look at the way in which labor shares in GDP evolved during the periods preceding and following these devaluations. The analysis concentrates only on these two variables since in these countries there are very limited data on primary income distribution indicators. In fact, according to data in the World Bank *World Tables*, most of the developing countries have data on the personal distribution of income for at most 2 out of the last 25 years.

Devaluations and Wages

In a nongrowing economy there is a direct relation between real exchange rate movements and real wage rate movements. In fact, real appreciations (depreciations) will imply increasing (decreasing) real wages expressed in terms of tradables. To illustrate this consider the following simple model:

$$\hat{P}_t = \alpha\hat{P}_{Tt} + (1 - \alpha)\hat{P}_{Nt}, \tag{8.23}$$

$$\hat{P}_{Tt} = \hat{E}_t + \hat{P}_{Tt}^*, \tag{8.24}$$

$$D^N(P_N/P_T) = S^N(W/P_N, \tau), \tag{8.25}$$

$$\hat{w} = \hat{W} - \hat{P}, \tag{8.26}$$

$$\hat{e} = \hat{P}_T - \hat{P}_N. \tag{8.27}$$

Equation (8.23) expresses percentage movements in the price level ($\hat{P}_t$) as a weighted average of changes in the price of tradables in home currency ($\hat{P}_{Tt}$) and the price of nontradables ($\hat{P}_{Nt}$). Equation (8.24) is the law of one price for tradables, where $\hat{P}_{Tt}^*$ is the rate of change in the world price of tradables and $\hat{E}$ is nominal devaluation. Equation (8.25) is the equilibrium condition for the nontradable goods market, where the demand for $N(D^N)$ depends negatively on the relative price of nontradables, and the supply is a negative function of the product wage rate (W/P_N) and of a parameter τ that captures the extent of technological progress and/or productivity gains. If there is no technological progress, $\hat{\tau} = 0$. Equation (8.26) defines changes in real wages w, whereas equation (8.27) gives us the evolution through time of the real exchange rate. As before, a real depreciation means that $\hat{e} = (\hat{P}_T - \hat{P}_N) > 0$.

Using equations (8.25) and (8.26) and assuming no technological change, the following expression is obtained:

$$\hat{e}_t = \left(\frac{\varepsilon}{\eta + \varepsilon}\right)\{\hat{P}_{Tt} - \hat{W}\}, \tag{8.28}$$

where ε is the elasticity of supply of N with respect to the product wage ($\varepsilon < 0$) and η is the elasticity of demand of N with respect to the relative price of N ($\eta < 0$). This equation states that if the real exchange rate appreciates ($\hat{e}_t < 0$), the nominal wage rate is increasing faster than the domestic price of tradables. The opposite will be true if there is a real depreciation: With no productivity gains, real depreciations necessarily will be related to declines in the *real product wage rate* for tradables. This, of course, is a reflection of the fact that the real exchange rate is a measure of the degree of competitiveness of domestically produced tradables. If, however, there are gains in productivity, it is possible to have a simultaneous real depreciation and real wage rate increases. This, indeed, has been the experience of Korea during much of the last 15 years (Collins and Park, 1987). When the real wage is measured relative to a basket of tradables and nontradables, as in equation (8.26), the following relation holds:

$$\hat{e} = -\left\{\frac{1}{\alpha + (\eta/\varepsilon)}\right\}(\hat{W} - \hat{P}).\qquad\qquad(8.29)$$

From this analysis it follows that one would generally expect a rapid increase in real wages in the period preceding a devaluation crisis, with a decline in real wages in those countries that successfully implement a real depreciation. Naturally, countries with very fast productivity improvements will provide an exception to this rule. Another way of looking at this relationship is by stating that unless productivity gains are large, countries that have real wage resistance—due to indexation mechanisms, for example— will fail to generate real depreciations after a nominal devaluation.

In this study, data on three types of wages were analyzed: (a) non-agricultural wages, (b) manufacturing wages, and (c) agricultural wages. These data were obtained from the International Labor Office (ILO), and are presented in tables 8.6–8.8. In figures 8.1–8.5 these real wage indexes are depicted for the 29 countries that had data. In these figures a plus sign (+) is used to represent agricultural wages, and asterisk (*) represents manufacturing wages, while a circle (o) is used to depict nonagricultural wages. Before turning to the analysis of these figures, a word of caution is needed regarding the quality of these data. In most developing nations the procedure for collecting wage information is quite deficient, making many of these indexes suspect. For this reason the figures presented here should be taken with a grain of salt and as only providing preliminary information.

The data contained in these tables and figures show a common pattern in a number of countries: Real wages exhibited an important increase in the year prior to the devaluation, experiencing declines in the years following the crisis. Notice, however, that the behavior of the three wage indexes is quite different, especially in the postdevaluation period, suggesting that there may be important sector distributional effects associated with devaluations and adjustment packages. The general tendency is for real agricultural wages to decline in a large number of postdevaluation episodes than do real manufacturing wages. This dissimilar behavior may be capturing important institutional differences across sectors. While in many countries manufacturing wages tend to be indexed, agricultural wages are usually set in a freer way, thus being able to absorb negative (real) disturbances. Unfortunately there are no cross-country data on the extent of wage indexation. This makes the analysis of wage rate behavior somewhat incomplete.

Table 8.6
Manufacturing real wage rate indexes in devaluing countries (year prior to
devaluation = 100)

Country	Year	3 years before	2 years before	1 year before	Year of devaluation	1 year after	2 years after	3 years after
Colombia	1962	n.a.	94.2	100	112.0	117.9	114.1	122.3
Colombia	1965	98.1	103.3	100	107.1	101.6	103.7	108.1
Cyprus	1967	80.5	86.5	100	96.2	98.6	107.9	113.7
Ecuador	1961	96.3	97.5	100	100.2	102.5	100.8	105.8
Ecuador	1970	70.8	74.2	100	103.5	106.7	117.9	114.4
Egypt	1962	100.5	99.7	100	99.5	114.6	118.9	118.1
Egypt	1979	92.5	97.5	100	107.8	n.a.	n.a.	n.a.
Guyana	1967	n.a.	n.a.	100	114.9	129.4	141.9	146.2
India	1966	105.6	97.9	100	97.7	92.5	97.1	100.9
Israel	1962	94.1	96.9	100	100.2	108.9	109.8	120.5
Israel	1967	85.7	94.0	100	102.1	107.8	107.8	112.9
Israel	1971	95.5	95.4	100	98.0	100.1	102.7	101.9
Nicaragua	1979	104.4	99.2	100	87.5	81.7	n.a.	n.a.
Pakistan	1972	116.3	109.2	100	101.2	145.2	122.5	118.4
Philippines	1962	100.7	98.7	100	99.8	98.6	93.9	94.7
Philippines	1970	98.7	97.7	100	99.4	98.5	100.2	96.4
Sri Lanka	1967	96.5	97.9	100	98.8	102.0	96.5	98.6
Yugoslavia	1965	74.0	85.8	100	103.7	112.8	116.5	122.1
Average		94.4	95.7	100	101.7	107.1	109.6	112.2
Chile	1982	78.5	89.1	100	100.4	106.3	103.1	n.a.
Colombia	1967	98.3	105.3	100	102.0	106.3	105.7	115.7
Ecuador	1982	83.3	104.4	100	92.2	n.a.	n.a.	n.a.
Kenya	1981	100.8	98.5	100	99.4	91.6	88.9	n.a.
Korea	1980	78.3	91.9	100	95.3	94.4	101.0	109.6
Mexico	1976	91.9	95.2	100	108.0	109.8	107.6	106.5
Mexico	1982	101.5	97.5	100	99.5	72.4	69.8	n.a.
Pakistan	1982	126.4	105.5	100	n.a.	n.a.	n.a.	n.a.
Peru	1975	84.3	94.2	100	85.1	81.5	71.5	62.0
Average		93.7	98.0	100	97.8	94.7	92.6	98.5

Source: constructed from data obtained from the International Labor Office and the International Monetary Fund.

Table 8.7
Agricultural real wage rate indexes in devaluing countries (year prior to
devaluation = 100)

Country	Year	3 years before	2 years before	1 year before	Year of devaluation	1 year after	2 years after	3 years after
Colombia	1962	89.4	95.7	100	109.2	107.4	109.4	109.8
Colombia	1965	99.7	98.1	100	100.3	99.9	95.6	95.2
Costa Rica	1974	95.5	105.1	100	99.2	94.3	108.4	117.6
Cyprus	1967	78.6	65.9	100	117.9	124.0	127.1	139.7
Guyana	1967	99.2	98.0	100	99.0	95.8	102.7	99.8
India	1966	101.0	93.7	100	103.7	102.5	101.7	104.3
Israel	1962	n.a.	n.a.	100	101.8	108.0	114.7	125.5
Israel	1967	74.1	91.5	100	95.8	95.8	98.6	97.7
Israel	1971	98.0	100.9	100	105.3	110.4	119.4	123.3
Nicaragua	1979	93.9	98.2	100	82.2	89.6	n.a.	n.a.
Pakistan	1972	88.6	102.5	100	99.6	141.0	152.5	120.5
Sri Lanka	1967	98.6	100.5	100	99.1	107.7	100.2	97.2
Yugoslavia	1965	79.5	87.3	100	108.0	126.2	137.9	137.5
Average		91.4	94.8	100	101.7	107.9	114.1	114.1
Chile	1982	82.5	83.4	100	101.2	81.4	69.6	n.a.
Colombia	1967	100.0	100.4	100	95.6	95.2	105.7	100.4
Kenya	1981	106.5	107.7	100	99.4	85.8	82.6	n.a.
Korea	1980	61.8	78.0	100	98.3	92.1	94.8	97.0
Mexico	1976	84.7	94.6	100	n.a.	111.2	109.4	111.8
Mexico	1982	96.5	95.9	100	109.5	95.5	73.9	n.a.
Pakistan	1982	72.5	76.3	100	96.8	114.0	181.8	n.a.
Average		86.4	90.9	100	100.2	96.5	102.3	103.1

Source: constructed from raw data obtained from the International Labor Office and the
International Monetary Fund.

Table 8.8
Nonagricultural real wage rate indexes in devaluing countries (year prior to devaluation = 100)

Country	Year	3 years before	2 years before	1 year before	Year of devaluation	1 year after	2 years after	3 years after
Cyprus	1967	95.4	96.3	100	103.4	106.3	116.9	126.7
Egypt	1962	99.7	101.5	100	99.7	113.7	116.6	117.6
Egypt	1979	91.7	99.8	100	111.0	n.a.	n.a.	n.a.
Guyana	1967	n.a.	n.a.	100	111.6	129.5	139.2	137.7
Israel	1962	n.a.	n.a.	100	103.1	109.5	111.8	126.4
Israel	1967	80.7	91.1	100	96.5	100.2	98.6	100.1
Israel	1971	97.5	98.5	100	102.0	103.8	109.3	107.5
Nicaragua	1979	106.0	99.2	100	84.6	80.5	n.a.	n.a.
Philippines	1962	99.9	101.1	100	96.0	92.0	88.8	91.9
Philippines	1970	99.7	98.1	100	94.6	88.8	89.1	87.6
Sri Lanka	1967	99.8	99.5	100	101.8	112.1	104.4	101.3
Trinidad	1967	96.1	100.4	100	100.2	96.2	98.8	101.2
Yugoslavia	1965	74.4	87.4	100	103.1	112.5	119.5	125.2
Average		94.7	97.6	100	100.6	103.8	108.5	111.2
Kenya	1981	100.8	101.7	100	104.7	91.8	87.4	n.a.
Korea	1980	78.1	92.1	100	95.8	95.4	102.9	110.5
Peru	1975	90.5	101.1	100	96.2	87.3	76.3	65.8
Average		89.1	98.4	100	98.9	91.5	88.9	88.2

Source: constructed from data obtained from the International Labor Office and the International Monetary Fund.

The data in tables 8.6–8.8 are quite revealing. Let us first focus on those countries with large real wage rate increases in the period prior to the crisis. Five out of the 25 countries with available data experienced rates of growth of real manufacturing wages that exceeded 10% per year during the 3 years prior to the devaluation—Chile (12.1% per year), Ecuador in 1970 (12.3%), Ecuador in 1982 (11.4%), Korea (15.8%), and Peru in 1975 (10.8%). All of these countries suffered substantial real appreciations (see table 6.2). In the case of Chile, the rapid growth of real wages prior to the devaluation reflected the economic "boom" of the late 1970s; Ecuador's wage rate behavior in the late 1970s and early 1980s was seen as a consequence of the oil driven growth; the Korean wages responded, at least partially, to productivity increases, while the Peruvian rapid real wage evolution was the result of the policies of the populist military government.

In 9 out of the 24 episodes that have data, the manufacturing real wage rate dropped after the crisis below its value in the year before the devaluation. In the case of the nonagricultural sector, there was a decline in real wages in 8 out of 15 episodes, whereas for agriculture, real wages dropped in 10 out of the 20 episodes with data.

Some countries experienced both a decline in real GDP and a reduction in at least some of the indexes of real wages in the period following the devaluation and stabilization programs: Chile in 1982, Ecuador in 1982, Korea in 1980, Mexico in 1982, and Nicaragua in 1979.

Although the data in these tables and figures do not provide conclusive evidence, they do suggest quite strongly that stabilization packages that include large devaluations as one of their components have been historically associated with fairly generalized declines in real wages. In many ways this is not too surprising given the observed increase in real wages prior to the devaluation and the close relation between real exchange rate movements and real wages established in equations (8.28) and (8.29).

It should be noticed, however, that the historical evidence indicates that reductions in real wages do not appear to be either a necessary or sufficient condition for a successful devaluation. For example, one of the most unsuccessful episodes, Peru in 1975, was followed by a massive drop in real wages. On the other hand, the devaluation of 1972 in Pakistan, a successful episode, was followed by an important increase in wages in the short run. In spite of these exceptions, the evidence reported in these tables is consistent with the hypothesis that successful devaluations require, in the short run, restraint in the evolution of wages. There is no doubt, however, that a full understanding of the important question of the effects of devaluations

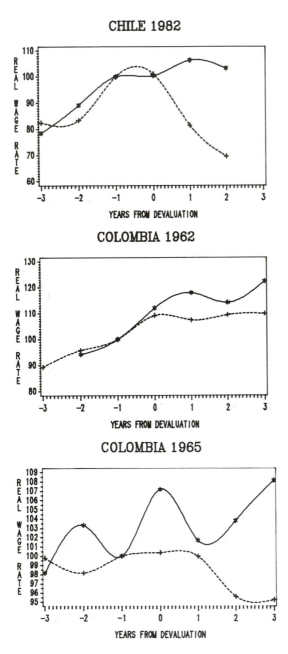

Figure 8.1
Real wage rates (year before devaluation wage = 100). Key to figures 8.1–8.5: +,
agricultural wages; *, manufacturing wages; o, nonagricultural wages. Source: constructed
from raw data obtained from the *IFS* and *ILO*.

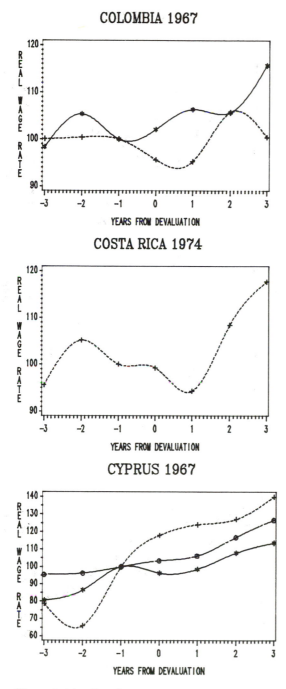

Figure 8.1 (continued)

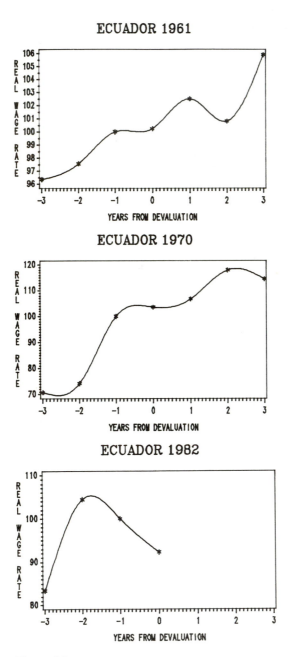

Figure 8.2
Real wage rates (year before devaluation wage = 100). Source: constructed from raw data obtained from the *IFS* and *ILO*.

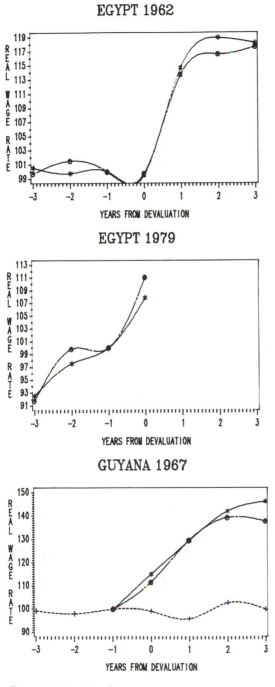

Figure 8.2 (continued)

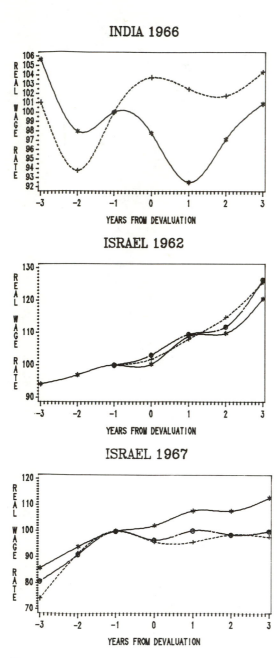

Figure 8.3
Real wage rates (year before devaluation wage = 100). Source: constructed from raw data
obtained from the *IFS* and *ILO*.

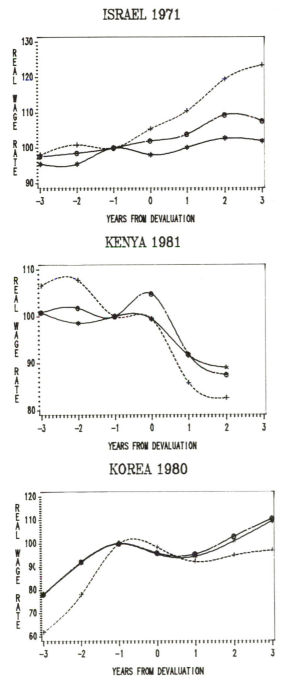

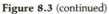

Figure 8.3 (continued)

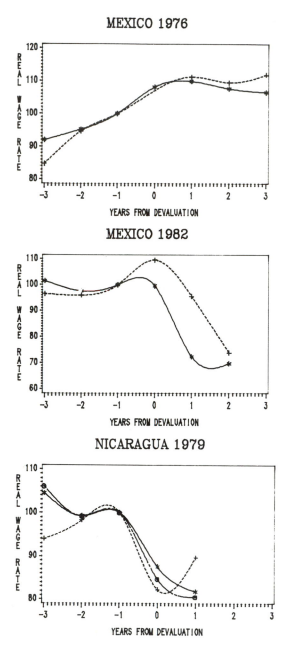

Figure 8.4
Real wage rates (year before devaluation wage = 100). Source: constructed from raw data obtained from the *IFS* and *ILO*.

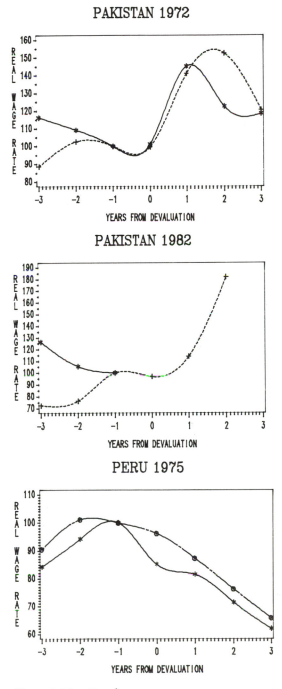

Figure 8.4 (continued)

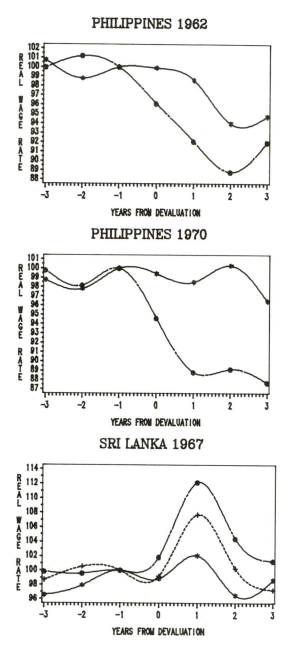

Figure 8.5
Real wage rates (year before devaluation wage = 100). Source: constructed from raw data obtained from the *IFS* and *ILO*.

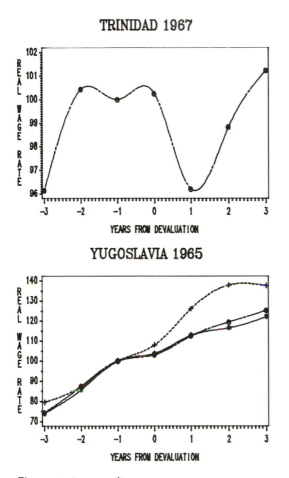

Figure 8.5 (continued)

on real wages requires additional empirical research, including (and perhaps what is more important, generating) the appropriate data.

Labor Share of GDP

Table 8.9 contains the evolution of labor's share in GDP in the period surrounding the crises for those episodes that have the appropriate data. These figures provide another useful piece of information in our attempt to solve the jigsaw puzzle of devaluations and income distribution. The main characteristic that emerges from these data is that for most countries, labor shares move very slowly through time, making the analysis of the effects of devaluations in factoral distribution of income rather difficult. For this reason, in this section we compare the average for the 4 years prior to the crisis with the 4-years average comprised by the year of the devaluation and the 3 years that follow. This comparison is done in two ways: First we have arbitrarily defined a *significant* change in the labor share as any movement that exceeds, either up or down, 1.5 percentage points. Second, we have used nonparametric tests (χ^2) to analyze whether there has been a statistically significant change in income distribution in the years surrounding the devaluation.

Using the first criterion, the data from table 8.9 show that in 15 out of 31 episodes there were no significant changes in income distribution in the period surrounding the devaluations; in 9 out of 31 cases there was a worsening in income distribution—Bolivia in 1972, Egypt in 1979, Israel in 1971, Jamaica in 1967, Jamaica in 1978, Peru in 1975, the Philippines in 1962 and 1970, and Sri Lanka in 1961; and in 7 out of the 31 episodes there were significant gains in the labor share of GDP—Bolivia in 1979, Colombia in 1962, Egypt in 1962, India in 1966, Korea in 1980, Mexico in 1976, and Pakistan in 1972.

With respect to the nonparametric tests, we compared each of the years following the devaluation that appear in table 8.9 to each of the years prior to the crisis. What this does is provide a very broad "before and after" view where no *a priori* commitment is made on any one pair of years as providing the most relevant comparison. The χ^2 obtained ranged from 0.6 to 3.0. Given that these statistics are distributed with two degrees of freedom, these tests clearly indicate that for these devaluations *as a group* there was no significant change in income distribution.

These findings are remarkably inconclusive, indicating that, from a historical point of view, and given the available information, it is not possible to make sweeping statements regarding the relation between devaluations

Table 8.9
Devaluations and income distribution (percentage of compensation to employees with respect to GDP)

	Year of devaluation	Year(s) before/after devaluation							
		−4	−3	−2	−1	0	+1	+2	+3
Argentina	1970	40	41	40	40	41	42	39	43
Bolivia	1972	37	37	34	36	35	32	30	33
	1979	33	34	35	35	36	36	n.a.	n.a.
	1982	35	36	36	n.a.	n.a.	n.a.	n.a.	n.a.
Chile	1982	39	36	38	40	n.a.	n.a.	n.a.	n.a.
Colombia	1962	n.a.	n.a.	34	36	38	38	36	37
	1965	36	38	38	36	37	36	37	36
	1967	38	36	37	36	37	36	38	38
Costa Rica	1974	47	48	48	45	45	46	47	45
Cyprus[a]	1967	87	87	88	87	88	88	88	88
Ecuador	1961	n.a.	n.a.	n.a.	28	29	29	29	28
	1970	27	27	28	28	29	30	28	26
	1982	28	28	32	30	29	n.a.	n.a.	n.a.
Egypt[b]	1962	n.a.	n.a.	39	41	42	42	40	41
	1979	46	39	38	37	33	34	n.a.	n.a.
Guyana	1967	47	47	48	49	49	49	48	49
India	1966	73	72	74	72	74	77	75	74
Indonesia[a]	1978	89	89	89	89	89	89	90	90
Israel	1962	n.a.	n.a.	44	44	44	44	45	48
	1967	44	45	48	50	50	46	44	47
	1971	50	46	44	47	46	43	45	43
Jamaica	1967	50	50	50	46	47	48	49	50
	1978	54	56	57	56	52	51	51	53
Kenya	1981	32	34	35	35	n.a.	n.a.	n.a.	n.a.
Korea	1980	32	33	37	36	37	35	38	n.a.
Malta	1967	49	50	49	47	47	47	47	50
Mexico	1976	37	36	37	38	40	39	38	38
	1982	38	38	36	37	36	n.a.	n.a.	n.a.
Nicaragua	1979	54	55	54	56	n.a.	n.a.	n.a.	n.a.
Pakistan[a]	1972	87	81	84	85	85	86	88	86
	1982	86	84	83	84	84	n.a.	n.a.	n.a.
Peru	1975	36	38	39	37	37	37	37	32
Philippines[a]	1962	n.a.	n.a.	88	87	87	86	86	86
	1970	86	86	86	86	84	83	83	82
Sri Lanka	1967	45	41	43	42	41	41	39	36
Venezuela	1964	45	45	42	43	43	43	44	45

Source: United Nations, *Yearbook of National Accounts Statistics.*
a. (Compensation to employees + operating surplus)/GDP.
b. Year beginning July 1.

and income distribution. Again, this analysis clearly suggests that an improvement in our knowledge on these important matters will not only require additional analysis but, and this is more important, the construction of appropriate data.

An important loose end refers to making these findings regarding labor shares consistent with the previous results related to real wages and real output behavior. The share of labor on GDP (s) is defined as $s = wL/y$, where w is the real wage, L is employment, and y is real GDP. Percentage changes in the labor share are then equal to $\hat{s} = \hat{w} + \hat{L} - \hat{y}$, where, as before, the circumflex denotes percentage changes. Once we recognize that changes in employment ($\hat{L}$)—which we have not analyzed—play a very crucial role in the adjustment, all our previous analysis—which dealt with $\hat{s}$, $\hat{w}$, and $\hat{y}$—can be made perfectly consistent.

Appendix A

Real Output: This was defined as real GDP, and the data were taken from line 99b.p of the *IFS*.

Nominal Money: A broad definition (M2) of money was used. Average yearly values constructed from data obtained from the *IFS* were used.

Fiscal Deficit: Data from line 80 of the *IFS* were used.

Terms of Trade: This was defined as the relative price of exports to imports, and was taken from the *IFS* supplement on international trade statistics.

Real Exchange Rate: This was defined as the relative price of tradables to non-tradables. This variable was proxied by a real exchange rate index constructed as the nominal exchange rate with respect to the U.S. dollar times the ratio of the U.S. wholesale price index (WPI) to the domestic consumer price index (CPI).

Government Expenditure: This was defined as current government expenditure, and was taken from line 91f of the *IFS*.

Notes

1. The developing countries' reluctance to devalue their currencies even when facing major external disequilibria has been documented many times. See, for example, Krueger (1978). See also *The Economist* (1986).

2. However, a problem with Cooper's analysis is that he does not give any information on what happened to the finance ministers of those countries that did not devalue!

3. This proposition has come to be known as the "contractionary devaluation" problem. See Diaz-Alejandro (1965), van Wijnbergen (1986), and Edwards (1986a).

4. Sachs (1988) has argued that the multilateral agencies, and in particular the IMF, have shown little interest in dealing with the income distribution ramifications of devaluations.

5. It should be noted that the model developed here has some limitations when compared with that of chapter 3. First, the current model is not dynamic, and second, it has a much simplified financial sector.

6. Adding imported intermediate inputs to the importables and exportables production process would complicate the algebra without adding much substance to the analysis.

7. As usual, the stability condition is found by analyzing the behavior of an expression for the dynamics of the price of home goods, $\dot{P}_N = b(N^d - N^s)$.

8. After log differentiating (8.10) and plugging in the expressions for $\hat{N}$, $\hat{X}$, and $\hat{M}$, an equation for $\hat{g}$ is derived. The integration of this expression yields equation (8.20), where *constant* combines all the constants of integration.

9. See, for example, Barro (1977), Hanson (1980), and Edwards (1983a). Barro (1977) discusses the assumptions implicit in the use of residuals as proxies for money growth surprises.

10. For each individual country, the following money creation equation was estimated:

$$\Delta \log M_t = a_0 + a_1 \Delta \log M_{t-1} + a_2 \Delta \log M_{t-2}$$
$$+ a_0 \Delta \log M_{t-3} + a_4 \operatorname{DEH}_t + \mu_t,$$

where M_t is broadly defined (M2) nominal money, DEH_t is the fiscal deficit term, and μ_t is a white noise term. In all cases the fits were quite good. In 10 of the 12 cases the coefficients of the fiscal deficit term DEH_t are positive, as expected. However, in only 4 cases—Greece, Israel, Brazil, and Colombia—this coefficient is significant at conventional levels. The approach followed here has well-known shortcomings, including the fact that by using data on all the sample to generate the money creation equation parameters, too much information is being considered (Barro, 1977). In the present case, however, the lack of long enough data series makes the use of rolling regressions or similar procedures impossible. As in much of this literature, the equations reported here are subject to the problems stemming from using generated regressors (see Pagan, 1984, 1986).

11. Since the number of time series observations were not the same for each country, it was not possible to estimate these equations using a random coefficient procedure. However, when some observations were dropped and the Fuller-Batesse (1974) procedure was used, results very similar to those reported here were obtained.

12. The instruments used included: DEH; $\log \operatorname{GCGDP}$, $\log \operatorname{GCGDP}_{t-1}$, $\log \operatorname{GCGDP}_{t-2}$; lagged, twice-lagged, and thrice-lagged real exchange rates; EXCRE; $\operatorname{EXCRE}_{t-1}$; nominal devaluation, lagged, twice-lagged and thrice-lagged

nominal devaluations; money surprises, lagged, twice-lagged, and thrice-lagged money surprises; country-specific dummy variables; country-specific time; growth in domestic credit, lagged, twice-lagged, and thrice-lagged growths in domestic credit; $\log \text{TOT}$, $\log \text{TOT}_{t-1}$, $\log \text{TOT}_{t-2}$, $\log \text{TOT}_{t-3}$; lagged, twice-lagged, and thrice-lagged capital flows ratios; lagged and twice-lagged real GDPs; lagged parallel market premium; and lagged and twice-lagged parallel market nominal exchange rates. As in chapter 5, a test was performed to analyze whether it was appropriate to pool these 12 countries. The results obtained suggest that indeed the two groups described in chapter 5 can be pooled for the estimation of these output equations. The F-statistics ranged from 1.55 to 2.35.

13. This contrasts with Edwards (1986a), who found that a short-run contractionary effect was fully reverted after 1 year. A possible explanation for this discrepancy is that in the current study we are using a much longer data set, which extends to the mid-1980s, and thus captures the effects of devaluations on the domestic currency (real) value of the foreign debt.

14. This is a much more controversial statement than at first may appear. In fact, it is not that easy to generate that kind of result with standard neoclassical equilibrium growth models. The problem, of course, relates to the difference between *levels* and *rates of growth*. See Lucas (1987).

15. Since BMPR is only a proxy for our ideal distortions index, it was treated as a variable measured with errors, and the instruments listed in note 12 were used in our two-stage regressions.

9   Conclusions

In chapter 1 two basic questions regarding exchange rates in the developing nations were asked: (1) How can we account for the large swings observed in real exchange rates in these countries. (2) Are devaluations an effective component of adjustment processes that help restore macroeconomic equilibrium in these countries? In the previous chapters we have tackled these questions from both theoretical and empirical perspectives. In this last chapter the main points made in the book are briefly summarized and the more important conclusions obtained are presented.

Real Exchange Rate Determination

According to the theoretical framework constructed in chapters 2 and 3, real exchange rate movements are the result of both real and monetary disturbances. While changes in real variables or "fundamentals" will result mainly in changes in the equilibrium real exchange rate, monetary disturbances will usually generate departures of the actual from the equilibrium real exchange rate, or real exchange rate misalignment. If inconsistent macroecomic policies are followed and not corrected in time, real exchange rate overvaluation will become unsustainable, until a balance of payments crisis will result.

The empirical analysis of chapters 4 and 5 provided ample support for the theory of real exchange rate determination developed in chapters 2 and 3. First, using a large cross-country data set, it was found that real exchange rates—measured using either official or parallel market nominal exchange rates—did not behave according to the purchasing power parity (PPP) theory. Second, using a data set for 12 developing nations, it was found that real and monetary factors have indeed affected RERs in the way predicted by the theory. In particular, these results show that with other things as given, "excessively" expansionary macroeconomic policies will result in real exchange rate overvaluation. These results also provide strong support for the view that *equilibrium* real exchange rates respond to real disturbances, such as terms of trade shocks, and can exhibit significant movements through time. Moreover, these regression results indicate that for most fundamentals it is important to make a distinction between temporary and permanent disturbances. Also, the results reported in chapter 5 suggest that domestic macroeconomic instability has been the main source behind the wide swings exhibited by actual real exchange rates.

Devaluations and Adjustment

The cross-country empirical investigation presented in this book very strongly indicates that, if properly implemented, devaluations are a powerful and effective macroeconomic tool; they can greatly help troubled countries to regain external equilibrium, reducing the costs of adjustment. This finding supports the theory of devaluations developed in chapter 3. According to that theory, although nominal devaluations are neutral in the long run, they can be very useful in countries that face the need to embark on an adjustment process. In particular, if wages or prices of nontradable goods are inflexible, nominal devaluations will speed up the adjustment, reducing unemployment and related costs during the transition.

However, not all devaluations are "properly implemented"; the data show that historically stabilization packages that include devaluations as one of their major components have not always "worked." There have been many instances—especially in Latin American—where soon after devaluing, the external sector variables revert to their predevaluation levels.

The empirical analysis undertaken in this book convincingly shows that those devaluations that have been "unsuccessful" have been the result of the inability to regain macroeconomic, and especially fiscal, discipline. On the other hand, those countries that have been able to implement corrective macroeconomic policies alongside the devaluations have generally succeeded in realigning their real exchange rates and generating important improvements in their external positions.

The empirical results reported in this book have also shown that historically devaluations have been closely related to changes in the degree of exchange and trade controls. In the majority of cases analyzed, devaluations have been accompanied by some type of liberalization measures. However, in many episodes these liberalizations have been short-lived, being reversed after a few months. This has typically been the case in those countries that, due to fiscal indiscipline, have been unable to sustain a real exchange rate depreciation. Our analysis strongly suggests the existence of a link between inconsistent monetary and fiscal policies, expectations of real exchange rate overvaluation and liberalization reversals. Interestingly enough, this link, which will operate mainly through the loss of credibility in the sustainability of the liberalization reforms, has not been analyzed rigorously in the literature on trade liberalization. Our empirical analysis, however, indicates that this is an important and promising area for future research on the economics of reform in developing nations.

Stepwise Devaluation or Crawling Peg?

A superficial look at the evidence presented in the preceding chapters would suggest that devaluations followed by the adoption of a crawling peg have outperformed stepwise devaluations. This proposition, however, does not stand closer scrutiny. Naturally, by the very nature of crawling peg regimes, countries that adopt them are able to maintain a depreciated real exchange rate; all they have to do is devalue at a faster rate than the ongoing rate of inflation. Of course, a problem with this strategy is that it can lead to a new equilibrium with a very high level of inflation. This means that when evaluating the effectiveness of a crawling peg regime, its inflationary consequences have to be taken into account. Once this is done, the notion that historically crawling peg regimes have generally done better than stepwise devaluations does not seem so evident.

Broadly speaking, our findings regarding crawlers are consistent with those for stepwise devaluers, and once again point toward the importance of maintaining fiscal and monetary discipline. If macroeconomic consistency is maintained, a crawling peg regime can indeed be very useful in helping countries to accommodate *major* disturbances affecting the equilibrium level of the real exchange rate, at the same time as they maintain the rate of inflation at manageable levels.[1] Moreover, a crawling peg regime can be particularly beneficial under the current international monetary arrangement where the major currencies float against each other, introducing major movements in multilateral exchange rates.[2]

Devaluations, Output, and the Costs of Disequilibrium

One of the most important empirical findings in this book (chapter 8) is that the (growing) disequilibrium situations that usually precede devaluations have had severe negative effects on output and growth. In particular, our regression analysis has shown that the imposition of exchange controls has had important negative effects on real growth. Although this finding will not surprise most economists, this is the first time that this proposition, which has been part of economists' beliefs for so many years, has been tested using regression analysis. The most typical scenario found in our empirical inquiry is one where overly expansive macroeconomic policies generate real exchange rate overvaluation, loss of reserves, and high inflation. The authorities usually tackle this situation by imposing (or hiking) exchange and trade controls in the hope that the international reserves drainage is stopped. These controls usually introduce severe inefficiencies and distortions that greatly affect economic performance. These are the *costs of not adjusting*. It is with these costs of not adjusting that the real effects of devaluations on output and real wages have to be compared. Indeed, a serious, and yet common, mistake made in the adjustment literature is to ignore the fact that not adjusting usually implies that there are costs. What this research has shown is that these costs can indeed be substantial, and that in view of these important considerations, devaluations appear to be, in most cases, a highly effective alternative.

Answering why some countries can exert fiscal discipline and others cannot is beyond the scope of this book. This is one of the most important unresolved questions in this study. Its answer, however, should not be sought exclusively in the narrowly defined domain of economics. In fact, we shall only be able to make progress in understanding this issue if we broaden our inquiry to take into account the political ramifications of adjustment policies. Here, questions pertaining to social pressures and income distribution will be the most important ones.[3]

Notes

1. Notice the emphasis on "major" disturbances. We are not advocating "fine tuning"; it is not only impractical but also highly ineffective.

2. See Edwards (1988b) for a discussion of the current international monetary system, exchange rate volatility, and economic performance in the developing countries.

3. Some recent efforts to understand the political economy of stabilization programs can be found in Haggard and Kaufman (1988).

Bibliography

Aizenman, J., "Adjustment to Monetary Policy and Devaluation under Two Tier and Fixed Exchange Rate Regimes," *Journal of Development Economics*, 18 (May 1985): 153–169.

Artus, J., "Methods of Assessing the Long-Run Equilibrium Value of an Exchange Rate," *Journal of International Economics*, 8 (May 1978): 277–299.

Bacha, E., and L. Taylor, "Shadow Exchange Rates: A Review of the Literature," *Quarterly Journal of Economics*, 85 (May 1971): 197–224.

Balassa, B., "The Purchasing Power Parity Doctrine: A Reappraisal" *Journal of Political Economy*, 72 (December 1964): 584–596.

Balassa, B., "Reforming the System of Incentives in Developing Economies," in B. Balassa (ed.), *Development Strategies in Semi-Industrial Economies*, Oxford University Press, 1982.

Barro, R., "Unanticipated Money Growth and Employment in the United States," *American Economic Review*, 67 (March 1977): 101–115.

Barro, R., "Real Determinants of the Real Exchange Rates," unpublished ms., University of Chicago, 1983.

Bean, C., "The Estimation of 'Surprise' Models and the 'Surprise' Consumption Function," *Review of Economic Studies*, 53 (1986): 497–516.

Beveridge, S., and Ch. R. Nelson, "A New Approach to Decomposition of Economic Times Series into Permanent and Transitory Components with Particular Attention to Measurement of the Business Cycle," *Journal of Monetary Economics*, 7(2) (March 1981): 151–174.

Bhagwati, J., "The Theory and Practice of Commercial Policy: Departures From Unified Exchange Rates," *Special Papers in International Economics*, 8, Princeton University Press, 1968.

Bhagwati, J., *Foreign Trade Regimes and Economic Development: Anatomy and Consequences of Exchange Control Regimes*, Ballinger Publishing Co., 1978.

Bhandari, J., and B. De Clauwe, "Stochastic Implications of Incomplete Separation between Commercial and Financial Exchange Markets," unpublished ms., 1983.

Branson, W., "Exchange Rate Policy After a Decade of 'Floating," in J. Bilson and R. Marston (eds.), *Exchange Rate Theory and Practice*, University of Chicago Press, 1984.

Branson, W., "Stabilization, Stagflation and Investment Incentives: The Case of Kenya 1975–1980," in S. Edwards and L. Ahamed (eds.), *Economic Adjustment and Exchange Rates in Developing Countries*, University of Chicago Press, 1986.

Buffie, E., "The Macroeconomics of Trade Liberalization," *Journal of International Economics*, 17 (August 1984): 549–580.

Calvo, G., "Fractured Liberalism," *Economic Development and Cultural Change*, 34 (April 1986): 511–534.

Calvo, G., "Balance of Payments Crises in a Cash in Advance Economy," *Journal of Money, Credit and Banking*, 19 (Feburary 1987): 19–32.

Calvo, G., and C. Rodriguez, "A Model of Exchange Rate Determination Under Currency Substitution and Rational Expectations," *Journal of Political Economy*, 85 (June 1977): 611–625.

Clague, C., "Determinants of the National Price Level: Some Empirical Results," *Review of Economics and Statistics*, 68 (May 1986): 320–323.

Cline, W., *The International Debt Problem*, MIT Press, 1983.

Collins, S., and W. A. Park, "External Debt and Macroeconomic Performance in Korea," unpublished ms., 1987.

Connolly, M., and D. Taylor, "The Exact Timing of the Collapse of an Exchange Rate Regime and Its Impact on Relative Price of Traded Goods," *Journal of Money, Credit and Banking*, 16 (May 1984): 194–207.

Cooper, R., "Currency Depreciation in Developing Countries," *Princeton Essays in International Finance*, 86 (1971a).

Cooper, R., "Currency Devaluation in Developing Countries," in G. Ranis (ed.), *Government and Economic Development*, Yale University Press, 1971b.

Cooper, R., "Devaluation and Aggregate Demand in Aid-Receiving Countries," in J. Bhagwati, et al. (eds.), *Trade, Balance of Payments and Growth*, North Holland, 1971c.

Corbo, V., "Chilean Economic Policy and International Economic Relations since 1970," in G. M. Walton (ed.), *The National Economic Policies of Chile*, JAI Press, 1985.

Corbo, V., and J. de Melo, "Overview and Summary of Liberalization with Stabilization in the Southern Cone of Latin America," Special Issue of *World Development*, 13 (August 1985): 863–866.

Corbo, V., and J. de Melo, "Lessons for the Southern Cone Policy Reforms," *The World Bank Research Observer*, 2 (July 1987): 111–142.

Corbo, V., et al., "What Went Wrong with the Recent Reforms in the Southern Cone," *Economic Development and Cultural Change*, 34 (April 1986): 607–640.

Corden, W., "The Exchange Rate, Monetary Policy and North Sea Oil," *Oxford Economic Papers*, 33 (July 1981): 23–46.

Corden, W., *Protection, Growth and Trade*, Blackwell, 1985.

Cotani, J., D. Cavallo, and M. S. Khan, "Real Exchange Rate Behavior and Economic Performance in Developing Countries," unpublished ms., The World Bank, 1987.

Cuddington, J., "Capital Flight: Estimates, Issues and Explanations," *Princeton Studies in International Finance*, 58 (December 1986).

Cuddington, J., and L. A. Winters, "The Beveridge Nelson Decomposition of Economic Time Series," *Journal of Monetary Economics*, 19 (1987): 125–127.

Cumby, R., and R. Levich, "On the Definition and Magnitude of Recent Capital Flight," NBER Working Paper #2275, 1987.

Denoon, D., *Devaluation under Pressure*, MIT Press, 1986.

Diaz-Alejandro, C., *Exchange Rate Devaluation in a Semi-Industralized Economy: The Experience of Argentina 1955–1961*, MIT Press, 1965.

Diaz-Alejandro, C., *Foreign Trade Regimes and Economic Development: Colombia* Columbia University Press, 1976.

Diaz-Alejandro, C., "Exchange Rates and Terms of Trade in the Argentine Republic, 1913–1976" in M. Syrquin and S. Teitel (eds.), *Trade, Stability, Technology and Equity in Latin America*, Academic Press, 1982.

Diaz-Alejandro, C., "The Latin American Debt: I Don't Think We Are in Kansas Anymore," *Brookings Papers in Economic Activity*, 2 (1984): 335–403.

Dixit, A., and V. Norman, *Theory of International Trade*, Cambridge University Press, 1980.

Dornbusch, R., "Tariffs and Nontraded Goods," *Journal of International Economics*, 4 (May 1974): 177–186.

Dornbusch, R., *Open Economy Macroeconomics*, Basic Books, 1980.

Dornbusch, R., "Equilibrium and Disequilibrium Exchange Rates," *Zeitschrift fur Wirtschafts und Sozialwissenshaften*, 102 (December 1982).

Dornbusch, R., "Real Interest Rates, Home Goods and Optimal External Borrowing," *Journal of Political Economy*, 91 (February 1983): 141–153.

Dornbusch, R., "Special Exchange Rates for Capital Account Transactions," *World Bank Economic Review*, 1 (September 1986a): 3–33.

Dornbusch, R., "Special Exchange Rates for Commercial Transactions," in S. Edwards and L. Ahamed (eds.), *Economic Adjustment and Exchange Rates in Development Countries*, University of Chicago Press, 1986b.

Dornbusch, R., and L. Helmers (eds.), *The Open Economy*, EDI Series in Economic Development, World Bank, 1988.

Eaton, J., and M. Gersovitz, "LDC Participation in International Financial Markets: Debt and Reserves," *Journal of Development Economics*, 7 (March 1980): 3–21.

Eckstein, Z., and L. Leiderman, "Estimating Intertemporal Models of Consumption and Money Holdings," Working Paper, 1988.

Edwards, S., "The Short Run Relation between Inflation and Growth in Latin America: Comment," *American Economic Review*, 73 (June 1983a): 477–488.

Edwards, S., "The Demand for International Reserves and Exchange Rate Adjustments: the Case of LDC's 1964–1972," *Economica*, 50 (August 1983b): 269–280.

Edwards, S., "The Order of Liberalization of the External Sector," *Princeton Essays on International Finance* #156, 1984.

Edwards, S., "Stabilization and Liberalization: An Evaluation of Ten Years of Chile's Experiment with Free Market Policies, 1973–1983," *Economic Development and Cultural Change*, 33 (January 1985a): 223–254.

Edwards, S., "Money, the Rate of Devaluation and Interest Rates in a Semi-Open Economy," *Journal of Money, Credit and Banking*, 16 (February 1985b): 59–68.

Edwards, S., "Exchange Rate Misalignment in Developing Countries: Analytical Issues and Empirical Evidence," CPD Working Paper, The World Bank, 1985c.

Edwards, S., "Are Devaluations Contractionary?," *Review of Economics and Statistics*, 68 (August 1986a): 501–508.

Edwards, S., "Tariffs, Terms of Trade and Real Exchange Rates in Intertemporal Models of the Current Account," NBER Working Paper, 1986b.

Edwards, S., "Commodity Export Prices and the Real Exchange Rate in Developing Countries: Coffee in Colombia," in S. Edwards and L. Ahamed (eds.) *Economic Adjustment and Exchange Rates in Developing Countries*, University of Chicago Press, 1986c.

Edwards, S., "Real Exchange Rate Variability: An Empirical Analysis of the Developing Countries Case," *International Economic Journal*, (Spring 1987): 91–106.

Edwards, S., "Economic Liberalization and the Equilibrium Real Exchange Rate in Developing Countries," in R. Findlay (ed.), *Debt, Stabilization and Development: Essays in Memory of Carlos F. Diaz-Alejandro*, Basil Blackwell, 1988a (forthcoming).

Edwards, S., "Implications of Alternative International Exchange Rate Arrangements for the Developing Countries," in H. G. Vosgerau (ed.), *New Institutional Arrangements for the World Economy*, Springer-Verlag, 1988b (forthcoming).

Edwards, S., "Exchange Controls, Devaluations and Real Exchange Rates: The Latin American Experience," *Economic Development and Cultural Change*, 1989a (forthcoming).

Edwards, S., "Tariffs, Capital Controls and Equilibrium Real Exchange Rates," *Canadian Journal of Economics* (1989b, forthcoming).

Edwards, S., "Temporary Terms of Trade Disturbances, Real Exchange Rates and the Current Account," *Economica* (1989c, forthcoming).

Edwards, S., "Real and Monetary Determinants of Real Exchange Rates: Theory and Evidence from Developing Countries," *Journal of Development Economics* (1989d, forthcoming).

Edwards, S., *Exchange Rate Misalignment in Developing Countries*, Johns Hopkins University Press, 1989e.

Edwards, S., "Structural Adjustment in Highly Indebted Countries," in J. Sachs (ed.), *The Developing Countries' Debt Crisis*, University of Chicago Press, 1989f (forthcoming). [Abridged version in J. Sachs (ed.), *Developing Countries Debt: The NBER Debt Project*, University of Chicago Press, forthcoming.]

Edwards, S., and L. Ahamed (eds.), *Economic Adjustment and Exchange Rates in Developing Countries*, University of Chicago Press for NBER, 1986.

Edwards, S., and A. Cox-Edwards, *Monetarism and Liberalization: The Chilean Experiment*, Ballinger, 1987.

Edwards, S., and P. Montiel, "Macroeconomic Policies, the Real Exchange Rate and Devaluation Crises in Developing Countries" NBER Working Paper, 1989.

Edwards, S., and F. Ng, "Trends in Real Exchange Rate Behavior in Selected Developing Countries," CPDTA Working Paper, The World Bank (1985).

Edwards, S., and S. van Wijnbergen, "Welfare Effects of Capital and Trade Account Liberalization," *International Economic Review*, (February 1986): 141–148.

Edwards, S., and S. van Wijnbergen, "Tariffs, the Real Exchange Rate and the Terms of Trade: On Two Popular Propositions in International Economics," *Oxford Economic Papers*, 39 (1987): 458–464.

Eichengreen, B., "A Dynamic Model of Tariffs, Output and Employment under Flexible Exchange Rates," *Journal of International Economics*, 11 (August 1981): 341–360.

Flood, R., and P. Garber, "Collapsing Exchange Rate Regimes: Some Linear Examples," *Journal of International Economics*, 17 (August 1984): 1–16.

Flood, R., and R. Hodrick, "Real Aspects of Exchange Rate Regime Choice with Collapsing Fixed Rates" *Journal of International Economics*, 21 (November 1986): 215–232.

Frankel, J., and R. Meese, "Are Exchange Rates Excessively Volatile?" Working Paper, University of California, Berkeley, 1987.

Frenkel, J. (ed.), *Exchange Rates and International Macroeconomics*, University of Chicago Press for NBER, 1983.

Frenkel, J., "Purchasing Power Parity: Doctrinal Perspective and Evidence from the 1920s," *Journal of International Economics*, 8 (1978): 169—191.

Frenkel, J., "The Collapse of Purchasing Power Parities during the 1970s," *European Economic Review*, 70 (1981): 145—165.

Frenkel, J., and M. Mussa, "Asset Markets, Exchange Rates and the Balance of Payments," in R. Jones and P. Kenen (eds.), *Handbook of International Economics*, Vol. II, North Holland, 1985.

Frenkel, J., and A. Razin, "The International Transmission and Effects of Fiscal Policies," *American Economic Review*, 76 (March 1986a): 330—335.

Frenkel, J., and A. Razin, "The Limited Viability of Dual Exchange-Rate Regimes," NBER Working Paper #7902, April 1986b.

Frenkel, J., and A. Razin, "Fiscal Policies and the Real Exchange Rates in the World Economy," NBER Working Paper #2065 November 1986c.

Frenkel, J., and A. Razin, *Fiscal Policies and the World Economy*, MIT Press, 1987.

Fuller, W., and G. Batesse, "Estimation of Linear Models with Crossed Error Structure," *Journal of Econometrics*, 2 (February 1974): 67—78.

Gylfason, T., and M. Radetzki, "Does Devaluation Make Sense in the Least Developed Countries?" *ILES Seminar Paper* 314, University of Stockholm, 1985.

Gylfason, T., and O. Risager, "Does Devaluation Improve the Current Account?" *European Economic Review*, 25 (1984): 37—64.

Gylfason. T., and M. Schmid, "Does Devaluation Cause Stagflation?" *Canadian Journal of Economics*, 16 (November 1983): 641—654.

Goldstein, M., and P. Montiel, "Evaluating Fund Stabilization Programs with Multicountry Data: Same Methodological Pitfalls," *IMF Staff Papers*, 33 (June 1986): 304—344.

Haggard, L., and R. Kaufman, "The Political Economy of Stabilization Programs," in J. Sachs (ed.), *The Developing Countries Debt*, University of Chicago Press, 1988.

Hanson, J., "The Short-Run Relation between Growth and Inflation in Latin America," *American Economic Review*, 70 (December 1980): 972—989.

Hanson, J., "Contracting Devaluation, Substitution in Production and Consumption, and the Role of the Labor Market," *Journal of International Economics*, 14 (February 1983): 179—189.

Harberger, A., "The Chilean Economy in the 1970s: Crisis, Stabilization, Liberalization, Reform," *Carnegie-Rochester Conference Series on Public Policy*, 17 (Autumn 1982): 115–152.

Harberger, A., "Welfare Consequences of Capital Inflows," paper prepared for a World Bank Conference, October 1983.

Harberger, A., "Economic Adjustment and the Real Exchange Rate," in S. Edwards and L. Ahamed (eds.), *Economic Adjustment and Exchange Rates in Developing Countries*, University of Chicago Press, 1986.

Harberger, A., and S. Edwards, "Lessons of Experience under Fixed Exchange Rates," in M. Gersovitz and C. Diaz-Alejandro (eds.), *The Theory and Experience of Economic Development*, Allen and Unwin, 1982.

Hirschman, A., "Devaluation and the Trade Balance: A Note," *Review of Economics and Statistics*, 16 (1949): 50–53.

Hooper, P., and J. Morton, "Fluctuations in the Dollar: A Model of Nominal and Real Exchange Rate Determination," *Journal of International Money and Finance*, 1 (April 1982): 39–36.

Huizinga, J., "An Empirical Investigation of the Long Run Behavior of Real Exchange Rates," paper prepared to the Carnegie-Rochester Conference on Public Policy, November 1986.

Judge, G., et al., *The Theory and Practice of Econometrics*, John Wiley and Sons, 1980.

Kamin, S. B., "Devaluation, External Balance, and Macroeconomic Performance," unpublished ms., MIT, December 1985.

Kaminsky, G., "The Real Exchange Rate in the Short Run and in the Long Run," unpublished ms., University of California, San Diego, 1987.

Katseli, L., "Devaluations: A Critical Appraisal of the IMF's Policy Prescriptions," *American Economic Review Papers and Proceedings* (May 1983): 359–364.

Khan, M., "Developing Country Exchange Rate Policy Responses to Exogenous Shocks," *American Economic Review*, 76 (May 1986): 84–87.

Khan, M., and M. Knight, "Determinants of Current Account Balances of Non-Oil Developing Countries in the 1970's: An Empirical Analysis," *IMF Staff Papers*, 30 (December 1983): 819–842.

Khan, M., and J. S. Lizondo, "Devaluation, Fiscal Deficits and the Real Exchange Rates," *World Bank Economic Review*, 1 (January 1987): 357–374.

Khan, M., and P. Montiel, "Real Exchange Rate Dynamics in a Small, Primary-Producing Country," *IMF Staff Papers*, 34 (December 1987): 681–710.

Kiguel, M., and J. S. Lizondo, "Theoretical and Policy Aspects of Dual Exchange Rate Systems," World Bank Discussion Paper No. DRD201, 1987.

Kimbrough, K., "Commercial Policy and Aggregate Employment under Rational Expectations," *Quarterly Journal of Economics*, 99 (August 1984): 567–586.

Kravis, I., and R. Lipsey, "Toward an Explanation of National Price Levels," *Princeton Studies in International Finance*, 52 (November 1983).

Krueger, A., "The Political Economy of the Rent Seeking Society," *American Economic Review*, 64 (1974): 291–303.

Krueger, A., *Foreign Trade Regimes and Economic Development: Liberalization Attempts and Consequences*, Ballinger Publishing Co., 1978.

Krueger, A., "Analyzing Disequilibrium Exchange Rate Systems in Developing Countries," *World Development*, 10 (December 1982).

Krueger, A., *Exchange Rate Determination*, Cambridge University Press, 1983.

Krugman, P., "A Model of Balance of Payments Crisis," *Journal of Money, Credit and Banking*, 11 (August 1979): 311–325.

Krugman, P., and L. Taylor, "Contractionary Effects of Devaluations," *Journal of International Economics*, 8 (1978): 445–456.

Larrain, F., and J. Sachs, "Contractionary Devaluation and Dynamic Adjustment of Exports and Wages," NBER Working Paper #2078, November 1986.

Lizondo, J. S., "Exchange Rate Differential and Balance of Payments under Dual Exchange Markets," *Journal of Development Economics*, 26: 37–53 (June 1987a).

Lizondo, J. S., "Unification of Dual Exchange Markets," *Journal of International Economics*, 22: 57–77 (1987b).

Lucas, R., "On the Mechanics of Economic Development," unpublished ms., University of Chicago, 1987.

Marris, S., *Deficits and the Dollar: The World Economy at Risk*, Institute for International Economics, 1984.

Marston, R. (ed.), *Misalignment of Exchange Rates: Effects on Trade and Industry*, University of Chicago Press for NBER, 1988.

McKinnon, R., "International Transfers and Non-Traded Commodities: The Adjustment Problem," in D. M. Leipziger (ed.), *The International Monetary System and the Developing Nations*, U.S. Agency for International Development, 1976.

Miller, S. M., "The Beveridge-Nelson Decomposition of Economic Time Series," *Journal of Monetary Economics*, 21(1) (January 1988): 141–142.

Morandé, F., "Domestic Currency Appreciation and Foreign Capital Inflows: What Comes First, Chile 1977–1982," paper presented at VI Latin American Meetings of the Econometric Society, Argentina, July 1986.

Mundell, R., "Flexible Exchange Rates and Employment Policy", *Canadian Journal of Economics and Political Sciences* 27, (November 1961): 509–517.

Mundell, R., "Devaluation," chapter 9 of his *Monetary Theory*, Goodyear Publishing Co., 1971.

Mussa, M., "The Theory of Exchange Rate Determination," in J. Bilson and R. Marston (eds.), *Exchange Rate Theory and Practice*, University of Chicago Press, 1984.

Neary, J. P., "International Factor Mobility, Minimum Wages Rates and Factor Price Equalization: A Synthesis," *Quarterly Journal of Economics*, 100 (1985).

Neary, J. P., and K. W. Roberts, "The Theory of Household Behavior under Rationing," *European Economic Review*, 13 (1980): 25–42.

Neary, J. P., and S. Van Wijnbergen, *Natural Resources and the Macroeconomy*, Cambridge, MA: MIT Press, 1986.

Obstfeld, M., "Balance-of-Payments Crises and Devaluation," *Journal of Money, Credit and Banking*, 16 (May 1984): 208–217.

Obstfeld, M., "Rational and Self-Fulfilling Balance-of-Payments Crises," *American Economic Review*, 87 (March 1986): 72–82.

Officer, L., *Purchasing Power Parity and Exchange Rates: Theory, Evidence and Relevance*, Contemporary Studies in Economic and Financial Analysis, vol. 35, JAI Press, 1982.

Pagan, A., "Econometric Issues in the Analysis of Regressions with Generated Regressors," *International Economic Review*, 25 (February 1984): 221–247.

Pagan, A., "Two Stage and Related Estimators and Their Applications" *Review of Economic Studies*, 53 (1986): 517–532.

Pfefferman, G., "Overvalued Exchange Rates and Development," *Finance and Development*, 22 (March 1985): 17–19.

Pigou, A. C., "The Foreign Exchanges," *Quarterly Journal of Economics*, 37 (November 1922): 52–74.

Pinto, B., "Black Markets for Foreign Exchange: The Case of Bolivia," CPD Working Paper, 1985.

Ricardo, D., *On the Principles of Political Economy and Taxation*, E. C. Donner (ed.), G. Gell and Sons, 1971 (originally published in 1821).

Rodriguez, C., "A Stylized Model of the Devaluation-Inflation Spiral," *IMF Staff Papers*, 25 (March 1978): 76–89.

Sachs, J. (ed.), *The Developing Countries Debt Crisis*, University of Chicago Press for NBER, 1988.

Svensson, L. E. O., and A. Razin, "The Terms of Trade and the Current Account: The Harberger-Laursen-Metzler Effect," *Journal of Political Economy*, 91 (1983): 97–125.

Tanner, E., "Exchange Rate and Reserve Regimes: Theory and the Latin American Experience," unpublished Ph.D. dissertation, University of California, Los Angeles, 1988.

Taylor, L., *Macro Models for Developing Countries*, McGraw-Hill, 1979.

Taylor, L., *Structuralist Macroeconomics: Applicable Models for the Third World*, Basic Books, 1983.

Urrutia, M., "Experience with the Crawling Peg in Colombia," in J. Williamson (ed.), *Exchange Rate Rules*, St. Martins, 1981.

van Wijnbergen, S., "The Dutch Disease: A Disease After All?" *Economic Journal*, 94 (March 1984): 41–55.

van Wijnbergen, S., "Taxation of International Capital Flows," *Oxford Economic Papers*, 37 (September 1985a): 382–390.

van Wijnbergen, S., "Capital Controls and the Real Exchange Rate," CPD WP # 1985-52, World Bank, 1985b.

van Wijnbergen, S., "Exchange Rate Management and Stabilization Policies in Developing Countries," in S. Edwards and L. Ahamed (eds.), *Economic Adjustment and Exchange Rates in Developing Countries*, University of Chicago Press, 1986.

van Wijnbergen, S., "Tariffs, Employment and the Current Account," *International Economic Review*, 1987.

Willet, T., "Exchange Rate Volatility, International Trade and Resource Allocation," *Journal of International Money and Finance*, Supplement (March 1986).

Williamson, J. (ed.), *Exchange Rate Rules*, St. Martins, 1981.

Williamson, J., *The Open Economy and the World Economy*, Basic Books, 1983a.

Williamson, J., *The Exchange Rate System*, MIT Press for the Institute of International Economics, 1983b.

Williamson, J., *IMF Conditionality*, MIT Press for the Institute of International Economics, 1983c.

Woo, W., and A. Nasution, "Indonesia Economic Policies and Their Relation to External Debt Management," unpublished ms., NBER, 1987.

Wood, A., "Global Trends in Real Exchange Rates: 1960–1984," unpublished ms., University of Sussex, 1987.

World Bank, *Towards Sustained Development in Sub-Saharan Africa*, Washington, DC, 1984.

Index

Africa, 1, 4
Appreciation, of the real exchange rate. *See* Real exchange rate misalignment
Argentina, 1, 259, 266, 278, 281
  crawling exchange rate in, 57–58
Autocorrelation functions, 118
Automatic adjustment, 78–79, 133. *See also* Real exchange rate misalignment, autonomous correction of

Balance of payments. *See* Current account; International reserves
Balance of payments crises. *See* Devaluation crises
Barro-Ricardo equivalence, 45
Beveridge-Nelson decomposition, 142, 147
Bilateral real exchange rate, 89, 90. *See also* Real exchange rate, measurement of
  before devaluation episodes, 169
  following devaluation episodes, 255, 259
Black markets for foreign exchange, 74–76
  in developing countries, 105, 107
Bolivia, 104, 105, 108, 252n5, 253n13, 239, 260, 263, 266, 278, 281, 289, 306, 308n3, 348
Box-Pierce statistic, 118, 122
Brazil, 132, 138, 283, 289, 326, 352n10
Bretton Woods system, 1, 90, 100, 104, 105, 123

Capital controls. *See also* Exchange controls and trade restrictions
  and the equilibrium real exchange rate, 40–41, 42, 51
  and foreign borrowing, 39, 42, 55n17
  proxies for, 136

Capital flight, 42, 253n8
  before devaluation episodes, 173, 192
  following devaluation episodes, 279, 309n7
  welfare costs of, 78
Capital mobility
  and the equilibrium real exchange rate, 39–40
  in model of dual nominal exchange rates, 61, 74
Capital transfers, and the equilibrium real exchange rates, 42–43, 52
C.E.S. production function, 315
Chile, 104, 108, 128, 132, 169, 176, 187, 260, 289, 337
  real exchange rate behavior in, 129–131
Cobb-Douglas production function, 315
Colombia, 104, 126n6, 128, 129, 132, 138, 169, 176, 177, 189, 253n13, 259, 260, 263, 264, 266, 281, 283, 288, 289, 326, 348, 352n10
  real exchange rate behavior in, 131–132
Commonwealth nations, 166, 175, 252n3. *See also name of specific country*
Consumer price index
  in computation of the real exchange rate, 87, 88, 89, 90, 118
  and price controls, 173, 253n7
Consumption rate of interest, 25, 48, 51
Contractionary devaluations, 311–312, 318, 324, 351n3. *See also* Nominal devaluation, output effects of
  empirical evidence of, 311, 327
Control group
  of developing countries, 162, 195
  macroeconomic policies in, 264
  methodology, 190, 252n1